CODE OF ORIENTAL CANON LAW

THE LAW ON PERSONS

RITES — PERSONS IN GENERAL — CLERGY AND HIERARCHY — MONKS AND RELIGIOUS — LAITY

ENGLISH TRANSLATION AND DIFFERENTIAL
COMMENTARY

By

VICTOR J. POSPISHIL, J.C.D., Sc. Eccl. Orient. L.

Archeparchy of Philadelphia

ST. MARY'S UKRAINIAN CATHOLIC CHURCH
FORD CITY, PA.
1960

NIHIL OBSTAT.

Philadelphia, Pa., December 2, 1959.

(Rev.) JOSEPH A. M. QUIGLEY, J.C.D., LL.D.

Censor Deputatus

No. 1529/59.

IMPRIMATUR.

Philadelphia, Pa., December 4, 1959.

† CONSTANTINE

METROPOLITAN, ARCHBISHOP

Printed by "AMERICA"—817 N. Franklin St., Philadelphia 23, Pa.

DEDICATED

TO

HIS EXCELLENCY

THE MOST REVEREND

KYR CONSTANTINE BOHACHEVSKY

ARCHBISHOP OF PHILADELPHIA

METROPOLITAN OF THE BYZANTINE RITE UKRAINIAN
ECCLESIASTICAL PROVINCE OF THE UNITED STATES

FOREWORD — HOW TO USE THIS BOOK

In response to many requests, especially from among the users of our book **Interritual Canon Law Problems in the United States and Canada,** we prepared this translation of those canons of the new codification of Oriental canon law which can be regarded as the most significant, namely the canons on the law on persons. This comprises the whole motu proprio **Cleri Sanctitati** and the larger part of the motu proprio **Postquam Apostolicis,** together 813 canons, and corresponds to the Second Book of the Latin Rite Code of Canon Law with 645 canons. It contains the constitution of the Catholic Church, a part of the ecclesiastical law where the Christian Orient deviates most conspicuously from the structural norms of the Western Church.

To the text of these canons we have added such explanations which we considered indispensable, and which regard all matters Oriental, and therefore cannot be found in other commentaries on canon law. We did not give a commentary on the canons or their parts that contain norms of law identical to those found in the Code of Canon Law, but limited ourselves strictly to problems not treated at all in the CIC, or which were added to, omitted from, or changed in **Cleri Sanctitati** and **Postquam Apostolicis.** Inconsequent improvements of a linguistic nature were not indicated, but only what constitutes change of law was recorded and commented.

Each section is preceded by a survey of the contents of each canon. Along with that, the relationship of that canon to the CIC was noted by the sign "=". If this sign is followed by the simple citation of a canon, as, e.g., "= c. 342 CIC", this means that there is no change involved to be taken notice of. If "=" is followed by "cf.", as, e.g., "= cf. c. 342 CIC", this signifies that some changes were made, and that the canons are not substantially identical. Whether the changes should be considered consequential can be found out from the subsequent commentary; also by turning to the text of the canon and by comparing it with the text of the corresponding canon of CIC. Whenever the difference need explanation, such information was given following the canon or some of its paragraphs or numbers. Whenever Oriental canons had no parallel in the CIC, this was designated by "new" after the sign "=". For legal institutions which as a whole are peculiar to the Christian East, and therefore are not found in the CIC, as, e.g., the patriarchate, no relationship could be indicated. Canons not transferred from the CIC into the new codification were mentioned in that place of the canons of the two motu propria where they could have been expected.

As to the translation of legislative documents, a word of caution is appropriate. It is commonly known how canonists frequently differ among themselves in respect to the interpretation of legislative texts in the original language. The differences of interpretation are not reduced in translations but rather enhanced and multiplied. It was the intention to render in this translation that sense of the respective law which is generally considered the correct one. For normal, practical use translations of the text of laws are sufficient; should problems of interpretation arise, reference to the original Latin texts will be indispensable.

Written among the travails of the pastoral ministry, far from a canonistic library, this book has no scholarly ambition. The reader who wishes to search deeper is referred to the works listed in the bibliography.

Corrections and suggestions are requested and will be sincerely appreciated.

Special gratitude is again due to the **Reverend Joseph A. M. Quigley, LL.D., J.C.D.,** Professor of the Theological Seminary of St. Charles Borromeus in Philadelphia, Pa., for numerous suggestions and corrections.

Should this work contribute to the awakening of an increased interest in the legal traditions of the Christian East among the clergy, the religious and the informed laity, the author will feel amply rewarded for the expended time and effort.

CONTENTS

THE LAW OF THE RELIGIOUS

GENERAL INTRODUCTION

THE MOTU PROPRIO POSTQUAM APOSTOLICIS

BIBLIOGRAPHY

Only the more important or easier accessible works have been listed here. For more complete references are recommended the books of **Coussa, De Meester, Milash, Pujol, Rezac, Wuyts.**

Coussa, A., **Epitome Praelectionum De Iure Ecclesiastico Orientali,** vol. I (Introductio, De ritibus orientalibus, De fontibus existendi iuris, De fontibus cognoscendi iuris, De ecclesiastica hierarchia), Grottaferrata, 1948.

—, **Epitome Praelectionum De Iure Ecclesiastico Orientali,** vol. II (I. De monachis et de aliis religiosis recentioris institutionis, II. De laicis), Venice (S. Lazzaro), 1941.

Dausend, Hugo, **Das interrituelle Recht im Codex Iuris Canonici,** Paderborn (Schoeningh), 1939.

De Meester, P., **De Monachico Statu iuxta Disciplinam Byzantinam** (Codificazione Canonica Orientale, Fonti II, fasc. X), Rome, 1942. (A nearly perfect collection of sources to the study of Oriental canon law on monachism).

Diederichs, Michael F., **The Jurisdiction of the Latin Rite Ordinaries over their Oriental Subjects.** The Catholic University of America Canon Law Studies, The Catholic University of America Press, Washington, D. C., 1946.

Duskie, John A., **The Canonical Status of Orientals in the United States.** The Catholic University of America Canon Law Studies, The Catholic University of America Press, Washington, D. C., 1928.

Ekklesia, Edited by Friedr. Siegmund-Schultze. 45. Lieferung: **The Orthodoxe Kirche of dem Balkan und in Vorderasien,** Leipzig (Leopold Klotz), 1939.

—, 46. Lieferung: **The Orthodoxe Patriarchate von Konstantinopel, Alexandrien, Antiochien, Jerusalem und das Erzbistum von Cypern,** Leipzig (Leopold Klotz), 1941.

Herman, Ae., De "Ritu" in Iure Canonico, **Orientalia Christiana,** XXXII (1933), 96-158.

—, De Conceptu "Ritu", **The Jurist,** 1942, 333-345.

—, De motu proprio "Postquam Apostolicis", **Monitor Ecclesiasticus,** vol. II, 1952, Rome, 233-260.

Janin, R., **Les Eglises Orientales et les Rites Orienteaux,** Paris, 1955.

Lover, N., New Law Affecting Our Dealing With Oriental Catholics, **The American Ecclesiastical Review,** 1958, 250.

The Melkite Church and the Code of Canon Law for the Oriental Church, **The Eastern Churches Quarterly,** 1958, 287-293.

Milash, N., **Pravoslavno Crkveno Pravo,** 3. ed., Belgrade, 1926.

Petrani, A., **De Relatione Iuridica inter Diversos Ritus in Ecclesia Catholica,** Turin (Marietti), 1930.

Ploechl, W., Non-solemn baptism and determination of rite, **The Jurist,** 1945, 359-388.

Pospishil, V. J., **Interritual Canon Law Problems in the United States and Canada,** Chesapeake City, Maryland (St. Basil's), 1955.

Rezac, J., **De monachismo secundum recentiorem legislationem russicam,** Rome (Pont. Institutum Orient. Stud.), 1952.

Vries, W. de, **Der Christliche Osten in Geschichte und Gegenwart,** Wuerzburg (Augustinus-Verlag), 1951.

Walsh, J. J., **The Jurisdiction of the Interracial Confessor in the United States and Canada.** The Catholic University of America Canon Law Studies, The Catholic University of America Press, Washington, D. C., 1950.

Wojnar, M. M., The Code of Oriental Canon Law **De Ritibus Orientalibus** and **De Personis, The Jurist,** 1959, 212-245; 277-299; 413-464.

Wuyts, A., **Le patriarcat russe au concile de Moscou de** 1917-1918, Rome (Orientalia Christiana Analecta, n. 129), 1941.

—, Il diritto delle persone nella nuova legislazione per la Chiesa Orientale, **Orientalia Christiana Periodica,** 1958, 175-201.

GENERAL INTRODUCTION

Please mak

- - - - - - - - - - - -

p.XVI: PUJOL, S.J., CLEMENS, De Religio-
        sis Orientalibus Ad Normam
        Iuris Vigentis, Rome, 1957.

THE CODIFICATION OF THE CANON LAW
OF THE EASTERN CHURCHES

The necessity of a unified Code of Oriental canon law, and in general of a thorough revision of the entire legislation, was recognized as early as in the last century. The successful codification of the law of the Latin Rite Church induced Pope Pius XI to begin in 1929 the preparation for such a codification. The commission of cardinals appointed to this end was headed by the great jurist **Cardinal Pietro Gasparri**, while the important task of co-ordinating the efforts of the co-workers was organized by the Secretary of the Commission, then Assessor of the Sacred Congregation for the Oriental Church, and at the present time its Secretary, **Cardinal Amleto Giovanni Cicognani**, professor at the School of Canon Law of the Lateran University. In the work of codification Monsignor Cicognani found a capable helper in the person of **Mons. Acacius Coussa**, a Basilian monk of the Melkites of the Byzantine Rite, professor of Oriental Canon Law at the same University, author of several text books on Oriental Canon Law, and presently Assessor of the Sacred Congregation for the Oriental Church, as well as Secretary of the Commission for the Codification of the Oriental Canon Law.

The difficult task of compiling the whole code is not yet terminated, chiefly because of the political situation following World War II. However, because of the urgent need of some communities of Oriental Rite, parts of the Oriental Canon Law have been already promulgated in the form of separate motu proprios, a way of introducing new law used also in the Latin Rite Church prior to the promulgation of the CIC. The relationship of these motu proprios to the future **Codex Iuris Canonici Orientalis** will be the same as was, e.g., that of the motu proprio **Ne Temere** concerning the ecclesiastical form of marriage to the respective canons of the C.I.C.

His Holiness Pope John XXIII has given expression of his desire to see the whole Oriental code as soon as possible promulgated.

Four motu proprios have been so far promulgated:

1. The Motu Proprio **Crebrae Allatae**

From a practical standpoint, this is the most important legislative act. It contains the matrimonial law of the Oriental Church, and was promulgated February 22, 1949 (AAS 1949, 89-119), taking effect from the 2nd of May of the same year.

As a whole, the motu proprio follows the CIC. It differs from it in several features: (1) The Latinity received more attention than did that of the CIC, and the terminology was corrected in some places. (2) Due consideration was given to the interpretations issued by the respective Papal Commissions since the promulgation of the CIC. (3) We find in several places additions which also clarify the meaning of the corresponding text of the CIC. Such additions and corrections, though formally issued only for Oriental Catholics, concern materially also Latin Rite Catholics, because they influence the interpretation of the corresponding passages of the CIC, clarifying disputed interpretations.

Crebrae Allatae established a common matrimonial law for all Orientals. At the present time, however, in evaluating marriages entered into before May 2, 1949, we are still obliged to go back to the former matrimonial legislation of the various Oriental Rites. Because of the plurality of Rites and groups, independent from each other in legislative matters, this is often an arduous task.

2. The Motu Proprio Sollicitudinem Nostram

This motu proprio was promulgated January 6, 1950 (AAS 1950, 5-120), and went into effect January 6, 1951. It contains the procedural law in 576 canons, a larger number than the 408 canons (cc. 1552-1959) of the CIC. A French translation with a brief commentary was published by **F. Galtier, S.J.** (Code Oriental de Procedure Ecclesiastique. Traduction annotée. Beyrouth, 1951).

3. The Motu Proprio Postquam Apostolicis

It was promulgated February 9, 1952 (AAS 1952, 65-150), and went into effect November 21, 1952. It concerns the following legal matters:

(1) Monks and Other Religious (cc. 1-231 = cc. 487-681 CIC).
(2) Temporal Property of the Church (cc. 232-301 = cc. 1495-1551 CIC).
(3) A Glossary of Canonical Terms (cc. 302-335).

The section on the Law of the Religious will be treated in this book, as well as most of the legal terms defined in the final canons of the motu proprio.

In regard to the section on the temporal goods of the Church, it must be said that it is the part which deviates least from the CIC. An innovation is the office of the (compulsory) Diocesan Econome, which is again redefined in the newest motu proprio on the Law of Persons.

4. The Motu Proprio Cleri Sanctitati

It was promulgated June 11, 1957 (AAS 1957, 433-603) to take legal effect from March 25, 1958. With this most recent statute the whole Law on Persons has been published. The motu proprio contains, after an introductory section on the Eastern Rites (cc. 1-15), the general norms concerning all physical and moral persons (cc. 16-37), the laws on clerics in general and in particular (cc. 38-526), and on the laity (cc. 530-558). The greater number of canons (558) in comparison with the CIC (442) was necessitated by the insertion of three chapters on the patriarchs, major archbishops, and their synods (136 canons).

The contents of this motu proprio and the first part on the Law of the Religious of the motu proprio **Postquam Apostolicis** are the subject of this book.

ORIENTAL RITE CATHOLICS AND THEIR HIERARCHICAL SUBDIVISIONS THROUGHOUT THE WORLD

There are 132 ecclesiastical districts of various hierarchical rank which can be classified in the following way:

Six patriarchs, besides being the heads of their respective Churches, administer each his own patriarchal diocese. Nine minor administrative units are ruled by the patriarchs with the help of patriarchal vicars, who usually are titular bishops.

The title of metropolitan is worn by 23 bishops, of whom only six have suffragan bishops, i.e., are heads of ecclesiastical provinces; the rest are titular metropolitans.

Eight bishops of dioceses are distinguished by the title of archbishop.

Simple residential bishops are numbered 53, in addition to 13 apostolic exarchs of episcopal rank, counting here also Latin Rite bishops who have such jurisdiction over Oriental Rite Catholics.

There are also two **ordinariates,** four apostolic administrators and visitors, and one exarchial monastery (abbey **nullius**).

I. THE RITE OF ALEXANDRIA

1. The COPTIC PATRIARCHATE OF ALEXANDRIA (Egypt) consists of four dioceses: The patriarchal diocese, and three others in Assiut, Minya, and Thebe (Luqsor).

2. The ETHIOPIAN APOSTOLIC EXARCHIES OF ADDIS ABEBA (Ethiopia) and of ASMARA (Erithrea).

II. THE RITE OF ANTIOCH (WEST SYRIAN RITE)

1. The SYRIAN PATRIARCHATE OF ANTIOCH comprises eight dioceses: The patriarchal diocese, the metropolitan dioceses of Aleppo, Bagdad, Damascus, Emesa and Mossul, and the (simple) dioceses of Hassatche and Mardin (Amida). The patriarch has in addition three vicars with episcopal rank in Egypt, Lebanon and Palestine.

2. The MARONITE PATRIARCHATE OF ANTIOCH has ten dioceses: The patriarchal diocese, the metropolitan diocese of Beyrouth, and the (simple) bishops of Aleppo, Baalbek, Cairo, Cyprus, Damascus, Gibail-Batrun, Saida-Tyre, Tripolis (Lebanon). There is also an Apostolic Administration of Laodicea for the Maronites.

3. The MALANKARIAN ECCLESIASTICAL PROVINCE in India has one metropolitan in Trivandrum and a bishop in Tiruvalla.

III. THE RITE OF CONSTANTINOPLE OR BYZANTINE RITE.

1. The MELKITE PATRIARCHATE OF ANTIOCH, ALEXANDRIA AND JERUSALEM is composed of the following administrative units: The patriarchal diocese; bishops with the title of metropolitans in Aleppo, Beyrouth (and Gibail), Bosra (and Haurun), Damascus, Emesa, Tyre. The Melkites in the Jordanian Kingdom are under the Archbishop of Petra and Philadelphia. There are bishops in Akka, Baalbek, Baniyas, Saida, Tripolis (Lebanon), Zahle. The patriarch also has vicars in Alexandria, Cairo, Jerusalem and Constantinople.

2. The DIOCESES OF THE UKRAINIANS AND OF OTHERS OF THE RUTHENIAN DISCIPLINE:

(1) UKRAINE (formerly Galicia): The Metropolitan-Archbishop of Lwiw had two suffragan bishops in Peremyshl and Stanislaviw. There was also an Apostolic Exarchy for the Ukrainians of the Lemkiwshchyna.

(2) The ECCLESIASTICAL PROVINCE OF CANADA is composed of the Metropolitan-Archbishop of Winnipeg and the bishops of Edmonton, Saskatoon and Toronto.

(3) The ECCLESIASTICAL PROVINCE OF THE UNITED STATES OF AMERICA comprises at the present time the Archeparchy of Philadelphia, Pa., and the Eparchy of Stamford, Conn.

(4) The Byzantine Rite faithful of the SUBCARPATHIAN REGION was organized in the dioceses of Munkachevo (Uzhorod), now in the Ukrainian Soviet Republic, and Preshow (Slovakia) and the Apostolic Exarchy of Miskolc (Hungary).

(5) The APOSTOLIC EXARCHY FOR THE RUTHENIANS from the Subcarpathian region, Hungary and Yugoslavia in the UNITED STATES OF AMERICA has its seat in Pittsburgh, Pa.

(6) The APOSTOLIC EXARCHY FOR THE UKRAINIANS IN AUSTRALIA, TASMANIA, NEW ZEALAND AND OCEANIA has a bishop who resides in Melbourne, Australia.

(7) The APOSTOLIC EXARCHY FOR THE UKRAINIANS IN GERMANY has a bishop whose seat is in Munich, Germany.

(8) The Ukrainians in Holland, Belgium, Sweden, and some other countries are under the spiritual care of the Apostolic Visitor, whose residence is in Rome, Italy.

(9) The Ukrainians of Brazil are under the jurisdiction of the Latin Rite Archbishop of Rio de Janeiro, who is the ordinary for all Oriental Rite Catholics in that nation. He has an Ukrainian titular bishop as Vicar General for his people.

(10) The Ukrainians in Austria are under the Latin Rite Archbishop of Vienna as ordinary of their parish in Vienna, the territory of which is the entire Austrian Republic.

(11) The Ukrainians in France are under the jurisdiction of the Latin Rite Archbishop of Paris in his capacity of ordinary for all Oriental Rite Catholics in the whole territory of France.

(12) The Ukrainians of England are subject to the Latin Rite Archbishop of Westminster, who has appointed a vicar general for them.

(13) The Ukrainians of Argentina are subject to the Latin Rite Archbishop of Buenos Aires, as ordinary for all Oriental Rite Catholics in that country.

3. The MAGYARS OF THE BYZANTINE RITE IN HUNGARY have a bishop and diocese in Haydudorog, with residence in Nyiregyhaza.

4. The CROATS, UKRAINIANS AND MACEDONIANS OF YUGOSLAVIA have a bishop in Krizhevtsy (Croatia).

5. The ROMANIAN ECCLESIASTICAL PROVINCE is composed of the Metropolitan-Archbishop of Fagarasi-Alba Julia, and the bishops of Cluj, Oradea Mare, Lugoj, and Maramures.

6. For the ITALIANS OF THE BYZANTINE RITE, who are remnants of the Greeks of Southern Italy and of Albanian settlers, there are two dioceses: Lungro (Calabria) and Piana degli Albanesi (Sicily), as well as the Exarchical Monastery (abbey **nullius)** of St. Mary of Grottaferrata.

7. For the GREEKS OF THE BYZANTINE RITE there are two apostolic exarchies with bishops as titulars in Athens (Greece) and Constantinople (Turkey).

8. The BULGARIANS OF THE BYZANTINE RITE are under an apostolic exarch with bishop's ranks in Sofia (Bulgaria).

9. For the RUSSIANS OF THE BYZANTINE RITE there is no episcopal jurisdiction extant at this time, but they are subject to the local Latin Rite ordinaries. A titular bishop is at the present time residing in Rome as ordaining prelate.

10. The APOSTOLIC ADMINISTRATOR OF SOUTHERN ALBANIA was in charge of the few Catholics of the Byzantine Rite in Albania.

IV. THE CHALDEAN OR EAST SYRIAN RITE

1. THE PATRIARCHATE OF BABYLON OF THE CHALDEANS in Irak, Iran, Lebanon, and other countries of the Near East, is composed, besides the patriarchal diocese, of four dioceses whose titulars are distinguished by the title of metropolitans, in Bagdad, Kerkuk, Mossul, Sena, Urmia. There is one archbishop of Bassorah, and nine dioceses with bishops in Akra, Aleppo, Amadia, Amida (Diabekir), Beyrouth, Mardin, Salmas, Seert, Zakho. The patriarch has vicars with episcopal rank in Constantinople and in Egypt.

2. The SYRO-MALABARIAN ECCLESIASTICAL PROVINC-
ES in India are composed of two metropolitans in Chanaganacherry
and Ernakulum, and five bishops in Kothamangalem, Kottayam,
Palai, Tellicherry, Trichur.

V. THE ARMENIAN RITE

1. The PATRIARCHATE OF CILICIA OF THE ARMENIANS
with residence in Lebanon has five archbishops in Aleppo, Bagdad,
Constantinople, Mardin and Sivas, and sixteen dioceses of Adana,
Alexandria, Amida (Diabekir), Ankara, Artwin, Beyrouth, Prusa,
Kayseri, Erzerum, Ispahan, Karnechlie, Karput, Marask, Mytilene,
Musk, Trebizond. Most of these dioceses are without titulars on
account of the extermination of the Armenians by the Turks during
World War I. There is a patriarchal vicar in Jerusalem. A patriarchal vicar represents the patriarch in the United States, without
exercising jurisdiction over clergy and faithful, who are subject
to the local Latin Rite bishops.

2. The Archdiocese of Lwiw (Western Ukraina).

3. The Ordinariate for the Armenians in Greece with residence
in Athens.

4. The Ordinariate for the Armenians in Romania with residence in Gherla.

RITES IN GENERAL

Various groups can be distinguished within the Church. If we
apply liturgical criteria and group the faithful in accordance with
the peculiar liturgical formularies, usages, ceremonies, etc., they
make use of in their worship, the division will be according to **liturgical** Rites. However, we are here primarily not concerned with the
liturgical divisions of the Church but rather with canonical divisions,
that it, with groups of the faithful who are governed by the same
rules and regulations of canon law, and which, being peculiar to
them, distinguish them from faithful who have — at least in some
matters — different canonical rules and regulations. Since these
groups may be differentiated from each other not only by a peculiar
system of canon law but also by peculiar forms of worship, the term
Rite is often used in a liturgical sense even where it denotes a canonical division. This is the cause of much confusion. We wish to state
that the term **Rite** will be here employed chiefly in the canonical
sense.

If within one of these Rites there exist subdivisions, i.e., groups
of faithful who have some common particular canonical order which
sets them apart from other groups of faithful belonging to the same
Rite, we call such a group a **discipline.** Futher subdivisions of a discipline are called by us **jurisdiction.** On the American continent such
a division exists in respect to the Ruthenian discipline of the Byzan-

tine Rite, the faithful of which discipline is divided into the two jurisdictions of the Ukrainian Ecclesiastical Province of Philadelphia and the Apostolic Exarchy of Pittsburgh.

The best definition of the term **Rite** from the canonical standpoint was given by **Emil Herman, S.J.** (De conceptu "ritus," p. 339):

> "A Rite is a group of faithful who are governed by laws and customs of their own, based on ancient traditions, not only in regard to liturgical matters, but also in respect to the canonical order, and which group is acknowledged by the Holy See as autonomous and distinct from others."

Rite, as referring to forms of worship, designates the whole system of ceremonies, texts, patterns, etc., of divine services of a certain group of faithful. Parallel to the development of a distinct liturgical Rite, a particular Church often evolved a distinct legal system also; thus the term **Rite** is applied to the sum of legal regulations peculiar to that particular Church.

All liturgical Rites do not possess a distinct system of canon law. The Latin Rite Church is the only one having but one system of law, represented by the Code of Canon Law, although, as far as the liturgical Rite is concerned the Latin Rite Church is divided in several Rites: The Roman, Ambrosian, Mozarabic, Carthusian, Dominican Rite, the Rite of Lyons, and others.

Among Oriental Rites we find Churches with the same liturgical forms but somewhat different legal systems, as the various disciplines within the Byzantine Rite, although these differences cede more and more to the unifying force of the recent codification of the Oriental Canon Law.

Language of worship is of no importance at all in defining a Rite. There are some Latin Rite Catholics who use the Roman Rite but in the Old-Slavonic language, and several Oriental Rites of disparate origins make use of the same language, Greek and Arabic.

The latest designation of **Rite** is to be found in c. 303 #1 of **Postquam Apostolicis,** where five Oriental Rites are enumerated:

"The Oriental Rites which the canons treat are the Alexandrian, the Antiochene, that of Constantinople, the Chaldean and the Armenian, and other Rites which the Church either expressly or tacitly recognizes as **sui iuris.**"

From this enumeration of Rites have been omitted groups of Oriental Catholics such as the Copts, Ethiopians, Maronites, Malabarians, and others, who very often have been called and treated in documents of the Holy See as autonomous Rites. This intentional omission was the reason why we in our book **Interritual Canon Law Problems in the United States and Canada** (p. 12) expressed the opinion that these subdivisions of the above mentioned five original Rites should be considered to be **disciplines** of the respective Rites, and not Rites themselves.

However, reappraisal of the use of the legislators intention, especially in many places of **Cleri Sanctitati,** induced us to admit that this does not apply in all instances. While, e.g., in the section concerning the interritual relationship, especially the transfer from one Rite to another, the term Rite can more strictly be conceded only to the five original Rites, in other sections it is used in such a way as to be applicable to the last subdivision of a Rite. It seems that the enumeration of c. 303 # 1 of five Rites is merely a historic reminiscence, with no practical consequences. The new codification has not removed the undefinite and ambiguous use of the term Rite encountered in so many legislative documents prior to the codification. We are again back to the definition of Father Herman, the last part of which, as the most significant, was taken into c. 303 #1, that a Rite is a "group acknowledged by the Holy See as autonomous and distinct from others."

We therefore continue to speak e.g., of the Byzantine Rite as an autonomous group, but at the same time we apply this criterion also to the Melkite Patriarchate which is only a part of the Byzantine Rite. We might find several autonomous groups within a Rite which were hierarchically separated from each other for centuries, but which were often treated as one unit by the Holy See in legislative matters. This was the case with the so-called Ruthenians, who comprise Ukrainian, Subcarpathian, Hungarian, and Croatian dioceses. Should we apply the term Rite to them as whole, or directly to each part, or to the whole as well as to each part?

Although the number of Rites will vary in accordance with the criteria adopted by various authors, we can say that this problem will lose its importance with the progressing codification of Oriental canon law. It is true that there are more matters in Oriental canon law relegated to particular law than in the Latin Rite canon law, but just as we do not consider parts of the Western Church to be separate Rites because they have their own particular law, so likewise we should not apply the category of Rite to every group of the Oriental Church. The codification, and the creation of a common code for all Oriental Churches, is at the same time also an unification of law, which implies also the elimination of certain differences among the Rites, and a reservation of the canonical term "Rite" to the more important subdivisions of the five liturgical Rites, in addition to some splinter groups which have severed their ties with their Mother Church in the East for many centuries.

ORIENTAL RITE CATHOLICS IN THE UNITED STATES AND CANADA

Catholics of various Eastern Rites in these two countries may be divided in two groups:

I. Those who are subject to the local Latin Rite ordinaries, viz., all Oriental Catholics with the exception of the Ruthenians. Such Orientals may again be placed in three classes:

1. Those who have parishes of their own Rite.

2. Those who belong to the local Latin Rite parish, although they are also visited and supervised by priests of their Rite under the jurisdiction of the local Latin Rite ordinary.

3. Those who have no ecclesiastical organization at all, i.e., who do not form groups numerically strong enough to constitute parishes.

II. Those who have their own ecclesiastical hierarchy: The Ruthenian discipline of the Byzantine Rite.

The terminology commonly used in denoting different groups of Eastern Rite Christians has no nationalistic or political significance, i.e., it does not imply any specific ethnical origin. **Melkites** and **Maronites,** although of different Rites, are of the same Arabian extraction, while under the name of **Ruthenians** are included Catholics from several nations.

Terms used for denoting national or ethnical extraction are often insufficient to distinguish various Eastern Rite Catholics from the Near East: **Lebanese,** as applied to those who came from the Lebanon Republic, could include besides Maronites also Melkites, Catholics of the Syrian discipline of the Antiochene Rite, and even Chaldeans. **Syrians** may be called all those who came from the Syrian Republic, regardless of Rite. The Arabian language is of no help in establishing the Rite to which a person belongs, since it is spoken by all Eastern Christians in Syria, Lebanon, Palestine, Iraq and Egypt, all of whom consider themselves as belonging to the Arabian nation.

SURVEY OF ORIENTAL RITE CATHOLICS IN THE UNITED STATES AND CANADA
THE UNITED STATES:
RITE OF ANTIOCH: M a r o n i t e s :

43 parishes in the following dioceses of the Latin Rite:

Albany, N. Y.	Gary, Ind.	Richmond, Va.
Atlanta, Ga.	Greensburg, Pa.	St. Louis, Mo.
Boston, Mass.	Hartford, Conn.	St. Paul, Minn.
Brooklyn, N. Y.	Los Angeles, Cal.	San Antonio, Texas
Buffalo, N. Y.	Manchester, N. H.	Scranton, Pa.
Chicago, Ill.	Mobile, Ala.	Springfield, Mass.
Cincinnati, Ohio	New York, N. Y.	Syracuse, N. Y.
Cleveland, Ohio	Philadelphia, Pa.	Wheeling, W. Va.
Detroit, Mich.	Pittsburgh, Pa.	Worcester, Mass.
Fall River, Mass.	Portland, Me.	Youngstown, Ohio
	Providence, R. I.	

RITE OF CONSTANTINOPLE or BYZANTINE RITE:
M e l k i t e s :

24 parishes in the following dioceses:

Atlanta, Ga.	Los Angeles, Cal.	Philadelphia, Pa.
Boston, Mass.	Manchester, N. H.	Providence, R. I.
Bridgeport, Conn.	Milwaukee, Wis.	Rochester, N. Y.
Brooklyn, N. Y.	Mobile, Ala.	Scranton, Pa.
Chicago, Ill.	New York, N. Y.	Syracuse, N. Y.
Cleveland, Ohio	Norwich, Conn.	Worcester, Mass.
Detroit, Mich.	Paterson, N. J.	

RITE OF CONSTANTINOPLE or BYZANTINE RITE:
Ruthenians:
The only group which has at this time its own hierarchical organization:

Archeparchy of Philadelphia: 132 parishes and missions in 21 states of the Union.

Eparchy of Stamford, Conn.: 56 parishes and missions in 5 states of the Union.

Apostolic Exarchy of Pittsburgh: 180 parishes and missions in 15 states of the Union.

RITE OF CONSTANTINOPLE or BYZANTINE RITE:
Romanians:
16 parishes in the following dioceses:

Cleveland, Ohio	Gary, Ind.	Trenton, N. J.
Detroit, Mich.	Pittsburgh, Pa.	Youngstown, Ohio
Erie, Pa.	Rockford, Ill.	

RITE OF CONSTANTINOPLE or BYZANTINE RITE:
Russians:
Three congregations are organized: Los Angeles and San Francisco in California, and in New York City.

CHALDEAN RITE: Two congregations are existing: Chicago, Ill., and Detroit, Mich.

ARMENIAN RITE: Five parishes in the following dioceses: Boston (Mass.), Detroit (Mich.), Paterson (N. J.), Philadelphia (Pa.), and Los Angeles (Cal.)

CANADA

RITE OF CONSTANTINOPLE or BYZANTINE RITE:

The Ukrainian (Ruthenian) Archeparchy of Winnipeg: 179 parishes and missions in the Province of Manitoba.

The Ukrainian Eparchy of Edmonton: 116 parishes and missions in the provinces of Alberta and British Columbia.

The Ukrainian Eparchy of Saskatoon: 163 parishes and missions in the Province of Saskatchewan.

The Ukrainian Eparchy of Toronto: 99 parishes and missions in the provinces of Ontario, Quebec and Nova Scotia.   ;

RITE OF ANTIOCH: MARONITES:

Three parishes and missions in the dioceses of Antigonish, London and Montreal.

RITE OF CONSTANTINOPLE or BYZANTINE RITE: MELKITES.

One church in Montreal.

THE BYZANTINE RITE HIERARCHY OF THE
RUTHENIAN (UKRAINIAN) DISCIPLINE
IN THE UNITED STATES AND IN CANADA

I. THE BYZANTINE RITE

The Byzantine Rite refers to those Catholics who follow the liturgical formularies developed in Constantinople, and who adopted the canon law of the Patriarchate of Constantinople. The ancient name of the city of Constantinople was Byzantion, which term is used to denote the whole culture which had its seat in this city during the Middle Ages. However, since during this epoch the city carried the name of Constantine the Great, the Rite developed in these centuries is more accurately called that of Constantinople. The term **Byzantine** is however so widely accepted for this period of history that we continue calling the Rite with this name.

Since the different groups of the Byzantine Rite created during the centuries particular laws, rules and regulations, for some sections of law at least, independently from each other, we have to distinguish different disciplines of the same Byzantine Rite. In the United States and in Canada the following disciplines of the Catholic Byzantine Rite are represented:

1. The **Ruthenian discipline,** numerically the most important, of which we shall say more in a separate chapter.

2. The **Melkite discipline.** Those Christians in Syria, Palestine and Egypt who remained loyal to the Byzantine Empire and the Byzantine Church when other natives fell away forming the dissident denominations of the Monophysites and Monothelites were called Melkites (royalists). The liturgical language of the Melkites is today mostly Arabic and partly Greek, and in this country also English.

3. The **Romanian discipline.** Byzantine Rite Catholics of this discipline on the American continent came from a section of Europe which prior to 1918 was a part of the Hungarian half of the former Austro-Hungarian Monarchy. After World War I their territory in Europe was united with Romania, and only a few remained in Hungary and Yugoslavia. Their liturgical language is the vernacular Romanian.

4. The **Russian discipline.** Approximately one thousand persons belong to this group in the United States and Canada.

II. THE RUTHENIAN (UKRAINIAN) DISCIPLINE

The word **Ruthenian** is not the best choice for the purpose of legal terminology. It seems to allude to some ethnical entity, but there is no such nation, people, language or country which could be designated by this name. It came in use only in modern times, in order to give a common name to those people of the Byzantine Rite who inhabitated a region in Europe situated roughly between Lithuania in the North and the Carpathian mountains in the South. During the last and the current centuries the nations which belong to this group grew in national conscientiousness and are known as White Russian (Byelorussians) in the North; Ukrainians, Carpatho-Russians, Rusines, Slovaks, in the South.

To make the confusion greater, the term Ruthenian, as far as canon law is concerned, was later extended to other peoples who are of entirely different origin, or merely distantly ethnically related, namely:

1. The **Magyars** of the Byzantine Rite, with the vernacular as their liturgical language. The Hungarians, or more correctly Magyars, were exposed to the cultural and ecclesiastical influence of the Byzantine Rite during the earlier part of the Middle Ages, and this Rite had its followers in Hungary, but later ceded entirely to the Latin Rite. By way of national assimilation a part of the Slavic peoples from the Carpathian mountains and of Romanians in the eastern part of Hungary became Magyars, introduced the vernacular as the liturgical language, and established their own ecclesiastical organization, the diocese of Haydudorogh.

2. The **Slovaks** of the Byzantine Rite, who are closely related, both in origin and language, to their Ukrainian and Subcarpathic neighbors.

3. The **Croats,** of the Byzantine Rite belong to the Slavic ethnical group, but are only distantly related to the Ukrainians and Slovaks. Croats live in Croatia, now a part of the federation of Yugoslavia. Being an isolated group of the Byzantine Rite, liturgically and canonically identical to the larger group of the Ukrainians, the Holy See included them in many, but not in all, legislative acts which were issued for the Ruthenians.

III. THE RUTHENIAN (UKRAINIAN) DISCIPLINE IN THE UNITED STATES AND CANADA

Byzantine Rite Catholics of this discipline have their own hierarchical organization in the United States and Canada. In Canada they are subject to the Ukrainian Ecclesiastical Province of Winnipeg, composed of the Archdiocese of Winnipeg, Man., and the dioceses of Edmonton, Alta., Saskatoon, Sask., and Toronto, Ont.

In the United States the Ruthenians are separated into two groups or jurisdictions, existing in the same territory, by a personal criterion:

1. The Ukrainian Ecclesiastical Province of Philadelphia, is composed of the Archdiocese of Philadelphia, Pa., and the Diocese of Stamford, Conn., and has jurisdiction over all Ukrainians who

trace their extraction to the Austrian half of the former Austro-Hungarian Monarchy.

2. The Byzantine Rite Apostolic Exarchy of Pittsburgh, Pa., has jurisdiction over those Catholics who came from the Hungarian half of the former Austro-Hungarian Monarchy .

During the last two decades of the XIX century a great number of Catholics of the Byzantine Rite from various provinces of the former Austro-Hungarian Monarchy immigrated to the United States of America, and consequently the Holy See created by the Apostolic Letter **Ea Semper** a bishopric for these people, which was territorially limited to the United States, but was not a diocese. The Most Reverend **Soter Stephen Ortynsky, O.S.B.M.**, titular bishop of Daulia, was appointed the ecclesiastical superior on May 12, 1907, and arrived in the United States on August 27, 1907. He was to receive the necessary jurisdiction for governing his flock by delegation from each single ordinary of the Latin Rite, to whom the faithful remained subject on the strength of Leo XIII's **Orientalium Dignitas** (November 30, 1894), and according to the decisions of the Sacred Congregation for the Propagation of the Faith.

It was not possible for Bishop Ortynsky to accomplish the task of organizing his clergy and faithful under such conditions. Therefore, the Sacred Congregation for the Propagation of the Faith granted to him on May 28, 1913, full ordinary jurisdiction and independence from the local ordinaries, under the vigilance, however, of the Apostolic Delegate in Washington. The new legal situation was then defined in the Decree **Cum Episcopo** of August 17, 1914.

After the premature death of Bishop Ortynsky on March 24, 1916, in the middle of World War I, when all communications with the dioceses of origin in Austria and Hungary were severed, the Holy See did not appoint a new bishop, but advised the Apostolic Delegate to appoint two temporary administrators, one for the faith ful who came from the ecclesiastical province of Galicia in Austria, and another for those whose origin was in some part of Hungary. This was done on April 11, 1916. This decision necessitated having the parishes divided according to the majority of the faithful. In 1924 the Holy See appointed two titular bishops as ordinaries for each of the two ecclesiastical circumscriptions which, therefore, have a common territory. Under the influence of the renewed Oriental canonical terminology the Holy See began to use the term "Exarchy" and "Exarch" for these subdivisions of the Church and their ordinaries.

The further development demanded new adjustments. Pope Pius XII created on July 20, 1956, the Apostolic Exarchy of Stamford, Connecticut, by separation from the Apostolic Exarchy of Philadelphia. Since the progress of the ecclesiastical organization continued to a state where a permanent hierarchy could be established in place of the Apostolic Exarchies, Pope Pius XII erected by the Apostolic Constitution **Apostolicam Hanc** of July 12, 1958, the Byzantine Rite Ecclesiastical Province of Philadelphia, consisting of the Archeparchy (archdiocese) of Philadelphia and the Eparchy (diocese) of Stamford, appointing at the same time the present apostolic exarchs to the two new residential sees.

The faithful of both jurisdictions, i.e., of the Ukrainian dioceses and of the Apostolic Exarchy of Pittsburgh, are of the same ethnic origin. Their language, with the exception of the Magyars, Croats and the Slovaks, is the same, save differences of dialect as occur in every language. With the exception of the Magyars, Croats and Slovaks, they are now politically united in Europe under the same government, the Ukrainian Soviet Republic. As to their national names — referring to their European extraction — among those of the Exarchy of Pittsburgh no common national name had been formed at the time of their migration to the United States, and we find among them Rusines, Russians, and, of course, Slovaks, Magyars (Hungarians), and Croats, although such distinctions become usually meaningless with the younger generation.

The faithful of the Archeparchy of Philadelphia and of the Eparchy of Stamford are Ukrainians. By far the largest group of Eastern Rite Catholics belong to the Ukrainian nation. The Ukrainians are a people of some forty millions who inhabit the southern part of East Europe, northward from the Black Sea. They are akin to other Slavic nations, as the Russians, Poles, Slovaks. The Ukrainian language belongs to the East Slavic language branch, distinguished from other languages of the same branch, e.g., the Russian language, in the same way as Italian, Spanish, French are differentiated among themselves. The Ukrainians are presently politically united in the Ukrainian Soviet Republic under communistic occupation. More than ten percent of the Ukrainians are Catholics of the Byzantine Rite, while the rest are dissidents.

As we said before, the group of Ukrainians, Rusines, Slovaks, Croats, Magyars, have in certain aspects of canon law the same particular law, and are in this respect only called by the name of **Ruthenians.** Some of them, especially the Ukrainians, object violently to the use of this term, since this was imposed on them by the former Austro-Hungarian Monarchy with the intention of separating them from those Ukrainians who were at that time under the rule of the Russian Czar. Considering, however, that no other term would be equally satisfying in canon law, this term cannot be discarded, provided any meaning of ethnical origin is excluded from it. This is the reason why the Apostolic See continues to use the term **Ruthenian** even in most recent documents, sometimes intermixed with Ukrainian.

Greek-Ruthenian is a pleonasm, the addition of **Greek** being unnecessary since all Ruthenians are of the same Byzantine (Greek) Rite.

Byzantine-Slavonic is incorrect, because it is derived from the liturgical language, which however is not common to all Ruthenians, some employing Magyar or English, and there are nations, belonging to the Byzantine-Slavonic group, as the Russians and Bulgarians, who do not belong to the Ruthenian canonical discipline.

It is also incorrect to use the designation of **Greek-Catholic** as synonym for **Ruthenian,** because Gree-Catholic applies to all Byzantine Rite Catholics, i.e., not only to Ruthenians, but also to Romanians, Melkites, and others.

16

The immigration of Ruthenian Catholics into Canada followed that of the United States. Their national composition was, however, different from that of those in the United States, because the great majority came from Western Ukraina (Galicia) and only a small number from Hungarian provinces. A division as found in the United States was therefore never considered advisable.

The Most Reverend **Nicetas Budka**, titular Bishop of Patara, was appointed July 12, 1912, the first ordinary with exclusive jurisdiction over all Ruthenians. He later returned to his native diocese and was replaced by **Bishop Basil Vladimir Ladyka**, O.S.B.M., who governed the Apostolic Exarchy till his death in 1956.

The territory of Canada was by the Constitution **Omnium Cuiusvis Ritus** of March 3, 1948 split up into three apostolic exarchies. The Apostolic Exarchy of Central Canada was again divided by the Constitution **De Ruthenorum in Canadensi** of March 21, 1951 into two exarchies, bringing their number to four apostolic exarchies.

By the Apostolic Constitution **Hanc Apostolicam Sedem** of November 3, 1956 (AAS 1957, 262-264) the four exarchies were elevated to dioceses and the Ukrainian Byzantine Rite Ecclesiastical Province of Winnipeg was established with Archbishop **Maxim Hermaniuk**, C.SS.R., as its first metropolitan.

PERSONS SUBJECT TO THE JURISDICTION OF THE BYZANTINE RITE HIERARCHY IN THE UNITED STATES AND IN CANADA

1. UKRAINIAN ECCLESIASTICAL PROVINCE OF PHILADELPHIA:

The Archdiocese of Philadelphia comprises the entire United States with the exception of the State of New York and the New England states, which are under the jurisdiction of the Diocese of Stamford, Conn.

The Ukrainian bishops have jurisdiction over:

1. All Byzantine Rite Catholics who immigrated to this country from Galicia and Bukovina, or some other part of the Austrian half of the former Austro-Hungarian Monarchy. This migration may sometimes have been accomplished in a circuitous way, i.e., that they came to this country after having been for a shorter or longer stay in some other country of Europe, or in Canada, South America, Australia, etc.

The original immigrants came from the following dioceses in Europe:

(1) Archdiocese of Lwiw (Lwow, Leopoliensis rit. byz., Lemberg).

(2) Diocese of Peremyshl (Premisliensis rit. byz., Przemysl).

(3) Diocese of Stanislawiw (Stanislaopoli, Stanislawow).

(4) Apostolic Exarchy of the Lemkiwshchyna (Lemkow-szczyna).

(5) Diocese of Maramures and its Vicar General in Czer-niwtsy (Bukovina) as far as Catholics of Ukrainian ethnical origin are concerned.

2. Descendents of such persons in accordance with can. 756 CIC.

3. Women married to men referred to under 1. and 2., if they comply with can. 98, 4, C.I.C., and join their husband in his Rite.

4. Those who in accordance with the pertinent regulations law-fully changed their Rite.

5. Converts received into the Church by priests of these dio-ceses.

6. Byzantine Rite Catholics of the Ruthenian discipline of other than Ukrainian extraction, if they are actually attached to parishes subject to the jurisdiction of these dioceses. When the Apostolic See permitted, in 1916, the division of the Ruthenian Ordinariate accord-ing to the European extraction of the faithful, this applied only to parishes. If a person or a group of persons were incapable of estab-lishing their own parish, they remain attached and subject to the existing parish of their Rite.

II. THE BYZANTINE RITE APOSTOLIC EXARCHY OF PITTSBURGH

The territory of the jurisdiction of this Exarchy is the entire United States. In respect to persons, the following are under the jurisdiction of the Apostolic Exarch:

1. Catholics of this Rite who immigrated to this country from Hungary and Croatia, or some other part of the Hungarian half of the former Austro-Hungarian Monarchy.

This refers to the following dioceses in Europe:

(1) Diocese of Munkacevo (Munkacs) with residence in Uzhorod (Ungvar), formerly in Hungary, then in Czechoslo-vakia, now belonging to the Ukrainian Soviet Republic.

(2) Diocese of Preshow (Presow, Prejasev, Eperjes), now in Slovakia, a part of the Czechoslovakian Republic.

(3) Diocese of Krizhevtsy (Crisio, Krizevci) in Croatia, a part of the Yugoslavian federation.

(4) Diocese of Haydudorogh in Hungary.

(5) Apostolic Exarchy of Miskolc (Hungary).

2. Descendants of such persons in accordance with can. 756 C.I.C.

3. Women married to men referred to in 1. and 2., if they join their husbands in their Rite.

4. Those who changed their Rite lawfully in accordance with can. 98, 3, C.I.C.

5. Converts to the Catholic Church received by priests of this Apostolic Exarchy.

6. Byzantine Rite Catholics of the Ruthenian discipline of other extractions, if they actually are attached to parishes subject to the jurisdiction of the Exarch of Pittsburgh.

The jurisdictional relationship of the Ukrainian dioceses and the

Apostolic Exarchy of Pittsburgh to each other follows the principles which apply to the relationship of one Latin Rite diocese to another. However, although their subjects are defined by personal consideration, instead of by territorial limits, the faithful of both groups are not separated from each other as exclusively and strictly as the subjects of the Latin Rite ordinaries are separated from the faithful of the two Ruthenian jurisdictions. From it follows that:

1. The faithful of one jurisdiction who are deprived of their own pastor do not become subject to the care of the local Latin Rite pastor but of the pastor of the other Ruthenian jurisdiction, provided one is in the place.

2. The faithful of one Ruthenian jurisdiction may come into a jurisdictional relationship with the ordinary of the other jurisdiction which may be compared with that of the **peregrinus** in other circumstances. Dispensations granted by an ordinary to subjects of a pastor of the other jurisdiction will not be invalid but at the most illicit, especially if based on faculties received from the Holy See.

III. THE UKRAINIAN BYZANTINE RITE HIERARCHY IN CANADA

The Ukrainian dioceses are territorially defined in the following manner:

1. Archdiocese of Winnipeg: Province of Manitoba.

2. Diocese of Edmonton: Provinces of Alberta, British Columbia, Yukon and the westerly part of the North West Territories.

3. Diocese of Saskatoon: Province of Saskatchewan.

4. Diocese of Toronto: Provinces of Ontario, Quebec, Nova Scotia, New Brunswick, Newfoundland and Prince Edward Island.

As to persons, all those Byzantine Rite Catholics who would be said to be subject to the Ukrainian dioceses in the United States as well as the Catholics subject to the Apostolic Exarchy of Pittsburgh come under the jurisdiction of the Canadian Ukrainian bishops. A division among the Ruthenians according to European extraction, as found in the United States, does not exist in Canada.

THE JURISDICTIONAL RELATIONSHIP BETWEEN THE BYZANTINE RITE (UKRAINIAN-RUTHENIAN DISCIPLINE) AND THE LATIN RITE HIERARCHIES IN THE SAME TERRITORY

Although we consider here the situation existing on the North American continent, the principles invoked by us apply to other parts of the world as well. Since the Byzantine Rite Catholics of the Ukrainian-Ruthenian discipline constitute a minority in this country and in Canada, their jurisdictional organization, be it a diocese or a parish, is often erroneously considered a personal one in contraposition to the territorial jurisdiction of the Latin Rite. Walsh (p. 14), for instance, is not correct when he states that

> "at the present time in the United States and Canada there are two distinct jurisdictions, namely, the **territorial** jurisdiction of the residential bishops of the Latin Rite and the **personal-territorial** jurisdiction of the ordinaries of the Ruthenian Rite."

Oriental Rite parishes are mistakenly put in the same category as the national parishes of the Latin Rite, and since the Latin Rite territorial pastors have cumulative jurisdiction with co-territorial national parishes, the same relationship is claimed in regard to Byzantine Rite parishes.

However, both jurisdictions are territorially and personally defined in the same manner. Latin Rite bishops have no jurisdiction over Ukrainian-Ruthenian Catholics, and the residential bishops or apostolic exarchs of the latter have no jurisdiction over Latin Rite Catholics.

It shall be mentioned that as far as Byzantine Rite Catholics of the Ukrainian-Ruthenian discipline are concerned in the United States and Canada, these both countries are according to the definition of can. 303 #1, 3, of **Postquam Apostolicis "territories of the Oriental Rite,"** since a hierarchy is established here for this particular Oriental Rite group.

In regard to parishes of any Oriental Rite on the American continent, whether under the jurisdiction of a Byzantine Rite bishop or a Latin Rite bishop, they are always territorial. It is of no importance that their jurisdiction is limited to the faithful of their own Rite, because so also is the jurisdiction of Latin Rite pastors. Oriental parishes have a certain territory whose boundaries are assigned explicitly or implicitly. It is of no consequence that such a parish has a territory co-terminal with the entire Latin Rite diocese. Such a parish does not lose its territorial character because no certain and definite limits have been assigned to it. Neither are such parishes national parishes in the meaning applied to Polish, German, Italian, Slovak, etc., parishes on the North American continent. Parishioners of such national parishes can leave them at any time and join the territorial parish. Such is not the case with Eastern Rite parishes and Catholics. They must be members of their respective Oriental Rite parish, and take part in its life, as long as the church is accessible to them without considerable hardship. The Latin Rite ordinary has no power to change this relationship once he has erected such an Oriental parish.

The characteristic of territorial, personal or national applies only to the inter-relationship of various parishes of the **same** Rite. Parishes of different Rite, although perhaps subject to the same ordinary, are always territorial when compared with each other. When contrasting, for example, a Melkite parish with an Italian (Latin Rite) parish of the same territory, both can be considered territorial.

THE MOTU PROPRIO

CLERI SANCTITATI

TITLE ONE:

EASTERN RITES IN GENERAL

1. PRESERVATION OF THE EASTERN RITES

CANON 1. # 1. The Eastern Rites, whose venerable antiquity is an illustrious ornament to the entire Church as well as an affirmation of the divine unity of the Catholic faith, shall religiously be preserved.

2. Patriarchs, archbishops and other hierarchs shall with great care promote the faithful preservation and accurate observance of their Rite, and they shall not permit or tolerate the introduction of any change into the Rite.

3. All clerics and religious shall not dare to give suggestion or advice to the clergy or the faithful of another Rite which could lead to contempt or lessening of respect for the laudable institutions of their Rite.

The Universal Church as well as each of her parts are living organisms; the development of new forms in various aspects of ecclesiastical activity is to be considered a normal and healthy phenomenon. The changes thereby necessitated will find a definition in the enactment of new laws and in the modification of old ones, of which the present motu proprio **Cleri Sanctitati** is a witness. The Eastern Catholic Churches are not exempt from this evolution. Various changes have been adopted in the legal systems of the Oriental Catholic Rites and disciplines. However, some of these innovations were introduced not because of some compelling need manifested in the play of everyday relationships, but by a blind imitation of institutions found in the numerically preponderant Latin Rite Church. The arrogant character of such unjustified copying is especially unreasonable in the liturgical sphere, where the Eastern Rites can proudly boast of having better preserved apostolic traditions than the Western Church was able to do. The Apostolic See has always opposed such changes, and in the most recent decades has even positively demanded that certain of them be eliminated and the respective Rite or discipline return to its genuine tradition.

2. OBSERVATION OF THE RITE

CANON 2. # 1. Every sacred minister shall accurately observe his Rite in the celebration of Divine Liturgy, in the administration of the sacraments and sacramentals, even though he may have faithful of another Rite under his administration.

Bi-ritualism and multi-ritualism is sometimes permitted by the Holy See to some priests who are called to minister to Catholics of several Rites. However, such priests are strictly enjoined from mixing the Rites.

2. Where there are several Rites, the faithful shall be advised often to frequent churches of their own Rite, especially on Sundays and holydays, and they shall not neglect to assist there at the divine services.

Although a Catholic may satisfy the precept of assisting at Mass on Sundays and holydays in any Catholic Rite (c. 1249 CIC), he has to give his regular parochial allegiance to the church of his own Rite, provided such one is available to him. His membership in such a congregation means that he generally assists at Mass and other divine services in his own Rite, and supports financially his own parish.

3. UNITY AMONG RITES

CANON 3. The sacred ministers shall beware lest the difference of Rite be an obstacle to them in keeping the unity of spirit in the bond of peace.

CANON 4. Local Hierarchs who exercise jurisdiction in the same territory shall in mutual agreement promote unity of action among the clergy of the various Rites, and they shall by concerted efforts work toward common goals, in order to advance more expeditiously the good of religion and to insure with better efficiency the discipline of the clergy.

The Byzantine Rite bishops and apostolic exarchs of the United States and Canada participate regularly in the meetings of the episcopal conferences of the hierarchy of their respective countries.

4. THE PREVALENT RITE

CANON 5. Clerics and religious, including exempt religious, who carry out their ministry in regions in which a Rite different from their own is the only existing one, or, on account of the number of the faithful, prevalent to such a degree that in public estimation it is considered as alone existing, shall depend on and be subject to the local Hierarch of that Rite in all matters pertaining to the sacred ministry.

1. GENERAL NORM

The normal care of souls is exercised by a pastoral ministry of two levels at least, namely, the immediate pastors or parish priests, and the supervisory pastors or bishops. This system of pastoral care must be an efficient one. If the number of the faithful of some Rite and of their parishes is so small as not to justify the erection of an episcopal authority of their Rite in the form of a diocese, apostolic vicariate, prefecture, exarchy, it becomes necessary to subject the faithful and pastors to the supervision of bishops of another Rite existing in that region.

Although this is normally the case with Oriental Rite Catholics in many countries of the Latin Rite, there are instances where the Latin Rite faithful and their pastors are subject to the local Oriental Rite bishop.

2. ORIENTAL RITE CLERGY AND THEIR LATIN RITE ORDINARY

Whenever Oriental Rite Catholics outside their patriarchate are in such a minority that no hierarchy of their own can be erected for them, they will, as a rule, be subjected to the local Rite ordinary (cf. also c. 22 # 3). The subjection of the Oriental clergy in such cases to the local Ordinary does not differ from that of the Latin Rite clergy. Only in matters pertaining specifically to Rite does there exist a right and duty on the part of the respective Oriental patriarchs to supervise clergy of their Rite in such places, as, e.g., in the United States and in Canada. This is a cumulative authority with that of the Latin Rite ordinary, and if therefore the latter possesses the necessary knowledge of a particular Oriental Rite, for instance, by employing a competent substitute, he is not prevented from exercising supervisional duties in such matters.

Since the jurisdictional relationship between Oriental clergy and their Latin Rite ordinaries is the same as that of the Latin Rite clergy to the same ordinary, no taxative enumeration of rights or duties is possible or advisable. It may be mentioned specifically that the Oriental clergy are subject to the disciplinary power of the Latin Rite ordinary, that the diocesan tribunal has jurisdiction over them, and that the Latin Rite ordinary may enforce in virtue of his coercive power not only his own disciplinary laws, but also those of that particular Oriental Rite and discipline. He alone is called upon to ensure by his coercive power the execution of decrees issued by Oriental patriarchs and their substitutes in matters pertaining to Rite.

In procedures involving Oriental Catholics their canon law is to be applied to all material questions, while the formal procedure has to follow the court's own law, that is, the C.I.C.

The Latin Rite ordinary is alone competent to appoint to or remove Oriental clergy from any ecclesiastical office. Considering the special supervision exercised by the Sacred Congregation for the Oriental Church over all these Orientals, his decision will have to be necessarily in agreement with the intentions of the same S. Congregation, which supervises the transfer of such clergy from the Near East to the American continent.

The clergy needed for the care of Orientals in Latin Rite dioceses could come from two sources: the Latin Rite ordinaries could educate Oriental clergy in their own seminaries, or at least in other suitable seminaries, who once ordained would be incardinated in their dioceses in the same way as other Latin Rite clergy. However, this is in general rarely done, because it is easier to receive priests for the small number of Oriental faithful from the respective patriarchates in the Near East. This shall be done in accordance with the decree **Qua Sollerti,** issued by the S. Congregation for the Oriental Church on December 23, 1929 (AAS 1930, 99-105). The chief principle to be followed in such appointments is that nothing can be done without the consent of the Sacred Congregation, which also carries on the necessary correspondence through the mediation of the Apostolic Delegates. Religious as well as secular clergy are eligible, the latter however must be celibates. Widowers, preferably without children, also may receive permission in special cases to come to America. Because of the absence of specific regulations in **Qua Sollerti,** we infer from its general tenor that such clergy cannot be incardinated in the Latin Rite diocese but remain always attached to their native dioceses, although their return or recall depends upon the written consent of the Sacred Congregation.

Should a Latin Rite ordinary not be able to procure Oriental priests from the Near East, or at least not immediately, he may ask Oriental priests from other dioceses in the same country to extend their care also to the faithful in the ordinary's diocese. These priests need to receive permission from their own Latin Rite ordinary, who will refuse it if an extension of work would be detrimental to the care of Orientals already placed under the care of these priests.

If an Oriental priest wishes to change from one Latin Rite diocese to another, he needs the consent of both ordinaries. The accepting ordinary must forward a notice through the Apostolic Delegate to the Sacred Congregation.

5. ACQUISITION OF RITE

CANON 6. # 1. **Among the various Rites a person belongs to that one according to the ceremonies of which he has been legitimately baptized.**

The principle enunciated here is of little practical value when the membership of children in a Rite is to be determined, since (1) the definition of what is a legitimate baptism is not given here but in the following canons, and (2) there are several exceptions in which the baptism might legitimately be administered in another Rite without producing the effect suggested in # 1. The rule is clearer if expressed by saying that a child who received baptism belongs to the Rite predetermined by law, irrespective of the Rite of the minister or the ceremonies.

Only in case the Rite of the parents cannot be established shall it be presumed that the Rite of baptism is the Rite to which the child belongs.

2. **If the baptism was administered by a minister of another Rite in case of grave necessity, when a priest of the proper Rite could not be present, or because of some other just reason with the permission of the proper Hierarch, or because of fraud, the person thus baptised shall be regarded as belonging to that Rite according to the ceremonies of which he ought to have been baptized.**

Every Catholic belongs as such to one of the ritual divisions of the Church, to one, and only to one, of the various Rites of the Church. In passing it should be said, that the Pope as head of the Church may be considered as belonging to all Rites, not only to the Latin Rite.

When becoming a member of the Church one acquires automatically also membership in one of the Rites. Baptism is the door to the Church and therefore also the mode of entering a Rite. Non-Catholics, as far as they are baptized, belong also in a sense not exactly defined to one of the Rites of the Church. Those who received baptism in a denomination which traces its origin to the Latin Church, as do the various Protestant groups, to the Latin Rite, while those who were baptized in one of the Oriental dissident Churches belong to the corresponding Catholic Rite.

1. ACQUISITION OF RITE BY ADULTS

(1) Formal Conversion

Adult converts may enter the Rite of their choice by accepting baptism in that Rite. In this matter, persons who have reached legal puberty, are adults (c. 17 # 2, **Cleri Sanctitati**).

The formal reception into a certain Rite of the Church may be affected also by a priest of another Rite, provided the person baptized has manifested the desire to join a Rite different from that of the receiving priest.

A non-Catholic who never belonged to the Church may make a free choice of Rite in entering the Church. This applies also to those non-Catholics who are children of Catholic parents. **Ploechl** (Non-solemn Baptism, 386) considers such persons obliged to enter the Church in the Rite of their parents, and though infidels, i.e., unbaptized, they have not "forfeited affiliation with a particular Rite of the Church." We do not think that there exists any affiliation in regard to persons who as non-baptized are entirely outside the reach of ecclesiastical legislation. They are bound only by the divine commandment of receiving baptism as a means of salvation. Children, as opposed to adults, have no choice and they follow therefore their parents in all things. We may say that c. 756 CIC (or c. 6 **Cleri Sanctitati**) imposes an obligation on parents but not on children. Once children are emancipated as far as matters of Rite are concerned, i.e., after puberty, they may freely choose the Rite in embracing the Faith. Such a freedom corresponds more to the actual situation in practice, and to the maxim to grant as much liberty as possible to those who wish to enter the Church.

Fallen-away Catholics in reconciling themselves with the Church have to return to the Rite to which they belonged before their apostasy. This follows from the general principles of law that one should not obtain by an illegal act what others can receive only as a grace, as well as from positive declarations of the Holy See, such as that of the Sacred Congregation for the Propagation of the Faith of July 15, 1876 (Collectanea, n. 1458).

(2) Informal Conversion

A non-Catholic who was baptized outside the Church may become a Catholic not only by going through the formal act of reception by profession of Faith, the regular and prescribed mode of joining the Church, but also by conclusive acts, which by their nature have the same meaning, that is, acceptance of the Faith and submission to the ecclesiastical authority. Such determinative acts will be the reception of sacraments. Such cases are not rare in practice, e.g., if Charles, a dissident Oriental, joins his stepmother in attending the Catholic Church, receiving sacraments, etc., without having sought the assistance of any priest.

We do not consider attendance at church services alone, even for a long time, **without** the reception of sacraments, as a conclusive act capable of proving one's decision to join the Church, because there is no true conviction and acceptance of faith if the reception of the annual communion is rejected. **W. L. Boudreaux** (p. 80) is satisfied with "a minimum of Catholic training from infancy even though they received no sacrament after baptism, provided that there was a total lack of heretical training." We cannot see how a non-Catholic who disobeyed the Church in the important matter of receiving — at least once — the sacraments of penance and Holy Communion can be called a Catholic in the absence of an explicit profession of Faith.

Practical implications of such a distinction result from the — now abrogated — second comma of c. 1099 # 2 CIC in respect to the "**ab acatholicis nati**" (cf. **Pospishil, Interritual,** 154-155).

2. ACQUISITION OF RITE BY CHILDREN

Children follow the Rite of their parents. We have to distinguish such cases:

(1) When both parents are Catholics belonging to the same Rite; all children are to be baptized in the Rite of their parents.

(2) When both parents, validly married, are Catholics, but of different Rites, all children, without distinction of sex, follow the father in his Rite. It is of no concern in which Rite the parents' marriage was contracted.

Exceptions which formerly existed in particular law, as, e.g.,

28

that established by the **Concordia,** entered into between the Latin Rite and Byzantine Rite hierarchy in Galicia (Western Ukraine) (1860), according to which children followed their parents' Rites in accordance with sex, are abolished by **Sanctitati Cleri,** in virtue of the invalidating clausel terminating the motu proprio.

The above rule applies also to the case when the father died before the child's birth. The same opinion was expressed by **W. Ploechl** (Non-solemn Baptism, 369) against **Michiels, Sipos** and **Dausend.** All these canonists, Ploechl not excluded, were implicitly referring to the case of a child who is the first-born of a couple, or at least the only remaining child. Our opinion, as well as that of **Duskie** (p. 87) and **Ploechl** is made even more reasonable if we consider the case where such a couple had already several children baptized in the Rite of the father. It is only natural that also the posthumous child should be baptized in the Rite of his father and his brothers and sisters.

(3) When one parent is a Catholic while the other is a non-Catholic, all children follow the Catholic parent in his Rite. Fallen-away Catholics, i.e., those who at the moment of the baptism of their children profess by positive acts adherence to some other faith or denomination, are to be considered non-Catholics in this matter. In case the apostate parent returns to the Faith (and to his former Rite) children as yet not emancipated in matters of Rite, i.e., before having reached legal puberty, follow the father in his Rite, or the mother, if he remains outside the Church, in analogy to the case with which c. 10 deals.

Should in a mixed marriage the non-Catholic parent — who never belonged to the Church — later become a convert and choose a Rite different from that of his wife, the children follow their father in the Rite he chooses if they have not yet reached legal puberty.

The principle that only the Rite of the Catholic parent is to be taken into consideration applies also to the case of a non-Catholic parent belonging to some dissident Oriental Rite group, who demands from his Catholic spouse that the child be baptized in the Catholic Oriental Rite corresponding to his own dissident affiliation but different from the Rite of the Catholic spouse. **Dausend** (p. 87) and **Petrani (De Relatione,** p. 63) permit baptism according to the wish of the non-Catholic father in order to avoid greater harm which perhaps could result from having the child baptized outside the Church. We cannot accept this view, because there are still other means for preventing such consequences, for instance, by lawful change of the mother's Rite, or by the permission of the bishop to have the child baptized in the other Rite without changing his ritual affiliation (c. 6 # 2).

(4) An illegitimate child follows the Rite of his mother. Should the mother later marry the father, the infant follows his Rite if the father is a Catholic. While common law has no provision for the case of illegitimate children, particular law follows our opinion, as that of the Ruthenians (Ukrainians) from Galicia (Fontes, VII, n. 4859), in the United States **(Cum Data Fuerit,** Art. 43) and in Canada **(Graeci-Rutheni Ritus,** Art. 48).

(5) Should the child of non-Catholic or unknown parents be offered for baptism to a Catholic priest, and he, morally certain that the child will be reared as a Catholic, administers baptism, the child will belong to the Rite of the administering priest, which means that non-Catholic parents may have their child baptized in the Rite of their choice, whether they themselves remain non-Catholics (**Duskie,** p. 90) or embrace the Faith in some other Catholic Rite.

If the baptism was administered in danger of death by a lay person, or, in the absence of a priest of the Rite selected by the non-Catholic parents, by a priest of another Rite, their intention alone is decisive (**Ploechl,** Non-solemn Baptism, 370).

(6) If several Catholics of different Rites come in some legal connections with a child of unknown parents, i.e., foundling, or if it is the case of a child not-yet baptized which is to be adopted, the child should be, according to our opinion, baptized in the Rite of that person or institution which is ultimately to assume the responsibility for his upbringing. This means that the mere accidental relationship as between the child and the person discovering or sheltering him for a short time is of no importance at all (**Ploechl,** Non-solemn Baptism, 370).

(7) Baptism administered to children of Catholics against the above rules does not influence their membership in a certain Rite. They belong not to the Rite in the ceremonies of which they were baptized, but to the Rite in the ceremonies of which **they should have been lawfully baptized** (c. 98 # 1 CIC). This applies also to the case when baptism had to be administered in the Latin Rite because no priest of the respective Oriental Rite was available.

(8) In case the baptism could be administered in the proper Rite without any difficulty, but for certain reasons, such as, e.g., to please relatives of whose good will the parents expect special benefits, it can be permitted that the child be baptized in a Rite other than that prescribed by law. The granting of a permission for such a baptism was, in the CIC, reserved to the Apostolic See, but in c. 6 # 2 it can be given now by the bishop in whose Rite the child ought to be baptized. The administration of baptism in these circumstances does not constitute a change of Rite, and the child will belong to the Rite prescribed by law.

Since c. 6 is not enumerated in c. 15 among those canons which oblige especially also Latin Rite faithful and clergy, the conclusion could be drawn that c. 6 regulates only the interrelationship among Oriental Rites, while that between the Latin Rite and Oriental Rites is still governed by c. 98 # 1 CIC. Consequently, the faculty given to local Hierarchs to permit that a child of their jurisdiction be baptized in another Rite would be restricted to Oriental Rites, and Oriental Rite Hierarchs could permit the baptism of one of their subjects in another Rite, but not in the Latin Rite. For the latter exception an indult of the Holy See would be required as specified in c. 98 # 1 CIC. This standpoint was tentatively taken by **Cecil L. Parres, C.M.,** in **The Homiletic and Pastoral Review,** March 1959, page 585. It would also follow that the Latin Rite ordinary could not grant such a permission either, namely, to have a Latin Rite child baptized in an Oriental Rite, but c. 98 # 1 CIC would have to be applied, i.e., an apostolic indult to be sought.

The different treatment of the relationship between various Rites in an inequal manner, as suggested by C. J. Parres, had a precedent in the previous law. While before **Cleri Sanctitati** for a transfer from the Latin Rite to an Oriental Rite and vice versa an apostolic indult was required, for that between at least some of the Oriental Rites the consent of local Hierarchs was sufficient. Such a simplified transfer could be accomplished only between Rites which make use of the same Eucharistic matter, i.e., leavened or unleavened bread respectively, as, e.g., between the Maronite and the Armenian Rite, in which the Eucharistic matter is unleavened bread as in the Latin Rite.

However, the opposite position seems to be preferable. As c. 98 # 1 CIC regulated the relationship between the Latin Rite and the Oriental Rites, by its very nature an interritual canon, so also c. 6 is an interritual law, which by its very essence must extend to all Rites. In the same way as the CIC, although enacted for the Latin Rite Church, was law also for the Oriental Churches if it was, e.g., a question of interritual relationship, as in c. 98 CIC, so also c. 6 could be considered to apply to the Latin Rite as well, although **Cleri Sanctitati** is admittedly primarily a law of the Oriental Churches. In consequence, the faculty granted to local Hierarchs to permit baptism in another Rite would be a change of law contained in c. 98 # 2 CIC, affecting all Rites without distinction.

This would also follow from the principle formulated in c. 22 CIC, where it is said that a subsequent law abrogates a previous law, among others, if its purpose is to order anew the entire respective legislative material, which was done in **Cleri Sanctitati.**

In addition, one could argue, assuming that we take the position whereby the faculty contained in c. 16 applies only to the relationship between Oriental Rites and is inapplicable to that between the Latin Rite and any of the Oriental Rites, that it seems strange that the legislator did not expressly say so, e.g., in c. 6, where it could easily have been done, removing any doubt. Therefore, in the same manner as the CIC, although a codification of the Latin Rite Church, in c. 98 # 2, regulated the relationship between the Latin Rite and Oriental Rites, so also c. 6 of **Cleri Sanctitati,** although a law enacted for the Oriental Church, regulates — besides the relationship of Oriental Rites among themselves — also the relationship between Oriental Rites and the Latin Rite, and consequently, the faculty granted in c. 6 to local Hierarchs is to be understood as applying to all interritual relationships without distinction.

6. CHANGE (TRANSFER) OF RITE — PROHIBITION OF PROSELYTISM

CANON 7. No one shall presume to induce in any manner anyone from among the faithful to join another Rite.

Not rarely it is possible to meet with the erroneous conviction that the unity of the Church would be advanced if all Rites would merge in the Latin Rite. This is wrong for many reasons:

(1) The Roman Pontiffs have on so many occasions expressed that this is not their desire, and have commanded that the other Rites of the Church, especially those of the East, preserve their separate existence. Any proselytism which would induce Catholics to request change of their Rite is forbidden and sinful (c. 7). Proselytism can be active, i.e., direct inducement, and passive, i.e., not resisting to the misguided persuasions of some Catholics who desire to change their Rite without the reasons approved by the Church. Priests of whatever Rite have a duty to persuade the faithful to obey the laws of the Church. In being approached with the wish of change of Rite against the intentions of the Church, they have an obligation to explain the contents of the law, and are forbidden to give assistance in effecting an unwarranted demand.

(2) Eastern Rites are of Apostolic origin, and therefore enjoy every right of continued existence.

(3) The Church aims at unity, not uniformity. The mistaken notion that unification of Rite could be to the advantage of the Church devaluates the meaning of the really important unity in doctrine and in the obedience to the Roman Pontiff as vicar of Christ on earth.

(4) The Church has received and will receive in the future spiritual inspirations and other benefits of a higher moral order from the Christian East, which are precious enlargements of the concepts of catholicity.

(5) The Church has been often accused of hypocrisy, namely, to desire the union of all Christians only to absorb them into the Latin Rite. Catholics who work against the intentions of the Church confirm such unfortunate incriminations.

(6) Catholics of every country have to learn to acquire an outlook more universal, transcending the situation of the Church in their own surroundings. It may be of little importance for the Church in a specific country whether the Eastern Rites continue to exist there, but not so for the universal Church.

(7) The majority of Oriental Rite Catholics have been subjected to the most cruel persecution by Communism, and are faced with annihilation for the only reason that they are Catholics, while at the same time the dissident communities enjoy freedom and sometimes even special privileges. Shall it be said that the Catholic Church of the Latin Rite duplicated the liquidation of the Eastern Catholicity in a manner only somewhat different from that employed by Communism, although aiming at the same goal?

(8) The Eastern Rites will be perhaps in a time not too far of great importance to the Church. Catholics should learn to see the life of the Church not only in the dimension of space, as an universal (= catholic) institution represented over the whole world, but they ought in addition to see her also projected into the dimension of time, i.e., what the Church will look like in one or more centuries. If the Eastern Rites have no great import for the Church at the present moment, they can be of utmost consequence in time to come.

7. AUTHORITY COMPETENT FOR GRANTING
A TRANSFER OF RITE

CANON 8. # 1. No one can validly transfer to another Rite, nor after a lawful transfer return to the former Rite, without permission of the Apostolic See.

No change of Rite is valid in the eyes of the law except if negotiated in conformity with the respective prescription of canon law. The reception of sacraments in another Rite, even if exclusive and protracted for a long time, does not effect a change of Rite (c. 98 # 4 CIC).

According to c. 8 # 1 the transfer or change from one Rite to another can be effected only by the Apostolic See, not counting here the exceptions mentioned in cc. 9 and 10. The different provisions for the transfer between Oriental Rites among themselves, especially those with the same Eucharistic matter, and between the Latin Rite and one of the Oriental Rites, are now abolished.

1. Transfer between Rites

As Rites are here understood the five Rites enumerated in c. 303 # 1 of **Postquam Apostolicis,** in addition to the Latin Rite. Even if **Cleri Sanctitati** accords the status of **ritus** sometimes to subdivisions of the original Rites, we do not consider them to be understood as independent Rites in the meaning of the present canon.

The permission of the Holy See is to be petitioned from and will be granted by the Sacred Congregation for the Oriental Church. The return to the former Rite is subject to the same rules as the transfer.

(2) Transfer between disciplines of the same Rite

In regard to change of Rite the concept **"Rite"** is taken from c. 303 # 1, of **Postquam Apostolicis,** where as Rites are enumerated: The Alexandrian, that of Antioch, that of Constantinople, usually called Byzantine, the Chaldean and the Armenian Rite. No change of Rite is involved when a Catholic transfer from one subdivision of a Rite to another, as (1) from the Coptic to the Ethiopian discipline, and vice versa, both subdivisions of the Alexandrian Rite; (2) from the Syrian to the Maronite or the Malankarian disciplines, all subdivisions of the Rite of Antioch; (3) from the Chaldean to the Malabarian discipline, which have a common origin; (4) from one discipline of the Byzantine Rite to another of the same Rite.

Though the passing from one such subdivision to another of the same Rite is not a change of Rite, the consent of the respective ordinaries will be necessary if both subdivisions have separate parishes, because the jurisdiction of the respective pastors is by explicit act limited and restricted to only one group.

In regard to conditions in the United States and Canada, we have to consider the following possibilities:

(1) An Oriental Catholic wishes to transfer himself from one discipline to another discipline of the same Rite, and both communities are subject to the same local Latin Rite ordinary, as, e.g., when

a Melkite wishes to join a Romanian parish, because there is no Melkite parish accessible to him. No permission is required in joining a parish of another discipline of the same Rite, provided there is no parish of one's own discipline accessible. However, if an Oriental Catholic does not wish to join the local parish of his discipline but one of another, he needs the consent of the local Latin Rite ordinary.

(2) An Oriental Catholic wishes to change one discipline of the same Rite with another discipline, but the two communities are under the jurisdiction of different ordinaries. Such a problem would arise if, for example, a Romanian of the Byzantine Rite wishes to join a parish of one of the Byzantine Rite dioceses. He needs the consent of both bishops.

In case the ordinary refuses his consent to the transfer, the interested persons may have recourse to the Sacred Congregation for the Oriental Church, provided they have sufficient reasons which are able to offset the basis of the ordinary's refusal.

(3) Transfer between different
jurisdictions of the same
discipline

Such a situation can arise in the United States where Byzantine Rite Catholics of the Ruthenian (Ukrainian) discipline are subject within the limits of a common territory to different resident bishops and apostolic exarchs in accordance with their European origin.

(1) If no parish or mission of his own jurisdiction is reasonably accessible to him, such a Catholic is obliged to join the parish of the other jurisdiction. This obligation, not mere permission, to join the other jurisdiction of his discipline is derived from the consideration of the jurisdictional origin of the Ruthenian discipline in this country. In permitting the separation into two jurisdictions it was the intention of the Holy See that it should be done not on the family level but on that of the parish. Thus if a community could not be conveniently divided into two new communitities in accordance with the European origin of the faithful, they continued to form one parish, which became subject to the jurisdiction of that ordinary to whom the majority of the parishioners belonged.

However, in many instances such a division was far from perfect. Some individuals who had lost any connection with the country of their extraction remained attached to a certain parish and did not follow other in their secession and establishment of their own parish of a different extraction. The intention of the Apostolic See was not so much to effect a neat division but to put an end to internal frictions by letting the faithful organize according to their liking.

While the faithful of the Ukrainian dioceses of Philadelphia and Stamford are in their entirety Ukrainians or of Ukrainian extraction, those of the Pittsburgh Apostolic Exarchy are of different national extractions. Besides Rusines, who are of the same national origin as the Ukrainians, there are found Slovaks, Magyars (Hungarians), and Croats. In some places the faithful of the Pittsburgh Exarchy are therefore divided into parishes in accordance with national origin, provided the number of such a group permits the establishment of a separate parish.

If a Ruthenian (Ukrainian) Catholic finds in a place a parish of his discipline and jurisdiction but of another national extraction, he is obliged to join that parish and not the Latin Rite parish. If there are several pastors of his discipline he comes under the jurisdiction of that who employs the liturgical language of his extraction, otherwise he comes under the care of the local pastor of his discipline without consideration of national extraction or liturgical language.

The introduction of the English language in the celebration of divine services and the progressive loss of ties with a specific country of extraction in Europe will solve many of the problems which could arise from such a multiplicity.

(2) If a Ruthenian (Ukrainian) Catholic wishes to join a parish of the other jurisdiction on a permanent basis, though a parish of his own jurisdiction is in the place, he needs the consent of both ordinaries.

(3) If in a certain place a parish of their own jurisdiction should be erected, the faithful of that jurisdiction are permitted to leave their affiliation and to join the new parish.

(4) Some aspects of illegal change of Rite

A change of Rite against the prescriptions of law is inefficacious, invalid, non-existent in the sphere of law. Though actually some one may have followed another Rite for a very long time the rules of prescription do not apply here, because the change of Rite is a favor to be obtained only by an indult of the Holy See (c. 1509, n. 2, CIC).

In spite of this, we find Catholics who do not in practice take heed of this rule, often without malice, and sometimes even unaware. Since such cases are encountered every day in many countries because of the relatively small number of Oriental Catholics, living isolated among a Latin Rite majority, the problem is not any more an academic one. A solution will be usually necessitated by the need to establish which pastor is competent to assist at a marriage of such a person.

The principle which should be employed in deciding the membership of such persons in a Rite is not easily found. The existing law deprives the faithful of the right to choose freely their Rite. The succession in the Rite of the father — as a general rule — is a necessary one, and contrary acts are null and void. By virtue of law a Catholic becomes the member of a certain Rite, even if he is entirely unaware of it, and he transmits the same Rite to his offspring. The necessity to give a practical solution to cases as the above mentioned demands that there should be some corrective regulation which would better conform to the needs of the actual situation. It is impossible to ignore the fact of a person's actually belonging to a certain Rite contrary to law only because nowhere is it decreed where the chain of obligatory membership in a certain Rite may be interrupted.

The just solution would be, according to our opinion, that by a legislative act of the Holy See it be established that children of Catholics, who themselves were baptized against the prescriptions of law in a different Rite, join the Rite in which they were baptized. This means that the third generation is able to effect a valid transfer. Since in the third generation no intention of willfully trespassing the law of the Church can be assumed, the fact that a certain goal was reached by unlawful means, will not be detrimental to the lawful public order.

It would seem that rigid application of the principle excluding permanently any change of Rite even in the future generations, except by actual Apostolic indult, is absurd. In practice we would have to dig into archives for centuries back to find out an individual's true Rite.

8. REASONS REQUIRED FOR A TRANSFER OF RITE

CANON 8　# 2.　Among the reasons on account of which transfer to another Rite is usually granted the return to the Rite of one's ancestors is eminent.

Since the interest of the Church demands the preservation of the various Rites, and in order to guarantee the peaceful relationship among the Rites, it is the desire of the Church that the faithful should not change from one Rite to another, except if such change is dictated by valid reasons. The clergy are especially forbidden to induce the faithful to change their Rite. Considering the possibility of one's conforming himself temporarily to any Catholic Rite, it will not be often necessary to change from one Rite to another.

The application for transfer to another Rite must be supported by valid reasons. Every true cause will be accepted. Reasons usually accepted are: The intention of entering a seminary or religious community of a different Rite, especially if the candidate was not reared in his native Rite because of peculiar circumstances; to render a mixed Rite marriage of one Rite only in places where there is no church of the husband's Rite available. The wish to return to the Rite of one's ancestors is the most acceptable to the Holy See, as expressly stated in the above canon.

The Holy See has understanding for the difficulties which Oriental Catholics experience when they are permanently living far from a church of their Rite, especially when entering marriage with a woman of another Rite. There is of course no need for a woman to apply for change of Rite before entering marriage with a man of a different Rite, since she will be permitted to change her Rite, without any special permission, once she has contracted marriage.

Defects in certain organizational situations with which sometimes Oriental Rite parishes are beset, but which can be overcome by applying Christian charity, cannot serve as valid reasons for a transfer of Rite, as, e.g., the fact that such a parish does not possess its own parochial school. Such children will certainly be accepted by the parochial school of another Rite without that the parents are forced to change their Rite. The lack of a school is no reason for Catholics to leave their parish, since the larger number of Latin Rite parishes in the United States and around the world have no parochial schools of their own.

The mere desire to change to another Rite if not supported by sufficient reasons cannot be taken into consideration. Canon law does not know the possibility that priests, bishops or the faithful can choose to obey laws according to their will.

9. SPECIAL CASES OF TRANSFER OF RITE

1. Transfer of wife to the Rite of her husband

CANON 9. A wife who belongs to another Rite is at liberty to join the Rite of her husband at the time of marriage or during its duration. When the marriage has been dissolved she is free to resume her own Rite.

A wife may aggregate herself to the Rite of her husband without needing any special permission. This is to be understood as a complete transfer of Rite, and not as a mere temporal accommodation to different liturgical rules and regulations, for which no authorization is required for anybody. She may make use of this privilege at the time of entering into marriage, but also at any other time during the duration of the marriage, and is entitled to return to her previous Rite after the dissolution of the marriage bond, regularly by death of the husband.

The declaration of transfer to the Rite of the husband made at the time of the wedding does not affect the laws governing the marriage form, i.e., the transfer takes legal effect from the moment of the exchange of vows, but not sooner (Commission on Interpretation April 29, 1940, AAS 1940, 212).

If the husband is a non-Catholic Oriental dissident, then of course the wife does not enjoy the privilege of changing to the Catholic Oriental Rite corresponding to her husband's Rite, but has to receive for this a special indult of the Apostolic See.

In making use of this privilege at a later time the formalities prescribed in c. 13 must be observed. However, if a bride chooses to change her Rite at the time of the wedding, the signing of such a declaration by her is sufficient, and no witnesses are needed. This could be done conveniently, e.g., by making a corresponding annotation in the marriage register to be signed by her.

2. Legal consequences for children of parents transferred to another Rite

CANON 10. If the father lawfully transfers to another Rite, or, in a mixed marriage, the Catholic mother, the children who have not yet reached the age of puberty are by law itself transferred to the same Rite.

Legal puberty is reached according to c. 17 # 2 by males when they have completed their fourteenth, by females when they have completed their twelfth year of age. In submitting a request for transfer of Rite, children under this age have not to be included in the petition, while those who are older must apply for themselves.

By analogy, illegitimate children of a non-Catholic father who himself becomes a Catholic in a Rite different from that of the mother of the children automatically change their Rite when the marriage of their parents is contracted, or at the time their father made his conversion, provided they did not yet reach puberty, in which case they would have to apply to the S. Congregation for themselves.

3. Conversion of dissident Orientals

CANON 11. # 1. Baptized non-Catholics of an Eastern Rite may embrace the Rite they prefer when they are admitted into the Catholic Church; however, it is desired that they retain their own Rite.

 # 2. A cleric who in virtue of delegated power received a baptized non-Catholic of an Eastern Rite into a Rite of the Catholic Church different from the cleric's own, shall inform the Hierarch of the Rite assumed. It is expedient also that he seek the advice of the mentioned Hierarch before he receives him.

Non-Catholic Orientals may choose in entering the Church any Rite, though they should be encouraged to remain in their native Rite. This possibility was also contemplated by Leo XIII in **Orientalium Dignitas** (Art. 11), when he mentioned Orientals entering the Church "with the stipulation interposed by them as necessary condition of joining the Latin Rite." The S. Congregation for the Oriental Church demands that such persons should be informed of the opportunity given them by the Church to remain in their native Rite. This was also emphasized in an instruction concerning the conversion of Russians, Ukrainians and Byelorussians issued by the same S. Congregation on August 26, 1929 (AAS 1929, 608).

Leo XIII ordered in **Orientalium Dignitas** also that if in the absence of a priest of the Oriental Rite Eastern dissidents embrace the Faith through the efforts of a Latin Rite priest, they have to return to their native Oriental Rite as soon as a priest of their Rite establishes a parish or mission among them.

However, should a convert allege that he was not made aware of the possibility of remaining in his native Rite, he cannot aggregate himself on his own authority to the Oriental Catholic Rite corresponding to that Rite he held as a dissident, but needs a permission of the Holy See, which in view of c. 8 # 2 will readily be granted.

4. Conversion of Protestants

The permission granted to baptized Oriental dissidents to choose any Rite in entering the Church could mistakenly be understood as granting them a special privilege which is denied to other non-Catholics, notably to baptized Protestants. This would be an erroneous conclusion for the following considerations:

Any person is free in all actions and omissions except if limitations have been set by divine or human law. This principle is valid also within canon law. Consequently, a validly baptized person, regardless of his religious affiliation, would be entitled to change from one Rite to another, were it not for certain limitations established by the Church. These restrictions of the freedom of persons ought to be interpreted strictly. Such curtailment has been established by c. 8. This canon speaks of "nobody" being able to transfer to another Rite without the permission of the Holy See. This is to be understood, in the light of preceding laws and the teaching of canonists, as regarding baptized Catholics only, i.e., baptized persons who are or have been at one time in communion with the Church, and excludes thereby dissident Orientals as well as Protestants and other non-Catholic Christians. No provision having been made for dissident Orientals and Protestants, they are free to change from one Rite to another, as long as they are outside the communion of the Church, or at the moment of aggregating themselves to the visible organization of the Church headed by the Roman Pontiff.

Canon 11 # 1 is not a special grant of a privilege to dissident Orientals, withheld from Protestants, but its insertion is to be explained by reference to the law preceding **Cleri Sanctitati**. The S. Congregation for the Propagation of the Faith had granted Oriental dissidents permission to choose any Oriental, but not the Latin Rite, in entering the Church. Leo XIII conceded in **Orientalium Dignitas** (1894) that they may become Latin Rite Catholics only if they made the aggregation to the Latin Rite a necessary condition of their joining the Church.

Since **Cleri Sanctitati** did not establish any specific limitation to baptized non-Catholics as to a free choice of Rite when they join the Church, the stipulation of c. 11 # 1 was not needed, strictly speaking. However, to prevent some canonists from invoking the above mentioned limitations decreed in the last century, and demanding that Oriental dissidents retain their native Rite, a reminder was appropriate, and was given in this place. Therefore, baptized non-Catholics, without consideration in which denomination they have received baptism, may choose any Rite in entering the Church. Oriental dissidents are urged to retain the Rite in which they were baptized, while no such exhortation was given for Protestants.

While there would be valid reasons for curtailing the freedom of Oriental dissidents in choosing a Rite, there are none as far as baptized Protestants are concerned, since they abandoned a long time ago all the genuine characteristics of the Latin Rite from which their denomination once originated. If the Church considered it justified to grant complete liberty to the Oriental dissidents in this matter, it was all the more appropriate to do the same in respect to Protestants or other baptized non-Catholics of Western extraction.

Oriental dissidents have not only faithfully preserved the common liturgical tradition, but have retained also the canonical structure which defines the separate existence of a Rite. Nothing similar can be found among Protestants, and a preservation of their status before conversion would be meaningless.

5. Conversion of infidels

CANON 12. A non-baptized person may freely choose the Rite in embracing the faith.

This canon disproves the sometimes advanced opinion that foreign missionary work is reserved to the Latin Rite.

10. FORMAL REQUIREMENTS OF TRANSFER OF RITE

CANON 13. # 1. Except when the rescript of the Apostolic See orders otherwise, the transfer to another Rite takes legal effect from the moment of the declaration made before the proper Hierarch or pastor of the new Rite or before a priest delegated by either of them and two witnesses, with the exception of a transfer which takes place at the time of entering marriage, which shall be preceded by a written declaration of the wife.

2. This declaration shall be recorded without delay in the baptismal register, and shall be brought by the pastor of the new Rite to the knowledge of the pastor of the parish where the baptism of the person who changed Rite was to be recorded according to Canon Law, in order that the change of Rite might be mentioned in the baptismal register, and in the case of a further transfer of Rite, also the pastor of the Rite which was held in the meantime shall be informed.

The question at which time the transfer of Rite becomes legally effective is now definitely answered. Except the S. Congregation should decree otherwise, the transfer is accomplished at the moment of the declaration of the applicant that he goes through with his intention.

1. The request for transfer to another Rite must be made in writing to the S. Congregation for the Oriental Church, whose prefect is the Holy Father himself; therefore the petition is to be addressed to him.

The application is a request of the persons interested, who therefore are to apply themselves. A priest may be of assistance to them in preparing the petition, if requested expressly and without solicitation on his part, and if the canonical reasons are present, but he cannot apply on their behalf, and they must consequently sign the documents themselves.

The request is normally forwarded to his chancery by the pastor of the Rite to which the petitioner wishes to affiliate. If both Rites, that a quo and that ad quem, are under the jurisdiction of the same Latin Rite ordinary, the latter can forward the petition at once to the S. Congregation together with his opinion. If it involves a transfer between the Latin Rite and, e.g., the Ukrainian dioceses of the United States and Canada or the Apostolic Exarchy of Pittsburgh, then the application is best submitted to the representative of the Apostolic See in that country, the Apostolic Delegate in Washington or Ottawa.

The Apostolic Delegate sends the request to the ordinary of the Rite from which the petitioner wishes to be transferred, in order to hear his opinion. The respective ordinary will normally seek further information from the pastor under his jurisdiction whose parish the applicant is about to leave. This perhaps tedious procedure has the advantage that possible falsehoods contained in the application will then be revealed.

After having formulated his own judgment, the ordinary returns the files to the Apostolic Delegate, who submits them to the Sacred Congregation.

2. If the S. Congregation decided favorably, the ordinary of the Rite **ad quem** will be informed. He will receive the decree and be notified of the fee to be paid for the document. The ordinary forwards the same information to the pastor, who in turn will request the petitioner to appear before him for making the declaration of transfer.

3. The applicant, possibly his wife, and all their children who are of legal puberty and had joined them in the request, will then in the presence of the pastor or a priest delegated by him and two other witnesses sign a short declaration to the effect that they accept the decree of the Holy See and that they will consider themselves from now on as belonging to this Rite. The applicant, the receiving priest and the witnesses affix their signatures. Any other ceremony or sacred rite, as, e.g., the reception of sacraments, cannot be joined with such a declaration because it would create the impression as if the transfer of Rite is a kind of conversion to the Faith, and debase the dignity of the Rite which was abandoned.

The signed declaration should then be preserved, preferably in the diocesan archives.

4. The transfer of Rite shall be recorded in the baptismal register of the church where it had taken place.

5. It is also a duty of the receiving pastor to notify the pastors of the churches where the applicants and their children have been baptized, and request them to make such an annotation in the baptismal register. They should not omit to forward the protocol number of the files and the date of issuance of the decree of the S. Congregation to have it recorded in the baptismal register. If this information is not furnished, the pastor is not bound to consider the information as genuine.

In the case of a convert baptized outside the church this notification is to be sent to the church where he was received into the Church.

6. The wife may join her husband in his Rite at any time during the marriage. She needs no permission of the Holy See, but she must make the same kind of declaration as other petitioners.

11. SUBJECTION TO ANOTHER RITE

CANON 14. The faithful of an Eastern Rite who are lawfully subject to a Hierarch or pastor of a different Rite continue to remain members of their own Rite.

12. OBLIGATION OF INTRODUCTORY CANONS

CANON 15. The prescriptions of canons 1 # 2, 3, 4, 5, 7, 10, 11 # 2, 13, oblige the clergy and faithful of any Rite whatsoever, those of the Latin Rite not excluded.

The canons enumerated in c. 15 refer to interritual relationships, and oblige all Rites. However, **Cleri Sanctitati** is the law for the Oriental Churches, and lest someone should draw the conclusion that these canons affect only all O r i e n t a l Rites and their reciprocal legal relations, the legislator has added **"latinis haud exclusis,"** i.e., that the relationship between any of the Oriental Rites on one side and the Latin Rite on the other is also ruled by these canons.

From the enumeration of c. 15 it does not follow that other canons of **Cleri Sanctitati** do not oblige Latin Rite faithful and clergy.

A certain number of canons of **Cleri Sanctitati** will effect the Latin Rite Church indirectly, since they contain new formulations of problems disputed in the CIC. Because of the complete analogy between the laws and the circumstances contemplated by the legislator, with canons nearly identical in wording, and since they originated from the same lawgiver, the Roman Pontiff, the corresponding canon of **Cleri Sanctitati** must be accepted as an authentic interpretation of the respective canon of the CIC. We have such an example in c. 35 # 1 (= c. 105 CIC) in respect to the question under what legal sanction, for validity or only lawfulness, the consent or advice of consultors of a superior is required.

Other canons of **Cleri Sanctitati** contain definitions of principles accepted in the canon law of the Latin Rite Church although they were not expressly codified in the CIC. As example may serve c. 142 # 1, in which the exercise of jurisdiction is limited to subjects. By enlarging the text of c. 201 CIC also **vagi** and **peregrini** were included, a principle derived already by canon law on the basis of other legislative maxims.

TITLE TWO:

PHYSICAL AND MORAL PERSONS

CHAPTER ONE: PHYSICAL PERSONS (cc. 16-26).

1. MEMBERSHIP IN THE VISIBLE CHURCH

CANON 16. # 1. By baptism man acquires in Christ's Church the character of a person.

2. A person in Christ's Church enjoys all Christian rights and is obliged to all Christian duties, unless, as far as rights are concerned, there is an obstacle impairing the bond of communion with the Church, or a censure pronounced by the Church.

2. AGE

CANON 17. # 1. A person who has completed the eighteenth year of age is of full age, save for a regulation in particular law which demands a more advanced age; a person below this age is a minor.

2. A minor of the male sex is considered to have attained puberty from the completion of the fourteenth year, and one of the female sex from the twelfth year.

3. 1. A person who is below puberty is called an infant or a child or a little one (parvulus) if he is younger than seven years, and he is not considered to be in full possession of mental faculties; after completing seven years he is presumed to have the use of reason.

2. Persons habitually devoid of the use of reason are held equal to infants.

Oriental canon law has lowered the age for reaching majority to eighteen years unless particular law stipulates a higher age. For the Ruthenian discipline of the Byzantine Rite, which comprises as the most numerous Oriental Catholic group, the Ukrainians, there is no particular law which would make such a demand, since the general norm was followed, and the new limit is therefore obligatory. A practical application might be found in cases of marriages of minors against the will of their parents (cf. c. 24 of **Crebrae Allatae**, or c. 1034 CIC).

CANON 18. **A person of full age has the complete exercise of his rights; the minor remains subject to the authority of the parents or guardians in the exercise of his rights, with the exception of matters in which the law considers minors exempt from parental authority.**

3. ORIGIN

CANON 19. # 1. **Place of origin for a child is that place in which the father — or if the child is of illegitimate birth and was not declared legitimate, or was posthumously born, that in which the mother — had a domicile, or, in defect of a domicile, a quasi-domicile at the time of birth.**

2. **In the case of a child of vagi, the place of origin is also the place of birth; if it is the case of an exposed child, it is the place where he was found.**

The definitions of c. 91 CIC for the terms **incola, advena, peregrinus,** and **vagus** are not found in the sequence of these canons, since they were defined in the foregoing motuproprio **Postquam Apostolics** (c. 304):

"**A person is called an incola in the place where he has a domicile; advena in the place where he has a quasi-domicile; peregrinus when he stays outside his domicile and quasi-domicile which he still retains; vagus if he has nowhere a domicile or quasi-domicile.**"

4. DOMICILE

CANON 20. # 1. **A domicile is acquired by residence in some quasi-parish, or at least in an eparchy. This stay is either connected with the intention to remain in a place permanently, provided nothing calls one away, or is actually continued for ten complete years.**

2. **A quasi-domicile is acquired by residence as defined in # 1, which is either connected with the intention to stay in a place at least for the greater part of the year, provided nothing calls one away, or is actually continued for the greater part of the year.**

3. **The domicile or quasi-domicile in a parish or quasi-parish is called parochial; if it is had only in an eparchy but not in a parish or quasi-parish it is called eparchial.**

CANON 21. # 1. **A wife, if not lawfully separated from the husband, retains the domicile of her husband; however, she can obtain her own quasi-domicile; if she is lawfully separated, perpetually or** for an indefinite time, she can acquire also a domicile after she has given up the domicile of her husband.

2. A minor shares the domicile of the person in whose charge he is; a minor after the years of infancy can acquire his own quasi-domicile.

3. An insane person shares the domicile of his guardian.

CANON 22. # 1. Unless law provides otherwise, everybody acquires the pastor and Hierarch of his own Rite either through a domicile or a quasi-domicile.

2. When the faithful of a Rite do not have a pastor of their own Rite, their Hierarch shall appoint a pastor of another Rite, who shall assume their care, after the same Hierarch has obtained the consent of the Hierarch of the appointed pastor.

5. HAVE LATIN RITE PASTORS SUPPLETORY JURISDICTION OVER ORIENTAL CATHOLICS IN A TERRITORY WITH MULTIPLE HIERARCHY?

This problem shall be discussed only insofar it applies to the situation encountered in the United States and Canada in respect to the Ruthenian (Ukrainian) discipline of the Byzantine Rite, which has its own hierarchy of seven dioceses and exarchies. Does the Latin Rite pastor acquire suppletory jurisdiction over subjects of these dioceses and apostolic exarchies in places where their own pastors are not available to them?

A practical implication of some importance concerns the validity of the assistance at marriage and the obligation of observing the ecclesiastical form of marriage. It must be stated at once that some cases of assistance at marriage are outside our consideration, since the problem of validity will not arise:

1. Marriages of Ruthenian (Ukrainian) Catholics before the Latin Rite pastor after he received proper delegation from the Byzantine Rite bishop or pastor.

2. Marriages of Ruthenian (Ukrainian) Catholics with Latin Rite Catholics, because the Latin Rite pastor possesses the necessary power of assistance even if the Byzantine Rite pastor ought have been approached for lawfulness.

3. Marriages of Ruthenian (Ukrainian) Catholics with baptized Protestants, since also in this case the Latin Rite pastor possesses jurisdiction over the baptized Protestant.

4. Marriages of Ruthenian (Ukrainian) Catholics with dissident Orientals who received baptism in a denomination the Catholic counterpart of which is under the jurisdiction of the Latin Rite ordinary. For example, the case of a dissident Syrian of the Byzantine Rite; the corresponding Catholic Oriental group, the Byzantine Rite Melkites, are subject to the Latin Rite bishops of the United States and Canada.

The validity of the following marriages will depend upon our answer to the question whether the Latin Rite pastor in the above circumstances has suppletory power:

5. Marriages between two Ruthenians (Ukrainians) of the

Byzantine Rite before a Latin Rite pastor without specific delegation.

6. Marriages between Ruthenian (Ukrainian) Catholics and non-baptized persons before a Latin Rite pastor without specific delegation.

In either case none comes under the regular jurisdiction of the Latin Rite pastor.

We maintained in our book **Interritual Canon Law Problems in the United States and Canada** (p. 21) that Oriental Rite Catholics are in case of inavailability of their own pastors subject to the Latin Rite clergy even in the territories where they have their own hierarchy. A study of **Cleri Sanctitati** did not disclose any specific principle of law which would support such an assumption. The lack in the most recent part of the codification of a provision which would grant by virtue of law itself to Latin Rite pastors suppletory jurisdiction in such situations should be an indication that the only source of such jurisdiction would be the authorization from the respective Ruthenian (Ukrainian) ordinary, granted in each single case, or for all cases in the meaning of can. 22 # 2. However, as far as it is known, general delegations have not been granted to Latin Rite pastors in this country and in Canada by the Ruthenian (Ukrainian) ordinaries.

Yet, there is one additional general principle of law which can be invoked, namely, legal custom. It has been always the conviction of the Ruthenian (Ukrainian) Catholic faithful as well as of the clergy of all Catholic Rites that in such a situation the faithful of one Rite is obliged to seek the ministrations of the clergy of another Rite, and that marriages entered into in the United States and Canada must always be witnessed by a priest.

In addition it must be said that the above mentioned two classes of marriages would be always valid if assisted at by Latin Rite pastors in the defined circumstances in virtue of c. 89 of **Crebrae Allatae** on the extraordinary ecclesiastical marriage form. The only remaining problem would be the case where marriages of classes 3, 4, 5 and 6 were entered into before a civil magistrate or a non-Catholic minister. We are inclined to regard them as invalid because we consider the Byzantine Rite Ruthenian (Ukrainian) Catholics obliged to have recourse to the Latin Rite pastors in such circumstances.

However, even such cases cannot easily arise if we adopt a modern view of the circumstances which are contemplated in the extraordinary ecclesiastical marriage form. The inavailability of the proper pastor, his inaccessibility, should be judged according to the circumstances of life in this time on the American continent. Consequently, considering on one hand the means of speedy transportation which are at the disposal of everyone at not too great an expense, and on the other hand the importance of marriage as a contract from which the parties will draw benefits for a whole lifetime, it is not to be regarded as a great inconvenience if we demand that they should approach a pastor or Hierarch of their jurisdiction, although either of them might reside hundreds of miles afar. The same diligence can be expected in this matter which is employed by average people when they seek a competent surgeon for a major operation. A similar expenditure of effort and time can be demanded from one entering into the holy state of matrimony. We need not feel sorry for him because of the possible inconvenience, since he can avoid it by approaching the local Latin Rite pastor who could easily obtain the necessary delegation.

In conclusion, our answer is the following: In places where Ruthenian (Ukrainian) Catholics have no pastor of their own jurisdiction available they come under the suppletory jurisdiction of the Latin Rite pastor in force of a legal custom observed before and since the independent Byzantine Rite jurisdiction on the American continent was established. For the lawfulness, and sometimes also for the validity, of dispensations needed for such marriages, the Byzantine Rite ordinary must be approached. Marriages entered into in such situations without the observance of the obligatory ecclesiastical marriage form will be invalid. The Latin Rite pastor needs for the lawful assistance at such marriages the permission of the Byzantine Rite bishop.

In respect to those Oriental Rite Catholics who are under the jurisdiction of the Latin Rite bishop, the situation might be different. Their bishop could have erected a parish of the Rite or discipline for the whole diocese or only for a limited part of it. He could have subjected these Catholics to the jurisdiction of the local Latin Rite pastor in places outside the territory or reach of their Oriental Rite pastor.

3. Outside the territory of their own Rite, in the absence of a hierarch of that Rite, the Hierarch of the place shall be regarded their proper Hierarch.

This norm is applied wherever no hierarchy of their own is established for a specific Oriental Rite group, as, for instance, for all Eastern Rite Catholics in the United States and Canada, with the exception of the Ukrainian (Ruthenian) Byzantine Rite Catholics, for whom seven dioceses and apostolic exarchies are erected.

A "territory of their own Rite" is one where at least an exarchy is established for that specific Oriental Rite group, as, e.g., in respect to the Ukrainians (Ruthenians) on the North American continent, the United States and Canada (cf. c. 303 # 1, n. 3, of **Postquam Apostolicis**).

Such an "Oriental territory" should be distinguished from an **"Oriental region,"** which are those places where the respective Oriental Rite was observed since ancient times, although no hierarchical structure does exist there at the present time.

It is a maxim of paramount import that faithful have tobe under the care of ecclesiastical superiors, who are their shepherds. This care is exercised not only by pastors, but also by bishops. Such supervision must be efficient, not nominal. Since most Catholic Orientals in the United States and Canada form only few and numerically small local groups, the erection of their own hierarchy was not advisable, except for the Ruthenians. Distance again prevents the respective hierarchy in the Near East from taking efficient care of the clergy and the faithful on the American continent.

Oriental Catholics are here assigned for this reason to the care of the local Latin Rite ordinaries, and, if necessary, of Latin Rite pastors.

The subjection of Oriental Rite Catholics to the local Latin Rite clergy is not decreed because of any preeminence of that Rite over Oriental Rites. We find the reversed situation for instance in Italy, where the Byzantine Rite bishops of **Lungro (Calabria)** and **Piana dei Greci (Sicily)** are not only ordinaries of their Byzantine Rite faithful, but also of Latin Rite Catholics residing in their episcopal cities.

Where there are several local ordinaries in the same place, the Apostolic See, or in exceptional cases the patriarch, will decide which of the local ordinaries is to be considered the one to whom the faithful of a certain Rite will be subject. In the United States and Canada we find two and even three local ordinaries in the same territory, namely the Latin Rite bishops, the Ukrainian Byzantine Rite bishop, and (in the United States) the Apostolic Exarch of Pittsburgh. By many acts of the Holy See it has been made clear that all Oriental Catholics, with the exception of the Ruthenians, are subject to the Latin Rite ordinaries.

The same principle may be indirectly deduced from other decrees of the various offices of the Holy See, especially those which state that the Ruthenians in the United States and Canada are exempt from the jurisdiction of the local Latin Rite ordinary, which subjection is therefore to be inferred as the normal rule. Other decisions of the same content may be found in Bouscaren (I, 4; 17-24, 39-42; II, 5-6).

The subjection of Orientals to the local Latin Rite ordinaries is however limited. All that concerns peculiarities of Rite are to be preserved, and interference of the ordinary is excluded. Catholics are held to the laws of their Rite everywhere. Orientals are therefore bound by the disciplinary laws of the local Latin Rite ordinaries only as long as the observance of these laws is not detrimental to their respective Rite. The Latin Rite ordinaries enjoy in regard to their Oriental Rite faithful the same dispensative power which ordinaries of their own Rite would enjoy. They are, therefore, entitled to dispense also from prescriptions of the particular law of that respective Rite, for instance, established by legal custom, provincial and patriarchal synods, etc.

4. **The proper pastor or Hierarch of a vagus is the pastor or Hierarch of his Rite of the place where the vagus actually stays; if there is no pastor or Hierarch of his Rite, the norms established in ## 2, 3, shall apply.**

5. **Also for those who have but an eparchial domicile or quasi-domicile the proper pastor shall be the pastor of the place where they actually stay.**

CANON 23. **Domicile and quasi-domicile are lost by departure from the place with the intention not to return, save for the prescription of canon 21.**

6. CONSANGUINITY

CANON 24. # 1. Consanguinity is computed by lines of descent and degrees.

 # 2. In the direct line there are as many degrees as there are persons, not counting the head of the line.

 # 3. In the branch line there are as many degrees as there are persons in both branches, not counting the head of the line.

Roman Law reckoned degrees of relationship by counting the persons in both lines, excluding the common progenitor. There were as many degrees as persons less one. This computation remained in the Eastern Churches and was also accepted by the civil law system of modern times. The Latin Rite Church adopted the Germanic computation, which is still preserved in the Code of Canon Law. Eastern Catholics follow the Eastern computation according to **Crebrae Allatae (c. 66 # 4).**

There is no difference in computing degrees in the direct line, but only in the collateral or branch lines. While Eastern computation counts in establishing the degrees of relationship the number of persons on both sides, Western computation reckons it by counting the persons of one line only, and if the lines are inequal, of the longer branch.

Both systems of computation have some shortcomings. The Eastern computation is sometimes vague, because, e.g., the fifth degree could be the first touching the fourth (¼) as well as the second touching on the third (⅔). Since, however, in practice a case of relationship ¼ (e.g. between a man and his great grandniece) will not likely happen, greater accuracy is not needed. The Western computation is also not accurate enough and has to be supplied by giving the number of persons of the other line, e.g., 3/2.

As to consanguinity, that in the direct line is a diriment and indispensable impediment (c. 66 # 1 **Crebrae Allatae**). In the collateral line it is in the Oriental matrimonial law a diriment impediment to the sixth degree inclusive (c. 66 #2). Some combinations, lateral line it is in the Oriental matrimonial law a diriment impediment in the Latin Rite at all, while in Oriental Rites it still prevents a valid marriage.

7. AFFINITY

CANON 25. # 1. 1. Affinity from digeneia arises from a valid marriage although not consumated.

2. It exists between each spouse and the blood relations of the other.

3. In that line and degree in which someone is a blood relation of one of the spouses, he is in affinity with the other.

Oriental marriage law knows three kinds of affinity. Paragraph 1 of c. 25 contemplates the first species of affinity arising from digeneia, and is the affinity between one spouse and blood relations of the other. This is the only one known in the present day Latin Rite canon law (c. 97 # 2 CIC). It arises from a valid marriage, whether it is consumated or not.

This species of affinity exists among all Orientals, and is an impediment in the direct line in all degrees, and in the collateral line to the fourth degree inclusive (c. 67 # 1, 1 **Crebrae Allatae**).

> # 2. 1. **By particular law affinity from digeneia mentioned in # 1, 1, arises also between the blood relations of the husband and the blood relations of the wife.**
>
> 2. **It is to be reckoned in such a manner that there are as many degrees as result from the sum of the degrees of consanguinity by which both affines are distant from the spouses from whose marriage the affinity arose.**

This kind of affinity is an impediment only to the fourth degree inclusive (c. 67 # 1, 2). It exists among the following Oriental disciplines and subdivisions of disciplines (cf. **Coussa, De matrimonio,** p. 133) : Chaldeans, Melkites, Rumanians, Bulgarians, Greeks from Greece and Turkey, Ethiopians. It is never a multiple impediment. The local ordinary has ordinary power to dispense from this kind of affinity in any degree (c. 32 #1, 2).

> # 3. 1. **By particular law affinity, moreover, results from trigeneia, that is, from two valid marriages, although not consummated, when two persons contracted marriage: (a) with the same third person, after the previous marriage had been dissolved, with one after the other; or (b) with two persons who were blood relations;**
>
> 2. **Affinity resulting from trigeneia exists between each of the spouses and those who are related in affinity with the other party by way of the second marriage on strength of digeneia;**
>
> 3. **This affinity between one spouse and those who are in affinity with the other is to be reckoned in such a manner that those who are by the second marriage in affinity with the husband by way of digeneia are in the same degree in affinity with the wife in trigeneia, and vice versa.**
>
> 4. **When this affinity exists between the blood relations of the one spouse and those in affinity with the other, it is reckoned in such a manner that there are as many degrees as result from the sum of degrees of the consanguinity as well as of the affinity from digeneia, by which both of the affines are distant from the spouses whose marriage the affinity arose from.**

The third species of affinity arises from two marriages but affects three marriages, namely, also the now contemplated and impeded. This impediment exists only among Catholic Russians, Bulgarians, and Greeks from Greece and Turkey (**Coussa, De matrimonio,** p. 133). It exists also among many dissident Oriental groups. The impediment does not exceed the first degree (c. 67 # 1, 3, **Crebrae Allatae**) and is never a multiple one. The local ordinary has the power of granting dispensations.

8. STATES

> CANON 26. **Among various persons in the Church some belong to the clerical state, others to the laical. Clerics as well as lay persons can be of the religious state.**

CHAPTER TWO:

MORAL PERSONS

Definition and Classification (c. 27 = c. 99 CIC).
Mode of Establishment (c. 28 = c. 100 CIC).
Requisites for Actions (c. 29 = c. 101 CIC)
Duration of Existence (c. 30 ## 1, 2 = c. 102 CIC;
    # 3 = new)
Provisions in Case of Extinction (c. 31 = new).

CANON 27. There are in the Church besides physical persons also moral persons, constituted by the public authority of the Church, which persons are distinguished into collegiate and non-collegiate moral persons.

CANON 28. # 1. The Catholic Church and the Apostolic See possess the nature of a moral person by divine ordinance. The other subordinate moral persons in the Church receive it either from the prescription of law itself or from a specific concession of the competent ecclesiastical superior granted by a formal decree for a religious or charitable purpose.

2. No collegiate moral person can be established that does not consist of at least three physical persons.

3. Moral persons, the collegiate ones as well as the non-collegiate ones, are held equal to minors.

CANON 29. # 1. Actions of collegiate persons are governed by the following rules: 1. Unless either common or particular law prescribes otherwise, that shall have legal force which was decided by absolute majority of those who cast votes, not counting invalid ones, or, after two indecisive votings, by relative majority in the third voting. If the number of votes cast on both sides was equal, the president can after the third balloting break the tie in virtue of his authority, or if it is the case of elections and the president declines to break the tie by his authority, he shall be regarded as elected who is the senior in sacred ordination, then the senior in first profession, and then the senior in age.

2. Matters that concern all members individually must be approved by all.

2. In respect to actions of non-collegiate moral persons, the norms of the common and particular law regarding such persons are to be followed.

CANON 30. # 1. A moral person is of its very nature perpetual. It may be extinguished by law if it is suppressed by legitimate ecclesiastical authority, or by having ceased to exist for a period of one hundred years.

2. If at least one member of the collegiate moral person remains, the rights of all rest with him, save for the prescription of # 3.

3. A collegiate person that is deprived of members enjoying active vote in the number required by law for the exercise of rights is

entrusted to the special care of the secular or religious ecclesiastical superior. Collegiate actions must be ratified by the superior, unless otherwise provided in common or particular law, and, for their validity, after consulting the members who enjoy active vote. Non-collegiate actions, for whose validity the intervention of a college is required in virtue of common or particular law, must receive for their validity the confirmation of the same superior.

CANON 31. # 1. 1. Unless otherwise provided in common or particular law, the property and rights of a collegiate person which is left without members must be conserved, administered or exercised, as in the case of a non-collegiate person, by that ecclesiastical superior who is entitled to dispose of them in the case of extinction. The superior must in accordance with the law take provisions that the obligations which affect this property be satisfied.

2. Members of such a moral person can, and according to circumstances must, be received by that eclesiastical superior who is entitled to the immediate management of the collegiate person, without prejudice to the norms of common and particular law. The same rule shall be applied if the members are in accordance with common or particular law incapable of performing the reception.

2. 1. The appointment of rectors and administrators of a non-collegiate person is entrusted to the immediate ecclesiastical superior when it cannot be performed in accordance with common or particular law.

2. It is also an obligation of the same superior to act as administrator according to the norms of # 1, until he has appointed a suitable administrator.

CHAPTER THREE:

RULES COMMON TO PHYSICAL AND MORAL PERSONS (cc. 32-37)

Force, Fear, Fraud (c. 32 = c. 103 CIC)
Error (c. 33 = c. 104 CIC)
Compensation for Causing Damage (c. 34 = new)
Acts of Superiors (c. 35## 1, 3, 4 = c. 105 CIC; # 2 = new)
Rules for Voting on Proposals of a Superior (c. 36 # new)
Precedence Among Persons (c. 37 = c. 106 CIC)

CANON 32. # 1. Actions that are taken by either a physical or a moral person on account of force, brought to bear upon from outside, which the person could not resist, are to be regarded as though they were not done.

2. Actions placed because of great fear which was caused unjustly, or because of deceit, are valid unless the law provides otherwise; they can, however, be declared null and void by a sentence of an ecclesiastical judge according to canonical norms either at the demand of the injured party or ex officio.

CANON 33. Error renders an action void when it concerns what constitutes the substance of the action, or amounts to sine qua non condition; otherwise the action is valid, unless law provides the reverse. In contracts, however, error may give the right to action for the rescinding of the contract.

CANON 34. Damage whatsoever caused through injustice is to be compensated by that person through whose malice or guilt it was done.

CANON 35. # 1. 1. When the law states that a superior needs the consent or the advice of some persons, the following rules obtain: If consent is required, the superior acts invalidly if he did not obtain the consent of these persons.

While the corresponding c. 105 CIC says "the superior acts invalidly a g a i n s t their vote," making it possible to act validly if no consultation at all had taken place, the present canon is more precise, stating that the act would be invalid if the superior did not actually obtain the consent of the persons entitled to it.

2. If only advice is required, by words like cum consilio consultorum, or auditis consultoribus, or similar expressions, nothing else is required for the validity of the action except that the superior consults these persons. Though he is not bound by any obligation to accept their advice, even if it be unanimous, he should nevertheless have great regard for such an unanimous vote where several persons have to be consulted, and he should not depart from it without a reason judged by him to be prevailing.

3. If the consent or the consultation not only of one or of two persons is required, but of several simultaneously, these persons shall be legally convened, in accordance with the norms of c. 104 ## 3, 4, on the convocation of electors, and then they shall manifest their mind.

2. If someone of those who are to be convoked, and whose consent is required, has been passed over, the superior acts validly, but on demand of the neglected person, who can prove the disregard and the absence, the competent superior or judge must rescind the actions, provided it is proven that the recourse was forwarded according to the norms of law at least within three days from the time knowledge was had of the planned meeting for the purpose of seeking the consent.

3. The superior may, if he considers it advisable and the importance of the business justifies it, oblige the persons mentioned in # 1 to take an oath of observing secrecy.

4. All persons whose consent or advice is sought shall with due respect, confidence and sincerity manifest their opinion.

CANON 36. The prescriptions of c. 29 # 1, 1, concerning actions taken by collegiate moral persons shall be observed also in respect to the vote mentioned in c. 35 # 1, 3, as well as in regard to other votings which are to be held either collectively or individually by several persons.

CANON 37. 1. The following rules shall apply to the question of precedence among various physical or moral persons, without prejudice to special norms that will be given in connection with the treatment of the respective matters: Whoever represents another person enjoys the right of precedence of that person. However, whoever participate in the capacity of proxies in synods or other similar gatherings shall sit after persons of the same rank who participate in their own right, save for a different norm of particular law.

2. Whoever exercises authority over physical or moral persons enjoys the right of precedence over these persons.

3. Among ecclesiastical persons of whom none has authority over the other the following rules apply: Whoever belongs to a higher rank precedes those who are of a lower rank. Among persons of the same rank but not of the same order: Whoever holds a higher order precedes those who are of a lower order. If they finally belong to the same rank and hold the same order, whoever was first promoted to the rank preceds the others; if they were promoted at the same time, whoever is senior in sacred orders, unless the junior in sacred orders has been ordained by the Roman Pontiff; and in case they received the order at the same time, whoever is senior in age.

4. In matters of precedence the difference of Rite is not considered.

5. Among various moral persons of the same kind and rank, that which is in peaceful quasi-possession of the precedence is entitled to precede, and if this is not determined, that which was established first in the place where the question arose. The right of precedence among the members of a college shall be determined by their lawful statutes, and if this connot be done, by the particular law; and if no norm can be found there, by the rules of common law.

6. It is the task of the Hierarch to determine in his eparchy the precedence among his subjects, in accordance with the principles of common law, the legitimate eparchial customs and the functions assigned to them. He shall also in truly urgent cases settle all controversies concerning precedence, even among exempt ones, insofar as they are to appear together with others as bodies. Every recourse in suspensivo is excluded, but without prejudice to the right of anyone.

7. In respect to the persons who belong to the court of the Supreme Pontiff, precedence shall be determined in accordance with the special privileges, the rules and the traditions of the same court.

TITLE THREE:

CLERICS IN GENERAL

INTRODUCTORY NORMS (cc. 38-43)

Classification of Hierarchies (c. 38 = c. 108 CIC)
Source of Power of the Hierarchies (c. 39 = c. 109 CIC)
Minor Clerics (c. 40 = new)
Prelatic Titles for Oriental Priests (cf. c. 110 CIC)
    Who Can Confer Titles (c. 41 # 1)
    To Whom They Can be Conferred (c. 41 ## 2, 3; c. 42)
Members of the Papal Household (c. 43 = c. 328 CIC)

CANON 38. # 1. 1. Those who have been assigned to the divine ministry by the sacred rite established in their own discipline are called clerics.

Tonsure is not mentioned here because not all Oriental Rites have it as a form of reception into the clergy. The Byzantine Rite, for instance, has a tonsure, but only as part of the double order of lector-cantor, which constitutes reception into the clergy. The genuine tradition of the East knew no rite of reception into the clergy which was not at the same time an order.

2. Clerics are by Divine institution distinguished from lay people.

2. They are not all of the same rank, but there is an ecclesiastical hierarchy by which one is subordinate to the other.

3. The ecclesiastical hierarchy of orders is composed by Divine institution of bishops, priests and ministers. The hierarchy of jurisdiction is composed of the Supreme Pontificate and the subordinate episcopate; by ecclesiastical institution also other degrees have been added.

CANON 39. Those who are received into the ecclesiastical hierarchy, or who have been received but are to be promoted to a higher degree, are not selected or promoted by consent or call from the faithful or the secular power, but are appointed to the grades of the power of orders by sacred ordination; in the Sureme Pontificate, by Divine Law itself through the fulfilling of the conditions of a lawful election and its acceptance; in all other degrees of jurisdiction by canonical mission.

CANON 40. In those Rites in which it is permitted to have clerics who will not be raised to the subdeaconate and to major orders, such clerics are governed solely by particular law.

While in the CIC only those candidates can be received into the clergy who are capable and willing to be promoted to the presbyterate (c. 973 #1), Eastern Churches have preserved the ancient tradition of ordaining clerics who for lifetime may remain in the lower degrees of cantor-lector, subdeacon or deacon. Canon 40 mentions those below a subdeacon, while c. 62 # 2 speaks of such deacons. The matter will be more fully treated in the yet to be promulgated section on holy orders.

CANON 41. # 1. 1. The patriarch can confer on priests of his Rite eminent on account of virtue and learning a prelatic title in order to honor them, observing the norm of c. 260 # 1, 1. However, they cannot make use of their insignia and privileges outside the patriarchate, except if they accompany the patriarch or represent his person in synods or other solemnities, or if they obtained the consent of the local Hierarch.

Priests who are employed in parishes outside the patriarchate, and therefore under the jurisdiction of the Latin Rite ordinary, are usually under the supervision of the patriarch or his representative in respect to liturgical matters. They are not rarely honored by the patriarch with a prelatic title, and it is an accepted custom that they make use of the title and the prerogatives which go with it. Because of their connection and dependence on the patriarch at least in some matters, they can be considered as belonging to those clergy whom the patriarch can distinguish with prelatic titles and privileges.

2. The same right belongs also to the bishop for his territory in the meaning of n. 1, save for the prescription of # 2, and for particular law according to which this right is reserved to the patriarch also in respect to secular clerics.

The various Eastern Rites each know several degrees of distinctions. To confer the higher ones is at least reserved to the patriarch, as, e.g., that of chor-bishop, archimandrite The lower ones can be conferred also by the local Hierarch. Latin Rite bishop would enjoy the same privilege in respect to their Oriental Rite priests, provided the dignity or title is one of that respective Rite, and conferred usually by a bishop.

2. Religious who are charged with an office outside their houses cannot receive titles of dignities of their Rite, except if the patriarch, after having consulted the superior, has granted his consent. With the surrender of the office the title of the dignity ceases also, except if the liturgical laws provide otherwise.

Most dignities are conferred by a liturgical act or blessing, which parallels in its meaning the minor orders, and is therefore considered perpetual; it cannot thus be lost when the reason for having received such a dignity should cease to exist. For the same reason such dignities, titles, insignia and prerogatives are made use of everywhere, not only in the territory for which they were conferred, or of the Hierarch who granted them.

3. The particular law shall be followed in respect to the privileges and insignia which come with the titles mentioned in # 1.

Eastern Churches have developed different systems of honorific dignities, titles and distinctions for their clergy below bishops. We shall here treat the Byzantine Rite, which is numerically by far the most preponderant.

Catholic Byzantine Rite Churches have under the influence of the Latin Rite Church often discontinued honors traditional in their Rite and adopted those of the Western Church. Since it is the desire of the Church that they return to their genuine tradition, we shall often refer to the customs of the dissident Churches.

I. INSIGNIA CONFERABLE ON PRESBYTERS

1. Mitre.

While in the Latin Rite the mitre of the bishops and abbots developed quite early from the headgear of the monks, i.e., before the first millenium was reached, in the Byzantine Rite of the early Middle Ages only the Patriarch of Alexandria was known to make use of a liturgical head cover. From the 15th century on the mitre in the form of a crown, first without a cross, came down from the patriarchs to the metropolitans and the bishops. The Ukrainian Church in the Polish Republic, Catholic as well as dissident, granted in the 17th century, in imitation of the Latin Rite abbots, the mitre and some other pontifical insignia to the archimandrites, the higher degree of monastery superiors. This spread from the Ukrainian ecclesiastical center in Kiew to Moscow and the Russian Church.

The mitre and the crozier were later granted by the Roman Pontiffs also to the first; and/or first two dignities of Ukrainian Romanian and Croatian Byzantine Rite archdiocesan and diocesan chapters of canons in the former Austro-Hungarian Moarchy. The use of these pontifical insignia was also permitted to some celibate or widowed priests by the Metropolitan of Lwiw on account of the special task with which they were charged. The same insignia were worn by priests whom the Holy See had honored with the dignity of Protonotary Apostolic.

In the Russian and Ukrainian dissident Churches the mitre can be conferred also on married priests, so-called **mitroforny protoyereyi,** while the mitre and the crozier are used by archimandrites.

The Byzantine Rite mitre was also accepted by the Armenian Rite, where however the bishops and higher abbots had assumed the Latin Rite mitre during the crusades, but was given to all priests and even to the archdeacon, the higher degree of clergy who permanently remain in the order of deacons.

2. Crozier.

The Byzantine Rite pastoral staff ends in a fork, the ends of which are bent down and decorated with snake heads. It is surmounted by a sphere, which has on its top a small cross. Many staffs have still the piece of brocade cloth fastened to the middle of the crozier where it is held by the bishop, as it may be seen on many pictures of medieval Latin Rite bishops.

The crozier in this form is carried by bishops of all degrees, and in the Catholic as well as dissident Ukrainian and Russian Churches also by archimandrites and protonotaries apostolic.

3. Hypogonation.

The hypogonation is a piece of quite stiff brocade or other precious material, and has the shape of a diamond, approximately one foot in length. It is suspended on one corner by a ribbon coming down from the left shoulder, placing the hypogonation at the height of the right knee. It was originally probably a piece of cloth used as a handkerchief for perspiration.

The hypogonation is worn by archpriests, hegoumeni, archimandrites, and all degrees of bishops.

4. Pectoral Cross.

The pectoral cross is not a sign of the episcopal dignity in the Byzantine Church of today. Bishops use a **panagia** (= allholy), i.e., a medallion of the Bl. Mother, richly decorated with gold and gems, pending on a golden chain, sometimes carried together with a cross. Higher bishops, as patriarchs and metropolitans, wear often two panagias.

Dignitaries who are only presbyters wear golden crosses. That of archpriests is simple, while archimandrites may have a cross decorated with precious stones. In the dissident Russian and Ukrainian Churches some priests may be distinguished with the privilege to wear two pectoral crosses. Simple priests in these Churches make use of a silver cross on a simple silver chain.

5. Color of Clerical Dress.

The ancient clergy wore a tunic, which was covered with a cloak or coat with wide sleeves when they were leaving the house. The tunic was as a rule of a fabric which was not yet dyed, because good and stable dyes were expensive. The bleached wool or linen tunic had the color of a dirty white or a white mixed with a yellow tint. This is the origin of the color of the white habit found in several Latin Rite orders, e.g., the Premonstratenses, the Dominicans, most Canons Regular of St. Augustine, and others. It is preserved also by the Roman Pontiff. The cloak or coat was usually dyed black, which is also preserved in this color in some orders, as, e.g., the Dominicans, Augustinian Hermits.

The general rule for the Byzantine Rite clergy is that the tunic or subrason, which corresponds to the cassock, can be of any color whatsoever. However, whenever the cleric appears in public, as on the street, in the church, he must wear over the subrason the rason, which is black in color.

The subrason is girded with a cincture, which for dignitaries is of purple or red color. Dignitaries, including bishops and patriarchs, may line the rason with purple or red silk.

Catholic Byzantine Rite Bishops in the United States, Ukraine, Hungary, Slovakia, Romania, Yugoslavia, distinguished priests with the right to wear such insignia as a purple cincture, purple biretta (kolpak), and a purple rabat.

II. HONORARY TITLES AND DIGNITIES

Dissidents of the Byzantine Rite distinguish the secular clergy with the dignity of archpriest, and as a higher decoration they permit such archpriests to wear a special pectoral cross.

Widowed priests, who decide not to make monastical profession but remain in the secular clergy, especially if they possess a higher education, are in some countries, as in Greece, distinguished with the dignity of archimandrite, which originally was exclusively reserved to superiors of more important monasteries. They are entitled to wear a pectoral cross, the hypogonation and make use of their kamelaukion or biretta during the celebration of Mass.

Dissident Byzantine Rite Churches ordain celibate clerics only if they took monastic vows, although they may be permitted to reside permanently outside convents, in the same way as the secular clergy of the Latin Rite. For the celibate monks, as well as for those who entered into this state as widowers, several dignities exist: (1) **Syncellus** is the lowest. When bishops were appointed from among monks — which today is the exclusive mode — they were obliged to take another monk who would live with them in the same residence as they were wont to do in their kellions or cells in the monastery. This companion became then the chief assistant of the bishop, a sort of vicar general. Among the dissidents the title of syncellus is mere honorary. (2) **Protosyncellus** is a higher degree of the same title. (3) **Hegoumenus** was the title of the monastery superior. Today it is often conferred as a title on monks-priests who are not superiors. Depending on the dissident Church, the hegoumenus might be entitled to wear such insignia as a pectoral cross, hypogonation, purple or red lining in his rason, purple or red cincture, and a crozier (in the Ukrainian and Russian Churches), which has preserved the most ancient form of a simple staff from a tree, ending in a fork, and pushed under the armpit like a crutch to support the body in a standing position during the long hours of the divine office. (4) **Archimandrite** is the highest dignity below that of a bishop. It is conferred upon priest distinguished usually by a higher education and upon prospective candidates to the episcopate. In the Ukrainian and Russian dissident Churches archimandrites wear the mitre, crozier, hypogonation, and pectoral cross. They are also entitled to wear the episcopal mandays, a wide silk cloak of purple color, with three horizontal stripes. However, while the episcopal mandyas has on its four corners in the front the pictures of the four evangelists, the archimandritic mandyas has four crosses. The archimandrites of the former Ukrainian Order of St. Basil the Great, and of the present Italian Order of the same name, had the same insignia. The superiors of the present Ukrainian Order of St. Basil the Great of St. Josaphat make use of only the titles of hegoumenus (monastery superior), protohegoumenus (provincial superior) and proto-archimandrite (superior general) during tenure of the office, without having any insignia attached to the titles.

The title and insignia of a hegoumenissa is conferred also on the superioresses of nuns, with the right to make use of a crozier and pectoral cross.

The Byzantine Rite Catholic dioceses of the former Austro-Hungarian Monarchy had, in imitation of the Latin Rite, chapters with residential and honorary canons and dignitaries, who wore various insignia analogous to Latin Rite canons, although in form adapted to the Eastern tradition. In these dioceses married and celibate clergy were often distinguished with papal honors, although the mitre was conceded only to celibate or widowed priests.

Those clerics who are destined to stay permanently in the order of deacons, and who might possess a higher education than other clergy, may also be the recipients in dissident Churches of the dignity of protodeacon, if secular clerics, or archdeacon, if monks.

CANON 42. # 1. The patriarch and bishops can confer an honorary prelatic title according to the norm of c. 41 on priests of another eparchy but of different Rite, the Latin Rite excepted. with the written consent of their Hierarchs.

2. Such prelatic titles do not confer the faculties connected with the titles in the Rite of the grantor, but they bestow only the right of wearing the honorary liturgical insignia in the liturgical ceremonies of the grantor's Rite.

CANON 43. The members of the court of the Roman Pontiff, those who enjoy a prelatic title as well as those who do not, shall be governed by the privileges, the rules and the traditions of the court of the Supreme Pontiff.

CHAPTER ONE

THE ASCRIPTION OF CLERICS TO AN EPARCHY
OR RELIGIOUS INSTITUTE (cc. 44-52)

Necessity of Ascription (c. 44 = c. 111 # 1 CIC)
Original Ascription into an Eparchy (c. 45 = 111 # 2 CIC)
Original Ascription into a Religious Institute
   (c. 46 ## 1, 2 = cc. 115, 585 CIC)
Change of Ascription by a Religious
   (c. 46 # 3; c. 47 = c. 112 CIC)
Who Can Grant Ascription and Dismissal (c. 48 = c. 113 CIC)
Ascription by Conferral of a Benefice (c. 49 = c. 114 CIC)
Rules for the Validity of Dismissal (c. 50 = c. 116 CIC)
Rules for the Lawfulness of Dismissal (c. 51 = c. 117 CIC)
Rules for Patriarchal Clergy (c. 52 = new)

CANON 44. Every cleric must belong either to some eparchy or some religious institute, save for the norm of c. 52.

CANON 45. By the sacred rite in which one becomes a cleric the cleric is ascribed to the eparchy for the service of which he was promoted.

There are three modes of enrollment of a cleric in an ecclesiastical juridical entity of the Oriental Church: (1) Ascription into an eparchy (c. 45) ; (2) Incardination in a religious institute (c. 46) ; (3) Incardination in the patriarchate as such, eliminating enrollment in a particular eparchy (c. 52) ; this manner exists only for the secular clergy.

The terms **incardinatio** and **excardinatio** of the CIC, which have a Latin Rite origin, were replaced by **adscriptio**, by us rendered as **ascription**, and **dimissio**, by us translated as **dismissal**.

Tonsure as a sacramental distinct from an order, by which a candidate is accepted into the clergy, exists only in the Armenian and Malabarian Rites, in imitation of the Latin Rite.

The Byzantine Rite has as initiation into the clergy a double order, cantorate-lectorate, in which rite also a tonsure is included.

The Syrians, Malankarians and Maronites receive into the clergy by the conferral of the cantorate as first order, later to be followed by the lectorate.

Chaldeans, Copts and Ethiopians have as first order the lectorate.

CANON 46. # 1. Through the sacred rite by which a religious becomes a cleric, even though temporarily professed in monasteries or in orders or congregations in which perpetual vows are taken, the religious becomes ascribed as a cleric to his institute.

2. A cleric who was lawfully received into the institute, and who has taken temporary vows, is subject as a cleric to the religious superior, although he remains ascribed to his eparchy. After he has taken perpetual vows, or after six years have elapsed from his first profession in an institute without perpetual vows, he loses his own eparchy.

3. Save for the norms of law concerning religious clerics of an order lower than subdiaconate who were dismissed from their institute, a religious cleric below a subdeacon, who was according to the norm of # 1 ascribed as a cleric in his institute, is dismissed in virtue of law from the clerical state if he leaves the institute, unless he be received and ascribed by some benevolent Hierarch into his eparchy.

CANON 47. With the exception of the case mentioned in c. 49, and the case of reception by a benevolent Hierarch of a religious who is a subdeacon or of a major order, and who has not lost his proper eparchy according to the norm of c. 46 # 2, it is necessary for a valid ascription of a cleric into another eparchy that he obtain letters, granted and signed by his Hierarch, of perpetual and unconditional dismissal, and letters likewise of perpetual and unconditional ascription, granted and signed by the Hierarch of the other eparchy.

CANON 48. A cleric cannot validly be ascribed into an eparchy or dismissed from an eparchy:

1. by the syncellus without a special mandate;

2. in patriarchates, by the administrator of the patriarchate who was temporarily appointed, without the consent of the permanent synod, and by the patriarchal exarch and the administrator of a vacant eparchy without the consent of the patriarch;

3. outside the patriarchate, by the archiepiscopal exarch, without the consent of the archbishop; and by the administrator of a vacant eparchy, except after one year's vacancy of the episcopal see and with the consent of the eparchial consultors.

CANON 49. A cleric who has obtained from the Hierarch of another eparchy a benefice of any kind which carries with it the obligation of residence, with the written consent of his own Hierarch, or with the permission granted by the same in writing to leave the eparchy perpetually, is considered in virtue of law dismissed from his eparchy and ascribed into the other eparchy.

CANON 50. Dismissal from an eparchy cannot take place without good reasons, and it does not take effect unless ascription into the other eparchy has followed, whose Hierarch shall inform the former Hierarch as soon as possible.

CANON 51. A Hierarch shall not ascribe an extraneous cleric to his eparchy unless the following conditions are met:

1. The necessity or utility of the eparchy demands it, and the prescriptions of law in regard to the canonical title of ordination are satisfied.

2. It is established by a legitimate document that a lawful dismissal from the eparchy was obtained, and in addition appropriate testimonials from the dismissing chancery have been obtained, s u b s e c r e t o if need be, on the background, life, moral character, and studies of the cleric, especially if the cleric who is to be ascribed is of a different language or nationality. The dismissing Hierarch, however, is gravely obliged in conscience to make sure that the testimonials conform to the truth.

3. The cleric has declared in writing his willingness to give his service to the new eparchy for all times according to the canons.

In the reception of a cleric from another eparchy of the Eastern Church it is not necessary to demand from him an oath to serve in the eparchy forever, as is demanded by the CIC, but his written declaration to this end is sufficient.

CANON 52. If in accordance with particular law clerics are ascribed not to a certain eparchy but to the patriarchate itself, their ascription as well as their dismissal is governed by the prescriptions of c. 44.

In the Armenian Patriarchate, for instance, celibate clergy can be ascribed, or incardinated, directly into the patriarchate, and not in a specific eparchy, with the result that they are at the sole disposition of the patriarch, who can send them where they are needed.

CHAPTER TWO

RIGHTS AND PRIVILEGES OF CLERICS (cc. 53-59)

Exclusive Rights of Clerics (c. 53 = c. 118 CIC)
Privileges:
    Privilegium Canonis (c. 54 = c. 119 CIC)
    Privilegium Fori (c. 55 = c. 121 CIC)
    Privilegium Immunitatis (c. 56 = c. 121 CIC)
Privilegium Competentiae (c. 57 = c. 122 CIC)
Loss of Privileges (c. 58 = c. 123 CIC)
Financial Aid to Retired Clerics (c. 59 = new)

CANON 53. Clerics alone can obtain the power of orders, or of ecclesiastical jurisdiction, and ecclesiastical benefices and pensions.

CANON 54. All the faithful owe the clergy reverence according to their various ranks and offices, and they are guilty of sacrilege if they do them bodily injury.

CANON 55. # 1. Clerics must be sued in all cases, both civil and criminal, before an ecclesiastical judge, unless for certain countries other provisions have lawfully been made, and save for the prescription of # 2.

2. The following cannot be sued before a lay judge:

1. Without the permission of the Apostolic See: the cardinals, legates of the Roman Pontiff, patriarchs, archbishops. In respect to matters pertaining to their offices: major officials of the Roman Curia, apostolic administrators and apostolic visitors. Outside patriarchates: bishops, even titular; exarchs with a territory of their own; apostolic exarchs; administrators of vacant eparchies, save for the norm of n. 3; supreme moderators of institutes of papal right, and superiors of independent monasteries endowed with papal exemption;

2. Without permission of the patriarch: bishops even titular, patriarchal exarchs, patriarchal syncelli, administrators of vacant eparchies, patriarchal delegates in respect to matters pertaining to their duties, supreme moderators of institutes of papal or patriarchal right, and superiors of exempt independent monasteries;

3. Without permission of the archbishop: archiepiscopal exarchs and administrators of vacant eparchies;

4. Without permission of the Hierarch in whose territory the action is to be adjudicated: all others who enjoy the privilegium fori, which permission the Hierarch, especially if the plaintiff is a lay person, shall not refuse without a good and grave cause, and particularly after he has unsuccessfully attempted to effect an agreement between the parties.

3. If they nevertheless have been called into court by one who had no permission, they can, out of necessity to avoid graver evils, accept the summons, but they shall inform the superior from whom the permission should have been obtained.

CANON 56. All clerics are immune from military service and from duties and public offices that are alien to the clerical state.

CANON 57. Clerics who are forced to satisfy their creditors are not to be deprived of what is necessary for their decent living, according to the prudent judgment of the ecclesiastical judge, but the obligation to satisfy their creditors as soon as possible remains intact.

CANON 58. A cleric cannot renounce the aforementioned privileges. He loses them, however, if he is reduced to the lay state, or punished with perpetual privation of the right to wear the ecclesiastical dress, according to the norm of c. 157 # 1. He regains them if the penalty is remitted, or if he is again readmitted to the clergy. The privileges are suspended if the cleric is temporarily deprived of the right of wearing the ecclesiastical dress.

CANON 59. # 1. The Hierarch shall see to it that a sum of money is set aside in his eparchy for granting pensions, in order to be able to support pastors and other secular clerics of the eparchy who have become incapable of discharging their duties on account of impaired health.

2. The following must contribute for the establishment and increase of this fund: the bishop's endowment or episcopal mensa, the parishes and quasi-parishes, each eparchial consultor, pastors, parish vicars, and if the eparchial statutes state so, all other clergy ascribed to the eparchy.

3. Several Hierarchs, for the purpose mentioned in # 1, may agree among themselves for the benefit of the clerics of all their eparchies.

CHAPTER THREE

OBLIGATIONS OF CLERICS

Positive Obligations (cc. 60-77)

Holiness of Life (c. 60 = c. 124 CIC)
Practice of Piety (c. 61 = c. 125 CIC)
Retreats (c. 62 = c. 126 CIC)
Relationship to Hierarchs (c. 63 = c. 127)
Obligation of Service (c. 64 = c. 128 CIC)
Continuation of Studies (c. 65 = c. 129 CIC)
Junior Clergy Examination (c. 66 = c. 130 CIC)
Deanery Meetings (c. 67 = c. 130 CIC)
Celibacy and Marriage:
    Preference of Celibacy (c. 68 = new)
    Candidates for the Episcopacy (c. 69 = new)
    Matrimonial Impediment of Holy Orders (c. 70 = c. 132 # 1)
    Ordination of Married Candidates (c. 71 = new)
    Effect of Unlawful Marriage and Ordination of Married Candidates (c. 72 = c. 132 ## 2, 3 CIC)
    Chastity as Obligation of all Clerics (c. 73 = new)
    Cohabitation with Women (c. 74 = c. 133 CIC)
    Common Life of the Celibate Clergy (c. 75 = c. 134)
Obligation of Reciting the Holy Office (c. 76 = c. 135 CIC)
Ecclesiastical Garb (c. 77 = c. 136 CIC)

CANON 60. Clerics must live an interior and exterior life higher than that of the laity, and they must excel them by the example of virtue and good deeds.

CANON 61. The local Hierarchs shall see to it in regard to all clerics:

1. That they frequently cleanse their conscience by receiving the sacrament of penance;

2. That they devote each day a suitable time for mediation on the teachings of the faith, the mysteries of the life of Our Lord Jesus Christ, and the obligations of their state; that they adore Christ the Lord present in the Divine Eucharist; that they honor the Virgin Mother of God with prayers customary in the Church; that they examine their

conscience, and that they assiduously read the Holy Scriptures of the Old and New Testament.

The enumeration of practices of piety recommended to the clergy was changed so as to exclude those which are peculiar to the Latin Rite as far as their historical origin is concerned, e.g., the Marian rosary, although they are in practical use among Catholic Eastern Churches as much as in the Latin Rite Church.

CANON 62. # 1. All secular priests must at least every third year make a retreat for a length of time to be specified by their Hierarch, in a pious or religious house designated by him. No one shall be exempted, except in a particular case, for a just reason, and with the explicit permission of the same Hierarch.

2. Those deacons who will not be promoted to the presbyterate are bound by the same obligation.

In this canon, as in several others, a significant distinction has been introduced. The Latin term **sacerdos** is applied to all three degrees of higher orders: diaconate, presbyterate and episcopate. Whenever there is a need to restrict the meaning to priests in the strict sense, the term **presbyter** is employed.

The second paragraph obliges also those deacons who are ordained to remain perpetually in that order. The reason for the existence of clerics who are not destined to be promoted to the presbyterate is the desire to enhance the celebration of the Divine Liturgy and other divine services by the participation of deacons, who play a very conspicuous part in the liturgical services of the Eastern Rites. Since they will not be called to participate in the care of souls, no special studies are necessary for them, except the possession of a good voice.

Among dissident Orientals not infrequently men of the secular or the regular clergy, although possessing perhaps a higher education, and possibly teaching theology, decide to stay forever in the order of deacons. They belong to the clergy, receive honorary titles and distinctions, and may enjoy precedence over many other priests of the diocese, except during divine services where they take their rank as deacons.

CANON 63. All clerics, but chiefly priests, are under the special obligation to show respect and obedience each to his own Hierarch. The Hierarchs, however, shall be mindful that they are fathers, not lords, and they shall therefore treat the clergy with fatherly affection.

The Western Church was profoundly influenced by the intrusion of elements of the Teutonic mentality into the ecclesiastical organization, especially in the empires established by the Franks in France and the Langobards in Italy. The bishops acquired a feudal status and became important vassals of the kings. The concept of the lord bishops and prelates was evolved. The aristocracy, and even the sons of kings, entered the ecclesiastical hierarchy chiefly for other than religious considerations. The East did not exalt the status of its ecclesiastical leaders in the civil sphere to such heights, and the bishops stayed closer to the ideal of the monasteries from which they were exclusively taken. A reflection of this different attitude is the addition (to the text found in c. 127 CIC) in this canon of the reminder that hierarchs should not forget that they are fathers and not lords.

CANON 64. As often and as long as the need of the Church requires it, in the judgment of their proper Hierarch, clerics are obliged, excepting a legitimate impediment, faithfully to carry out the duty with which they are charged by the Hierarch.

CANON 65. # 1. Clerics after being ordained must not neglect their studies, especially of the sacred sciences, in which they should always follow the sound doctrine handed down by the Fathers and universally received by the Church, and shall avoid profane novelties of expression and what is incorrectly called scientific.

2. They shall, according to their capability, endeavor to understand the Catholic doctrine in matters of faith and morals to such an extent as to be able to teach it to others, and in order to become in time better and better prepared to give spiritual guidance to the faithful.

3. They shall also not omit to acquire even in profane sciences, especially those which are more intimately connected with the sacred sciences, such knowledge as is regarded fitting for educated men.

CANON 66. # 1. All priests, unless they have been exempted by the local Hierarch for a good reason, must every year for three years after the completion of their curriculum of studies undergo an examination in various sacred sciences, conveniently designated in advance, according to the order determined by the same Hierarch.

2. In the appointment to ecclesiastical offices and benefices those ought to be preferred who, all other things being equal, have surpassed the others in these examinations.

Canon 130 # 1 CIC refers the obligation of the triennal examinations to **sacerdotes,** while **Cleri Sanctitati** has to be more accurate, and uses the word **presbyteri** in order to exclude clergy who permanently hold an order lower than the presbyterate, as, e.g., deacons in some Oriental communities, who may have only a very rudimentary education, since their exclusive duty consists in liturgical assistance.

CANON 67. # 1. In the episcopal city and in each protopresbyterate meetings shall be held several times each year on days appointed by the decree of the local Hierarch, which are also called discussions or conferences, on questions of moral theology and liturgy, to which other exercises can be added which the Hierarch considers suitable for promoting the learning and piety of the clergy.

2. If it is difficult to hold such meetings, written solutions to the questions shall be submitted, according to the norms established by the local Hierarch.

3. All secular priests, and also the religious who are charged with the care of souls, even though they are exempt, and, if such conferences are not held in their houses, all religious who received jurisdiction for hearing confessions from the Hierarch, must participate

in the meeting, and, in case no meeting is held, must submit a written solution of the questions.

CANON 68. The celibacy of the clergy, which corresponds and fits better with their state and the celebration of the divine mysteries, as it is witnessed by the unanimous tradition of both the Eastern as well as the Latin Church, shall be held in esteem by all.

The Christian East retained the apostolic custom of ordaining married candidates, but hand in hand with this indulgence to human frailty a high appreciation of the celibate state was no less an ideal in the East than in the West.

The reference to the appropriateness of celibacy in relation to the celebration of the divine mysteries is probably an allusion to the demand of the liturgical rubrics in most Eastern Rites, directed to the married clergy, to abstain from marital intercourse before the celebration of Mass, i.e., from the preceding evening. Mass is as a rule among dissidents still celebrated only on Sundays and holydays. The Catholic married clergy followed the custom of the Latin Rite of celebrating daily, and could not comply with the request of the ancient tradition.

According to a decree of the Apostolic See celibate clergy must be given preference over the married clergy in appointments to parishes (S. Congregation for the Propagation of the Faith, September 2, 1647).

CANON 69. No one can be promoted to the episcopal order who is not celibate or lawfully freed from bonds of marriage.

From St. Paul's admonition that bishops shall be but men who have been married once, and from other ancient sources, we know that bishops were often married men, engaged in secular business, living with their families. However, married bishops disappeared in the East quite early, and in later centuries the episcopacy was exclusively recruited from among the monks.

The reunited Catholic Orientals followed in the beginning this practice, but after a vaccilation returned to the custom of the postapostolic era, permitting candidates for the episcopacy to be assumed from among the celibate or widowed secular clergy, as well as from the religious.

CANON 70. Subdeacons and all clerics ordained to major orders are forbidden to marry to the extent that according to law they become incapable of contracting marriage.

Candidates who are to be ordained as married men must enter into marriage before the reception of the subdiaconate. The subdiaconate was definitely established as a diriment matrimonial impediment by **Crebrae Allatae** (c. 62) ; it remains, however, a minor order. Widowed priests, deacons or subdeacons are not permitted to remarry, nor can they validly do so.

CANON 71. In regard to married men who wish to be admitted to the subdiaconate or major orders, either absolutely or with a dispensation either from the patriarch or the local Hierarch, but not from a syncellus, or even to those who are to be excluded from their reception, these Apostolic Letters do not change anything in the present discipline of each Eastern Rite. '

The Apostolic See has rarely demanded or authoritatively suggested to groups of Oriental Catholics to follow the Latin Rite example and to introduce obligatory celibacy. However, the preeminence of the celibate state influenced individuals and the episcopate of various Catholic communities of the East to adopt either exclusive celibacy, or make the ordination of celibate candidates the normal case, while the exceptional ordination of a married man is permitted only with a special dispensation either of the patriarch or of the bishop.

Emil Herman, S.J., distinguishes the various C a t h o l i c Oriental Church into three groups ("Celibat des clercs", II. en droit oriental, in Dictionaire du Droit Canonique, III. v., column 155):

1. **Total** or **absolute** celibacy exists among the Malabarians in India, where it was introduced by custom, under the influence of the Latin Rite.

2. **Limited** or **relative** celibacy is observed in various Rites. Married men are admitted to higher orders only with a foregoing dispensation, preference being given to celibate candidates:

(1) Among the Ethiopians the Hierarch can dispense.

(2) Among the Syrians a dispensation from the patriarch is needed for the diaconate and presbyterate, while married candidates who will stay forever subdeacons can be ordained without patriarchal dispensation (Synod of Sharfeh, 1888).

(3) Among the Copts permission for ordination of married men must be obtained from the patriarch (Synod of Alexandria, 1898).

All these Churches receive into the clergy married priests and deacons who come from dissident Oriental groups.

3. **Without general laws on celibacy**: The other Oriental Catholic groups have no prohibition, which would uniformly apply to all dioceses, to ordain married candidates, and follow the ancient tradition of the Christian East. Regional prohibitions are known, as for the United States and Canada, where only celibate or widowed candates may be ordained.

Among the Byzantine Rite Catholics in Italy, Greece and Turkey recently celibate candidates only were ordained. In some other Rites the major part of the clergy remains celibates, since preference is given to such candidates, as among the Maronites, or the number of clerics belonging to religious institutes surpasses that of the secular clergy, as among the Melkites.

Among Romanians, Croats, Ruthenes in the Subcarpathic region, Magyars (Hungary), Bulgarians, Armenians, Chaldeans, the majority of the clergy are married men.

The situation in the three Ukrainian dioceses of Western Ukraine (Lwiw, Peremyshl, Stanislawiw) was somewhat different. In the diocese of Peremyshl and Stanislawiw only celibate candidates were ordained since after World War I. In Lwiw preference was given to celibate candidates, but married ones were also ordained, provided the support of the future family was assured, usually by the prospect of a vacant benefice to be conferred on the candidate, in addition to a corresponding dowry possessed by his wife.

Such a change of the lawful order, usually decreed by the hierarchy assembled in a synod, must be distinguished from the decision of single bishops, although perhaps assembled in an episcopal conference, to give preference to celibate candidates to the extent that married men were wholly excluded from ordination in that diocese or dioceses. Such was the situation, e.g., in the two Ukrainian dioceses of Peremyshl and Stanislawiw (Western Ukraine). This kind of arrangement can be changed at any time by the respective bishop, especially if the number of celibate candidates should become insufficient to provide for the needs of the faithful.

Canon 71 does not change the present situation, but leaves it in the sphere of particular law, although the conclusion must be drawn that the Holy See does not wish to impose celibacy on the Eastern Catholic Churches as an obligatory measure. However, whenever the exclusion of married candidates is not absolute, but depending on a dispensation to be granted by the patriarch or bishop, such dispensations shall not be granted by the syncellus, and consequently the bishop or patriarch shall not assign such power to his syncellus, but should exercise it in person.

The question of married or celibate clergy in the United States and Canada was and still is a difficult problem, that has not yet found a solution. The Holy See demanded from the very beginning of the immigration of Oriental Rite clergy into these two countries that they be celibate, or if they were widowers, that they come without their children. This rule was adopted on the request of the Latin Rite hierarchy, but proved to be disastrous for the future of the Oriental Catholics on the American continent, especially the Ukrainians. Since the number of celibate clerics in the countries where the immigrants came from was very scant, and they were mostly in positions of higher responsibility, only married priests could come to minister among their nationals, and even they only in a limited number. They were often rejected by the Latin Rite clergy and ordinaries. The faithful sought refuge in schismatic churches organized by the Russian Orthodox Church. The Russian bishops provided them with priests by ordaining simple men from among them, who had no schooling except some training in liturgical singing. The dearth of priests among the Catholics was the decisive reason why so many left the Church, and why more than four fifths of the Slavic non-Catholic Orientals in America are former Catholics and their descendants.

The situation is such today that in the United States and in Canada only celibate or widowed candidates are ordained. However, still the majority of the Ukrainian clergy are married. After World War Two, because no other region was capable of accepting and employing several hundred married Ukrainian priests, refugees from behind the Iron Curtain, the Sacred Congregation for the Oriental Church suspended the prohibition and permitted married priests to come with their families to the United States and Canada, directing the few celibates to other countries with Ukrainian immigrants where married clergy could not be accepted, as Australia, Argentina, Brazil.

Because of the lack of celibate candidates in Canada, and the great need of priests in the wake of the new immigration, several married men, who were graduates of the School of Theology of the Ukrainian Seminary in Lwiw (Western Ukraine) before World War Two, but had not been ordained for lack of available employment, have been recently (1958) ordained in Europe by Ukrainian bishops with the permission of the Sacred Congregation, in order to return for work in Canada. The letter of the prohibition of ordaining candidates on the American continent was thus preserved.

CANON 72. 1. In those Rites in which married clergy are not permitted, clerics below subdeacons can indeed enter into a marriage, but, unless the marriage was invalid on account of their being forced or because of fear, they cease by law itself to belong to the clerical state.

2. A married man who without apostolic dispensation received the subdiaconate or major orders, even though in good faith, is forbidden to exercise such orders.

CANON 73. Clerics, even those married, must excel in the virtue of chastity. Those who sin against chastity shall be punished according to the rules of law.

CANON 74. # 1. The clergy shall take care not to have in their houses, nor to visit in any way, women who could give reason for suspicion.

2. Save for what is said in c. 71, they are allowed to live in the same house only with those women concerning whom there can be no suspicion either on account of the natural bond, as mother, sister, aunt, or about whom because of their moral character, in addition to a more advanced age, all suspicion is removed.

3. It is left to the local Hierarch to decide whether the retention or visiting of women, even of those who commonly would not be considered suspicious, could in a particular case be a cause of scandal, or lead to the danger of incontinence, and it is his duty to forbid clerics such retention or visiting.

4. Contumacious clerics are presumed guilty of concubinage.

CANON 75. The custom of community life among the celibate clergy is praiseworthy and is to be encouraged, and where it is followed it shall be continued as far as possible.

The common life of the clergy is praised only in respect to the celibates among them. The living together in one household of celibate and of married clergy, or of celibate clerics and widowers with their children, is against the tradition and the spirit of the Church, even with the consent of the celibate cleric, excepting the case of very close blood relationship.

CANON 76. Clerics who are ordained subdeacons or in major orders, with the exception of those mentioned in cc. 157, 158, are obliged to recite the divine office publicly or privately in accordance with the norms of particular law.

As the subdivisions of the Latin Rite, so also the Eastern Rites possess as a magnificent heritage from Christian antiquity a rich and extensive divine office, structured according to the same principles as that of the Latin Rite. It is divided in eight parts: matins, lauds, prime, tierce, sext, none, vespers, compline; and in some Rites, as the Byzantine, also a midnight hour (mesonyktion) exists.

The divine office of the Eastern Rites has not undergone a systematic shortening as that experienced by the Latin Rite when the Breviary was reformed. The changing texts in the Byzantine Rite, for instance, are still so extensive that they are for convenience sake distributed in twelve volumes. The length of the daily canonical office has therefore never led to the idea of imposing its recitation as an obligation on one sole person. Some Catholic communities were induced to emulate the Latin Rite also in this respect and prescribed that certain parts be recited by their clergy under the same definition and sanction of the obligation as accepted in the Latin Rite. They had necessarily to make a limited selection from the liturgical treasures, which usually was accomplished only in defiance of the natural laws of liturgical growth. Wherever particular law decrees such an obligation, canon 76 does not change it, but leaves it in the sphere of particular law.

The legislative efforts of some synods in respect to the introduction of daily private recitation of the divine office by the clergy were not always successful, as, e.g., among the Ukrainians. The Synod of Lwiw of 1891 had a strongly worded decree to this effect, but its validity was disputed from the very beginning. The synod had assumed that its decrees would receive papal confirmation and thereby also legislative force (**"accedente praesertim S. Sedis confirmatione"**), at least as far as the question of the private recitation of the divine office was concerned, and used such loose language as to make it doubtful whether the synodal fathers themselves had at all intended to enact a law, or had left that to the Holy See. The Apostolic See granted the confirmation, but only in **forma communi,** which is of no more legal value than the permission for publication of a book granted by a bishop. These and other reasons made the whole law of doubtful validity and therefore without obligatory force.

The attitude of the Holy Se in the matter of the recitation and celebration of the divine office is today in line with the strict preservation of the Oriental tradition, once common with the West. The obligation of public recitation of the divine office rests with the clergy of certain churches and monasteries as an obligation affecting the community as such in solidum (cf. c. 401; also c. 157 of **Postquam Apostolicis**). The superior assigns a sufficient number of the clergy or religious for the correct celebration or recitation. Members not participating have no obligation of private recitation, with the exception of those Oriental Rite orders and congregations which have adopted the respective Latin Rite rule in this matter.

Oriental Rite members of Latin Rite religious institutes that have an obligation of private recitation of the breviary either in virtue of profession or of major orders, are generally instructed by their superiors to recite any part of the canonical hours of their

Rite for a certain amount of time each day, e.g., thirty to forty minutes, if their small number does not permit them to recite the office publicly.

From c. 76 we hear that the secular clergy can be obliged to the public recitation of the canonical hours, which does not exist in the Latin Rite except for the canons of cathedral or collegiate chapters. However, we must know that the recitation of the office is in Oriental Rites not reserved to the clergy. Since most Eastern Rites either make use of the vernacular or an older form of the vernacular, the divine office can be recited and sung also by persons without any specific schooling. Actually all Eastern Rite parish churches have at least one professional cantor who, on the average, is better acquainted with the intricate music and rules of the divine office than most clerics. Also many lay persons are capable of participating in the divine office. The public celebration of the matins and lauds and vespers on Sundays and holydays is in many churches customary. Where such a custom prevails, the clergy can be obliged by the bishop to continue and actively to participate in the public celebration of the divine office.

CANON 77. # 1. Clerics shall wear a becoming ecclesiastical garb in accordance with the legitimate customs of the region and with the rules defined by the local Hierarch. The hair of the head shall be kept simply. Concerning the wearing of a beard, the local customs and the norms of the local Hierarch shall be observed.

 # 2. They shall not make use of a ring, except if it is permitted to them either by common or particular law, or by a privilege.

 # 3. Clerics below a subdeacon who against the prescription of # 1 have on their own authority, without a lawful reason, ceased to wear the ecclesiastical garb, and, although admonished by the Hierarch, have not obeyed within one month, can be returned to the lay state.

The simplicity of hair style is not necessarily equivalent with the shortening of the hair on the head, since in some Oriental Rites the clergy wears the hair long down to the shoulders.

The local Hierarch is not only empowered to permit the cultivation of a beard, but is entitled to force clerics to wear a beard if particular law demands it.

The sometimes mentioned prohibition of wearing a wig refers to the hair style of the 17. and 18. centuries, as it is still retained by the judges and attorneys of the British judicial system when they act in court. It does not prohibit the use of permanent toupees or wigs worn for cosmetic purposes.

Because minor clergy among Orientals are not only those who prepare themselves for the priesthood and pastoral work, but also individuals who might stay forever in the order of lector or subdeacon, the refusal to wear ecclesiastical garb is not punished by automatic expulsion from the clerical state, as in the CIC, but is left to the discretion of the local Hierarch.

Negative Obligations (cc. 78-87)

CANON 78. Clerics are forbidden to furnish bond, even with their own property, without consulting the local Hierarch.

CANON 79. Clerics must completely abstain from all things that are unbecoming to their state. They shall not exercise unbecoming arts; nor play games of chance for money; nor carry weapons, unless there is justified cause for fear; nor indulge in excessive hunting, and never participate in clamorous hunting; nor visit taverns and other similar places without necessity or for any other good reason approved by the local Hierarch.

CANON 80. # 1. The clergy shall avoid also those things which, although not unbecoming, are nevertheless alien to the clerical state.

2. Without apostolic indult they shall not: practice medicine or surgery; act as public record keepers or notaries public, except in ecclesiastical offices; accept public offices that impart secular jurisdiction or duties of administration, without prejudice to the prescription of c. 260 # 1, 2, b.

3. Without permission of the local Hierarch they shall not: act as agents in property transactions of lay persons, or assume secular offices that impose the obligation of rendering an account; exercise the office of procurator or lawyer, except in the ecclesiastical court, or in civil court when there is a question of their own cases or of their churches. Clerics shall not have any part at all in criminal cases in lay courts where grave penalty is imposed, not even that of witnesses, unless they are forced to act as such.

4. They shall not strive for or accept the office of senators or legislative representatives, also called deputies, without permission of the patriarch or archbishop, which can be granted only if there is no objection on the part of the Hierarch of the cleric; without permission of his Hierarch as well as of the Hierarch of the area where the election is to be held, if it is outside the patriarchate or archiepiscopate; and in places for which the Apostolic See has issued a prohibition without its permission.

CANON 81. Clerics shall not attend performances, dances and shows which are unbecoming to their state, or where their presence would cause scandal, especially in public theaters.

CANON 82. # 1. They shall not volunteer for military service, unless they do so with the permission of their Hierarchs in order sooner to discharge their obligation. They shall in no way contribute to internal wars and perturbations of the public order.

2. A cleric below a subdeacon who against # 1 voluntarily enlists into the armed forces service ceases thereby to belong to the clergy.

CANON 83. Clerics are forbidden to engage in business or trading either by themselves or through others, whether for their own benefit or for that of others.

CANON 84. Clerics, even though they have no benefice or office requiring residence, are forbidden to be absent from their eparchy for a not too brief period of time without at least the presumed permission of their own Hierarch.

While c. 84 demands the permission for an absence **"per tempus non breve,"** c. 143 CIC used the term **"notabile."** The period of time seems thereby to be shortened, but clarity on the legislator's intent has not increased.

CANON 85. # 1. Permission to reside outside Oriental regions can be granted to clerics by the local Hierarch, but not for longer than six months, unless the reason is to pursue studies, without prejudice to the prescription of # 3.

2. The granting of permission for protracted residence is reserved to the Apostolic See, save what is said in c. 260 # 3.

The limitation of # 2, that the absence of a cleric from his diocese over six months can be permitted only by the Apostolic See, applies only to Oriental regions, that is, to dioceses in the Near East, since c. 303 # 1, 2, of **Postquam Apostolicis** defines Oriental regions as "all places, although not contained in an eparchy, province, archiepiscopate, or patriarchate, where the Oriental Rite was observed since ancient times."

The Byzantine Rite bishops, for instance, in the United States and Canada are not bound by this limitation, and can permit their clerics a longer absence.

3. With the exception of cases of superior authority, and save for the norms in regard to the collecting of alms, or when approved statutes decree otherwise in regard to the exercise of the sacred ministry under the obedience of superiors — superiors cannot permit subjects to stay outside the house of their own institute except for a grave and justifiable reason, and then only for a time as short as possible in accordance with the statutes. For an absence, however, exceeding six months, unless for reasons of studies, permission of the patriarch is required, or, outside of the patriarchate, that of the president of the monastic confederation or the supreme superior of the institute.

As for Latin Rite clergy, so for Oriental Rite clergy limitations are established by the Holy See in respect to travel to both Americas from Europe and Asia. The decree **Non Raro Accidit** of January 3,

1930 (AAS 1930, 106; English translation cf. Pospishil, Interritual Canon Law Problems, 230-232):

> "on members of the Eastern clergy, secular or regular, who emigrate from Oriental territories or dioceses to North, Central or South America, or to Australia, not in order to give spiritual ministrations to the faithful of their own Rite, but for some other reason, economic or moral, or that they may live there for a short time,"

contains the norms according to which Oriental Rite clergy may visit the American and Australian continents.

CANON 86. Those who with the permission of their Hierarchs transfer to another eparchy remain ascribed in their eparchies and can be called back for a just reason and with the observance of natural equity. The Hierarch of the other eparchy can for a just reason revoke the permission to continue residence in his territory, except if he has conferred a benefice on the cleric.

CANON 87. A cleric who is to reside for a protracted period of time outside his own eparchy for reason of teaching, studies, or for another similar purpose, shall present himself without delay to the local Hierarch, whom he shall treat as his own Hierarch in all matters that regard the obligations of his state, and he shall stay under his vigilance, authority and disciplinary power.

This is a new definition of an old legislative principle which excludes the existence of clerics who have no actual superior; the so-called **clericus vagus** or **acephalus** (i.e., headless), that is one without a Hierarch, has been eliminated from canon law.

CHAPTER FOUR

ECCLESIASTICAL OFFICES

Article One:

APPOINTMENT TO ECCLESIASTICAL OFFICES IN GENERAL
(cc. 88—93)

Definition of Canonical Provision (c. 88 = c. 147 CIC)
Kinds of Canonical Provisions (c. 89 = c. 148 CIC)
Determination of Qualification (c. 90 = c. 149)
Provision of Non-Vacant Office (c. 91 = c. 150 CIC)
Appointment to a Non-Vacant Office (c. 92 = c. 151 CIC)
Effect of Fear, Fraud, Error and Simony (c. 93 = c. new)

The definition of the term **ecclesiastical office,** by which the Fourth Title of the CIC is introduced, is not found at the beginning of this section, corresponding to cc. 145 and 146 CIC, but was earlier published in **Postquam Apostolicis,** in the third part containing the definitions of canonical terms:

CANON 305. # 1. An ecclesiastical office, in the broad sense of the word, denotes any employment which is lawfully exercised for a spiritual purpose. In the strict sense, it is a stable position established either by divine or ecclesiastical ordinance, to be conferred according to the rules of canon law, and carrying with it either some participation of ecclesiastical power of orders or of jurisdiction, or some other public ecclesiastical power.

2. Unless the contrary is stated, the term ecclesiastical office is to be understood in the strict sense.

Significant is the addition of the phrase "aliam publicam ecclesiasticam potestatem," thus indicating as office holders also those who do not possess jurisdiction or orders but still exercise some ecclesiastical authority, often with important juridical sequels, as superiors of religious institutes of both sexes.

CANON 88. # 1. An ecclesiastical office cannot be validly obtained without a canonical appointment.

2. By canonical appointment is understood the conferring of an ecclesiastical office by the competent ecclesiastical authority, according to the canons.

The adjective sacrorum modifying the noun canonum, contained in c. 147 CIC and in other places, was deleted as unnecessary. The term canon designated always exclusively the ecclesiastical law in opposition to nomos, the civil law.

CANON 89. Appointment to an eclesiastical office is performed either as a free conferring (libera collatio) by the legitimate superior; or as investiture (institutio), granted by him after there has preceded a presentation exercised by a founder, or a nomination; or as a confirmation or admission, conferred by him after an election or postulation has preceded; or by a simple election and acceptance by the elected if the election does not require confirmation.

The legal term of patronus in c. 148 CIC was replaced here by fundator. The law of patronage came into the ecclesiastical law under the influence of Teutonic institutions. If the owner of the land erected a church on his property, he was considered its proprietor and the church his property (Eigenkirche). This included the obligation of supporting the clergy, repairing the edifice, etc., but also the right to appropriate for himself the excess of the income of the church, to appoint and depose the clergy, etc. The Church fought a long and fierce battle until the demands of the patrons were reduced to honorary privileges, to the right of presentation of the clergy, and to a charitable support if he or his successors should be in want.

The Christian East was not exposed to the influence of the Teutonic law, and never developed the right of patronage. However, special rights were granted to founders, who could make certain stipulations which became by-laws for their foundations.

The right of patronage, and the resulting privilege of presentation of the titular, was in force in the Byzantine Rite dioceses of the former Austro-Hungarian Monarchy, later on in Western

76

Ukraine, Hungary, Czechoslovakia, Romania, Croatia (Yugoslavia). Many parishes in these dioceses were under the patronage of the lord of the manor, who for the duty of maintaining the church building and the rectory was vested with the privilege to present to the bishop suitable candidate for appointment as pastor.

CANON 90. Those who have been elected, postulated, presented or nominated to ecclesiastical offices by whatever persons shall not be confirmed, admitted, or invested before their own Hierarch has found them qualified, possibly through an examination, if the law or the nature of the office demands it, or the Hierarch considers it appropriate.

CANON 91. # 1. The appointment to an office which is not vacant according to law as defined in c. 125 #1 is automatically void, and it does not become valid when the vacancy later occurs.

2. The promise of such an office by anyone has no legal effect whatsoever.

CANON 92. An office vacant according to law, which perhaps is unlawfully in the possession of a cleric, can be conferred, provided this possession was declared illegal according to the canons, and that mention of this is contained in the letters of appointment.

CANON 93. The appointment to an office made because of unjust and grave fear, fraud or substantial error, or with simony, is automatically void.

1. Free Appointment (cc. 94-101).

Appointing Hierarch (c. 94 = c. 152 CIC)
Qualifications of the Appointee:
    In General (c. 95 = c. 153 CIC)
    Presbyterate for Pastoral Offices (c. 96 = c. 154 CIC)
Time Limit for Appointments (c. 97 = c. 155 CIC)
Incompatibility of Offices (c. 98 = c. 156 CIC)
Appointment to Offices Vacant by Renunciation or Removal
    (c. 99 # 1 = c. 157 CIC; # 2 = new)
Extraordinary Appointing Superior (c. 100 = c. 158 CIC)
Provision to be in Writing (c. 101 = c. 159 CIC)

CANON 94. # 1. The local Hierarch, but not the syncellus without a special mandate, is entitled in virtue of common law to appoint in his own territory to ecclesiastical offices, unless it is otherwise provided.

2. The same right belongs to the patriarch in stauropegial places, and to the patriarch or archbishop in places of the patriarchate or archiepiscopate where eparchies or exarchies have not been established.

Concerning the law of **stauropegium** cf. c. 263.

CANON 95. # 1. The person to be appointed to a vacant office must be a cleric, endowed with those qualifications which are required for this office by common or particular law or by the by-laws of the foundation.

2. The candidate who, taking everything into consideration, is better suitable shall be appointed, without any personal preference.

3. If the appointed cleric lacks the required qualifications, the appointment is void if common or particular law or the by-laws of the foundation so order; otherwise it is valid, but can be rescinded by a sentence of the legitimate superior.

CANON 96. Offices that have attached to them the care of souls, either in the external or in the internal forum, cannot validly be conferred on clerics who are not priests.

CANON 97. Appointment to offices, if no time limit is established by special law, shall never be deferred beyond six months, to be computed from the time when the vacancy became known, save for the prescription of c. 499.

CANON 98. # 1. No one shall be appointed to two offices which are incompatible.

2. Offices are incompatible which, on account of the duty of residence or other obligations attached to them, cannot be discharged simultaneously by the same individual.

3. Save for the prescription of c. 130, 3, the appointment to another office made by the Apostolic See is not valid, unless the first incompatible office is mentioned in the petition, or a clause repealing the prohibition is added to the document of appointment.

CANON 99. # 1. An office that has become vacant either through renunciation or by a sentence depriving the cleric of the office cannot be validly conferred by the Hierarch who accepted the resignation or pronounced the sentence on his or the resigning cleric's relations, either by blood or by marriage, up to the fourth degree inclusive, save for the prescription of # 2.

2. An office that has become vacant in one of the ways defined in # 1 cannot be validly conferred by the Hierarch who accepted the renunciation or pronounced the sentence on those mentioned in the same # 1 without the consent of the patriarch or archbishop. If the patriarch or archbishop himself accepted the renunciation or pronounced the sentence, the consent of the permanent synod is required for a valid appointment of the mentioned person to such an office.

CANON 100. He who in supplementing another's negligence or incapacity appoints someone to an office does not acquire thereby any authority over the appointee, whose legal status therefore is determined in the same way as if the appointment had taken place according to the usual norms of law.

CANON 101. Appointment to any office shall be made in writing.

2. E l e c t i o n (cc. 102-120).

There was no reason to introduce changes in the formulation of the CIC on the general legal rules for elections. The corresponding canons of **Cleri Sanctitati** contain the same text we find in cc. 160-178 CIC, with one minor restriction: Whenever there is a time limit established for the acceptance of the election (c. 117 # 2) or for petitioning of confirmation (c. 119 # 1), particular law can reduce the eight days to a shorter period of time.

CANON 102. The election of the Roman Pontiff is solely governed by the apostolic constitutions enacted in this matter. In other ecclesiastical elections the rules of the canons that follow shall be observed, and the special statutes which possibly were enacted for particular offices.

CANON 103. If a college of persons enjoys the right of electing the appointee to an office, the election shall not be deferred beyond three months, to be computed from the time the vacancy became known, unless the law prescribes otherwise. If this time limit has elapsed to no purpose, the ecclesiastical superior who is entitled to confirm the election or successively enjoys the right of appointment shall freely confer the vacant office.

CANON 104. # 1. Save for a different norm of particular law, the president of the college shall, observing the established manner, place and time suitable to the electors, summon all members of the college. Whenever a citation is to be addressed to individuals, it is valid if it is served in the place of domicile or quasi-domicile or in the place of actual sojourning.

2. If any of the electors has been overlooked, and has therefore been absent, the election is valid, but on his demand, having

proved his being passed over and his absence, the competent superior must rescind it, even after confirmation, provided it is proved according to law that the recourse was taken at least within three days from the time he became aware of the proposed election.

3. If more than one third of the electors were passed over, the election is automatically null.

4. The defect of convocation is ineffective if the persons passed over nevertheless took part therein.

5. Where an election is to an office that will be retained for life, the convocation of the electors before the vacancy of the office has no legal effect.

CANON 105. If the convocation was lawfully done, the right of electing pertains to those who are present at the day appointed in the convocation, in such a way that the votes cannot be cast either by letter or by proxy unless particular law decrees otherwise.

CANON 106. Although someone should be entitled to vote in his own name from several titles, he cannot cast more than one vote.

CANON 107. No one who does not belong to the college can be admitted to the vote, save for privileges lawfully acquired; otherwise, the election is automatically void.

CANON 108. If lay persons should interfere in any way with the canonical liberty of action in an ecclesiastical election, the election is automatically void.

CANON 109. # 1. A vote cannot be cast by these:
1. who are incapable of human actions;
2. who have not reached puberty;
3. who have incurred a censure or legal infamy, after a declaratory or condemnatory sentence;
4. who have joined or publicly declared their allegiance to an heretical of schismatical sect;
5. who are deprived of active voice either by legitimate sentence of a judge or by common or particular law.

2. If one of these is admitted, his vote is null, but the election is valid, unless it is established that the elected has not obtained the required number of votes, or that one excommunicated by declaratory or condemnatory sentence was knowingly admitted to vote.

CANON 110. If one of the electors present in the house where the election is held is unable to participate in the election because of impaired health, his vote in writing shall be received by the tellers unless particular law determines otherwise.

CANON 111. # 1. A vote is null unless it was:
1. free; therefore a vote is invalid if the elector was compelled directly or indirectly by grave fear or fraud to elect a certain person or several of them separately;
2. secret, certain, absolute, determined.

2. Conditions which were added to the vote before the election are to be regarded as not stipulated.

CANON 112. No one can validly cast a vote for himself.

CANON 113. # 1. Before the beginning of the election two tellers shall be appointed from among the members of the college by secret vote, if they are not already designated by their own statute, who together with the president, if he himself is a member of the college, shall take an oath faithfully to fulfill their duty and to keep the secret even after the election has been completed in regard to what occurred in the meetings.

2. The tellers shall see that the votes be cast by each elector secretly, diligently, one by one, and with observance of the order of precedence. After the last ballot is collected they shall establish, in the presence of the president of the election, according to the manner determined in their own particular law, whether the number of ballots corresponds with the number of electors, and then they shall inspect the ballots themselves, and shall make public how many votes each has obtained.

3. If the number of ballots surpasses the number of electors, nothing has been accomplished.

4. The ballots shall be burned at once after each voting, or after the meeting if in the same meeting several votings have taken place.

5. Accurate minutes shall be drawn up concerning everything that was done during the election by him who discharges the function of the actuary, and having been signed at least by the actuary, the president, and the tellers, they shall carefully be preserved in the archives of the college.

CANON 114. # 1. An election can also be performed, unless law stipulates differently, by a compromise, namely, when the electors by unanimous consent, expressed in writing, transfer the right of election for that case to one or several suitable persons, either of the college or from among outsiders, who shall elect on behalf of all in virtue of the mandate received.

2. In the case of a clerical college, the persons appointed by compromise must be clerics in major orders, otherwise the election is invalid.

3. In order that the election be valid, the persons appointed by compromise must observe the conditions stipulated in the compromise which are not contrary to common law. If no conditions were stipulated, common law norms on elections are to be observed; conditions that are against the law shall be regarded as not stipulated.

4. If the electors entered into a compromise selecting only one person by compromise, he cannot nominate himself; if several have been designated by compromise, none of them can assent by his vote to his own election by the others in order that the number of votes required for election be completed.

CANON 115. The compromise ceases to exist and the right of election returns to the compromisers:

1. If the college revokes the compromise while the matter is still not acted upon;

2. If a condition stipulated in the compromise was disregarded or not observed;

3. If the election was performed invalidly by the persons appointed by compromise.

CANON 116. He who received the required number of votes in accordance with c. 29 # 1, n. 1, shall be considered as elected and declared as such by the president of the college.

CANON 117. # 1. Save in the cases mentioned in c. 235 # 3, c. 253, the elected shall at once be notified of his election.

2. The elected must manifest, at least within eight days, to be computed from the receipt of the notification, save for any law, even a particular one, that stipulates a shorter length of time, whether he accepts his election, or not; otherwise he loses every right acquired from the election.

CANON 118. # 1. If the elected renounces his election he loses every right that he acquired through the election, although he may later regret the renunciation; but he can be re-elected. The college however must proceed to a new election within one month from the time the renunciation became known.

2. By the acceptance of the election, if he needs no confirmation, the one elected obtains at once all rights; otherwise he acquires nothing but the right to demand the conferring of the title according to the norm of c. 119 # 2.

3. The elected is not permitted before he has received the confirmation to interfere, under the pretext of having been elected, in the administration of the office, either in spiritual or in temporal matters, and actions accidentally taken by him are null.

CANON 119. # 1. The one elected must, if the election needs confirmation, request confirmation not later than eight days, counting from the day of acceptance of the election, save for any law, even a particular one, that stipulates a shorter length of time, from the competent superior in person or through another; otherwise he is deprived of any right, unless he proves having been prevented from requesting confirmation by a justifying impediment.

2. The superior cannot refuse confirmation if he finds the one elected qualified, and if the election was performed according to law.

3. The confirmation must be granted in writing.

4. With the receipt of the confirmation the elected acquires the full right in the office, unless otherwise stipulated in law.

CANON 120. If the election was not performed within the prescribed time, or the college was deprived, as a penalty, of the right of election, the free appointment to the office devolves on that superior by whom the election should have been confirmed or to whom successively belongs the right of appointment.

3. Postulation (cc. 121-124)

Definition (c. 121 = c. 179 CIC)
Requirements (c. 122 = c. 180 CIC)
Time Limit (c. 123 = c. 181 CIC)
Rejection and Acceptance (c. 124 = c. 182 CIC)

The only change of the text contained in the corresponding canons 179-182 of CIC is the addition to c. 122 #1, by which the postulated candidate is excluded from consideration in the third balloting if he did not receive the required majority of votes in the first or second.

CANON 121. # 1. If there is an impediment from which dispensation can, and usually is, granted, preventing the election of a candidate whom the electors consider better qualified and therefore prefere, they can by vote request him from the competent superior, unless the law stipulates differently, although it is an office for which the one elected does not need confirmation.

2. Persons appointed by compromise cannot postulate unless this was expressly stated in the compromise.

CANON 122. In order that a postulation have legal force, it is necessary that the majority of votes be cast for it, indeed, if it is concurrent with votes for election, a majority of at least two thirds is required; otherwise that eligible person will be considered elected who in the third balloting has obtained the relative majority of votes, with the exclusion of the one postulated.

2. The vote for a postulation must be expressed by the word "I postulate" or one of equivalent meaning. The formula "I elect or postulate," or anything equivalent, is valid for an election, if there is no impediment, otherwise for a postulation.

CANON 123. # 1. The postulation must be forwarded as soon as possible (not later than) within eight days, to the superior who is to grant the confirmation of an election, if he has the power to dispense from the impediment, otherwise to the Roman Pontiff or someone else who has the power.

2. If the postulation has not been forwarded within the prescribed time, it becomes by this fact void, and the electors are deprived for this time of the right of election or postulation unless they prove to have been prevented from forwarding the postulation by a justifiable cause.

3. The postulated candidate does not acquire by postulation any right, and the superior is free to reject him.

4. The postulation forwarded by the electors to the superior cannot be revoked, except with the consent of the superior.

CANON 124. # 1. If the postulation was rejected by the superior, the right of election returns again to the college, unless the electors have knowingly postulated a candidate who is excluded because of an impediment from which dispensation cannot be granted, or usually is not granted; in this case the appointment devolves to the superior.

83

2. If the postulation was admitted by the superior, the postulated candidate shall be notified, and shall give his reply according to the norm of c. 117. If he accepts the election he acquires full right in the office.

Article Two:

THE LOSS OF ECCLESIASTICAL OFFICES (cc. 125-137).

Modes of Losing Office (c. 125 = c. 183 CIC)
Renunciation:
   Right of Renunciation (c. 126 = c. 184 CIC)
   Effect of Fear, Fraud, Error, and Simony
      (c. 127 = c. 185 CIC)
   Formal Requirements (c. 128 = c. 186 CIC)
   Requirement of Acceptance (c. 129 = c. 187 CIC)
   Tacit Renunciation (c. 130 = c. 188 CIC)
   Rules for the Superior (c. 131 = c. 189 CIC)
   Vacancy of Office (c. 132 = c. 190 CIC)
   Withdrawal of Renunciation — Acceptance
      (c. 133 = c. 191 CIC)
Removal from Office:
   Kinds of Removal — Formal Requirements
      (c. 134 = c. 192 CIC)
Transfer to another Office:
   Formal Requirements (c. 135 = c. 193 CIC)
   Vacancy of Office (c. 136 = c. 194 CIC)
Persons Incompetent for Effecting Removal
   (c. 137 = c. 195 CIC)

CANON 125. # 1. An ecclesiastical office is lost by renunciation, deprivation, removal, transfer, and by expiration of a predetermined term.

2. The incumbent is not deprived of an office by whatever loss of official status incurred by the superior who appointed him to it unless the law states differently, or if in the appointment the stipulation was added "at our pleasure" or equivalent words.

CANON 126. Everyone who is in possession of his mental faculties can renounce an office for a good reason, unless by a special prohibition such renunciation is forbidden to him.

CANON 127. A renunciation submitted under the influence of grave fear, unjustly brought to bear, or fraud, or substantial error, or simony, is invalid by the law itself.

CANON 128. In order that a renunciation be valid, it must be submitted by the one renouncing the office, either in writing or orally, before two witnesses, or also through a proxy who has been given a special mandate. The document of renunciation shall be preserved in the archives of the office.

CANON 129. # 1. Except the law stipulates differently, in order that a renunciation be valid, it must be submitted to him who is empowered to accept it, or, if there is no need of acceptance, to him from whom the cleric received the office, or who is in his place.

2. If the office was conferred by confirmation, institution or admission, the renunciation must be submitted to the superior who by his official authority is entitled to grant the confirmation, institution or admission.

CANON 130. Any office whatsoever becomes vacant by one of the following facts in virtue of tacit renunciation admitted by law itself, and without further declaration, if the cleric:

1. makes a religious profession, save for the prescription of law in regard to the forfeiture of a benefice that the cleric enjoyed who makes the profession;

2. neglected to enter into the possession of the office to which he was appointed within the time stipulated by law or determined by the Hierarch in case of lack of such a law;

3. accepted another ecclesiastical office that is incompatible with the former one, and obtained peacefully its possession;

4. publicly abandoned the Catholic faith;

5. contracted or attempted marriage against the norm of c. 70, although only a so-called civil marriage;

6. although married, received the subdiaconate or a major order contrary to the norm of c. 71;

7. voluntarily joined the armed services contrary to the norm of c. 82 # 1;

8. ceased to wear the ecclesiastical dress on his own authority against the prescription of c. 77, without a good reason, and has not resumed, although admonished by the Hierarch, clerical dress within one month after he received the admonition;

9. unlawfully deserted the residence to which he was obliged by law, and after he received the admonition of the Hierarch has not obeyed within the time determined by the Hierarch, nor submitted the reason of his absence, although he was not prevented by a lawful impediment.

CANON 131. # 1. Superiors shall not accept renunciations without a good and commensurate cause.

2. The renunciation shall be accepted or rejected by the local Hierarch within one month. But although one entire month from the date of the renunciation has elapsed, the Hierarch can validly accept the renunciation, unless the renouncing office-holder has revoked the renunciation before its acceptance, and has notified the Hierarch of the revocation of the renunciation.

CANON 132. # 1. When a renunciation was lawfully submitted and accepted, the office becomes vacant when the renouncing office-holder was notified of the acceptance.

2. The renouncing office-holder remains in the office as long as he has not ascertained that the superior has granted his acceptance.

CANON 133. # 1. After a renunciation has been lawfully submitted and accepted, there is no more time for consideration, although the renouncing office-holder may obtain the same office in virtue of another title.

#2. The acceptance of a renunciation shall be timely brought to the attention of those who have any right in the appointment to the office.

CANON 134. # 1. One can be deprived of an office either by law itself, or by the decision of a lawful superior.

2. The Hierarch cannot deprive a cleric of an irremovable office except through procedures in accordance with law.

3. The removal from a removable office can be decided by the Hierarch for any good cause whatsoever, on his prudent judgment, even if there is no offense on the part of the cleric, with observance of natural equity, and he is not obliged to follow any established manner of procedure, save for existing particular law on the manner of procedure in the removal of removable pastors; the removal, however, has effect only after it has been announced by the superior. Recourse to the Apostolic See is allowed from the decree of the Hierarch, save for the prescription of c. 260 # 2.

The removal of a cleric from an irremovable benefice against his will is to follow the special procedure prescribed by law. To the present time no such procedure has been promulgated as part of the codification of the Oriental canon law, and thus the procedural rules of particular law are to be applied. Such a procedure existed for the Ukrainians and Ruthenians in the European dioceses, and was identical with that for the Latin Rite. It was not applied in the United States or Canada because parishes in these two countries were all removable benefices till the promulgation of **Cleri Sanctitati.** With the new rule that parishes are generally irremovable benefices, the procedure of particular law as applied in the dioceses of the same discipline in Europe is to be used also in the removal of pastors on the American continent.

The same is to be said of removable benefices, but only if particular law knows a special procedure of involuntary removal of removable pastors. Whenever there is no such procedure, such pastors can be removed without the observance of any formal rules, but always taking into consideration canonical equity or justice, and positive requirements of canon law.

CANON 135. # 1 The transfer to another ecclesiastical office can be decreed only by him who enjoys the right both to accept the renunciation as well as to remove from the first office and promote to the second.

2. If a cleric is transferred with his own consent, any good reason is sufficient; if against the will of the cleric, practically the same reason and the same manner of procedure is required as is prescribed for a removal, save for particular law of procedure in the transfer of pastors.

CANON 136. # 1. In a transfer, the former office becomes vacant when the cleric has canonically assumed the administration of the other, unless law provides otherwise or the legitimate superior decides differently.

\# 2. The income from the first office accrues to the transferred cleric until he occupies the second one.

CANON 137. Those who elected or postulated or nominated a cleric to an office, cannot deprive him of it, or remove him from it, or transfer him to another office.

CHAPTER FIVE

ORDINARY AND DELEGATED JURISDICTION (cc. 138-154)

Jurisdiction in the External and Internal Fora
    (c. 138 = c. 196 CIC)
Ordinary and Delegated Jurisdiction (c. 139 = c. 197 CIC)
Rules for Delegation and Subdelegation (c. 140 = c. 199 CIC)
Interpretation as to the Limits of Jurisdiction
    (c. 141 = c. 200 CIC)
Limitations as to Persons and Places (c. 142 = c. 201 CIC)
Relationship of the Two Jurisdictional Fora
    (c. 143 = c. 202 CIC)
Limits of Delegation (c. 144 = c. 203 CIC)
Order Among Hierarchs in Jurisdictional Actions
    (c. 145 = new)
Relationship of Higher and Lower Superior
    (c. 146 = c. 204 CIC)
Delegation of Several Persons:
    Simultaneous Delegation (c. 147 = c. 205 CIC)
    Successive Delegation (c. 148 = c. 206 CIC)
Expiration of Jurisdiction:
    Delegated Jurisdiction (c. 149 = c. 207 CIC)
    Ordinary Jurisdiction (c. 150 = c. 208 CIC)
Suspension of Jurisdiction (c. 151 = c. 208 CIC)
Jurisdiction Supplied by the Church (c. 152 = c. 209 CIC)
Public Eclesiastical Authority Subject to Rules of Jurisdiction (c. 153 = new)
Transmission of the Power of Order (c. 154 = c. 210 CIC)

CANON 138. The power of jurisdiction or government which is in the Church by Divine institution is to be distinguished into that of the external forum and that of the internal forum or of the conscience, which again can be sacramental and extra-sacramental.

CANON 139. \# 1. Ordinary jurisdiction is that which by law itself is attached to the office; delegated jurisdiction, which is committed to the person.

\# 2. Ordinary jurisdiction can be either proper (exercised in one's own name) or vicarious.

We would expect in this place the definitions of c. 198 CIC. However, they were published five years earlier in the glossary of canonical terms of **Postquam Apostolicis,** where they were joined with some other definitions in one canon:

CANON 306. # 1. Prelates are secular or religious clerics who possess ordinary jurisdiction in the external forum.

This definition corresponds to c. 110 CIC.

2. 1. Under the term of Hierarch, besides the Roman Pontiff, are understood, unless expressly excluded, in relation to the territory of each of them: the resident bishop; the exarch who is in charge of his own territory; the apostolic as well as the patriarchal and archiepiscopal exarch who is in charge of a territory not his own; the permanently appointed apostolic administrator; the syncellus, the judicial power excepted unless he has received a special mandate; the temporarily appointed apostolic administrator; and all those who in case of vacancy in these offices are to succeed in the government according to rules of law or approved statutes. In respect to their subjects, the major superiors in exempt monasteries and in exempt clerical institutes are also Hierarchs.

2. By the term of local Hierarchs are meant all persons enumerated above except the religious superiors.

3. Exarchy is included in the term eparchy, and in the term bishop also every exarch, except there be some special prescriptions in respect to the exarch, or something else follows from the text and context of the law or the nature of the matter.

The generic term for prelates with episcopal or quasi-episcopal jurisdiction of the Latin Rite "ordinarius" was replaced with "Hierarch," which corresponds better with the Eastern tradition. The same matter is treated in c. 215 # 2 CIC.

CANON 140. # 1. He who has ordinary jurisdiction can delegate it to another either totally or in part, unless the law expressly provides the contrary.

2. Even jurisdictional power delegated by the Apostolic See can be subdelegated either for one act or also for habitual use, unless the person was delegated by reason of his personal qualities, or if subdelegation was forbidden.

3. Power delegated by one who is below the Roman Pontiff, and who enjoys ordinary jurisdiction, can be subdelegated in single cases if it was delegated for all cases in general; if it was delegated in specific cases, it can be subdelegated only in virtue of an express concession; delegated judges can subdelegate non-judicial acts even without an express commission.

4. No subdelegated power can be further subdelegated unless this was expressly granted.

CANON 141. # 1. Ordinary jurisdiction and that delegated for a universality of cases are to be interpreted liberally; all other jurisdiction strictly. To whom, however, jurisdiction was delegated, to him it is understood all power was granted without which it cannot be exercised.

2. He who claims to possess delegated power has the burden of proving his delegation.

CANON 142. # 1. The power of jurisdiction can be exercised directly over subjects only, unless expressly stipulated otherwise.

Subjects are persons who come into a jurisdictional relationship to the superior by having their domicile or quasi-domicile in his territory. The addition in c. 142 # 1, differing from that in c. 202 # 1 CIC, of **"nisi expresse aliter statuatur"** refers to **vagi** and **peregrini,** who, although not having a domicile or quasi-domicile in the territory, nevertheless come in certain aspects under the jurisdiction of the superior in whose territory they actually are staying.

2. The judicial power, both ordinary and delegated, cannot be exercised for one's own advantage, nor outside the territory, except if it is the case of absolving own subjects in virtue of ordinary power, which can be exercised also outside the territory, or of a judge who was expelled by force from his territory or prevented from exercising his jurisdiction there.

3. Unless the nature of the case or the law decree otherwise, one can exercise non-judicial power also for one's own advantage, or if sojourning outside the territory, or in favor of a subject who is absent from the territory.

CANON 143. # 1. An act of the power of jurisdiction granted for the external forum, whether ordinary or delegated, is valid also in the internal, but the reverse does not hold.

2. The power granted for the internal forum can be exercised also in the non-sacramental internal forum, unless the sacramental has been specified.

3. If the forum for which the power was granted, was not specified, the power is understood to have been granted for both forums, unless its nature indicates otherwise.

CANON 144. # 1. The delegate who exceeds the limits of his mandate, either in regard to the matters or the persons, acts invalidly.

2. The delegate, however, is to be considered not to have exceeded the limits if he performed that to which he was delegated in a different manner, contrary to the wishes of the one who delegated him, unless the manner itself has been prescribed by the same as a condition.

CANON 145. Without prejudice to the right of every member of the faithful in the whole Catholic world directly to address the Apostolic See because of the primacy of the Roman Pope, and freely to communicate with it, in forwarding recourses that are permitted by law the following order shall be followed, unless expressly stipulated otherwise: from the decrees of the local Hierarch who is subject to a patriarch or archbishop, the recourse shall be forwarded to the patriarch or archbishop; but from the decrees of a local Hierarch who is not subject to a patriarch or archbishop, as well as from the decrees of the patriarch or archbishop himself, to the Apostolic See.

CANON 146. If a person applies to a superior, passing over an inferior, the non-judicial power of the inferior, whether ordinary or delegated, is thereby not suspended; but once the matter has been brought before the superior, the inferior shall not interfere, unless for a grave and urgent reason, in which case he shall immediately notify the superior.

CANON 147. # 1. If several individuals have received delegated jurisdiction for the same matter, and doubt arises whether the delegated power was given to be exercised by each individually or by all jointly as a body, it is to be presumed to have been granted to be exercised by all jointly in judicial matters, while in others as an individual power.

2. If several persons were delegated individually, he who first makes use of his power excludes thereby the others, unless the first is either subsequently impeded or does not wish to continue to act in the matter.

3. If several persons were jointly delegated, all must act together in the affair in order that their action may be valid, unless the mandate provides otherwise.

CANON 148. If several persons have been delegated at different times, the one first delegated must take care of the matter, unless the later mandate explicitly revoked the former.

CANON 149. # 1. 1. A delegated power ceases: when the mandate has been complied with; when the time has expired or the number of cases has been exhausted for which it was granted, save for n. 22; when the motive for granting the delegation has ceased to exist; by revocation of the mandate directly intimated by the delegating superior to the delegate; or by renunciation of the delegate, directly intimated and accepted by the superior; but not by the passing out of office of the delegating superior, unless it follows from the conditions stipulated in the rescript of the Apostolic See, the patriarch or the local Hierarch, or the rescript contains power delegated to an individual in order that he might grant a favor to some persons named therein, and the matter is still not taken care of.

2. Power granted for the internal forum is still validly exercised if through inadvertence it was not noticed that the stipulated time limit had expired or the stipulated number of cases was exhausted.

2. When several persons are jointly delegated, all lose their delegated power if one fails to act, unless the contrary follows from the contents of the delegation.

CANON 150. Ordinary power does not cease with the retirement of the superior who appointed to the office to which it is attached, according to the norm of c. 125 # 2; it ceases, however, when the office is lost.

CANON 151. # 1. Unless law states otherwise, ordinary or delegated power of jurisdiction is suspended in the case of a legitimate appeal, except if the appeal is only with devolutive effect.

2. This power is not suspended in the case of a recourse, except if expressly stipulated by law.

CANON 152. The Church supplies jurisdiction both for the external and the internal forum in case of common error, or in a positive and probable doubt of fact as well as of law.

CANON 153. The norms of c. 139-152 in respect to the power of jurisdiction are to be observed in regard to every public ecclesias-

tical authority, unless the nature of the matter or the text or context
is opposed.

Superiors of an exempt clerical religious institute enjoy ecclesiastical jurisdiction in the external as well as in the internal forum. Superiors of other religious institutes have only dominative power in virtue of the religious profession or another act by which one places himself under the authority of the superior. Such dominative power, even when exercised by a woman superior, can have effects not less far-reaching than jurisdiction, as, e.g., when the validity of admission to the novitiate or profession is dependent on its legitimate exercise.

The Code Commission had declared on March 26, 1952, that this **potestas dominativa**, or, as it is better called, **public ecclesiastical authority**, in order to differentiate it somewhat from the simple dominative power of parents, follows in everything the rules of law for ecclesiastical jurisdiction, except when the nature of the matter or the text and context of the law demands something different.

> CANON 154. **The power conferring order which was by the legitimate ecclesiastical superior either attached to an office or committed to a person cannot be delegated to others unless this was expressly granted by law or in the indult.**

CHAPTER SIX

THE RETURN OF CLERICS TO THE LAY STATE (cc. 155-158).

> Return to the Lay State (c. 155 = c. 211 CIC)
> Readmission to the Clerical State (c. 156 = c. 212 CIC)
> Effects of Reduction to the Lay State (c. 157 = c. 213 CIC)
> Holy Orders Received under Grave Fear (c. 158 = c. 214 CIC)

> CANON 155. # 1. **Although sacred ordination once validly received can never be invalidated, a subdeacon and a cleric of a major order may be reduced to the lay state by a rescript of the Apostolic See, by a decree or sentence according to c. 158, and, finally, by the penalty of major deposition.**

> # 2. **A cleric below a subdeacon can be reduced to the lay state ipso facto, for reasons defined in law, or by a decree issued by the Hierarch for a just reason, namely, if the Hierarch, having considered the matter, prudently judges that the cleric could not with due respect to the clerical state be promoted to the subdiaconate or to major orders; or he may return to this state of his own accord, having beforehand advised so the local Hierarch.**

> CANON 156. # 1. **A cleric below a subdeacon, who has returned or has been reduced to the lay state for whatsoever reason, cannot be readmitted to the clergy, unless the local Hierarch, who is to consider this matter a grave obligation in conscience, has sought the advice of the Hierarch of the eparchy, or of the superior of the**

religious institute to which the cleric belonged before his reduction or return to the lay state, and after a careful inquiry into the life and morals of the individual, and a suitable period of trial, enabling him to conclude that the cleric is fit for the sacred ministry.

2.   1.   A subdeacon or cleric in major orders who was reduced to the lay state by the Apostolic See can be readmitted to the clergy only by the Apostolic See.

2.   However, if he was reduced to the lay state by a superior below the Roman Pontiff, he needs the permission of the Apostolic See in order to be readmitted to the clergy, without prejudice to can. 260 # 1, 2, c.

CANON 157.   # 1.   All clerics who lawfully have been reduced or have returned to the lay state thereby lose the offices, benefices, rights and clerical privileges, and are forbidden to wear the ecclesiastical garb.

2.   A subdeacon and a cleric in major orders, who was not lawfully united in marriage before the ordination, is bound by the law of celibacy when he is reduced to the lay state, without prejudice to c. 158.

CANON 158.   The cleric who received the subdiaconate or a major order out of grave fear, and has not later, when the reason for the fear has disappeared, ratified the ordination, at least tacitly, by the exercise of the order with the intention of subjecting himself thereby to the clerical obligations, can be returned to the lay state, with no clerical obligations, by the sentence of a judge, provided the lack of liberty and the absence of ratification has been proved.

The mentioning in c. 214 CIC of celibacy and canonical hours as obligations from which a cleric who was ordained under the influence of great fear will be relieved, had to be changed into the generic expression of **clerical obligations** so as to fit married clerics. It could happen that a widowed priest make use of the provision of c. 158, since in all Rites subdiaconate is a diriment impediment to marriage, which is not removed simply by a return **(reductio)** to the lay state even in the case of a widowed cleric.

TITLE FOUR

CLERICS IN PARTICULAR
TERRITORIAL DIVISIONS:

Larger Territorial Divisions (c. 159 = c. 215 # 1 CIC)
Parishes and Quasi-Parishes (c. 160 = c. 216 CIC)
Protopresbyterates (c. 161 = c. 217 CIC)

CANON 159. The erection or renewal, change or suppression of patriarchates, archiepiscopates, provinces, eparchies, exarchies with a proper territory, and apostolic exarchies, is the exclusive competence of the Roman Pontiff or the ecumenical synod, without prejudice to what is prescribed in cc. 248; 347 # 1; 328.

Concerning patriarchates see cc. 216 sq.; archiepiscopates, cc. 324 sq.; ecclesiastical provinces, cc. 315 sq.; eparchies cc. 392; exarchies with a territory of their own, cc. 362 sq.; apostolic exarchies, cc. 366 sq. Patriarchs and archbishops can establish quasi-dioceses, the so-called patriarchal or archiepiscopal exarchies, which are treated in cc. 388-391.

The contents of c. 215 # 2 CIC are found in the glossary of canonical terms promulgated by **Postquam Apostolicis:**

CANON 306. # 2. The exarchy is included in the term eparchy, and also every exarch in the term bishop, except if there are some special prescriptions in respect to the exarch, or from the text and context of the law or the nature of the matter the contrary is certain.

CANON 160. # 1. The territory of each eparchy shall be divided into distinct parts, and each part shall have assigned its own church, with its own faithful; and a particular rector shall be appointed in the capacity as their own pastor for the necessary care of souls.

2. Exarchies shall be divided in the same manner, when this can be done conveniently.

3. The sections of an eparchy mentioned in # 1 are parishes; the sections of an apostolic, patriarchal or archiepiscopal exarchy are called quasi-parishes if they have their own rector.

4. 1. Without a special apostolic indult there cannot be established parishes for difference of the language of the faithful of the same Rite in the same city or territory, nor parishes for certain

families or certain persons. In regard to such already established parishes nothing shall be changed without the advice of the Apostolic See.

2. The permission and advice mentioned in n. 1. can be granted by the patriarch and archbishop in accordance with the law, each in his territory.

Oriental Rite parishes are territorial parishes even if the faithful are assigned to them according to the personal criterion of membership in a certain Rite. There is no difference in general between Latin Rite and Oriental Rite parishes in this respect: both are limited to the faithful of their own Rite.

If Oriental Rite parishes of the same Rite, discipline, or jurisdiction are coexistent with each other within the same territory, but separated from each other by such criteria as liturgical language, or European national extraction (Rusine, Magyar, Croatian), or difference of calendars (Julian and Gregorian), their relationship to each other is that of personal parishes, but the relationship of each of them to the local Latin Rite parishes, or to those of another Oriental Rite, is one of territorial parishes among themselves.

CANON 161. # 1. The bishop shall divide his territory into districts consisting of several parishes, which are known under the name of protopresbyterates.

2. 1. If such a division seems, on account of the circumstances, impossible or inadvisable, the bishop shall seek the advice of the Apostolic See.

2. In the circumstances mentioned in n. 1, a bishop in a patriarchate or archiepiscopate shall seek the advice of the patriarch or archbishop.

PART ONE

THE SUPREME AUTHORITY AND THOSE WHO IN CANON LAW TAKE PART IN ITS EXERCISE

CHAPTER ONE

THE ROMAN PONTIFF

Source, Definition, Limits (c. 162 = c. 218 CIC)
Mode of Acquisition (c. 163 = c. 219 CIC)
Major Causes (c. 164 — c. 220 CIC)
Renunciation (c. 165 = c. 221 CIC)
Liturgical Commemoration by Other Hierarchs (c. 166 = new)

CANON 162. # 1. The Roman Pontiff as the successor to the primacy of Saint Peter has not only the prerogative of honor but also the supreme and full power of jurisdiction over the universal Church, in matters of faith and morals as well as in those that pertain to the discipline and government of the Church throughout the whole world.

 # 2. This power is truly episcopal, ordinary and immediate, and extends over each and every Church as well as over each and every pastor of souls as well as over the faithful, and depends on no human authority.

CANON 163. The Roman Pontiff, after his legitimate election, obtains at once from the moment he accepts the election, by divine right, the full power of his supreme jurisdiction.

CANON 164. Affairs of greater importance, which are reserved exclusively to the Roman Pontiff either by their very nature or by law, are called major causes.

CANON 165. If the Roman Pontiff should resign, it is not necessary for validity that the cardinals or any other persons accept his resignation.

CANON 166. The Roman Pontiff must be commemorated in the divine services of all Rites by the patriarchs, bishops, and other Hierarchs and all clerics.

The commemoration of the Roman Pontiff and of other Hierarchs during divine services of Oriental Rites cannot be compared with that in the Latin Rite, since the latter is a silent mentioning of the name, except in the infrequent case of an **oratio imperata pro papa,** while in the Oriental Rites it is a public manifestation, heard by all present at Mass or other services. During the Mass of the Byzantine Rite the Roman Pontiff is mentioned at least three times by exhorting the faithful to offer their prayers "for our Most Holy and Universal Archpriest N., the Pope of Rome." Thus the commemoration of any Hierarch, or its omission, has a distinct dogmatical and legal connotation.

CHAPTER TWO:

THE ECUMENICAL SYNOD (cc. 167-174).

The Roman Pontiff and the Ecumenical Synod
(c. 167 = c. 222 CIC)
Participants:
Personal Participation (c. 168 = c. 223 CIC)
Representation by Proxy (c. 169 = c. 224)
Prohibition of Leaving (c. 170 = c. 225 CIC)
Object of Discussions (c. 171 = c. 226 CIC)
Confirmation by Roman Pontiff (c. 172 = c. 227 CIC)
Authority of the Ecumenical Synod c. 173 = c. 228 CIC)
Suspension at Death of Roman Pontiff (c. 174 = c. 229 CIC)

CANON 167. **# 1.** There can be no ecumenical council unless it is convoked by the Roman Pontiff.

 # 2. It is the right of the Roman Pontiff to preside, either in person or through others, at the ecumenical council, to determine the matters which are to be discussed, and to establish and designate the order to be followed, to transfer, suspend, or dissolve the council, and to confirm its decrees.

CANON 168. # 1. The following persons are to be called to the council, and shall have the right to a decisive vote:

1. The cardinals of the Holy Roman Church, even if they are not bishops;

2. The patriarchs, primates, archbishops, residential bishops, even if they have not yet received the episcopal consecration;

3. The abbots or prelates nullius or exarchs who are in charge of a proper territory;

4. The abbot primate, the president of the consociation of monastic confederations endowed with papal exemption, the abbots superiors of monastic congregations, the presidents of monastic confederations endowed with papal exemption, and the supreme superiors of clerical religious institutes endowed with papal exemption, but not of other institutes, unless the decree of convocation should stipulate otherwise.

2. Even titular bishops enjoy a decisive vote if called to the council, unless it is stipulated otherwise in the convocation.

3. Theologians and experts of canon law, if they have been invited to the council, have only a consultative vote.

CANON 169. # 1. If any one of those summoned to the council according to c. 168 # 1 cannot attend on account of some just impediment, he shall send a proxy and furnish proof of the impediment.

2. If the proxy is one of the fathers of the council, he has not a double vote; if he is not, he shall be allowed to be present solely at the public sessions, but without a vote; and after the conclusion of the council, he is entitled to subscribe the acts of the same.

CANON 170. No one of those who must be present at the council is allowed to leave before the council is officially declared closed, unless he received permission to leave from the president of the council, who has investigated and approved of the reason for leaving.

CANON 171. The fathers may add other questions to those proposed by the Roman Pontiff, after they have been approved by the president of the council.

CANON 172. The decrees of the council have no definite binding force unless they have been confirmed by the Roman Pontiff and promulgated by his command.

CANON 173. # 1. The ecumenical council has supreme power over the whole Church.

2. From the judgment of the Roman Pontiff there is no appeal to the ecumenical council, nor a recourse from other acts.

CANON 174. If it happens that the Roman Pontiff dies during the celebration of a council, it is thereby suspended by law until the new Pontiff shall have ordered its resumption and continuation.

CHAPTER THREE:

THE CARDINALS OF THE HOLY ROMAN CHURCH (cc. 175-187)

CANON 175. The cardinals of the Holy Roman Church constitute the senate of the Roman Pontiff and they assist him in the governing of the Church as his principal advisers and aides.

CANON 176. # 1. The Sacred College is composed of three orders: The episcopal order, to which belong only the six cardinals who are in charge of the suburbicarian churches; the priestly order, composed of fifty cardinals; the diaconal order, composed of fourteen cardinals.

2. To each cardinal of the priestly and diaconal orders a titular church or a deaconry in Rome will be assigned by the Roman Pontiff.

CANON 177. # 1. Cardinals are freely selected by the Roman Pontiff from the whole world and from every Rite, and they shall be men who have received at least priestly ordination, and who are eminent for their learning, piety and wisdom in matters of administration.

2. From the dignity of a cardinal are excluded:

1. Illegitimates, even though legitimated by a subsequent marriage; likewise, others who are irregular or who have an impediment in respect to the reception of the subdiaconate or major orders according to the canonical sanctions, although they received lawful dispensations for orders and dignities, even the episcopal;

2. Who have children, though begotten in a valid marriage, or grandchildren;

3. Who are related by blood to another living cardinal up to the fourth degree inclusive.

CANON 178. # 1. Cardinals are appointed and nominated by the Roman Pontiff in consistory, and cardinals appointed and nominated in this manner obtain the right to elect the Roman Pontiff and the privileges named in c. 185.

2. If the Roman Pontiff announced the appointment of a cardinal in consistory, but retained the name in petto, the appointee does not enjoy meantime any of the rights and privileges of cardinals, but once his name has been published by the Roman Pontiff, he enjoys them from the date of publication, but his right of precedence begins with the date of the reservation in petto.

CANON 179. A cardinal promoted while absent from the Roman Court must at the reception of the red biretta take an oath to visit the Supreme Pontiff within one year, unless he is prevented thereof by a legitimate impediment.

CANON 180. Eastern Rite clerics promoted to the dignity of cardinal retain their own Rite. They shall, however, abstain from the use of those privileges which are not in agreement with their Rite.

There were only a few cardinals from Oriental Rites. The major reason was that the dignity of cardinal was rather unknown in the Near East; to be one of seventy seemed always a lesser honor than to be invested with the ancient dignity of patriarch. The following Oriental Rite prelates were elevated to the dignity of cardinals:

Bessarion of Nicea (1403-1472), Byzantine Rite Archbishop of Nicea 1437, made cardinal in 1439, appointed titular Patriarch of Constantinople in 1463, died in Ravenna 1472.

Isidor (1380-1463), of Greek birth, Byzantine Rite Metropolitan of Kiew (Ukraine) 1437, elevated to the cardinalate 1439, Patriarch of Constantinople 1455, Archbishop of Cyprus, 1461, died in Rome 1463.

Michael Lewytsky, Byzantine Rite Metropolitan of Lwiw (Ukraine) 1816-1858, created cardinal in 1856.

Sylvester Sembratowych, Byzantine Rite Metropolitan of Lwiw (Ukraine) 1882-1892, promoted to the cardinalate 1895.

Antonius Peter IX Hassun (1809-1884), Armenian Patriarch, made cardinal 1880, died in Rome 1884.

Ignatius Gabriel Tappouni, Syrian Patriarch of Antioch, born 1879, cardinal since 1935.

Gregory Peter XV Agagianian, Patriarch of Cilicia of the Armenians, born 1895, created cardinal 1946.

CANON 181. Unless otherwise stipulated by the Apostolic See, not only do all dignities, churches or beneficies which the newly promoted held by the very fact of his promotion to the sacred purple become vacant, but also all ecclesiastical pensions are forfeited.

CANON 182. # 1. Cardinals of the priestly order can, with the observance of the priority of order and promotion, by option submitted in a consistory and approved by the Roman Pontiff, transfer to another titular church, and cardinals of the diaconal order to another deaconry, and if they have completed ten years in the diaconal order, also to the priestly order.

2. A cardinal of the diaconal order who transfers by option to the priestly order takes his place before all those cardinals priests who were elevated to the honor of the sacred purple after him.

3. If a suburbicarian see is vacant, cardinals of the priestly order, who at the moment of the vacancy are present at the Roman Court, or are temporarily absent because of a charge committed to them by the Roman Pontiff, may claim it by option in consistory, with the observance of the priority of promotion.

4. Cardinals to whom one of the suburbicarian churches was assigned cannot adopt another; however, when a cardinal has reached the dignity of dean, he joins with his church that of Ostia, which latter thus is always joined in the person of the dean of the cardinals with one of the suburbicarian churches.

CANON 183. # 1. The Sacred College of Cardinals is presided over by the dean, who is the oldest by reason of promotion to one of the suburbicarian sees. He has no jurisdiction over other cardinals, but is to be regarded as the first among equals.

2. If the position of dean is vacant, by law the sub-dean succeeds, whether he at the time of the vacancy is present at the Roman Court, or resides in his suburbicarian see, or is temporarily absent because of a charge committed to him by the Roman Pontiff.

CANON 184. # 1. Cardinals are bound by the obligation of residing at the Roman Curia, and they cannot leave it without the permission of the Roman Pontiff, without prejudice to ## 2, 3.

2. This obligation binds also the cardinals suburbicarian bishops, but they do not require a permission to go to the churches committed to their care as often as they see it fit.

3. Cardinals who are bishops of one of the non-suburbicarian churches are exempt from the law of residing at the Roman Curia; but when they come to Rome they shall present themselves to the Supreme Pontiff, and shall not depart from Rome before having obtained his permission to leave.

CANON 185. # 1. All cardinals enjoy, besides other privileges established by law, the following faculties from the date of their promotion in a consistory:

1. To hear confessions anywhere in the world, even of the religious of either sex, and to absolve from all reserved sins and censures, with the exception of those reserved to the Apostolic See s p e c i a l i s-s i m o   m o d o   and those incurred by revealing the secret of the Holy Office;

2. To choose for themselves and the members of their household a priest as confessor, who, if he should lack jurisdiction, obtains it by law, also in respect to sins and censures, even if reserved, with the exception only of the censures mentioned in n. 1;

3. To preach the word of God everywhere;

4. To celebrate, or allow another to celebrate in his presence, one Divine Liturgy on Holy Thursday and three on Christmas Night;

5. To bless everywhere by the sign of the cross alone, with all the indulgences which the Apostolic See usually grants, crosses, rosaries, and other crowns of prayer, medals, statutes; scapulars approved by

the Apostolic See, and to impose them without the obligation of having the names inscribed;

6. To erect the Stations of the Cross with one blessing in churches, oratories, even private ones, and in other pious places, with all the indulgences granted to those who make this devout exercise; also to bless crucifixes with the indulgences of the Way of the Cross for the use of the sick and those who are in any other way legitimately impeded from visiting the Stations of the Cross;

7. To celebrate on a portable altar not only in their own residences but wherever they are staying, and to allow that another Divine Liturgy be celebrated in their presence;

8. To celebrate on the ocean observing the proper precautions;

9. To celebrate according to their own calendar the Divine Liturgy in all churches and oratories;

10. To enjoy daily the personal indult of the privileged altar;

11. To gain in their own oratories the indulgences for the gaining of which is prescribed a visit to some church or public oratory of the city or town in which the cardinal stays, and the members of his household can likewise enjoy this indult;

12. To bless the people in any place in the manner of bishops, but in Rome only in churches, pious institutions and at gatherings of the faithful;

13. To wear the insignia of bishops, and to make use of the mitre and the crozier;

14. To celebrate Divine Liturgy in any private oratory without prejudice to the one who enjoys the indult;

15. To celebrate according to the manner of bishops with throne and canopy in all churches outside Rome, and in case of a cathedral, after he has previously informed the Hierarch;

The exercise of pontifical functions was defined in **Postquam Apostolicis:**

CANON 307. The exercise of pontifical functions is to be understood to refer to sacred functions which in accordance with liturgical laws must solemnly be performed by the bishop vested with all pontifical insignia. Such functions are especially the solemn entrance into a church, the solemn celebration or assistance at Divine Liturgy and other divine services, the solemn blessing of the faithful, solemn conduction of processions, the administration of holy orders, to act as bishop assistant in an episcopal consecration, to consecrate a church, altar, or other places, an antimensium, iconostasis, and to consecrate the chrism (cf. c. 337 § 2 CIC).

16. To receive everywhere the honors which are usually accorded to local Hierarchs;

17. To authenticate in the external forum the oral pronouncements of the Supreme Pontiff;

18. To have a private oratory which is exempt from the visitation of the Hierarch;

19. To dispose freely, also by last will, of the income of their

benefice, save for the exception in respect to cardinals who died while they had a domicile in Rome;

20. Of consecrating and blessing everywhere churches, altars, sacred utensils, abbots and superiors of independent monasteries, and the like, except the consecration of the Holy Oils, if the cardinal lack the episcopal character, in accordance with the law;

21. To have precedence over all prelates, patriarchs and papal legates not excluded, unless the legate be a cardinal residing in his own territory; a cardinal legate a l a t e r e outside of Rome precedes all others;

22. To confer first tonsure and minor orders, provided the candidates has dismissorial letters of his own Hierarch;

23. To confer the sacrament of confirmation with the obligation of having the name of the confirmed entered in the record as required by law;

24. To grant an indulgence of three hundred days, to be gained t o t i e s q u o t i e s, in places or institutions for persons under his jurisdiction or protectorate; also in all other places, but to be gained solely by those present and once only each day.

2. The dean of the cardinals enjoys the privilege of ordaining the elected Pontiff, if he needs to receive the priestly or episcopal ordination, and he then makes use of the pallium. In the absence of the dean this privilege belongs to the subdean, and if the latter is absent, to the oldest suburbicarian cardinal bishop.

3. Finally, the cardinal protodeacon places on behalf of the Roman Pontiff the pallium upon archbishops and bishops who enjoy the privilege, and their proxies, and he announces to the people the name of the newly elected Pontiff.

CANON 186. # 1. After a cardinal, promoted to the suburbicarian see, has canonically assumed its government, he is a true bishop of his church, and he possesses the power which is obtained by other residential bishops in their own eparchy or diocese.

2. Other cardinals can do in their titular churches and deaconries, after they have assumed their government according to law, all what local Hierarchs can do in their churches, with the exception of judicial matters and of any jurisdiction over the faithful, but without prejudice to their authority in those matters which pertain to the discipline, the correction of morals and the divine service in the church.

3. A cardinal of the priestly order can in his titular church celebrate in the manner of bishops with throne and canopy, and a cardinal of the diaconal order can in his deaconry assist in the manner of bishops at divine services, and no one else can do the same without the cardinal's consent; in other churches in Rome cardinals cannot make use of a throne and canopy without permission of the Roman Pontiff.

CANON 187. The Sacred College of Cardinals and the Roman Curia have during the vacancy of the Apostolic See no other power than that defined in the apostolic constitutions enacted in this matter.

CHAPTER FOUR
THE ROMAN CURIA (cc. 188-210)

General Structure (cc. 188-191)

Composition of the Roman Curia (c. 188 # 1 = c. 242 CIC)
Competence in Affairs of Oriental Catholics
(c. 188 # 2 = new)
General Norms for Transaction of Business
(c. 189 = c. 243 CIC)
Relationship to Roman Pontiff (c. 190 = c. 244 CIC)
Controversies of Competence (c. 191 = c. 245 CIC)

CANON 188. # 1. The Roman Curia consists of the sacred congregations, tribunals, and offices, as they are enumerated and described below.

2. Without prejudice to the right of the Congregation of the Holy Office, apart from all the other sacred congregations, affairs of Orientals are transacted by the Congregation for the Oriental Church, unless it is expressly stated otherwise.

CANON 189. # 1. In each of the congregations, tribunals and offices, the order is to be observed and business is to be transacted according to the general and particular norms which the Roman Pontiff has enacted for them.

2. All who belong to the congregations, tribunals and offices of the Roman Curia must observe the secret within the limits and according to the manner determined by the customs of each.

CANON 190. # 1. Nothing grave or extraordinary shall be transacted in these congregations, tribunals and offices unless the moderators of the same shall have notified the Roman Pontiff of the matter.

2. All concessions and resolutions need papal approval, except those for which special faculties have been granted to the moderators of the offices, tribunals and congregations, and except the sentences of the Sacred Roman Rota and the Apostolic Signatura.

CANON 191. Any controversy that arises between sacred congregations, tribunals or offices of the Roman Curia concerning competency shall be decided by a committee of cardinals of the Holy Roman Church, whom the Roman Pontiff will designate in each case.

Article One

THE SACRED CONGREGATIONS (cc. 192-203)

General Structure of Congregations (c. 192 = c. 246 CIC)
The Congregation of the Holy Office (c. 193 = 247 CIC)
The Consistorial Congregation (c. 194 = c. 248 CIC)
The Congregation for the Oriental Church
(c. 195 # 1, 1; # 2 = c. 257 CIC; # 1, 2-4 = new)
The Congregation of the Sacraments (c. 196 = c. 249 CIC)

The Congregation of the Council (c. 197 = c. 250 CIC)
The Congregation of the Religious (c. 198 = c. 251 CIC)
The Congregation of the Propagation of the Faith
    (c. 199 = c. 252 CIC)
The Congregation of Rites (c. 200 = c. 253 CIC)
The Ceremonial Congregation (c. 201 = c. 254 CIC)
The Congregation of Extraordinary Ecclesiastical Affairs
    (c. 202 = c. 255 CIC)
The Congregation of Seminaries and Universities
    (c. 203 = 256 CIC)

CANON 192. A cardinal prefect presides over each of the congations, but if the Roman Pontiff himself presides, a cardinal secretary directs them. With these other cardinals are associated whom the Pontiff sees fit to appoint, together with other necessary assistants.

CANON 193. # 1. The Congregation of the Holy Office, over which the Supreme Pontiff himself presides, guards the doctrine of faith and morals.

2. It judges crimes which according to its own law are reserved to it, with the power to judge these criminal cases not only in the instance of appeals from a tribunal of a local Hierarch, but also in the first instance, if they have been directly brought before it.

3. The Holy Office has exclusive jurisdiction in all what either directly or indirectly, in law or in fact, concerns the so-called Pauline Privilege and the matrimonial impediments or disparity of worship and mixed religion. Likewise, to it belongs the power to dispense from these impediments. Therefore, all such questions are to be brought before that congregation, which, however, may, if it sees fit and the circumstances advise it, remit the question to another congregation or to the Tribunal of the Sacred Roman Rota.

4. To the Holy Office belongs the task to examine carefully books which have been denounced to it, and, if necessary, to prohibit them, and to grant dispensations from the prohibition. It is also the duty of the same to investigate ex officio censurable writings of any kind which are published, and to remind the Hierarchs that they must conscientiously proceed against pernicious writings and denounce them to the Apostolic See according to the norm of law.

5. The Holy Office alone is competent in all questions which concern the eucharistic fast for priests in the celebration of the Divine Liturgy.

CANON 194. # 1. The prefect of the Consistorial Congregation is the Roman Pontiff himself. Besides other cardinals, the Cardinal Secretary of the Holy Office, the Cardinal Prefect of the Congregation for Seminaries and Universities, and the Cardinal Secretary of State belong to it ex officio. Along its consultors are always the Assessor of the Holy Office, the Secretary of the Congregation for Extraordinary Affairs, and the Prelate Secretary of the Congregation for Seminaries and Universities.

2. The work of this Congregation is not only to prepare the agenda for consistories, but in addition to erect in places which are not subject to the Congregations for the Oriental Church and for the

Propagation of the Faith, new dioceses and provinces, and both cathedral and collegiate chapters; to divide existing dioceses; to propose for appointment bishops, apostolic administrators, coadjutor and auxiliary bishops; to prepare the canonical investigation or the inquiry in respect to individuals who are to be promoted, and diligently to evaluate the results, and to examine their doctrinal standing, without prejudice to the norms of c. 202.

3. This Congregation is in charge of all matters pertaining to the erection, preservation and welfare of dioceses. Therefore, it invigilates the observation and the neglect of obligations to which ordinaries are bound; renders decisions in reports submitted in writing by bishops in respect to the condition of their dioceses; it orders apostolic visitations and examines the reports of the same, transmitting in either case to the respective congregations for their deliberation those matters which pertain to their sphere of activity.

CANON 195. # 1. 1. To the Congregation for the Oriental Church, which is presided over by the Roman Pontiff, are reserved all matters of whatsoever kind which regard either the faithful or the discipline or the Rites of the East, even those of a mixed nature, that is to say, such as affect partially matters or persons of the Latin Rite. For that reason it possesses for the Churches of the Oriental Rites all those faculties which the other congregations enjoy for the Churches of the Latin Rite, without prejudice to the right of the Congregation of the Holy Office according to c. 193, of the Congregation of the Sacred Rites according to c. 200 # # 2, 3; of the Congregation for Extraordinary Ecclesiastical Affairs according to c. 202; and of the Congregation of Seminaries and Universities according to c. 203 # 1, in those matters that concern higher schools, that is, universities and colleges; and of the Sacred Penitentiary according to c. 204;

2. It is the duty of this Congregation to approve for all Eastern Rites liturgical books, and to resolve questions in regard to their texts and translations; also to supervise and decide all questions concerning rubrics and ceremonies of the Divine Liturgy, the sacraments, sacramentals and the divine office;

3. In addition, in all those regions in which this Sacred Congregation possesses full and exclusive jurisdiction, the same enjoys not only over the faithful of Eastern Rites but also over the faithful of the Latin Rite, their hierarchy, organizations, institutions, pious associations, those faculties which other congregations possess in respect to the faithful of the Latin Rite outside of these regions, without prejudice, however, to the right of the Congregation of the Holy Office, and preserving their authority in those matters which are still reserved to the Congregation for the Discipline of the Sacraments, the Congregation for Seminaries and Universities and the Sacred Penitentiary.

4. In regard to members of Latin Rite religious institutes, missionaries in regions alluded to in n. 3, this Congregation has power over them in their capacity as missionaries, both as individual persons as well as collectively. However, whatever concerns them insofar as they are religious, both as individuals as well as collectively, shall be remitted or left to the authority of the Congregation for Religious.

2. This Congregation decides controversies in administrative

procedure; those which it remits to judicial procedure shall be decided by the Congregation itself or be submitted to the ordinary tribunals of the Apostolic See.

The general characteristic of the jurisdiction of the Sacred Congregation for the Oriental Church does not differ from that of the other S. Congregations. It was sometimes incorrectly labeled as personal jurisdiction, and thereby opposed to the alleged territorial jurisdiction of the other S. Congregations, because it affects primarily Catholics of Oriental Rites. However, in the same measure as the S. Congregation for the Oriental Church is limited in its jurisdiction by the criterion of membership of persons in a certain Rite, so also the Latin Rite congregations are limited in their jurisdiction.

However, by the motuproprio **Sancta Dei Ecclesia** of March 25, 1938 (AAS 1938 p. 154) the S. Congregation for the Oriental Church received exclusive jurisdiction over all Catholics without distinction of Rite, even those of the Latin Rite, including their hierarchy, institutions, religious organizations, etc., in certain regions, mostly where Oriental Catholics are in the majority, and where Oriental Rites have been since antiquity. These countries are: Egypt, with the Sinai Peninsula, Erythrea, the northern part of Ethiopia, Iran, Irak, Lebanon, Palestine, Syria, Jordan, Cyprus, Turkey, Greece, with all surrounding islands, the southern part of Albania, and Bulgaria. The competence of the Holy Office, the S. Congregations of the Sacraments, the Rites, for Seminaries and Universities, and of the S. Penitentiary have remained untouched.

CANON 196. # 1. The Congregation for the Discipline of the Sacraments is in charge of the entire legislation concerning the discipline of the seven sacraments, without prejudice to the right of the Congregation of the Holy Office in regard to the matters mentioned in c. 193, and of the Congregation of the Sacred Rites in respect to the rites and ceremonies which must be observed in the celebration, administration and reception of sacraments.

2. Under its authority come also all those matters which customarily are decided and conceded in the discipline of matrimony, as well as in the discipline of the other sacraments, and also in the celebration of the Eucharistic Sacrifice, with the exception of those reserved to other congregations.

3. This Congregation decides also exclusively concerning the fact of non-consummation of marriage, on the existence of reasons for granting the dispensation, and whatever is connected with it, although it can remand the decision on all these questions to the Sacred Roman Rota if it considers it expedient. Also questions concerning the validity of marriage can be referred to it, which, however, shall be submitted to a competent tribunal if they require a more accurate inquiry or investigation. It is also its duty to decide on the obligations connected with major orders, and to examine questions of the validity of sacred ordination, or to remand them to a competent tribunal. The same is to be said in respect to the other sacraments.

CANON 197. # 1. To the Congregation of the Council there is committed the entire discipline of the secular clergy and the Christian people.

2. Therefore, it is its duty to see that the precepts of Christian life be observed, and it has the faculty of granting to the faithful dispensations therefrom. It is its duty to moderate those matters that concern pastors and canons; or that regard pious associations, pious unions (even though they depend on religious institutes or are erected in their churches and houses), pious bequests, pious works, stipends of liturgies (Mass stipends), benefices and offices, personal and real church property, diocesan contributions, fees of episcopal curiae, and the like. There is reserved to it the faculty of granting exemptions from the conditions required for obtaining benefices when the appointment belongs to ordinaries; to approve settlements with those who have occupied church property, also those pertaining to religious institutes; to permit to the faithful to acquire church property which has been usurped by civil governments.

3. This Congregation decides all questions concerning ecclesiastical immunity and controversies in respect to precedence, without prejudice to the Congregation for the Rites and the Congregation for Ceremonies.

4. It is charged with the direction of all matters pertaining to the holding and approval of councils and of meetings and conferences of bishops outside the regions subject to the Congregations for the Oriental Church and for the Propagation of the Faith.

5. This Congregation is also competent to render decisions in all controversies that concern matters which have been committed to it which it judges should be transacted in administrative procedure; the others shall be submitted to a competent tribuanl.

CANON 198. # 1. The Congregation in charge of the Affairs of the Religious takes exclusive care of matters pertaining to the government, discipline, studies, property and privileges of the religious of both sexes bound by any kind of public vows, and of those who lead a common life after the manner of religious, although without vows, and also of the third orders of the faithful, without prejudice of the right of the Congregations for the Oriental Church and that of the Propagation of the Faith.

2. Therefore, this congregation shall decide all questions belonging to its competence in administrative procedure, submitting questions to be treated in judicial procedure to a competent tribunal, and always without prejudice to the right of the Congregation of the Holy Office and the Congregation of the Council concerning matters with which they are charged. However, if there is a question between a religious and a person not belonging to the religious state, the congregation may also, if it deems it proper, especially on request of a party, submit the question to another congregation or a tribunal.

3. Finally, to this congregation is reserved the granting of dispensations to religious from general laws, save for the norm of c. 193 # 5.

CANON 199. # 1. The Congregation for the Propagation of the Faith is in charge of the missions for the preaching of the Gospel and the Catholic faith, and appoints and changes the necessary ministers, and possesses the faculty to manage, transact and execute everything considered necessary and appropriate in this matter.

2. It takes care of all matters pertaining to the holding and approval of councils in regions which are subject to it.

3. Its jurisdiction is limited to those regions where the ecclesiastical hierarchy has not yet been established, and the status of mission still perdures. To this Congregation are also subject regions which, even though a hierarchy has been established, are still in their initial stage. Likewise, it also has charge over societies of ecclesiastics and seminaries which were exclusively organized for the purpose of educating candidates for the foreign missions, especially in what concerns their rules, administration and opportune concessions in connection with the sacred ordination of their students.

4. This Congregation must however refer to the competent congregations all those matters which pertain to faith, matrimonial causes, or the general norms concerning the teaching and interpretation of the discipline of sacred rites.

5. In respect, however, to the religious, this Congregation claims jurisdiction over all matters which concern the religious as missionaries, taken individually or collectively. Whatever concerns the religious as such, taken individually or collectively, shall be remanded and submitted to the Congregation of Religious.

CANON 200. # 1. The Congregation of Sacred Rites has the right to supervise and regulate all matters strictly pertaining to sacramental rites and ceremonies of the Latin Church, but not those which in a wider sense refer to sacred rites, such as are the right of precedence and others of that kind, which are to be determined in either the judicial or administrative order. Its duty is, therefore, to invigilate that the sacred rites and ceremonies be accurately observed in the celebration of the Holy Sacrifice, in the administration of sacraments, in the recitation of the divine office, and finally in all those matters which regard the worship of the Latin Church; to grant appropriate dispensations; insignia and privileges of honor, personal and temporary as well as local and perpetual, which are connected with the sacred rites and ceremonies, and to make sure that they be not misused. In these transactions it makes use of the Liturgical Section.

2. This Congregation is also charged with all matters that concern the beatification and canonization of servants of God, taking into consideration # 3, or in any manner concern sacred relics. These questions are reserved to another section under the direction of the Promotor General of the Faith.

3. For the causes of the servants of God in which no testimony from contemporary witnesses can be obtained, nor authentic documents containing such testimony, properly obtained in their time, are available a third section is at hand, which is called the historical. This section also is to render in addition decisions concerning the correction and republication of liturgical books. It is headed by the Relator General.

CANON 201. The Congregation of Ceremonies regulates the ceremonies which are followed in the Papal Chapel and Court, and the sacred functions which the cardinals perform outside the Papal Chapel. It decides also questions concerning precedence among the cardinals as well as among the envoys whom the various nations send to the Apostolic See.

CANON 202. The Congregation for Extraordinary Ecclesiastical Affairs is in charge of erecting or dividing of dioceses and of promoting suitable candidates to vacant dioceses and of promoting suitable candidates to vacant dioceses whenever such matters must be taken up with civil governments. Moreover, this Congregation takes care of matters which the Supreme Pontiff assigns to its examination through the Cardinal Secretary of State, especially those connected with civil legislation, and those which concern the pacts entered into with nations.

CANON 203. # 1. The Congregation for Seminaries and Universities supervises all matters concerning the government, discipline, the administration of temporal property, and the studies of seminaries, without prejudice to the right of the Congregation for the Oriental Church and that of the Propagation of the Faith. To this Congregation is likewise committed the supervision of the government and the studies in universities and faculties of higher learning depending on the authority of the Church, not excepting those which are conducted by the members of some religious institute. The Congregation examines and approves new institutions, grants the right of conferring academic degrees, and prescribes the norms according to which they may be conferred. In the case of a man distinguished for exceptional learning, it may itself confer them.

2. To this Sacred Congregation belong among other cardinals the Cardinal Secretary of the Consistorial Congregation and among the consultors the Assessor of the same Congregation.

Article Two:

THE TRIBUNALS OF THE ROMAN CURIA (cc. 204-205)

The Sacred Penitentiary (c. 204 = c. 258 CIC)
The Sacred Roman Rota and the Supreme Tribunal of the Signatura Apostolica (c. 205 = c. 259 CIC)

CANON 204. # 1. The Sacred Penitentiary is headed by the Cardinal Major Penitentiary. The jurisdiction of this tribunal is limited to matters pertaining to the internal forum, the non-sacramental included. Therefore, this tribunal grants favors for the internal forum alone, such as absolutions, dispensations, commutations, sanations, condonations; in addition, it also examines and decides questions of conscience.

2. Moreover, it belongs to this Congregation to make decisions in matters pertaining to the use and the concession of indulgences, without prejudice to the right of the Holy Office to decide dogmatic questions on matters concerning indulgences or new prayers and devotions.

CANON 205. Cases that require judicial procedure are in charge of the Sacred Roman Rota and the Supreme Tribunal of the Signatura

Apostolica within the limits and according to the norms enacted for them, save for the right of the Congregation of the Holy Office and the Congregation of Sacred Rites in respect to matters of their competence, and without prejudice to c. 195 # 2, concerning the right of the Congregation for the Oriental Church.

Article Three:

THE OFFICES OF THE ROMAN CURIA (cc. 206-210).

The Apostolic Chancery (c. 206 = c. 260 CIC)
The Apostolic Datary (c. 207 = c. 261 CIC)
The Apostolic Camera (c. 208 = c, 262 CIC)
The Office of the Secretary of the State (c. 209 = c. 263 CIC)
The Secretaries of Briefs to Princes and of Latin Letters
(c. 210 = c. 264 CIC)

CANON 206. # 1. The Apostolic Chancery, in charge of the Cardinal Chancellor of the Holy Roman Church, has the task of dispatching the apostolic letters or bulls issued for the appointment to benefices and offices made in consistories, for the erection of new provinces, dioceses and chapters, and for other more important affairs of the Church.

2. These letters and bulls shall not be dispatched except by orders of the Congregation of the Consistory or that for the Oriental Church in those matters over which they have authority, or by orders of the Supreme Pontiff in regard to all other affairs, with observation of the terms contained in each single mandate.

CANON 207. The Apostolic Datary, in charge of the Cardinal Datary of the Holy Roman Church, has the duty of investigating the qualifications of candidates who are to be appointed to non-consistorial benefices reserved to the Apostolic See; of drawing-up and dispatching letters for such appointments; of granting exemptions from the conditions required for the appointment to a benefice whenever the appointment does not constitute a right of the Hierarch; and to provide for the pensions and obligations the Supreme Pontiff has imposed in the appointment of the aforesaid benefices.

CANON 208. The Camera Apostolica, over which presides the Cardinal Chamberlain of the Holy Roman Church, has the care and administration of the temporal property and rights of the Apostolic See, especially for the time of vacancy; in which case the norms contained in the apostolic constitutions enacted on this matter must exactly be followed.

CANON 209. The Office of the Secretary of State, which is headed by the Cardinal Secretary of State, is divided into three sections:

1. The first section, which is presided over by the Prelate Secretary of the Congregation for Extraordinary Ecclesiastical Affairs, attends to those matters which must be referred to this Congregation

according to c. 202, while other matters shall be transmitted, in accordance with their nature, to the respective congregation;

2. The second section, under the direction of the Substitutus, attends to ordinary affairs;

3. The third section is in the charge of the Chancellor of the Apostolic Briefs, and attends to the dispatching of briefs.

CANON 210 The Secretaries of Briefs to Princes and of Latin Letters have the duty of writing in Latin the acts of the Supreme Pontiff which he has committed to them.

CHAPTER FIVE

LEGATES OF THE ROMAN PONTIFF (cc. 211-215)

The Right of the Roman Pontiff to Appoint Representatives
    (c. 211 = c. 265 CIC)
Kinds of Legates:
    Legates a l a t e r e (c. 212 = c. 266 CIC)
    Nuncios and Internuncios (c. 213 # 1 = c. 267 # 1 CIC)
    Apostolic Delegates (c. 213 # 2 = c. 267 # 2 CIC)
Termination of Office (c. 214 = c. 268 CIC)
Relationship of Legates to Patriarchs and Bishops
    (c. 215 = c. 269 CIC)

CANON 211. The Roman Pontiff has the right, independently of any civil power, to send legates to any part of the world, either with or without ecclesiastical jurisdiction.

CANON 212. A legate a l a t e r e is a cardinal sent by the Supreme Pontiff as an a l t e r e g o; he enjoys only such power as the Supreme Pontiff has granted to him.

CANON 213. # 1. Legates who are sent with the title of nuncio or internuncio:

1. Maintain according to the rules accepted by the Apostolic See the relations between the Holy See and the civil governments where they act as permanent legates;

2. In the territory assigned to them they watch over the condition of the Churches and submit reports thereon to the Roman Pontiff;

3. They usually receive in addition delegated faculties.

2. Those who are sent with the title of apostolic delegates have but the ordinary power mentioned in # 1, n. 2, besides other delegated powers committed to them by the Apostolic See.

CANON 214. # 1. The office of the legates, with the faculties committed to them, does not expire at the vacancy of the Apostolic See, unless the contrary be stated in the papal appointment.

2. It ceases, however, when the mandate has been carried out, by revocation made known to them, and by renunciation accepted by the Roman Pontiff.

CANON 215. # 1. The legates are not to impede the patriarchs and local Hierarchs in the free exercise of their jurisdiction.

2. Though they may lack episcopal consecration, they precede all Hierarchs who are not distinguished with the dignity of cardinals.

DECISION OF THE COMMISSION FOR THE CODIFICATION OF THE ORIENTAL CANON LAW
of June 23, 1958, published in AAS 1958, p. 550.

QUESTION: Do legates, who, in virtue of c. 215 # 2 "although they have not episcopal consecration, nevertheless enjoy precedence over all Hierarchs who are not distinguished with the dignity of cardinals," have precedence over patriarchs?

ANSWER: In the negative, since the term of Hierarch does not comprehend the patriarch, in accordance with the Apostolic Letters P o s t q u a m   A p o s t o l i c i s   L i t t e r i s of February 9, 1952, c. 306 ## 2, 4.

His Holiness, Our Lord Pius XII, Pope by Divine Providence, ordered that the special norm, which was proposed by this Papal Commission, be inserted into c. 215 # 2 and that the same norm shall hence enter into legal force.

This norm is the following:

"Although they have not episcopal consecration, they nevertheless enjoy precedence over all Hierarchs who are not distinguished with the dignity of cardinals or of patriarchs, provided the patriarch is in his own territory and presides over ceremonies or services of his own Rite; however, even in such a case, legates have precedence over patriarchs if a special mandate with right of precedence for certain acts was granted by the Supreme Pontiff."

3. Though they might lack episcopal consecration, they can without permission of the Hierarchs celebrate divine service, also in the manner of bishops, in all their churches of whatever Rite, except the cathedral.

The corresponding c. 269 # CIC mentions as right of legates "to bless the people," and that they may perform pontifical ceremonies, not excluding "the use of throne and canopy." The public blessing of the faithful is so intimately connected in the minds of the Christians of the Near East with the possession of the fullness of the priesthood, i.e., episcopal consecration, that simple priests, even if of highest rank, would not be considered qualified for such a blessing. It is true that precedence was accorded during the ecumenical councils of the early Church, all celebrated in the Near East, even to simple priests and deacons over bishops if they represented the Roman Pope and Patriarch, but this was outside the celebration of liturgical services.

The Eastern Christians have also special seats or thrones in their churches reserved exclusively for bishops, but this reservation is connected with the possession of the episcopal consecration and less with any specific hierarchical position. The use of the throne is a requirement of the rules of the respective liturgical service, and is not reserved to the bishop under whose jurisdiction the church is placed. Once a prelate is entitled either in virtue of law, as the papal legates, or by grant of the local Hierarch, to celebrate pontifical services in the church, he automatically has also to make use of the episcopal throne.

Canon 270 CIC has no equivalent in **Cleri Sanctitati,** since there are no prelates in the Christian East who have the title of papal legates attached to their office.

CHAPTER SIX

PATRIARCHS

GENERAL NORMS (cc. 216-220)

Dignity of Patriarchs (c. 216 # 1)
Definition of Patriarch (c. 216 # 2, n. 1)
Relationship to Faithful Outside the Patriarchate
(c. 216 # 2, n. 2)
Patriarchal Titles (c. 217)
Place of Residence of Patriarchs (c. 218)
Order of Precedence Among Patriarchs (c. 219)
Patriarchal Apocrisiaries at the Roman Curia (c. 220)

The term of **patriarch** was applied to the father or chief of a clan or family. The word occurs in the Greek translation of the Old Testament, the Septuagint, for the chiefs of the tribes. In the New Testament it denotes Abraham as a version of his "father of many nations," also King David and the twelve sons of Joseph.

The Christian Church first used the same term as a title of respect given to various bishops without consideration of a possible hierarchical rank. However, soon the title of patriarch became reserved to the bishops of the principal centers of Christianity. After several centuries of ambiguous use, the bishops of Constantinople, Alexandria, Antioch and Jerusalem were exclusively designated as patriarch, as we learn from a letter of Emperor Justinian II to Pope John V (687). The Roman Pontiff was naturally understood to be the first patriarch, but this title was absorbed in his higher rank as supreme head of the Church. It must be mentioned that the title of pope is not the exclusive designation of the highest hierarch of the Church, since the same title is a prerogative also of the Patriarch of Alexandria since the earliest times, although the only Catholic Patriarch of Alexandria, i.e., the Coptic, seems not to make use of this title at the present time.

The number of patriarchs became multiplied by the various heresies of Christian antiquity. The title of Patriarch of Antioch was claimed by the orthodox as well as by the Monophysites, and later by a third group, the Monothelites. The see of Alexandria was contested by the orthodox, who remained faithful to the Byzantine Empire, and the Monophysitic native element, the Copts. The heads of all these groups considered themselves the rightful patriarchs of their sees.

In the Middle Ages the number of patriarchs was raised through assumption of the title by heads of national Churches, as that of the Armenian Church, the Georgian Church, the Nestorians in Mesopotamia, the Bulgarian Church, the Serbian Church, the Russian Church, and in the West by the conferral of the title to the bishops of Aquileia, later transferred to Venice.

Later centuries saw a new increase of hierarchs with the title of patriarch. From nearly every dissident Oriental community a part returned to the Catholic Church, and their chief bishops considered themselves the rightful heads and patriarchs of their Churches. The Latin Rite established also new titular patriarchates, or continued to confer the mere title of Oriental patriarchates of the Latin Rite, and also among the dissident Orientals new national Churches were organized whose heads were distinguished with the title of patriarch.

The following hierarchs carry today the title of patriarch:

Catholic Patriarchal Titles:

1. R o m e : The pope has also the title of Patriarch of the West.

2. C o n s t a n t i n o p l e : The title was conferred only on Latin Rite prelates who resided at the Roman Curia, but was discontinued in the last decades.

3. A l e x a n d r i a : There is one resident Catholic patriarch, the Patriarch of Alexandria of the Copts. The title was also given to some Latin Rite prelates at the Roman Curia, but for some decades no new appointment was made.

4. A n t i o c h : There are four possible Catholic patriarchs of this title: The Byzantine Rite (Melkite) Patriarch, the Syrian Patriarch of Antioch, and the Patriarch of Antioch of the Maronites. The Latin Rite title has not been conferred for a number of years. The Byzantine Rite (Melkite) Patriarch of Antioch enjoys also the personal title of Patriarch of Alexandria and of Jerusalem.

5. J e r u s a l e m : One prelate has this title, the only resident Latin Rite patriarch in the Orient, the Patriarch of Jerusalem. He has no true patriarchal jurisdiction, but only that of a bishop. His territory comprises Palestine, Transjordania and Cyprus.

6. A r m e n i a n   C h u r c h : Patriarch of Cilicia of the Armenians, who resides in Lebanon; at the present time it is Gregory Peter XV Cardinal Agagianian.

7. C h a l d e a n (East-Syraian) C h u r c h : Patriarch of Babylonia of the Chaldeans, who resides in Iraq.

8. V e n i c e : The Archbishop of Venice was distinguished with the title of patriarch when the see was transferred from Aquileia to Venice. The patriarchal title was first assumed by the Bishop of Aquileia-Grado in 607, and by Pope Nicholas V transferred in 1451 to Venice.

9. L i s b o n : The Archbishop of Lisbon and Primate of Portugal was made a patriarch by Clement XI in 1716.

10. P a t r i a r c h o f W e s t I n d i e s is the title of the or-

dinary of the Spanish Armed forces, at the present time the Bishop of Madrid. This title was created by Pope Leo X.

11. Patriarch of East Indies is the title of the Archbishop of Goa, a Portuguese colony in India. It was established by Pope Leo XIII in 1886 to end the Goanese schism.

Non-Catholic Patriarchal Titles:

1. Constantinople: (1) The Byzantine Rite (Orthodox) Patriarch, who calls himself the "ecumenical patriarch,' i.e., of the whole Byzantine Empire. (2) The Armenian Patriarch of Constantinople, who is under the nominal jurisdiction of the Katholikos-Patriarch of Etschmiadzin (Soviet-Armenia).

2. Alexandria: (1) The Byzantine Rite Pope and Patriarch of Alexandria; (2) The Copt Patriarch.

3. Antioch:(1) The Byzantine Rite Patriarch of Antioch; (2) The Syrian Patriarch of Antioch.

4. Jerusalem: (1) The Byzantine Rite Patriarch of Jerusalem; (2) The Armenian Patriarch, who is under the nominal authority of the Katholikos-Patriarch of Etschmiadzin (Soviet-Armenia).

5. The Patriarch of the Serbian Church in Yugoslavia.

6. The Patriarch of Moscow and of all Russia.

7. The Romanian Patriarch.

8. The Bulgarian Patriarch.

9. The Katholikos-Patriarch of the Armenian Church, with residence in Etschmiadzin (Soviet-Armenia).

10. The Armenian Patriarch of Cilicia, with residence in Syria, who is under the nominal authority of the Katholikos-Patriarch of Etschmiadzin (Soviet-Armenia).

11. The Nestorian Katholikos-Patriarch of the Chaldeans of the Orient, who resides now in the United States.

CANON 216. # 1. Special respect is due to the patriarchs of the East, in accordance with the oldest tradition of the Church, since they preside each his own patriarchate or Rite as father and head with the most ample powers, granted or recognized by the Roman Pontiff.

2. 1. The title of patriarch is given to a bishop to whom the canons assign jurisdiction over all other bishops, including metropolitans, the clergy and the faithful of a territory or Rite, to be exercised under the authority of the Roman Pontiff, according to the norms of law.

2. Patriarchs possess authority over the faithful of the same Rite who reside outside the boundaries of their territory to the extent it is determined expressly in general or particular law.

Patriarchal powers were either granted by the Roman Pontiff, cr by ecumenical councils but subsequently recognized by the popes. The jurisdiction of the patriarchs was always limited as to the territory, which goes back to the political territorial division of the late Roman Empire. This is theoretically acknowledged also by the dissident canonists, although they dispute among themselves concerning the jurisdiction over the faithful who presently live outside the boundaries of the ancient Roman Empire, especially in North and South America and in South Africa. While some would reserve it to the Patriarch of Constantinople in his capacity of Ecumenical Patriarch, to whom jurisdiction over Mission territories was once assigned, others dispute it, and as a result there is a double — and with other immigrant national churches — a multiple dissident ecclesiastical jurisdiction everywhere.

The Roman Pontiff exercises jurisdiction outside the limits of the ancient patriarchal territories in virtue of his primatial power. He may share it with a patriarch to the extent he sees fit. Actually, Oriental patriarchs have been granted certain supervisory authority over the faithful outside their patriarchates. Since matters of Rite are exempt from the local Latin ordinaries, primarily because of lack of the knowledge required in such matters, and because the Oriental Rite faithful cannot be without proper ecclesiastical supervision in matters of Rite, the Holy See has granted to the highest authority of each Rite the right to exercise some supervision over matters strictly pertaining to the Rite even over the faithful outside the respective dioceses and territories of the patriarchate. This is the reason why Oriental patriarchs are entitled to supervise the faithful of their Rite even on the American continent as far as matters of Rite are concerned, as, e.g., the use and the editing of liturgical books, the observance of liturgical regulations, laws of fasting, time for Easter Communion, holydays of obligation, etc.

The S. Congregation for the Oriental Church supervises this capacity of the patriarchs. Since the patriarchs have no coercive power over the clergy and faithful outside their patriarchates, in order to enforce their decrees they must employ the assistance of the respective local Latin Rite ordinary.

The patriarchs may delegate their authority in such matters to others. Actually, several patriarchs have appointed **patriarchal vicars** from among the clergy of their Rite in the United States.

The following patriarchs have faithful in the United States organized in parishes:

1. The Patriarch of Antioch of the Maronites, for the Maronites.

2. The Patriarch of Antioch, Alexandria and Jerusalem of the Byzantine Rite, for the Melkites.

3. The Katholikos-Patriarch of Cilicia, for the Armenians.

4. The Patriarch of Babylonia, for the Chaldeans.

Other divisions of Oriental Rites with patriarchs have no communities established in these two countries, as the Syrians and the Copts.

CANON 217. # 1. The title of the Church attributed or granted to each patriarchate can be changed only by the Roman Pontiff or the ecumenical council.

2. Personal titles, which are granted to patriarchs as individual persons, are to be considered as adjunct and accessory titles, and in regard either of their use or time fixed for their use, they are to be judged strictly according to the stipulations contained in the grant.

At the present time only the Melkite (Byzantine Rite) Patriarch of Antioch enjoys the personal title of Patriarch of Alexandria and of Patriarch of Jerusalem. These are not mere empty titles but correspond to actually existing dioceses in those territories, and both patriarchates are listed in the **Annuario Pontificio** as separate ecclesiastical entities.

> **CANON 218.** # 1. 1. Each patriarchate must have a fixed place of residence.
>
> 2. The place of residence cannot be transferred except for very grave reasons, with the consent of the patriarchal synod or the bishops according to c. 224 # 1, and the previous approval of the Apostolic See.
>
> # 2. The place of residence shall be fixed in the principal city from which the patriarch derives his title, or, if this cannot be done, in the patriarch's own eparchy.

Because of conditions existing in the Near East, not one patriarch resides in the city from which he wears the title, but usually somewhere nearby.

> **CANON 218.** # 1. 1. The order of precedence among the ancient patriarchal sees of the East is the following: The precedence belongs to the Patriarch of Constantinople, after whom follow that of Alexandria, then that of Antioch, and after him that of Jerusalem.
>
> 2. Among the patriarchs who are of different Rites but of one and the same title, precedence is obtained by him who was first promoted to the patriarchal dignity, and if they were promoted at the same time, to him who is the senior in age.
>
> # 2. Among the other patriarchs of the East precedence is regulated by the norm of # 1, 2.
>
> # 3. 1. In churches or divine services of his own Rite every patriarch preceeds other patriarchs, though they may have a higher title or priority of promotion.
>
> 2. A patriarch who possesses actual jurisdiction precedes, outside the Roman Curia, patriarchs of any Rite, also the Latin, who possess only the title.

The original order of precedence among the apostolic sees was: Rome, Alexandria, Antioch. When Constantinople emerged as a new ecclesiastical center, it took the last place. However, the splendor and importance of the new imperial residence raised also the status of the Bishop of Constantinople, and so the Second Ecumenical Council (381) in Constantinople assigned to him the second rank, after the See of Rome. This was explained by the idea that with the transfer of the imperial capital from Old Rome to Constantinople, to which Constantine the Great had given the official name of **New Rome,** the factual primacy of that bishop was established. This situation was reaffirmed at the Council of Chalcedon (451), but was again rejected by the popes until the times of the Crusades, when the Patriarch of Constantinople became a Latin Rite prelate. The Ecumenical Council of Florence (1438) also confirmed the rank of the Patriarch of Constantinople as the first after the Roman Pontiff.

The patriarchal sees of Alexandria and Antioch are followed by that of Jerusalem, which at the Council of Chalcedon (451) was made independent from all other ecclesiastical authority, especially that of the Metropolitan of Cesarea (Palestine), and consequently acquired first the highest rank and later also the patriarchal title.

Since the see of Alexandria has precedence over that of Antioch, it seems that the Melkite Patriarch is the highest ranking patriarch of the Catholic Oriental Churches, although not the highest ranking prelate, there being at the present time two cardinals of Eastern Rites. However, the conferral of the two personal titles of Patriarch of Alexandria and of Jerusalem would be connected with some restrictions, since each patriarch has to apply for himself to the Holy See.

CANON 220. A patriarch can have an apocrisiary at the Apostolic See, appointed by him with the advice of his permanent synod and the previous consent of the Apostolic See.

Apocrisiaries were called envoys of some ecclesiastical authority to some other hierarch or civil government in Christian antiquity. The various Eastern patriarchs had their apocrisiaries at the imperial court in Constantinople, and some metropolitans kept such envoys at the seat of their patriarch. The popes had permanent or temporary apocrisiaries at the imperial court in Constantinople and at that of the Exarch of the Byzantine Emperor in Ravenna (Italy). Pope Gregory the Great was as a deacon such an apocrisiary in Constantinople.

Article One:

THE ELECTION OF PATRIARCHS (cc. 221-239)

The Synod of Election (c. 221)
Place of Election (c. 222)
Time Limit for Election (c. 223)
Right of Active Vote (c. 224)
Obligation of Participation (c. 225)
Procedure of Election:
    Quorum Required for Election (c. 226 # 1)
    Mode of Voting (c. 226 # 2)
    The Presidency of the Election (c. 227)
    Tellers (c. 228 # 1)
    Actuaries (c. 228 # 2)
    Oath of Secrecy (c. 228 # 3)
    Form of Ballots (c. 229 # 1)
    Oath of Electors (c. 229 # 2)
    Required Majority (c. 230)
Qualifications of Candidates (c. 231)
Default of Right of Election (c. 232)
Notification of the Elected:
    Mode of Notification (c. 233)
    Time Limit for Acceptance (c. 234)
Procedure After Election:

In Case of Renunciation of the Elected (c. 235 # 1)
In Case of Acceptance of an Elected Who is a Bishop
    (c. 235 # 2)
In Case of Acceptance of an Elected Who is not a Bishop
    (c. 235 ## 3, 4)
Notification of Apostolic See (c. 236)
Minutes of Election (c. 237)
Effect of Enthronization (c. 238)
Oath of Secrecy (c. 239)

CANON 221.   The patriarch is to be designated by the synod of the bishops of his patriarchate in a canonical election, which was lawfully convoked by the administrator of the patriarchate according to c. 308, n. 3, and duly inaugurated.

CANON 222.   The synod must be held in the patriarchal residence itself, or in another place which was designated by the administrator of the patriarchate with the advice of the fathers of the synod, obtained perhaps by way of correspondence.

CANON 223.   The synod shall be held not later than one month from the day of vacancy, save for particular law which establishes a shorter time.

CANON 224.   # 1.   In the election of the patriarch all and only the bishops of the same patriarchate, including titular bishops, enjoy an active vote, if they have been lawfully elected and confirmed, although they have not yet received episcopal consecration, with the exclusion of those enumerated in c. 109 # 1.

2.   Clerics who lack the episcopal dignity are absolutely excluded from the synod, save for c. 228 ## 1, 2.

3.   Lay persons of whatever position or authority cannot interfere in the election of the patriarch, either by participation in the synod, or by recommendation of candidates, or in any other manner, every contrary custom being hereby abolished, and any contrary privilege whatsoever being revoked.

All Catholic Oriental patriarchs were formerly found in the Turkish Empire, which recognized the chiefs of the various Catholic and dissident religious communities as civil heads of their people. This made them supreme judges even in temporal matters in cases involving their own subjects. They were as ethnarchs charged with the collection of taxes, out of which they had to pay their contribution to the Sublime Porte for themselves and their people. They were the supreme administrators of all schools, foundations, institutions of their Rite. Because of this mixture of secular obligations with ecclesiastical ones, it could hardly be avoided that the laity demanded a voice not only in the management of the secular aspects of their patriarch's official duties, but also of ecclesiastical matters, which were inextricably joined with the former. So-called national councils were formed with the lay members in the majority, and which arrogated to themselves the right to elect the patriarch and bishops. While this situation held sway more among the dissident Christian communities, the Catholic ones had also to go through

118

rather troublesome developments. However, the abolition of the theocratic califate in Turkey and the expulsion of the Turks from the Near East eliminated the dual role of the patriarchs, returned them to the ecclesiastical sphere, and removed the laity from intervention, at least as far as Catholics are concerned, in the appointment of the patriarchs and bishops.

Canon 224 # 3 is a legal definition of the Catholic principles in this matter.

CANON 225. # 1. All bishops invited have a serious obligation to participate in the election.

2. If they consider themselves prevented because of a reasonable impediment, they shall submit in writing their reasons to the synod, whose decision they must follow.

CANON 226. # 1. After a lawful convocation, if two thirds of those who enjoy active voice and who are not prevented by a true impediment are present in the place designated in accordance with c. 222, the synod shall be declared canonical and the election can be held.

2. Save for the norm of c. 110, the right of casting votes is reserved to those present in the place of the election, excluding thereby the possibility of casting a vote either by letter or by proxy.

CANON 227. Unless the Apostolic See has decreed differently in a particular case, the synod for the election of the patriarch is presided by him who is the senior by episcopal consecration among the bishops subject to the patriarch, without prejudice to particular law.

CANON 228. # 1. 1. Two tellers shall be appointed before the election by secret ballots, who together with the president carry out the duties mentioned in c. 113.

2. These tellers shall be taken from among the fathers of the synod or from priests according to the norms of particular law.

2. Besides the tellers, a secretary shall be appointed by the president of the synod, with the advice of the two who are seniors by episcopal consecration among the bishops present.

3. 1. All those mentioned in ## 1 and 2 must take an oath faithfully to discharge their duties, and to keep the secret concerning all that is transacted in the meetings, also after the termination of the election.

2. The tellers are forbidden by the sanctity of their oath to reveal the name of those who have cast certain ballots, even to the fathers of the synod themselves.

CANON 229. # 1. The ballot shall be made up according to the norms of particular law; the votes shall be cast according to the rules of common law, without prejudice however to particular law.

2. Before the election of the patriarch begins, each of the fathers must promise by oath that he will elect in each voting him whom he considers should be elected according to the will of God.

CANON 230. # 1. He is to be considered elected who has obtained two thirds of the votes, after invalid votes have been removed.

2. The balloting must be repeated until two thirds of the votes have been cast for a candidate.

CANON 231. In order that a candidate may be considered qualified for the patriarchal dignity, in addition to the requirements for the episcopal dignity according to c. 394 # 1, 1,, 2, 5, 6, he must be:

1. At least forty years of age;

2. At least ten years in the priesthood.

CANON 232. If the election is not performed within fifteen days from the beginning of the synod, the designation of the person of the patriarch devolves for this time upon the Roman Pontiff.

CANON 233. If the election has been performed according to law, it shall immediately be made known to the one elected by the president, and if the president was elected, by him who is to act in his stead, on behalf of the whole synod, according to the form and manner customary in each Rite, save for the rule of c. 235 # 3, 1.

CANON 234. The one elected must manifest within two days from the receipt of the notification whether he accepts or refuses the election; otherwise he loses every right deriving from the election.

CANON 235. # 1. If the one elected renounces, the electors must proceed to a new election.

2. If the one elected accepts, the synod shall proceed, according to the regulations of that Rite, to his proclamation and enthronement, provided he is a bishop, not excluding an elected or designated and duly confirmed bishop although he has not yet received the episcopal consecration, but excluding bishops who canonically have resigned or have been deposed from the episcopal office, and those mentioned in c. 109 # 1.

3. 1. If the one elected is not such, the synod shall immediately notify the Roman Pontiff of the result of the election, which suspends the proclamation and enthronement of the one elected. The fathers and all others who in whatsoever capacity participated in the election, or have by whatever means come to know of the result of the election, must keep secrecy in regard to the result, also in relation to the one elected, until the confirmation has arrived and lawfully has been made public.

2. The fathers of the synod may in the meantime return to their residences, but shall be ready to return to the synod when the answer of the Roman Pontiff arrives.

3. After the confirmation from the Roman Pontiff is received, they shall proceed to the solemn proclamation and enthronement of the patriarch.

4. If the elected did not obtain the confirmation of the Roman Pontiff, they shall proceed at once to a new election.

4. A candidate elected to the patriarchal dignity who lacks episcopal consecration, if it is one of whom # 2 treats, shall be consecrated bishop before the enthronement; but if he is one spoken of in # 3, n. 1, he can be ordained bishop only after confirmation by the Roman Pontiff.

CANON 236. # 1. The new patriarch must send a report to the Roman Pontiff concerning the election, together with the documents, signed by himself, the profession of faith made by him according to approved forms in the presence of the synod, and the oath of fidelity, and at the same time request ecclesiastical communion and the pallium, which is an insignia of the fulness of the pontifical office.

2. The synod shall forward at the same time by a synodal letter a report to the Roman Pontiff on the manner in which the election was held in accordance with the norms of law, and that the new patriarch has made the profession of faith and taken the oath of fidelity and signed them in the presence of the synod, and they shall request likewise for the patriarch ecclesiastical communion and the pallium.

CANON 237. # 1. 1. The minutes of the election, after they have been concluded and signed by the president, the tellers and the clerk, shall carefully be preserved in the secret archives of the patriarchate.

2. It is praiseworthy that all fathers of the synod add their signatures to the above mentioned signatures, if particular law demands it.

2. A certificate attesting the election, and signed according to the norm of # 1, shall be given to the new patriarch.

CANON 238. # 1. The patriarch elected and enthroned according to c. 235 obtains full right to his office, save for # 3.

2. The patriarch elect mentioned in c. 235 # 3, who in whatsoever manner has to come to know of the election, is in no way permitted to interfere, on the pretext of the election, in the administration of the office of the patriarch, be it in spiritual or in temporal matters, before the confirmation of the election was obtained from the Roman Pontiff; and decisions peradventure made by him before the mentioned confirmation are void.

3. The patriarch who was lawfully elected and enthroned, is forbidden to call together the patriarchal synod mentioned in c. 340 # 1, and to elect or consecrate bishops before he has solemnly received confirmation in a consistory and the pallium.

The pallium is today considered a liturgical vestment of the Latin Rite although it is paralleled in some Eastern Rites by a vestment of similar shape and symbolic significance, the **omophorion**. Both go back to a shoulder garment, scarf or shawl, which was in general used by both sexes among the ancient Roman and Greeks, as we know from mosaics and statues of those times. It cannot be established at what time the pallium — omophorion — began to be considered an exclusive ecclesiastical garment. However, today the omophorion is worn in the Byzantine and Syrian Rites by every bishop, while the pallium is reserved to certain classes of bishops. The **Liber Pontificalis** tells us that Pope Mark, who died in A.D. 336, conferred the right of wearing the pallium on the Bishop of Ostia, since he had the prerogative of consecrating the new-elected pope if the latter was not a bishop; the last time this happened was in 1846 at the election of Gregory XVI.

The pallium of the sixth century, as we know it from the mosaics preserved in various churches in Ravenna (Italy), had the form of a long, moderately wide, white band, ornamented at its extremity with a black or red cross, and finished off with tassels. It was draped around the neck, shoulders and breast in such a manner that it formed a "V" in front, and the ends hung down from the left shoulder, one in front and one behind. In the eighth century it became customary to let the ends fall down, one in the middle of the breast and the other in the middle of the back, and to fasten them there with pins, the pallium becoming thus "Y"-shaped. Later on the band, which had hitherto been kept in place by the pins, was sewed into the "Y"-shape, without however being cut. Even to this day the pallium is doubled on the left shoulder, and a loop for a pin is provided on the left, but not on the right, shoulder, a remnant of the ancient form.

The two vertical bands of the present circular pallium were very long until the fifteenth century, but were later shortened until they have now a length of only about twelve inches. The pins, which at first served to keep the pallium in place, were retained as ornaments even after the pallium was sewed in the proper shape, although they no longer served a practical purpose. The insertion of small leaden weights in the vertical ends of the pallium was customary at least since the thirteenth century.

The pallium, as it is now conferred by the Holy See, is a circular band about two inches wide, worn about the neck, breast, and shoulders, and having two pendants, one hanging in front and one behind. The pendants are about two inches wide and twelve inches long, and are weighted with small pieces of lead covered with black silk. The pallium is decorated with six black crosses on the breast, the back and the left shoulder, and on each pendant. The crosses on the breast, back and left shoulder are provided with a loop for the reception of a gold pin set decorated with precious stones.

The pallium is made of white wool, part of which is supplied by two lambs presented annually as a tax by the Lateran Canons Regular of St. Augustine to the Chapter of Canons of the first church in Christendom, St. John in the Lateran Palace in Rome. The two lambs are solemnly blessed on the feast of St. Agnes at the main altar of the basilica after a pontifical Mass, and then offered to the pope. After the palliums have been made by the nuns of St. Agnes in Rome, they are blessed on the evening of the feast of SS. Peter and Paul, and are then kept in a silvergilt chest near the grave of St. Peter in St. Peter's basilica.

The pallium symbolizes the fullness of the pontifical office. Worn by patriarchs and independent metropolitans, it typifies their share in the supreme pastoral authority of the pope. The use of the pallium is reserved to the pope, patriarchs and metropolitans who are independent of a patriarch. The pope may distinguish some simple bishops by granting them the pallium, which does not increase their power or jurisdiction, nor give them precedence over other bishops.

The pope may use the pallium at any time and occasion. Patriarchs and metropolitans use it only in their respective territory, and there only on the days and occasions designated in liturgical books or according to statutory provisions.

Since the various Oriental Christian Churches had their own pallium, the omophorion, worn by every bishop, it was only during the Crusades, when the first Latin Rite patriarchs were appointed to sees in the Near East, that the Roman Pontiffs conferred upon them also the Latin Rite pallium. This was later continued when Oriental Rite patriarchs and metropolitans reunited their Churches with the Roman See. Because of the great difference in size between the Byzantine Rite omophorion and the Latin Rite pallium of our time it did not seem incongruous from a liturgical stand-point to wear the latter on top of the former, i.e., two vestments identical as to historical origin and nearly equivalent in their hierarchical symbolism. Some patriarchs ,as the Byzantine Rite (Melkite) Patriarch of Antioch, rarely make use of the pallium. The Maronite Patriarch wears one or the other, but not both together.

After the Holy See has appointed a metropolitan, or confirmed the election of a patriarch, he makes a formal request for the pallium in the first consistory held by the pope. It may be presented in person or through a proxy, usually a priest of his Rite living in Rome. The pallium is then either delivered to the proxy or laid upon the metropolitan or patriarch by the Cardinal Protodeacon.

The twin of the pallium, the omophorion, is used today in three different forms. The original form is retained by most bishops of the Byzantine Rite, Catholics and dissidents. It is a broad band, eight to ten inches wide, decorated with crosses, and draped loosely over the neck, shoulders, and breast, the two ends pending from the left shoulder down below the knees, often to the ankles. Ukrainian Catholic bishops, and Catholic bishops in Hungary and Romania, have sometimes adapted the form of the omophorion to that of the Latin Rite pallium by letting the ends fall down in the middle of the breast and back, and fastening them there with buttons, which changes the form from a "V" to a "Y". The same veestment has in the Syrian Rite the form of a straight band, about ten inches wide and eight feet long, with a hole for the head, reminding one of the scapular of some Latin Rite orders. There is also a so-called little omophorion; it is used by Byzantine Rite bishops during liturgical functions whenever the grand omophorion becomes cumbersome in the execution of rites and ceremonies. It is nothing else than the grand omophorion folded at the middle, and then laid on the shoulder over the neck.

CANON 239. Each and every person participating in a synod must take an oath to maintain secrecy, even after the termination of the election, in relation to the one elected, and to matters which either directly or indirectly concern the balloting.

Article Two:

RIGHTS AND OBLIGATIONS OF PATRIARCHS (cc. 240-282)

General Principles (cc. 240-244)

A general survey of the principles underlaying the patriarchal authority and the organs by which it is exercised should be of advantage.

The patriarch shares in the supraepiscopal jurisdiction of the Vicar of Christ on earth and Successor of St. Peter by concession of the Roman Pontiff, granted directly, or indirectly by confirmation of decrees of ecumenical synods, and to the extent it has been determined in law, notably **Cleri Sanctitati.** The patriarch enjoys legislative, judicial and coercive power in spiritual as well as temporal matters, within the limits of the entire patriarchate. Although his jurisdiction is ordinary in the patriarchate, he is not the local Hierarch of the whole patriarchate in the strict sense, but has only mediate power, more in the nature of an intermediary between his Church, the bishops, clergy, religious, faithful, and the Holy See of Rome. Depending on the person and circumstances of time and place, the patriarch's authority and influence might be felt in the life of his Church to a much greater degree than the limitations established by canon law would permit us to assume.

The jurisdiction of Catholic Oriental patriarchs is considerably more extensive than that conceded to dissident patriarchs. Catholic patriarchs are under the supervision and paramount jurisdiction of the Roman Pontiff, but dissident patriarchs are under the strict tutelage of their permanent synods, in which often simple priests have statutory membership. In addition, the laity has a say in every question of some importance, even if it is a purely spiritual matter. Because most dissident Oriental Churches have the character of national Churches, the civil government has subjected the Church to its supervision and obedience, reducing thereby the role of the patriarch to a mere high-ranking state official.

Subject to the patriarch are all metropolitans, bishops and exarchs. At the present time there are no ecclesiastical provinces established among Catholic as well as dissident Oriental Churches, and all rights and duties of metropolitans are exercised by the patriarch himself. Bishops with title of metropolitans enjoy only honorary precedence, and have no greater jurisdiction than that of local Hierarchs over their respective dioceses.

The patriarch is in the exercise of his power dependent on the cooperation of several organs:

1. The **patriarchal synod,** an assembly of all the bishops and supreme superiors of monks and clerical religious institutes, to be convoked at least every twenty years (c. 340 sqq.).

2. The **synod of election of a patriarch,** composed of all the bishops (c. 221 sqq.).

3. The **synod of election of bishops** (c. 251 sqq.).

4. **Conference of the bishops** of the patriarchate, to be summoned every year (c. 247).

5. **Permanent synod,** composed of the patriarch and four bishops (cc. 288-295), his chief advisory body, whose consent is necessary in all business of some importance.

6. **Patriarchal council** is a body composed of the patriarch and two bishops, and is to be constituted in circumstances where the permanent synod cannot be established (cc. 296-297).

7. The **patriarchal curia** comprises:
    (1) The permanent synod.

(2) The **patriarchal tribunal,** the highest court in the patriarchate, at the present time only of second instance. From the sentence of a diocesan tribunal appeal cannot be taken to a metropolitan court, because there are no ecclesiastical provinces existing at the present time (c. 298), but the appeal must be brought before the patriarchal court (cf. c. 72 sqq. of **Sollicitudinem Nostram).**

(3) The **patriarchal econome,** who is in charge of the administration of property belonging to the patriarchate as such (c. 299).

(4) The **patriarchal chancellor** and his assistant, who are the executive branch of the patriarch's office (cc. 300, 301).

(5) The **patriarchal liturgical commission** (c. 302).

(6) **Patriarchal consultors** are theologians and experts in law whose counsel the patriarch may request whenever he or other patriarchal organs need advice (c. 303). They form no body or college, but are heard individually, and should not be confused with the consultors of the patriarchal eparchy.

Limits of Patriarchal Jurisdiction (c. 240)
Prohibition of General Delegation (c. 241)
Relationship to Metropolitans (c. 242)
The Patriarch as Legislator (c. 243)
Relationship to Laws of Apostolic See (c. 244)

CANON 240. # 1. The Patriarch exercises ordinary power in the entire patriarchate, and therefore it is his right and duty to exercise, according to the norms of the canons and legitimate customs, jurisdiction over the bishops, the clergy and the faithful, who all must show him canonical obedience and respect.

2. This power can validly be exercised only in the patriarchate, unless on account of the nature of the matter or of law the opposite is true.

CANON 241. The authority of the patriarch is personal to the extent that he cannot appoint a syncellus for the whole patriarchate.

CANON 242. Until the exercise of the rights and duties in their provinces shall have been restored to the metropolitans according to c. 316, the patriarch is to exercise the rights and to fulfill the duties of the metropolitans.

CANON 243. # 1. Laws which are not contrary to the universal law of the Church and to those which the Apostolic See enacted for the patriarchate, and which concern the whole patriarchate, or some part thereof, or a group of persons, can be made by the patriarch only in the patriarchal synod mentioned in c. 340 # 1.

2. The patriarch must zealously provide for the promulgation of the laws enacted in the patriarchal synod, save for c. 350 # 1.

3. The authentic interpretation of laws of the patriarchal synod until the next synod is a right of the patriarch, to be exercised with the advice of the permanent synod.

4. 1. The patriarch is entitled to dispense from laws of the patriarchal synod for a good reason, in individual cases, even for the entire patriarchate. If the dispensation exceeds individual cases, the patriarch cannot grant it except for a grave reason and with the consent of the permanent synod;

2. A dispensation from a law of the patriarchal synod, which was refused by the local Hierarch, shall not be granted by the patriarch, except for a good reason and after having heard the Hierarch.

CANON 244. # 1. Pronouncements of the Supreme Pontiff issued for the patriarchate, for the Eastern Church, or for the universal Church, must be communicated by the patriarch, unless the Apostolic See has directed otherwise, after he has been informed thereof by the Sacred Congregation for the Oriental Church, to the bishops and others to whom it may be of concern, and when it is in the interest of the faithful, he must order their public reading in the churches.

2. Prescriptions which are contained therein and which concern the patriarchate itself shall faithfully be carried out by the patriarch.

RIGHTS OF PATRIARCHS
(cc. 245-250)

Teacher of the Hierarchs and Faithful (c. 245)
Visitation of the Patriarchate (c. 246)
Episcopal Conferences (c. 247)
Larger Territorial Divisions of the Patriarchate — Appointment, Transfer and Removal of local Hierarchs (c. 248)
Supervision of Vacant Eparchies:
    Exercise of Patriarchal Prerogatives (c. 249 # 3)
    Exercise of Metropolitan Prerogatives (c. 249 ## 1, 2)
    Care of the Property of Vacant Eparchies (c. 250)

CANON 245. # 1. The patriarch is entitled in virtue of his own power to:

1. enact decrees, mandates and general ordinances, even for the entire patriarchate, to define the application of laws, and to urge their execution;

2. direct instructions to the clergy and the people for the purpose of explaining sound doctrine, of promoting piety, of correcting abuses, and of promoting and recommending practices that are advantageous to the spiritual welfare of the faithful;

3. address encyclical letters to the entire patriarchate concerning questions pertaining to his own Church and Rite.

2. The patriarch can command the bishops, the clergy and the religious to have his ordinances, instructions and letters read and and explained publicly in churches, or in the houses of ecclesiastics and religious.

CANON 246. # 1. Without prejudice to the right and duty of each bishop to visit his own eparchy, the patriarch has the right and duty to visit by ordinary visitation every ten years the entire patriarchate in person or through somebody else.

2. The patriarch may conduct for a grave reason also an extraordinary visitation in some church, city or eparchy.

3. The patriarch can perform during the visitation everything to which the Hierarch is entitled in a canonical visitation.

CANON 247. The patriarch shall not omit to call together for a conference every year, with the exception of those years in which the patriarchal synod mentioned in c. 340 # 1 is held, the bishops and other local Hierarchs either of the entire patriarchate or of some province or region, in which later case this shall be done in such a way that there is no one who is not invited at least once in a period of five years.

CANON 248. # 1. The patriarch can with the consent of the patriarchal synod or of the bishops in accordance with c. 224 # 1, for a grave reason:

1. establish provinces and eparchies, change their boundaries, unite, divide, abolish or change their hierarchical rank, and transfer an episcopal see, provided that the Apostolic See confirms it;

2. transfer resident or titular metropolitans and bishops from one to another residential or titular eparchy;

3. accept the resignation of bishops submitted to him;

4. assign a coadjutor or auxiliary to a resident bishop, observing however cc. 251-255 if the appointee does not possess the episcopal dignity.

2. The patriarch can with the consent of the permanent synod establish exarchies, change their boundaries, and abolish them.

3. The patriarch shall as soon as possible notify the Apostolic See of the decisions of the synod concerning the matters mentioned in # 1, nn. 2-4; # 2.

CANON 249. # 1. Concerning vacant eparchies, the patriarch is charged with:

1. notifying the Apostolic See of the vacancy of a see;

2. caring for a vacant eparchy;

3. supplying for the neglect of a college of eparchial consultors, if they are entitled, according to c. 469, to elect an administrator;

4. appointing the administrator of a vacant eparchy, with the advice of the bishops who hold office with residence at the patriarchal curia, if according to c. 469 the appointment of an administrator is a right belonging to the patriarch.

2. The removal of the administrator, who was appointed by the patriarch according to the norm of # 1, n. 4, can be decided by the same patriarch, for a just reason, with the advice of the bishops who hold office with residence at the patriarchal curia.

3. It is the right and the duty of the patriarch to provide that the vacant see receive as soon as possible, within the time limits established by common law, a worthy and qualified shepherd.

CANON 250. The patriarch shall see during the vacancy of a see that the property of the eparchy, and those assets of the late bishop which are to devolve to the Church, are preserved and faithfully administered. They all must be delivered in their entirety and in the prescribed manner to the future bishop after his enthronement.

APPOINTMENT OF BISHOPS
(cc. 251-257)

Appointment of Residential Bishops:
The Synod of Election (c. 251)
Mode of Election (c. 252)
Confirmation by Roman Pontiff (c. 253)
Previous Approval of Candidates (c. 254)
Election by Letter (c. 255)
Appointment of Metropolitans (c. 256)
Appointment of Titular Bishops (c. 257)

CANON 251. The bishops are canonically elected in the synod according to the norms of the following canons, contrary privileges and customs being abrogated, save for c. 255.

CANON 252. # 1. In respect to the appointment of bishops:
1. The patriarch collects the information and documents which according to the norms of common law and the special instructions of the Apostolic See are necessary or appropriate for properly establishing the qualifications of candidates according to c. 394;
2. The patriarch shall, if he sees fit, request the opinion, to be kept secret, of pastors and other priests of the vacant eparchy, approaching them one by one and employing the necessary precautions, and he shall ask them whether they can propose a suitable candidate.

2. 1. He shall call together the bishops mentioned in c. 224 # 1 to a synod for the election of bishops, and preside over it; in which synod no one has the right to cast votes by letter or by proxy.
2. The fathers gathered in the synod shall freely elect him whom before God they regard worthy and qualified above others, to whom the care of the Christian flock can be committed, without prejudice to particular law which reserves to the patriarch the right of providing the names of candidates.
3. For a valid election there is required an absolute majority, not counting the invalid ballots;
4. Secrecy concerning the voting is to be kept after the election.

CANON 253. # 1. Save for the provision of c. 254 # 1, the patriarch shall immediately submit a report on the election to the Roman Pontiff in order to obtain the confirmation of the elected according to c. 392 # 2.

2. It is not permitted to reveal the name of the one elected to anybody, not even to the elected himself, before the authentic notification of the granting of the confirmation has arrived.

CANON 254. # 1. In order to expedite the appointment to vacant eparchies, a list can be prepared, to be approved by the Apostolic

See, of priests qualified for the office of a bishop. No one's name can be included unless he was found qualified for this office according to the opinion of the patriarch and the bishops gathered in synod, and expressed in a secret vote by absolute majority.

2. 1. If one lawfully elected by the synod for a certain residential or titular eparchy is among those enumerated on the list, it can be proceeded further immediately after the election, except if in the meantime the name of a candidate has been stricken from the list by the Apostolic See;

2. The Apostolic See shall at once be informed that the election has taken place.

CANON 255. # 1. Whenever a synod cannot be called together according to c. 251, the patriarch, having obtained the permission of the Apostolic See, shall ask by letter for the votes of the bishops. The patriarch must for the validity of the procedure make use of the aid of two bishops as tellers, who shall be appointed in accordance with particular law, or, if there is no such law, by the patriarch with the consent of the permanent synod. The tellers shall together with the patriarch take an oath according to c. 113 # 1 faithfully to discharge their duty and to preserve secrecy, and then open the letters of the bishops, count the votes, and together with the patriarch subscribe to a written report of the election.

2. The votes cast by letter must be kept secret.

CANON 256. # 1. To the patriarch belongs the right;

1. to ordain metropolitans in person, or, if he should be impeded, through other bishops;

2. to grant patriarchal letters of canonical appointment, as mentioned in c. 395 # 1, to a metropolitan or bishop;

3. to enthrone in person or by a delegate a metropolitan, after the latter has received episcopal consecration, though the metropolitan has canonically taken over the administration of the eparchy, through another person.

2. The patriarch must within three months confer on the elected one episcopal consecration and grant to him the document of canonical appointment referred to in # 1, n. 2; mention is to be made in this document of the appointment or confirmation granted by the Roman Pontiff.

CANON 257. The patriarch can cause that a few titular bishops, but not more than three, be nominated in the election synod, in accordance with c. 251, provided their livelihood is assured. He shall assign to them an office with residence in the curia, and he shall consecrate them after he has obtained their confirmation from the Apostolic See, except if it is the case of one elected according to c. 254 # 2.

THE SUPERVISION OF THE HIERARCHY AND CLERGY

CANON 258. The patriarch is entitled:

1. to permit to local Hierarchs subject to him, in addition to the instances mentioned in c. 403 # 2, to be absent from their eparchies, taking into account the gravity of the reasons;

2. by devolutive right to supply for the negligence of metropolitans, according to the norms of law;

3. during the vacancy of a metropolitan see to exercise the right of the metropolitan and to fulfill his obligations in the entire province.

CANON 259. # 1. The patriarch shall show to all bishops who are subject to him due reverence and treat them with brotherly charity; and all bishops shall display toward the patriarch as their lawful superior respect and devotion, and shall render to him due obedience.

2. If among them a controversy should arise, they shall submit it to the judgment of the patriarch, without prejudice to the right of referring the controversy at any time or phase to the Apostolic See.

3. In extraordinary matters or those which present special difficulty the bishops shall not fail to ask the patriarch's opinion, nor shall the patriarch fail to seek the advice of the bishops.

4. 1. Matters that concern several eparchies and those which have a connection with civil authorities can be reserved by the patriarch for his decision. However, he cannot render a decision concerning them before he has heard the opinion of the interested local Hierarchs, and with the consent of the permanent synod;

2. If the matter is urgent and there is no time to call together the bishops who are members of the permanent synod, the bishops who have office with residence in the patriarchal curia shall take their place.

CANON 260. # 1. It is a right and duty of the patriarch:

1. To supervise the clergy of the entire patriarchate. If any seems to deserve punishment, the patriarch shall admonish his Hierarch; and if the admonition should have been made in vain, he himself shall take steps against the cleric according to the norms of law;

2. If particular law so stipulates:

(a) to send priests of his Rite into an eparchy of the patriarchate if dearth of priests exists there, with the consent of the Hierarch of the eparchy; and to commit to any cleric the duty of caring for ecclesiastical or secular affairs of the patriarchate, with the consent of his Hierarch. The patriarch can remove such a cleric also from the jurisdiction of his Hierarch for the duration of the mission;

(b) to grant the indult mentioned in c. 80 # 2;

(c) to readmit, with the consent of the permanent synod, a cleric to the clerical state who was returned to the lay state according to c. 156 # 2, 2;

(d) to designate the Hierarch for faithful of his Rite who reside outside the patriarchate, provided the care of such faithful has been committed to the patriarch in virtue of particular law, and he has obtained the consent of the Apostolic See;

(e) to receive the oath of obedience to the patriarch from a candidate mentioned in c. 395 # 2;

(f) to exercise the faculty mentioned in c. 494 # 3 with the advice of the permanent synod.

3. To honor with a prelatic title a cleric belonging to any of the eparchies of the patriarchate, with the advice of his Hierarch.

2. The recourse mentioned in cc. 134 # 3, 494 # 5, 547 # 1, must be taken to the patriarch, without prejudice to the norm of c. 145.

3. The permission mentioned in c. 85 # 2 is to be granted by the patriarch; likewise, the indult referred to in c. 490 # 1, but with the consent of the permanent synod.

4. To enact regulations concerning military chaplains.

RELATIONSHIP TO FAITHFUL OUTSIDE THE PATRIARCHATE:

Sending of Priests to such Faithful (c. 261)
Appointment of Visitors for such Faithful (c. 262)

Between the patriarch and the faithful of his Rite there can exist various jurisdictional relationships:

The faithful who are living within the territorial limits of his patriarchate can be directly subject to the patriarch in his own eparchy, where he is not only their patriarch but also their bishop. A similar relationship exists in respect to the faithful residing in such parts of his patriarchate where no dioceses are established, and for whom the patriarch has erected patriarchal exarchies. The patriarchal exarchs govern their faithful with ordinary power, but as vicars of the patriarch.

Over the faithful living within dioceses of the patriarchate, the patriarch enjoys only mediate jurisdiction, to be exercised primarily through the local Hierarch.

Concerning the faithful of his Rite outside the patriarchate, two possibilities can be verified: If their care is a right of the patriarch, the rules of cc. 261, 262, apply. The patriarch has the initiative in organizing their pastoral care, although his activity is subject to the supervision of the Apostolic See. However, the faithful are not under the jurisdiction of the patriarch, but of that of the local Hierarch who has been charged with their care by the Apostolic See or the patriarch himself (cc. 5; 22 # 3; 260 # 1, 2, d).

Sometimes ecclesiastical provinces and dioceses of a Rite exist which have no jurisdictional connection whatsoever with the patriarch of the Rite. The two ecclesiastical provinces of the Malabarians in India are completely separated from the Patriarch of Babylonia of the Chaldeans, the chief hierarch of their Rite. The same is to be said of the Malankarian Ecclesiastical Province in India and the Syrian Patriarch of Antioch, and of the Armenian Patriarch on one hand and the Archbishop of Lwiw (Ukraine) of that Rite, the Apostolic Administrator of Gherla for the Armenians in Romania, and that for the Armenians in Greece.

CANON 261. # 1. The patriarch can send a suitable priest to the communities of faithful of his Rite who reside outside the territory of the patriarchate with the consent of the Apostolic See, to assume their care, if the power over such faithful belongs to him according to c. 216 # 2, 2.

2. 1. This priest shall present himself, before he begins to exercise his duties, to the local Hierarch, and shall submit to him the documents by which he was designated, in order to receive the appropriate faculties;

2. The local Hierarch shall not refuse the faculties to the priest without a grave reason; otherwise he shall notify the Apostolic See of the refusal and the reasons for the same;

3. This priest is subject in the exercise of his ministry to the local Hierarch according to the norms of law;

4. He shall in the exercise of his duty faithfully adhere to the norms defined by the decree of appointment or by the Apostolic See; he shall accordingly promote the Christian life of the faithful committed to him, and shall accurately observe the regulations of his Rite;

5. At the end of every year, to be computed from the date of the decree of appointment, this priest must submit a written report on his personal status, on the religious status of his faithful, and on the exercise of the sacred ministry, to the Sacred Congregation for the Oriental Church, either directly or through the legate of the Roman Pontiff, as well as to the patriarch.

3. 1. The priest mentioned in # 1 who is enrolled in a certain eparchy reverts at once to the jurisdiction of his Hierarch when he returns in his patriarchate; but in the meantime he is exempt from the power of his own Oriental Hierarch and is subject to the patriarch;

2. He can be recalled by the patriarch, in which case the Apostolic See is to be notified; however, he cannot be transferred to another place outside the patriarchate except with the consent of the Apostolic See.

CANON 262. # 1. 1. The patriarch is entitled to send, with the consent of the Apostolic See, as often as he considers it appropriate, a suitable secular or religious priest to communities of faithful residing outside the patriarchal territory, if he has power over these faithful according to the norm of c. 216 # 2, 2, which priest shall paternally visit them and report everything to the Sacred Congregation for the Oriental Church as well as to the patriarch;

2. The visitor shall before taking over his duty present himself to the local Hierarch and submit to him the document of his appointment.

2. The canonical visitation of these faithful is a right only of the Apostolic See, without prejudice to the rights and duties of the local Hierarch.

In regard to the pastoral care of Oriental Catholics in the United States and in Canada who have no hierarchs of their own in these countries, which comprises all Orientals with the exception of the so-called Ruthenians, among whom the great majority are the Ukrainians, the Holy See has enacted the decree **Qua Sollerti** of December 23, 1929 (AAS 1930, 90-105; for an English translation cf. Pospishil, Interritual Canon Law Problems, 220-226). It would seem that this decree should be changed in some details. More initiative is relinquished to the patriarchs. Nothing is said that the priest chosen by the patriarch needs to be approved by the S. Congregation for the Oriental Church once the same S. Congregation consented that the patriarch send suitable priests to his communities. These priests can directly approach the local Hierarchs, and they are not bound to await the intervention of the S. Congregation or the Apostolic Delegate. Their documents can be made out by the patriarch, and the local Hierarch must communicate with the S. Congregation only in case he has some objections. The authority of the local Hierarch will not extend so far as to the transfer or the removal of the priest without the patriarch's consent. The transfer from one diocese to another needs not only the consent of both bishops but also that of the patriarch.

The patriarch can exercise his authority, at least in part, through a representative residing in these two countries, who is appropriately titled **Patriarchal Vicar.**

OTHER POWERS AND PRIVILEGES OF THE PATRIARCH

The Privileges of the Stauropegium (c. 263)
Power in Respect to Holy days and Fast-Abstinence (c. 264)
Power of Dispensation:
    Concerning Impediments to Ordination (c. 265, n. 1)
    Concerning Fast-Abstinence (c. 265, n. 2)
    Concerning Ecclesiastical Penalties (c. 265, nn. 3, 4)
Power of Sanation:
    Of the Appointment to Benefices (c. 266)
    Concerning the Sacrament of Matrimony (c. 267)
    Concerning Judicial Acts (c. 268)
Right to Financial Support (c. 269)
Appointment of Confessors and Preachers (c. 270)
Personal Statutes (c. 271)
Liturgical Commemoration (c. 272)

CANON 263. # 1. The patriarch has the right for a grave reason and with the consent of the permanent synod, at the time of its foundation, to declare exempt from the jurisdiction of the local Hierarch and subject to himself an ecclesiastical place or institution dedicated to works of religion or spiritual and temporal works of charity, save for the prohibition of law to grant the privilege of stauropegium to a house of an order or congregation.

2. All persons whatsoever who do not belong to the stauropegial place or institution are exempt from the jurisdiction of the local Hierarch for the time during which they are attached to that

place or institution, and are subject to the patriarch only, in all matters which concern their duty or office or discipline of the place or institution.

3. The rights and duties of the local Hierarch in respect to the administration of the temporal property of the Church and contracts are, in stauropegial institutions, attributed only to the patriarch.

The term **stauropegium** denotes in Greek the erection or implanting of a cross, and refers to the rite of the cornerstone laying of a church. A wooden cross, sent or blessed by the bishop, is set up or implanted in the soil on the spot where the future altar will stand. When the cross is sent by the patriarch, the church, and other buildings belonging to it, such as a monastery, hospital, etc., come under the immediate jurisdiction of the patriarch, and are thereby exempt from that of the local Hierarch. Sometimes patriarchs sent a cross to be set up in a church or monastery already in existence, and granted thereby exemption from the jurisdiction of the bishop.

This privilege is very old, and cannot be traced today to its origin, since it developed rather through custom than by positive legislation. It belongs only to those chief hierarchs who have the title of patriarchs, and solely within the limits of the territory of the patriarchate.

The right of **stauropegium** grants local exemption, and separates the place completely from the territory of the surrounding diocese. Only the patriarch's name is to be commemorated, and all juridical acts usually reserved to the local Hierarch are to be performed by the patriarch or his delegate. How far the privilege affects persons is defined in c. 260 # 2: If they are religious, the exemption follows their persons. If they are only persons attached to the stauropegial place, their exemption is circumscribed by their duties in that place.

The **stauropegium** may be conferred on various institutions, such as (1) a monastery, which is the most common recipient. Monastic stauropegial rights will be discussed below together with c. 164 of **Postquam Apostolicis:** (2) a church, perhaps a sanctuary and center of pilgrimages; (3) a hospital, orphanage, or other institution dedicated to works of religion; (4) an organization set up for the achievement of some scope of religion. In this last class belong the stauropegial rights granted to ecclesiastical associations composed in the majority of lay members. In such a case there may not be a local or personal, but only a real exemption, insofar as only the activity of the organization as such is exempt from the interference of the local Hierarch, while the seat of the association does not participate in the exemption, although a church owned by the association might be included in the stauropegial exemption. Officers of the association are exempt only in respect to their duty and its discharge, but not as private persons.

Such institutional stauropegia were granted by various dissident patriarchs in the 16th and 17th centuries to confraternities in Ukraine and in Byelorussia, in order to assist them in their resistance against their bishops, who at that time tried to reunite their faithful with the Holy See of Rome. These confraternities became rich on account of bequests made to them by the pious faithful, and were important through the schools and printing houses they maintained. One of them, the Stauropegial Confraternity of Lwiw (Ukraine) received this privilege from Patriarch Joachim of Antioch in 1587. It became the owner of the monastery of St. Onuphrey, which participated with its community of monks in the exemption. When the Confraternity later returned to the Catholic Church, the stauropegial privilege was confirmed by Pope Clement XI in his Constitution **Pastoralis Officii** of April 5, 1709, and the Confraternity together with the monastery subjected directly to the Holy See, although the latter appointed the local Hierarch, the Bishop, later Archbishop, of Lwiw, as delegate. In virtue of this privilege, the two chief officials of the Confraternity, both laymen, received recognition as participants at the Provincial Synod of Lwiw in 1891, where they were admitted with the right of observing and being present at the sessions, held under the presidency of a papal legate.

The right of granting the stauropegium is limited in c. 263 # 1 to the time when the monastery or institution is founded. This should not be restricted to the first erection of a monastery, but could be applied also to the act by which it is set up as an independent monastery (**sui iuris**), although it might have existed before as a dependency or filial convent of another monastery.

Can the patriarch grant the stauropegium to a church or institution already in existence? Only if the church, sanctuary, institution, etc., should be reconstituted with a different legal character, e.g., if a parish church should lose this quality to another church, and then be declared as the church of a hospital, orphanage, or as a patriarchal shrine.

CANON 264. It is a right of the patriarch to order for a grave reason and with the advice of the permanent synod feast days of obligation, days of abstinence and fast, in extraordinary cases as well as in individual instances.

CANON 265. The patriarch is entitled:

1. To dispense from all impediments which hinder the reception of sacred orders and from irregularities originating from delicts or from defects, without prejudice to the right of the Congregation of the Holy Office;

2. To dispense from laws of abstinence and fast, for one year at a time, and for a good reason, either for a part of the patriarchate or for the entire patriarchate;

3. To absolve or dispense from censures and vindicative penalties, decreed by law, for the internal as well as the external forum, but excluding cases that had been brought into court, and excepting those that are reserved to the Apostolic See and those connected with the violation of a secret of the Holy Office;

4. To dispense from infamy of law and from the penalties of disqualification and deprivation of active and passive voice, provided no censure reserved to the Apostolic See is connected with the delict, and, in case active or passive voice is to be restored to a bishop, after having obtained the consent of the permanent synod.

CANON 266. The appointment to an office conferred by the

local Hierarch on his subject invalidly because of the vice of simony is reserved to the patriarch.

CANON 267. The patriarch enjoys the faculty to grant the s a n a t i o i n r a d i c e if the invalidity of the marriage is due solely to the defect of form of the celebration or to an impediment from which he himself can dispense.

CANON 268. The patriarch can grant a sanatio to procedures which are void by virtue of law, because they were not signed by the actuary or because they were conducted without the participation of the promotor of justice or the defender of the bond, provided they cannot easily be repeated, and the parties have given their consent, and with the approval of the promotor of justice, and likewise of the defender of the bond in matters in which his presence is required.

CANON 269. # 1. The patriarch is empowered:

1. to accept for the patriarchate bequests, inheritances, donations, subsidies, from his subjects as well as from extraneous persons, which shall be invested according to the pious bequests of the benefactors and according to canonical norms, and also in case of necessity to obligate them;

2. to demand from local Hierarchs of his patriarchate a moderate canonical subsidy, and from the faithful and from moral persons the customary tithes, offerings and collections, without prejudice to the norms concerning the imposition of taxes on holders of benefices, or concerning other contributions from benefices and other ecclesiastical institutions.

2. To determine which tithes, offerings and collections must be paid or given to the patriarch according to # 1, n. 2, is reserved to the patriarchal synod.

CANON 270. The patriarch can approve confessors and preachers for the entire patriarchate, who, however, are not empowered to exercise their ministry without the consent of the Hierarch.

CANON 271. # 1. Personal statutes must be observed in regions where they are in force not only in matters in which they agree with canon law, including the particular law, but also in other matters, provided there is no specific norm of canon law regarding the respective matter, and the personal statutes are not contrary to divine or canon law.

2. If several patriarchs make use in the same locality of the power given to them in personal statutes, it is advisable that they take counsel with each other in resolving matters of importance.

3. The patriarch may exercise the authority of a civil magistrate if this is in accordance with the approved custom.

Personal statutes are in existence in most countries where Islam is the religion of the majority of the population. According to the teaching of Mohammed and Islam there is no distinction between the civil and the religious spheres, and no priesthood is admitted. All citizens of the country should be of the faithful, although possessors of the sacred books, the Jews and Christians,

136

should be granted tolerance. Because of the theocratical character of such a society, there is no need, e.g., of a state law on marriage, because such laws are already provided by religion, i.e., Islam. Naturally, it was realized that citizens who are Jews and Christians could not be obliged to the same laws as Mohammedans, especially those laws which concern domestic relationships, as marriage, inheritance, parent-children relations, etc. It was therefore permitted to the various Jewish and Christian communities to regulate such matters of their adherents according to their own laws, the so-called personal statutes. The idea of modern European legal systems, that the same laws should oblige all citizens without distinctions, is still alien to such countries as Egypt, Syria, Lebanon, Irak, Israel, etc. In the most recent times, some branches of law, as, e.g., commerce, criminal offenses and their punishment, have been codified in one or the other country, but when, e.g., a Christian desires to have his marriage declared null, he can achieve it only before an ecclesiastical court of his denominations, since there is strictly speaking no civil court having jurisdiction over him in this matter.

Because there are no ecclesiastical superiors in the Islamic society, and religion is represented only by teachers, whatever hierarchs were encountered by the Mohammedans when they conquered Christian countries were regarded as civil heads of their communities. That they were only superiors in the realm of religion was beyond the understanding of the Islamic conquerors. The Arabs and Turks acknowledged the patriarchs as supreme heads of their people even in civil matters, and ruled the Christians and Jews even in civil affairs not directly, but mediately through their religious superiors, the patriarchs and bishops. The hierarchy, especially the patriarchs, achieved the status of high-ranking civil magistrates, gained great power, prestige and responsibility, and became true ethnarchs of their people. They not only administered justice even in criminal cases, but became also the tax collectors, and as such responsible to the civil government.

The whole legal situation for each community was defined in the **Personal Statutes,** so called because they regulated their personal status, and they concerned them only as persons belonging to that community, without consideration of the territory. A large part of the laws coming under the heading of personal statutes for Oriental Catholics are contained in the codification of the Oriental canon law. The reason the marriage law was promulgated as the first part of the codification was the necessity of speedily providing a unified law for all Eastern Catholics at a time when there was the dangerous threat that the state, e.g., Egypt, could place them under a state marriage law which would have been nothing else than the Islamic religious law. The state could have made use of the excuse that the Catholics had no such clearly codified statute as is needed for a normal dispensation of justice.

Since nearly all countries of the Near East have communities of several Oriental Catholic Rites, it is of importance that their interpretation and application of common laws belonging to personal statutes be the same, lest the situation of Catholics be jeopardized before the Islamic state because of divergencies in the application of laws that have legal force also in the civil sphere. Patriarchs are therefore urged to achieve this harmony by taking mutual counsel (c. 270 # 2).

CANON 272. The patriarch must be commemorated in divine services after the Roman Pontiff by all bishops, other Hierarchs, and, if particular law orders so, by the clergy.

The liturgical commemoration of hierarchs as practiced in Eastern Rites has no accurate analogy in the Latin Rite. It is a public and solemn affirmation of ecclesiastical communion and submission, and therefore of great legal significance.

DUTIES OF THE PATRIARCH (cc. 273-282)

Subjection to the Roman Pontiff:
  Oath of Allegiance (c. 273 # 1)
  Visit after Election (c. 273 # 2)
  Liturgical Commemoration of the Roman Pontiff (c. 274)
  Quinquennial Report (c. 275 # 1)
  Ad Limina Visit (c. 275 # 2)
Duty of Residence (c. 276)
Application of Mass for Faithful (c. 277)
Supervision of Hierarchs (c. 278)
Supervision of Divine Worship (c. 279)
Supervision of Administration of Church Property (c. 280)
Direction of Relationship with Civil Authority (c. 281)
Duties in the Patriarchal Eparchy (c. 282)

CANON 273. The patriarch has the obligation:

1. to profess to the Roman Pontiff, the successor of St. Peter and vicar of Christ on earth, full obedience, faithful subjection and filial respect, and to renew the oath of allegiance whenever the patriarchal synod is held, and when profession of faith is demanded by law;

2. to come within one year from his election to Rome in order to venerate the graves of the Saint Apostles Peter and Paul, and to present himself to the Supreme Pontiff.

CANON 274. The patriarch must commemorate the Roman Pontiff in the Divine Liturgy and other divine services, according to the liturgical laws, and to assure that this is faithfully done also by the metropolitans, bishops, other Hierarchs and clergy of the patriarchate.

CANON 275. # 1. The patriarch is obliged to make a report every five years on the condition of the patriarchate to the Supreme Pontiff according to the approved formulary.

2. 1. He shall in the same year in which he submits the report come to Rome to perform the visit mentioned in c. 273, n. 2.

2. If the patriarch is unable to perform the visit in person, he may perform it according to the norm of c. 408 through an auxiliary bishop, if he has one, or through a specially delegated priest, distin-

guished by an ecclesiastical dignity, who habitually resides in the patriarchate.

CANON 276. The patriarch must reside in the patriarchal see, from which he cannot be absent except for a canonical reason.

CANON 277. The patriarch shall not omit to apply the Divine Liturgy for the people of the entire patriarchate on Christmas, Epiphany of Our Lord Jesus Christ, Easter, Pentecost and Assumption of Bl. V. M., without prejudice to c. 404. If he on these feast days must, according to the aforementioned c. 404, apply the Liturgy for the people of his eparchy, the patriarch satisfies by the application of the Divine Liturgy for the people of the entire patriarchate also his obligation toward his own eparchy.

CANON 278. # 1. The duties of bishops mentioned in c. 400 bind the patriarch for the entire patriarchate, notwithstanding the duty of each single bishop.

2. The patriarch shall diligently see that the bishops and other local Hierarchs faithfully satisfy their pastoral obligations, and that they reside in their eparchies. He shall enkindle their zeal. If they are lax in some duty, he shall not omit to admonish them, and if the admonitions do not have the desired effect, he shall proceed according to the norms of law.

CANON 279. # 1. In respect to prayers and pious devotions, the patriarch enjoys in the entire patriarchate that power to which local Hierarchs are entitled, with the advice of the permanent synod if it is a matter of importance.

2. It belongs to the patriarch to approve editions of liturgical books, and he must be responsible for the fidelity and integrity of the text and its agreement with the approved text; and, once the authenticity is proven, he is empowered to grant the permission for publication. However, the first approval of liturgical texts is reserved to the Apostolic See.

CANON 280. # 1. The patriarch must assiduously supervise the administration of ecclesiastical property in the entire patriarchate.

2. The patriarch shall admonish a metropolitan who has not appointed an econome according to cc. 429 # 2, 438, and if the admonition remains ineffective, the patriarch himself shall appoint an econome according to the norm of c. 258, n. 2.

CANON 281. The patriarch can, with the previous consent of the Apostolic See, enter with the civil authority into agreements which are not contrary to common law or the law enacted by the Apostolic See for that specific Rite, after having obtained the consent of the permanent synod. The patriarch cannot, however, put these agreements into effect without having obtained the approval of the Apostolic See.

CANON 282. The patriarch must observe in his own eparchy, and also in other places where no eparchy nor patriarchal exarchy is erected, the regulations of the canons concerning the power, rights and obligations of resident bishops.

PRIVILEGES OF THE PATRIARCH (cc. 283-285)

Honorary Privileges According to Common Law (c. 283)
Privileges in Respect to Sacraments (c. 284)
Privileges According to Particular Law:
Delegation of Pontifical Functions to a Priest
(c. 285 # 1, 1)
Ordination of Monks (c. 285 # 1, 2)
Use of White Supracamelaucium (c. 285 # 1, 3)
Consecration of the Holy Chrism (c. 285 # 2)

CANON 283. Besides other privileges of common law, granted or recognized by the Roman Pontiff, all patriarchs enjoy, after the enthronement has been performed according to c. 235, the following faculties and privileges:

1. to hear everywhere the confessions of the faithful of Oriental Rites, also of the religious of both sexes, and to absolve from all sins and censures, including reserved ones, with the exclusion of those excepted in c. 185 # 1, 1;

The patriarch has therefore jurisdiction to absolve in the confessional: (1) all Catholics of whatever Oriental Rite, in any place, even if subject to the exclusive jurisdiction of a Latin Rite ordinary; (2) all Latin Rite Catholics who approach him for the same purpose while he is lawfully engaged in hearing confessions (cf. cc. 881 # 1, 905, CIC). If he were to hear the confessions of Latin Rite Catholics only, he would need to receive delegation from the Latin Rite ordinary if it is a place subject to the exclusive jurisdiction of the latter.

Priests having jurisdiction for hearing the confessions of the faithful from their own ordinary may validly and licitly absolve all Catholics of any Rite who approach them (c. 881 # 1 CIC). However, if in the same territory there exists another ecclesiastical jurisdiction, they may not validly exercise such jurisdiction in places and buildings which are under the jurisdiction of another ordinary, as churches, chapels, seminaries, convents, even though these buildings are within the territorial limits of their own jurisdiction and the penitents their subjects (S. Congregation for the Oriental Church, August 26, 1932). This decree of the S. Congregations for the Oriental Church and of the Propagation of the Faith (cf. Bouscaren, Canon Law Digest, II. vol., 1943, p. 218) mentions only churches and oratories, but this should include every place legally recognized for the valid hearing of confessions, provided the place is "subject to the exclusive jurisdiction of the ordinary (and pastor)" (cf. Coussa, Epitome, III, p. 197), as "churches, bishop's residence, rectories, hospitals, diocesan schools in the strict sense (i.e., erected by the authority of the bishop chiefly for the faithful of his Rite)."

2. to preach the word of God everywhere;

3. to bless everywhere merely with the sign of the cross, with all the indulgences which the Apostolic See usually grants, crosses, rosaries and other prayer beads, medals, statues, scapulars approved

by the Apostolic See and impose them without the obligation of inscribing the names of the persons invested;

4. to grant an indulgence of three hundred days, even t o t i e s q u o t i e s, in all places of his patriarchate, also exempt ones, in churches of his Rite outside the boundaries of the patriarchate, and everywhere to the faithful of his Rite;

5. to declare one of the altars in any church of his Rite, even outside the patriarchate, forever a daily privileged altar;

6. to make use, in accordance with liturgical laws, of the pastoral staff and pallium in the entire patriarchate, not excluding places that are exempt from his jurisdiction; of the pastoral staff alone, also outside the patriarchate, but only in churches of his Rite;

7. to celebrate in the manner of a bishop in churches of his Rite even outside an Oriental region or territory, with the use also of the pastoral staff, but having informed the local Hierarch if it is the case |of a cathedral;

The crozier or pastoral staff is in most Oriental Rites not a symbol of jurisdiction, as it is in the Latin Rite, but more an appurtenance of the pontifical way of celebrating the divine services. It would be inappropriate of a bishop, even if only an auxiliary, that he solemnly celebrate in any place without using the pastoral staff.

8. to make use in documents given by him, if this is the lawful custom, of a specific formula of blessing, even calling it apostolic, excluding formulas exclusively used by the Roman Curia;

The Roman Pontiff is not the only Hierarch entitled to the designation of "apostolic". The patriarchs at least of Alexandria, Antioch, and sometimes also that of Jerusalem, vindicate themselves the same prerogative, and this is recognized in this canon. The Apostolic See of Antioch was founded by St. Peter, while that of Alexandria had also St. Peter as its originator, who sent there in his stead his disciple St. Mark. The Apostolic See of Jerusalem goes back to St. James the Greater, cousin of Our Lord.

The Patriarchs of Constantinople began quite late to favor the legend of the founding of that see by St. Andrew, who was older than his brother Peter, and was moreover called before him to the apostolate. Since this is not historically supported, the apostolic title would be an usurpation on the part of Constantinople.

The Patriarch of Alexandria could also make use of the title of **pope,** which was given to him quite early in the history of the Church.

9. to make use of the insignia and decorations of his dignity also outside an Oriental region or territory;

The various parts of the clerical garb among Oriental Catholic clergy were enumerated under c. 41 # 3. As far as patriarchs and other prelates are concerned, there are three different forms of dressing, depending on the occasion. When the patriarch appears in public in his private character, he wears over the cassock the rason, a black coat of silk, of the same length as the cassock. It has very wide sleeves, and is lined with red silk. A bishop wears at least the panagia or encolpion, a medallion of Our Lord or the Blessed Mother, richly decorated with stones, hanging from a golden chain. Relics may be inclosed. He might in addition have a pectoral cross. Patriarchs wear often two panagias and one cross.

The prelate covers the head with the camelaucium, a tall hat of cylindrical shape, hidden under a veil of thin silk, the **supracamelacium**, which in patriarchs could be white (cf. c. 285 # 1, 3). He makes use of a black cane or stave of wood, four feet high, topped by a knob of ivory or gold.

When officiating at extra-liturgical rites, a Byzantine Rite patriarch dons the mandyas, which corresponds to the **cappa magna** of the Latin Rite. This is a large, wide cloak of red color. Four squares with the pictures of the evangelists are sewn at the four corners in front of the breast and feet **(pomata)**. Three horizontal stripes divide the mandyas, and are called **potamoi** (rivers). In his hand he carries the crozier. He wears no mitre with this attire, but the supracamelaucium.

At liturgical functions the patriarch wears the same vestments other bishops use: (1) sticharion (alb), (2) epitrachelion (stole), (3) zone (cincture), (4) epimanikia (cuffs), covering the end of the sticharion sleeves, (5) sakkos, which has the form of a dalmatic, (6) epigonation, at the right knee, (7) omophorion, (8) pallium, (9) panagia or encolpion, (10) mitre. He carries a (11) crozier, and (12) often also a hand-cross. Catholic patriarchs wear also a ring, as other prelates do.

Oriental Catholic prelates have often adopted Latin Rite liturgical and extra-liturgical vestments, or colors, or have introduced some other changes. The Armenians accepted the Latin Rite mitre during the Crusades, since they had not yet developed a liturgical headgear. The same was done by the Maronites, Syrians, Chaldeans, etc. A return to the genuine liturgical tradition of each Rite is a desire of the Holy See.

10. the title of B e a t i t u d e;

In divine services the patriarch is often called "most sacred". The title of **beatitude** is especially to be used in extra-liturgical circumstances.

11. to take precedence, also outside an Oriental region or territory, over all primates, archbishops and other metropolitans, bishops of whatsoever Oriental Rite, although they are each in his own territory;

The right of precedence of an Oriental Catholic patriarch over other hierarchs depends on whether he is among Oriental or among Latin Rite Catholics. He has everywhere precedence over all Oriental Rite prelates, even if they are of a different Oriental Rite, and although they are in their own territory, province or diocese. In respect to Latin Rite bishops, the patriarch enjoys no precedence in their own territory, but c. 347 CIC applies, in virtue of which "a bishop precedes in his territory all archbishops and bishops, with the exception of cardinals, papal legates, and their own metropolitan."

12. to be an assistant at the throne of the Roman Pontiff in public divine services and other papal ceremonies, with observance of the order of precedence;

13. to appoint procurators or delegates who are to represent his person or act in his name in business transactions of the patriarchate, without prejudice to c. 260 # 1, 2.

CANON 284. The patriarch may in the entire patriarchate, observing the canonical prescriptions, and with the obligation of recording according to canonical regulations:

1. Administer the sacraments of baptism and confirmation;

2. Assist at or bless the betrothal and the celebration of marriage.

The power of assistance at marriage outside the patriarchal eparchy or patriarchal exarchies cannot be delegated to another cleric, since it is a personal privilege of the patriarch, granted to him because of his exalted dignity, as the others enumerated in this section of **Cleri Sanctitati.** A general delegation would be excluded by c. 87 # 1, 2, of **Crebrae Allatae.**

CANON 285. # 1. The patriarchs are in addition empowered, if in virtue of particular law this is granted to them, to make use of the following privileges and faculties:

1. To delegate to a priest who is distinguished by a dignity the blessing of churches and altars, the administration of minor orders, the consecration of chalices, patens and portable altars;

Such faculties are granted by particular law to the Patriarch of the Maronites, that group among Orientals which was longest under Latin Rite influence. He can permit to simple priests to consecrate churches and altars, to administer confirmation, to make use of the mitre and crozier, and to confer minor orders (cf. Coussa, I, p. 278).

Particular law granting such privileges to the patriarch can be enacted also in the future, although the granting of such authority to simple priests merely by a jurisdictional act, and not through ordination **(cheirotonia)** or benediction **(cheirotesia),** is against the tradition of the Christian East. In addition, the blessing of liturgical utensils was taken over from the Latin Rite, and a reservation is therefore not necessary; they become consecrated by being put into liturgical use.

2. To promote monks of any monastery which is not of papal right to the first order as well as from one order to others, even the presbyterate, with the advice of the superiors and because of necessity;

This rule is concurrent to the minute regulations on the ordination of monks and religious in cc. 131-134 of **Postquam Apostolicis,** and seems rather superfluous. We consider it therefore a special privilege in virtue of which the patriarch can ordain monks even if they should not be able to fulfill all requirements of law, e.g., concerning the normally prescribed scholastic curriculum, provided there is a need for such clerics. The patriarch can have such monks ordained also through another prelate of his choice.

3. To make use of the white supracamelaucium.

The ancient monks of the Thebais used to cover themselves on frigid winter days as well as on hot summer days with a sheep skin. The hide covered the head and fell down over the shoulders, the legs dangling at the sides. This was later exchanged for a cloth hood fashioned according to the shape of the previously used sheep skin. It is now an oblong silk sheet of about three by four feet, which is fastened at one end around the **camelaucium**, a head covering in the form of a cylinder and about eight inches high, while the other end and the two side streamers fall down over the shoulders. This cover of the camelaucium is called **epanokamelaukion**, or in Latin, **supracamelaucium.**

The camelaucium was formerly worn also in the West, especially by the popes. From it developed the Latin Rite mitre, when the top was pushed inward, and the papal tiara, when it was decorated and stiffened.

The supracamelaucium is worn by all monks or religious of both sexes, who have received the so-called **minor scheme.** It is now always of black color; only the dissident patriarch and the metropolitans of the Russian Church, and the dissident patriarchs of Yugoslavia, Romania, and Bulgaria wear it in white. According to one tradition, this was the color once employed by those patriarchs of Constantinople who were of the secular clergy.

If particular law knows the white supracamelaucium, then the patriarch may wear it as a sign of his dignity. The supracamelaucium of a cardinal of an Oriental Rite is crimson, as was decided at the creation of the Armenian Patriarch Cardinal Gregory Peter XV Agagianian in 1946.

2. It is the patriarch's exclusive right, if in particular law this is reserved to him, to consecrate the chrism, which is to be distributed to the Hierarchs of the patriarchate without recompense.

The **holy myron** or chrism corresponds to the chrism of the Latin Rite, and is used for the same rites, namely: (1) as sacramental matter in the administration of confirmation; (2) in the consecration of altars and antimensia, which are the equivalent of the portable altars of the Latin Rite; (3) in the consecration of churches performed by a bishop; (4) in the crowning of a ruler.

The chrism of the Oriental Rites is composed, besides olive oil and some wine, of a large number of aromatic substances, thirty or forty or even more in number. It is prepared during the first days of Holy Week, in the church itself, where the ingredients are mixed and cooked for days while priests and deacons read the gospels and parts of the divine office. It is blessed on Holy Thursday, once every few years.

The consecration of the chrism became very early in the East a right reserved to patriarchs, which they later had to grant also to the heads of other national Churches, as it was done, e.g., by the Patriarchs of Jerusalem and Antioch in the 9th century to the Catholicus of Georgia (Caucasus). Today this is a privilege reserved among all dissident Orientals to the patriarchs or chief hierarchs of a Church. Among Catholics it is also a patriarchal right. Among those Oriental Catholics who have no patriarch, as the Byzantine Rite groups, with the exception of the Melkites, all bishops consecrate the chrism every year in imitation of the Latin Rite custom.

Article Four:
THE PATRIARCHAL CURIA (cc. 286-305)

GENERAL NORMS:

Definition (c. 286)
Composition (c. 287)

CANON 286. # 1. The patriarch must establish for the government of the entire patriarchate a patriarchal curia, and when adequately established, he must preserve it, distinct from the curia of the patriarch's own eparchy. Offices of the two curiae shall not be joined, as far as possible, in the same persons.

2. To the patriarchal curia belong all those who aid the patriarch in the government of the entire patriarchate, and who may be taken from the whole patriarchate and from the secular and the religious clergy.

3. The patriarchal curia shall be located at the residence of the patriarchate.

CANON 287. # 1. The patriarchal curia is composed of the permanent synod or the council mentioned in cc. 288, 296, the patriarchal tribunal, the patriarchal office of the administration of church property, the patriarchal chancery and the patriarchal consultors.

2. Besides the persons who are required according to common and particular law to belong to the aforementioned offices and councils, bishops who have an office in the curia with residence must also be considered as members.

3. In those matters in which common or particular law has no provision in respect to the patriarchal curia, the norm to be followed, unless the nature of the matter presents an obstacle, is to be taken from among those which regulate the eparchial curia.

THE PERMANENT SYNOD (cc. 288-295)

Definition (c. 288)
Members c. 289)
Rules of Business Transaction (c. 290)
Secretary and Archivist of the Synod (c. 291)
Secrecy on Voting (c. 292)
Recourse from Synodal Decisions (c. 293)
Relationship to Other Synods of the Patriarchate (c. 294)
Terms of Sessions (c. 295)

Patriarchs do not enjoy anything of the kind of the plenitude of the primatial authority of the Roman Pontiff. Although being superiors of their bishops, they are not bishops or hierarchs of the patriarchate, as the Roman Pontiff can be considered to be of the whole Church. Their authority over the patriarchate is superior to that of the bishops, but it can be exercised only mediately.

It was felt from the earliest times that the higher hierarchs, especially the patriarchs, needed some advice in the enactment of ordinances for the patriarchate, in the disposition of recourses taken to them against decisions of subordinate hierarchs, in replying to inquiries concerning doubtful matters, etc. The summoning of formal synods of their bishops was not always possible. They made use of the permanent or temporary presence of bishops in their city, and with the addition of the neighboring bishops, they formed a council which received the name of **permanent synod.** This assembly of bishops in Constantinople (**synodos endemousa**), the civil and ecclesiastical capital of a great nation, was especially occupied with the many problems submitted from all parts of the Byzantine Empire.

The permanent synod was never a mere advisory organ, as the Sacred Congregations of the Roman Curia are. Although the patriarch could not render decisions against the majority of the members, the permanent synod, even if unanimous, could not accomplish anything without the patriarch.

Today two kinds of permanent synods exist:

1. A permanent synod which is the governing body of the Church. The patriarch or other head of the Church needs the consent of the majority of its members for every act of patriarchal jurisdiction. This is the constitution of nearly all dissident Churches. In the Patriarchate of Constantinople, for instance, acts have validity only if signed by at least six members of the synod, besides the patriarch, and if sealed with the patriarchal seal, which consists of six wedges, each kept by one of the members, and the circular frame, kept by the patriarch.

2. A permanent synod which limits the exercise of the patriarchal jurisdiction only in matters of some importance. This is the system adopted by Catholic Oriental Churches, as evidenced from these canons of **Cleri Sanctitati.**

The problems brought before the patriarch are then divided according to their significane:

(1) Matters of routine, which are resolved by the patriarch alone.

(2) Matters to be brought before the permanent synod either for its advice or consent.

(3) Matters of major importance reserved to the patriarchal synod.

(4) Matters to be placed before the Roman Pontiff.

Since the Catholic form of the permanent synod need not be always in attendance at the patriarchal residence, it is a periodic assembly, to be convened whenever their is business to be transacted, at least three times a year.

The permanent synod concerns only affairs of the patriarchate, and has no authority over the patriarch's government of his own eparchy, where he has the rights and duties of a resident bishop.

CANON 288. The patriarchs must have a synod permanently established, which is to aid them in transacting matters of importance and in the deciding of questions which concern the patriarchate.

CANON 289. = 1. The permanent synod consists of the patriarch as president and four bishops appointed for five years.

2. Of these two must be resident bishops, designated according to priority of date of episcopal consecration.

3. 1. Of the other bishops, one shall be appointed freely by the patriarch; the other shall be elected according to the norm of law by the bishops subject to the patriarch. These bishops can be reappointed to the same office after their term of five years has expired.

2. At the same time, according to the same manner, shall be designated the bishop who is to substitute for an impeded member of the permanent synod appointed by the patriarch or elected by the bishops.

4. Those mentioned in c. 109 # 1 cannot be members of the permanent synod.

CANON 290. # 1. If the patriarch is prevented from taking part in the permanent synod, the sessions of the synod are presided over, without prejudice to particular law, by that member from among the bishops of the synod who is senior by date of episcopal consecration, while at the same time the number of five members is to be restored by the participation of the alternate bishop designated by the patriarch according to the norm of c. 289 # 3, n. 2.

2. 1. When a bishop, a member of the permanent synod, is prevented from taking part in the sessions of the synod, he shall be substituted for by the bishop who follows according to the established order, if he is one of the two bishops mentioned in c. 289 # 2; if he is one of the other two, he shall be substituted by the bishop mentioned in c. 289 # 3, n. 2;

2. If the bishop, a member of the synod, elected by the patriarch or by the bishops, as well as his substitute are prevented from taking part in the session of the synod, and the matter demands a decision, that bishop shall send his vote to the patriarch by letter, which is to be opened in the session of the synod.

3. When the permanent synod has to decide a matter that affects the person of a bishop-member of the synod or his eparchy, he indeed, shall be heard, but he is to be substituted for in the synod by another bishop according to the norm of # 2.

CANON 291. # 1. The office of the secretary of the permanent synod is to be fulfilled by one of the synodal bishops designated by this synod, but the minutes of the sessions must be signed by the president and all members of the synod.

2. It belongs to the patriarch to select the priest who shall care for the archives of the permanent synod, and also to remove him from office.

CANON 292. The permanent synod decides by vote which must be secret.

CANON 293. From the decisions of the permanent synod given outside judicial procedure and regarding matters that are reserved to it by law recourse is permitted to the Apostolic See with devolutive effect.

CANON 294. If any matter that comes under the competence of the permanent synod has to be decided during the celebration of a patriarchal synod or when a synod of election is being held, the decision of the matter remains reserved to the permanent synod.

CANON 295. The permanent synod must be called together three times a year, at predetermined times, and also whenever matters are to be transacted the decision of which requires according to law the consent or the advice of this synod.

The Patriarchal Council:
  Definition (c. 296)
  Membership (c. 297)
The Patriarchal Tribunal (c. 298)
The Patriarchal Econome (c. 299)
The Patriarchal Chancellor (c. 300)
The Patriarchal Notaries (c. 301)
The Patriarchal Liturgical Commission (c. 302)
The Patriarchal Consultants (c. 303)
The Patriarchal Archives (c. 304)
The Upkeep of the Patriarchal Curia (c. 305)

CANON 296. Where for a grave cause a permanent synod cannot be established, there shall be constituted, for as long as the cause perdures, a patriarchal council, having in advance informed the Apostolic See, which shall take the place of the permanent synod in all things.

CANON 297. # 1. The patriarchal council shall consist:

1. of the resident bishop who among the bishops subject to the patriarch is senior by virtue of episcopal consecration;

2. of a bishop elected according to the canons by the resident bishops.

2. After a period of five years, the resident bishop who is the next in seniority by virtue of episcopal consecration shall replace the bishop designated because of his precedence in virtue of episcopal consecration; but the bishop elected by the resident bishops can be reelected by them to the same office.

CANON 298. # 1. In the patriarchal curia a patriarchal tribunal must be established according to the norms of law, distinct from the tribunal of the patriarch's own eparchy.

The norms of law referred to in the above canon are contained in the motu proprio **Sollicitudinem Nostram,** where cc. 32 to 93 deal with the various kinds and degrees of tribunals.

2. The patriarchal tribunal shall have its own judges, a promoter of justice and a defender of the bond, and shall be provided with auditors, notaries, and other necessary ministers.

148

3. With the exception of the judges, auditors and the promotor of justice, the others mentioned in # 2 may simultaneously belong to the patriarchal and to the eparchial tribunal.

CANON 299. # 1. A special office shall be established in the patriarchal curia for the administration of the property of the patriarchate, distinct from the office which is in charge of the administration of the property that belongs to the patriarch's own eparchy, and which shall consist of an econome, an accountant and other necessary ministers.

2. 1. The patriarchal econome is in direct charge of this administrative office and he manages the property of the patriarchate according to the canonical norms;

2. The office of patriarchal econome shall be committed to a trustworthy, diligent cleric of proven virtue and an expert in the management of temporal property; it cannot be validly conferred on persons who are related to the patriarch by consanguinity or affinity up to the fourth degree inclusive;

3. He shall be appointed and removed by the patriarch, to whom he is subject in the exercise of his duty, with the consent of the permanent synod;

4. The office of the patriarchal econome can be joined, with the consent of the permanent synod, with the office of econome of the patriarch's own eparchy.

3. The patriarchal econome must submit an annual report in writing on his administration to the permanent synod, or whenever so requested by it. The synod shall have examined the accounting submitted by the econome by at least two synodal bishops, who shall audit the available cash, shall undertake or order appropriate inspections by others, even unexpectedly, of the real estate, documents, securities, and shall diligently make provisions for the conservation, protection and increase of the patriarchal patrimony.

CANON 300. # 1. A patriarchal chancellor shall be appointed for the patriarchal curia by the patriarch with the advice of the permanent synod, who shall be a priest above exception.

2. The chancellor heads the patriarchal chancery and the patriarchal archives, and he is by virtue of his appointment the first notary of the patriarchate.

3. The patriarch can appoint an assistant or substitute, who also can function as an official notary.

CANON 301. # 1. According to the norm of c. 440, the patriarch can appoint, besides the chancellor and his substitute, other notaries, even for the entire patriarchate.

2. Canons 440, 441, are to be applied to the patriarchal notaries.

CANON 302. A council or so-called commission on liturgical matters is to be established by the patriarch for the editing and printing of liturgical books, according to the norm of c. 279 #2, and for dealing with all matters that concern the liturgy.

CANON 303. The patriarch can with the advice of the permanent synod appoint some theologians and experts in law as patriarchal consultants from among both clergy who are distinguished for learning and prudence, that they assist in solving the more difficult problems submitted to them.

CANON 304. The archives of the patriarchate in the patriarchal curia shall be diligently arranged, filed and preserved in accordance with cc. 442 sqq.

CANON 305. The expenditures of the patriarchal curia shall be defrayed from the funds the patriarch can use for this purpose. If they are insufficient, the eparchies shall individually concur in bearing the expense, according to the extent determined by the patriarchal synod, as outlined in c. 340 # 1.

Article Five:

THE PATRIARCHATE DURING VACANCY AND IN CASE OF HINDRANCE IN THE EXERCISE OF THE PATRIARCHAL JURISDICTION (cc. 306-314)

Kinds of Vacancies (c. 306)
The Administration of the Vacant Patriarchate:
    Designation of the Administrator (c. 307)
    Duties of the Administrator (c. 308)
    Rights of the Administrator:
        In the Patriarchal Eparchy (c. 309)
        In the Patriarchate:
            Positive Limits (c. 310)
            Negative Limits (c. 311)
    Privileges of the Administrator (c. 312)
    Report (c. 313)
    Obstacles to the Exercise of the Patriarchal Jurisdiction
        (c. 314)

CANON 306. The patriarchal see becomes vacant according to the norm of c. 468 # 1.

CANON 307. During the vacancy of the patriarchal see, if the Apostolic See has not appointed an administrator, and without prejudice to particular law, the administration of the patriarchate passes to the bishop who is the senior by episcopal consecration among those who have an office with residence in the patriarchal curia.

Particular law could perhaps establish that the metropolitan senior in rank be the administrator of the patriarchate during a vacancy. Such a metropolitan or bishop is sometimes called a **protothronos**, i.e., because he occupies the first throne among the bishops of a patriarchate. Cf. what is said concerning the **maphrian** in c. 335 # 2.

CANON 308. It is the duty of the administrator of the patriarchate:

1. to send at once an announcement of the vacancy to the Apostolic See and to every single bishop of the patriarchate, titular bishops included, and other local Hierarchs, with the exception of syncelli;

2. to execute accurately, and to see that others execute, the special norms enacted by common or particular law or by an instruction of the Apostolic See for the specific circumstances in which the vacancy occurred;

3. to convene the synodal fathers according to the norm of c. 221, and diligently and faithfully to prepare everything which is needed for the synod that is to elect the patriarch.

CANON 309. The administrator of the patriarchate during the vacancy of the patriarchal see in the patriarch's own eparchy and in other places of the patriarchate where no eparchies or exarchies are constituted has the same rights and is bound by the same duties that are prescribed for the administrator of a vacant eparchy.

CANON 310. # 1. Provided the nature of the matter or the prescription of law do not decree otherwise:

1. the ordinary jurisdiction of the patriarch in spiritual and temporal matters passes, during the vacancy of the see, to the administrator of the patriarchate, without prejudice to c. 311;

2. the administrator can execute rescripts of the Apostolic See which were addressed to the patriarch; and as a rule the habitual faculties granted to the patriarch by the Apostolic See also belong to him.

2. The administrator of the patriarchate shall make no innovations during the vacancy.

CANON 311. # 1. All those matters which cannot be acted upon without the consent or advice of the bishops convened for a patriarchal synod or a synod of election are excluded from the competence of the administrator of the patriarchate during the vacancy of the see.

2. The administrator of the patriarchate during the vacancy of the see cannot remove from office or transfer anywhere the syncelli of the patriarch, even though they lack the episcopal dignity.

3. He does not enjoy the privileges mentioned in cc. 283, 285.

CANON 312. The administrator of the patriarchate during the vacancy of the see has precedence over metropolitans, archbishops, bishops, and other Hierarchs of the patriarchate, but not in the synod convened for the election of the patriarch.

CANON 313. The new patriarch must request from the administrator of the patriarchate an account of his administration.

CANON 314. # 1. When the patriarchal see is impeded in its function, in accordance with the norm of c. 467:

1. In respect to the government of the patriarch's own eparchy, the norms of the same c. 467 shall be observed;

2. The government of the entire patriarchate shall be carried on by that resident bishop, subject to the patriarch, who is first according to the rules of precedence, unless the patriarch, because of circum-

stances, has designated another bishop, or even a priest from among those who are outstanding;

3. If the patriarch should have failed in one of the cases referred to in c. 467 # 4, the bishop, subject to the patriarch, who is first in accordance with the rules of precedence shall at once approach the Apostolic See for the necessary steps.

2. In respect to the bishop or priest mentioned in # 1, n. 2, the norms of cc. 310, 311, shall be observed.

3. He who has assumed the government shall as soon as possible advise the Apostolic See that the see is impeded and the administration has been assumed.

CHAPTER SEVEN

ARCHBISHOPS AND OTHER METROPOLITANS (cc. 315-339)
METROPOLITANS (cc. 315-323)

Definition (c. 315 = c. 272 CIC)
Metropolitans in Patriarchates (c. 316)
Liturgical Commemoration of the Metropolitan (c. 317)
The Metropolitan Eparchy (c. 318 = c. 273 CIC)
Rights of the Metropolitan:
    Metropolitans Within Patriarchates (c. 319 = c. 274)
    Metropolitans Outside Patriarchates
      (c. 320 = cf. 274, 3, 4 CIC)
The Pallium:
    Metropolitans (c. 321; cf. cc. 275-277 CIC)
    Other Bishops (c. 322)
Suppletory Metropolitans (c. 323 = c. 285 CIC)

CANON 315. The metropolitan heads an ecclesiastical province, and this dignity is united with an episcopal see by decree or recognition of the Roman Pontiff or an ecumenical council.

CANON 316. The restoration of metropolitan sees or the exercise of the rights and duties of metropolitans is in patriarchates reserved to the patriarch, with the consent of the bishops gathered in a patriarchal synod or a synod of election, and with the confirmation of the Apostolic See.

The grandeur of the ancient patriarchates has vanished for many centuries, among the Catholics as well as among the dissidents. Today they are reduced in number of the faithful to such an extent that the existence of even true dioceses, with subjects in a number comparable to dioceses in the Western Church, is questionable. To interpose between the patriarch and the bishops the intermediary hierarchical organization of ecclesiastical provinces headed by metropolitans is impossible. **Cleri Sanctitati** leaves room for the reestablishment of ecclesiastical provinces, but even if the number of faithful should increase considerably, there would be the question whether a hierarchy of four degrees (bishop, metropolitan, patriarch, pope) in the Church of today, with its facility of momentaneous or rapid communication, has not become impractical.

To preserve the glamour of the patriarchal dignity, dissidents have given the title of metropolitan to every resident bishop, and have simple bishops only in the character of auxiliary or vicar bishops. This is the situation in Greece, the four ancient patriarchates, Cyprus, etc.

In the Ukraine and in Russia the title of archbishop was granted to bishops as a personal distinction, while the title of metropolitans was reserved to bishops of the larger cities, without giving them any jurisdiction over other bishops. The same system was adopted in the Serbian Patriarchate of Yugoslavia.

In Catholic patriarchates there exist titular archbishops and metropolitans, always attached to a certain see, but they have no suffragans, since all bishops are under the immediate jurisdiction of the patriarch, who exercises all metropolitan rights.

CANON 317. The metropolitan is to be commemorated by the Hierarchs of his province in the Divine Liturgy and other divine services according to the rules of liturgical laws.

CANON 318. Without prejudice to cc. 321, 339, the metropolitan has in his own eparchy the same obligations and the same rights that a bishop has in his.

CANON 319. The metropolitan who is subject of a patriarch is entitled in the eparchies of his province, besides that what is conceded to him in common law, to:

1. ordain the bishops of his province within the time defined in c. 396 # 1, n. 1, and to enthrone them;

The canon law of the Latin Rite Church reserves not only the appointment of bishops, but, since the XV century, also their consecration to the Roman Pontiff. In the document of appointment is usually stated whether a certain bishop has been designated ad hoc by this **mandatum pontificium.** In the Oriental canon law only the appointment of bishops is reserved to the patriarch or pope, while the law itself provides who is to administer the episcopal consecration: the patriarch in the patriarchate where no ecclesiastical provinces are established; the metropolitan in the ecclesiastical province.

2. see that the faith and ecclesiastical discipline be accurately observed, and to notify the patriarch of abuses;

3. invest candidates, presented by founders, with benefices if a Hierarch of the province omitted to do that within the time determined by law although not prevented by a true impediment; also to appoint the econome of an eparchy of the province if its Hierarch, although admonished, neglected to appoint one;

4. to perform the canonical visitation if the Hierarch neglected it, the cause having been previously approved by the patriarch. He can, during the visitation, preach, hear confessions, hold inquiries on the life and conduct of clerics; denounce clerics found of ill repute to

their Hierarchs that they punish them; punish with just penalties, not excluding censures, notorious and manifest offenses done to him as well as to his retinue;

5. to celebrate as bishop in all churches, even if exempt, notifying the bishop beforehand if it is the case of the cathedral; to bless the people in the manner of a bishop who is in his own territory, but not to exercise other functions that require jurisdiction; to perform the same functions in a stauropegial church with at least the presumed permission of the patriarch;

6. to grant indulgences of 200 days, as in his own eparchy.

CANON 320. # 1. The metropolitan outside the patriarchate is entitled in the eparchies of his province, besides what is conceded to him in common law:

1. to substitute for the neglect of the college of eparchial consultors if they did not elect within the prescribed time the administrator of the vacant see;

2. to see that the faith and ecclesiastical discipline accurately be observed, and to notify the Roman Pontiff of abuses, save for the provision of n. 5.

3. to conduct the canonical visitation if the Hierarch neglected it, the cause having been previously approved by the Apostolic See, save for the prescription of n. 5; during the visitation he can perform the functions mentioned in c. 319, n. 4.

4. to avail himself of the rights mentioned in c. 319, nn. 1, 3, 5, 6;

5. to notify the archbishop in an archiepiscopate of the abuses mentioned in n. 2, and in order to obtain from him the approval of the cause mentioned in n. 2.

2. 1. The metropolitan who is not subject to a patriarch or archbishop is in addition obliged to communicate decisions of the Supreme Pontiff for his province, as well as those for the Oriental or the Universal Church, to the bishops and other persons concerned, unless the Apostolic See has specifically made a pertinent provision; and to see that the prescriptions contained in these decisions faithfully be executed;

2. To such a metropolitan are to be applied the prescriptions of c. 249, n. 1, c. 259 # 3, and also, with the advice of the bishops of the province, c. 279, # 2.

CANON 321. # 1. The metropolitan outside a patriarchate is obliged to request from the Roman Pontiff within three months from the episcopal consecration or, if he was a bishop, from the canonical provision in the consistory, in person or through a proxy the pallium, which is the sign of the metropolitan authority.

Concerning the pallium conferred upon patriarchs and independent metropolitans cf. the commentary to c. 238.

Catholic Oriental Rite metropolitans, independent of the jurisdiction of patriarchs, are at the present time heads of several provinces: the Byzantine Rite Ukrainian Ecclesiastical Provinces of Lwiw (Ukraine), Winnipeg (Canada) and Philadelphia (U.S.A.) ; the Byzantine Rite Romanian Ecclesiastical Province of Alba Julia (Romania) ; the Malabarian Ecclesiastical Provinces of Ernakulum and Changanacherry (India); and the Malankarian Ecclesiastical Province of Trivandrum (India).

2. The metropolitan cannot hold a synod and consecrate bishops before the imposition of the pallium.

3. The metropolitan can use the pallium in episcopal divine services on the days predetermined in any church of his province, even exempt, but under no condition outside his province, not even with the consent of the local Hierarch.

The enumeration of the occasion and days when the pallium can be used is left to particular law, which will follow the principles of the Latin Rite, where the pallium originated.

CANON 322. The pallium which the Roman Pontiff has bestowed perpetually upon a bishopric, or upon a bishop as an honorary distinction, does not grant any jurisdiction, nor the archiepiscopal or metropolitan title, unless the Apostolic letters decree otherwise.

CANON 323. Bishops who are not subject to a patriarch, archbishop or metropolitan, exarchs with a territory of their own, and apostolic exarchs, shall designate, with the previous approval of the Apostolic See, a neighboring metropolitan, to whom permanently are assigned all rights and obligations to which a metropolitan so designated is entitled according to common law.

MAJOR ARCHBISHOPS (cc. 324-339)

Definition (c. 324)
Appointment (c. 325)
Rights (cc. 326, 327 # 1)
Permanent Synod or Council (c. 327 # 2)
Erection of Exarchies (c. 328)
Other Rights (c. 329)
Liturgical Commemoration (c. 330)
Apocrisiary (c. 331)
Honorary Privileges:
 Some of the Patriarchal Privileges (c. 332)
 Dignity of Assistant to the Papal Throne (c. 333)
 Supracamelaucium c. 334)
The Catholicus (c. 335 # 1)
The Maphrian (c. 335 # 2)
Vacancy of the Archiepiscopate:
 Rights and Duties of the Administrator (c. 337)
 Designation of the Administrator (c. 336)
Titular Archbishops and Metropolitans (c. 338)
Rules of Precedence (c. 339; cf. c. 280 CIC)

CANON 324. Among metropolitans that archbishop is preeminent whose dignity is united to a metropolitan see situated outside the patriarchate either by decree or recognition of the Roman Pontiff or by an ecumenical council.

Those chief hierarchs of a Church who are independent of any patriarch, and who have as subjects metropolitans with their own ecclesiastical provinces, are also called archbishops. This title was given to all patriarchs, and also to the heads of some other Churches who did not acquire the patriarchal title later. The Bishop of Constantinople, for instance, styled himself "Archbishop of Constantinople and Ecumenical Patriarch." The Ecumenical Council of Chalcedon (451) granted to the Archbishop of Cyprus independence from the Patriarch of Antioch, and made him therefore independent head of a Church.

In the Patriarchate of Constantinople the title of archbishop was in later centuries conferred on bishops who were not metropolitans, but who thereby received an independent status. Such was, e.g., the granting of this title to the bishop of Nowgorod in Russia in 1335, which gave him a somewhat independent position in relationship to his metropolitan in Kiew (Ukraine), to whom he remained subject.

In order to distinguish this class of archbishops from those who enjoyed quasi-patriarchal jurisdiction, the latter are called by A. Coussa major archbishops.

There are no major archbishop among Catholic Oriental hierarchs at the present time. The Byzantine Rite Metropolitan-Archbishop of Lwiw and Galicia (Ukraine), as legal successor to the Metropolitan of Kiew, came closest to this dignity. The late Archbishop-Metropolitan Sheptytsky considered himself entitled to and within his right when he, in World War I, due to interrupted communications with Rome, appointed and consecrated a bishop for a reestablished diocese. The Byzantine Rite Romanian Archbishop-Metropolitan of Alba Julia exercised in some aspects a power of a major archbishop.

Among the dissident Orientals there are several major archbishops: The Archbishop of Cyprus and the Archbishop of Athens, the head of the Church of Greece. Also the chiefs of the other autocephalus Churches, whatever title they may use, can be regarded to belong to the class of major archbishops.

The Byzantine Rite patriarchs of the dissident Churches of the Near East grant the title of archbishop to the heads of their semi-independent exarchies in North and South America, in Western Europe and in South Africa, which were formed for the emigrants of their faith from the Near East and from Greece. These archbishop-exarchs govern flocks more numerous than those of their patriarchs, and are usually assisted by a synod of at least two other bishops.

The Ukrainian and Russian dissident Churches have followed the example of the Latin Rite, which came to them through the Catholic Ukrainian Church of the 17th century, and have only titular archbishops, who follow metropolitans in rank.

Major archbishops enjoy patriarchal rights in nearly all aspects, with the exception of those that are an immediate reflection of the patriarchal dignity.

156

CANON 325. # 1. The Roman Pontiff freely appoints the archbishop, or confirms a lawfully elected one, and puts him in charge over the respective Church.

2. In the election of the archbishop the norms of cc. 221-239 for the election of the patriarch shall be observed, save for the prescription of # 3.

3. 1. The synod of election is to be called together by the highest ranking metropolitan, or if there are no provinces in the archiepiscopate, by the first bishop.

2. It is not permitted to procede to the proclamation and enthronement of the archbishop elect before confirmation by the Roman Pontiff.

CANON 326. # 1. Besides those matters which belong to him in his province in his capacity as metropolitan according to the norm of c. 320, it is the task of the archbishop:

1. to preside at the election of bishops of his archiepiscopate, observing the norms of cc. 251-255. However, where the appointment of bishops is reserved to the Roman Pontiff, the archbishop is charged, according to the instructions of the Apostolic See, to propose to the Roman Pontiff, with the cooperation of the bishops of the archiepiscopate, the names of qualified candidates;

2. to ordain metropolitans within the time determined in c. 396 # 1, n. 1, and to enthrone them;

3. to see that the metropolitans assiduously safeguard the faith and ecclesiastical discipline and that they be safeguarded by the clergy and the faithful, and to notify the Roman Pontiff of abuses. And also to admonish metropolitans who are negligent in the fulfilling of their duties, and to denounce to the Roman Pontiff those who do not obey the admonition;

4. to supply by devolutive right the negligence of metropolitans in respect to the matters treated in cc. 319, n. 3, 320 # 1, n. 3, as well as to appoint the administrator of a vacant metropolitan see if the college of eparchial consultors has not elected one within the prescribed time;

5. to address by encyclical letters all Hierarchs of his territory, who are obliged to have them publicly read and explained;

6. to see to the efficient promulgation of the laws passed in an archiepiscopal synod, without prejudice to c. 350 # 1;

7. to interpret authentically the laws of the archiepiscopal synod with the consent of the permanent synod, until a future synod passes a decision on the matter;

8. to call together every year, except that in which an archiepiscopal synod is held, the local Hierarchs either of the whole archiepiscopate or of a province or region, for the purpose of a conference, but in such a way that, in the latter instance, there is nobody during a period of five years at least who has not been invited;

9. to dispense from the matrimonial impediments which, according to common law, can be removed by patriarchs;

10. to perform what is contained in c. 319, 5, 6;

11. to exercise the rights and perform the duties mentioned in c. 320 # 1 during the vacancy of a metropolitan see in the whole province;

12. to accept recourses in cases in which the canons permit that recourse be taken to the patriarch.

2. Unless by the nature of the matter or according to law the contrary is true, the archbishop can validly exercise his authority only in the archiepiscopate.

CANON 327. # 1. Unless particular law decrees otherwise, the power accorded in c. 248 # 1 to the patriarch in a patriarchal synod or a synod of election belongs also to the archbishop in an archiepiscopal synod or a synod of election; however, the decisions in each of these matters cannot be made public, nor can they be put into effect, before confirmation has been obtained from the Apostolic See.

2. 1. The archbishop shall have a permanent synod established, or a council, in respect to which the norms of cc. 288-297 concerning the permanent synod or council must be observed;

2. The archbishop can accomplish with the permanent synod only those things which are expressly determined in law.

CANON 328. The archbishop can, with the consent of the permanent synod, establish an exarchy, change its boundaries, and abolish it, having beforehand notified the Apostolic See.

CANON 329. The norms of cc. 242, 244, 258, 259, ## 2, 3, 269, 273, 275, 279, 298, 299, 302, 305, in regard to the patriarch apply also to the archbishop.

CANON 330. # 1. The archbishop is obliged to commemorate the Roman Pontiff in the divine liturgy and other divine services, and to take care that this obligation be fulfilled in accordance with the liturgical rules by all metropolitans, bishops and other Hierarchs and clerics of his territory.

2. Metropolitans, bishops and other Hierarchs of the entire archiepiscopate must commemorate the archbishop in the divine liturgy and other divine services after the Roman Pontiff.

CANON 331. The archbishop can have an apocrisiary at the Apostolic See, who is to be appointed with the advice of the permanent synod and with the prior consent of the Apostolic See.

Concerning apocrisiaries cf. what is said in the commentary to c. 220 on patriarchal apocrisiaries.

CANON 332. The archbishop enjoys in the archiepiscopate the privilege granted in c. 283, 1, 6, to the patriarch.

CANON 333. The archbishop has by law the use of the privilege to be prelate assistant to the papal throne.

CANON 334. The archbishop may, if there is such a custom, make use of the white supracamelaucium.

CANON 335. # 1. The catholicus who does not have the title of patriarch is equal to an archbishop.

The title of **catholicus** was given to the chief hierarch of a Church either because he made use of the universal **(katholikos)** jurisdiction of a patriarch, or was considered a delegate of the patriarch **ad universitatem causarum.** The title of patriarch was not assumed by a catholicus as long as the bond with the mother-Church remained intact.

The head of the Nestorian Church in Persia, the Metropolitan of Babylon (Seleucia-Ktesiphon), was honored with the title of catholicus-patriarch in the Synod of 544, when the bond with Antioch was definitely severed. The chief bishop of the Armenian Church was styled catholicus even earlier. The Archbishop of the Gregorian Church received this title in the second half of the 5th century. Also the Syrian (Monophysitic) Metropolitan of Mossul, the representative of the Syrian Patriarch of Antioch in Persia, was titled "Catholicus of the East."

Today there is no Catholic catholicus who is not also a patriarch, namely, the Catholicus-Patriarch of Cilicia of the Armenians, and the Catholicus-Patriarch of Babylonia of the Chaldeans. They enjoy all patriarchal rights and prerogatives.

Among dissidents the title is given to the Catholicus-Patriarch of Georgia (U.S.S.R.), to the three Armenian Catholicuses of Etshmiadzin (Soviet-Armenia), Constantinople and Jerusalem, and to the Nestorian Catholicus-Patriarch of Babylonia (Seleucia-Ktesiphon), now residing in the United States.

2. The metropolitan who has the title and dignity of a m a p h r i a n is equal to an archbishop, without prejudice to the duties which come from his subjection to the authority of the patriarch, and excluding the rights mentioned in cc. 331, 334, and others regarding the pallium.

When the Syrian (Monophysitic) Church was divided in two parts, one within the Byzantine Empire, the other in the empire of the Sassanides in Persia, the Syrian Patriarch of Antioch appointed the foremost metropolitan in Persia as his delegate, to whom he ceded the right to appoint and consecrate metropolitans and bishops, and to bless the holy chrism, and who therefore was called **maphrian** (fructiferous) as a source of the ecclesiastical authority. Being the chief hierarch of his Church after the patriarch, the maphrian was entitled to consecrate and enthrone the Patriarch of Antioch.

The title is recognized both by Catholics and dissidents, but was not conferred for many years because of the dwindling number and significance of the Syrian Churches.

CANON 336. During the vacancy of the archiepiscopate, it belongs to the highest-ranking metropolitan, or, if there are no metropolitans in the archiepiscopate, to the first bishop, to do what in c. 308 is assigned to the administrator of the patriarchate during vacancy of the see.

CANON 337. # 1. The norms of cc. 310-314 concerning the administrator of the patriarchate when the see is vacant or impeded are to be observed also in respect to the administrator of the archiepiscopate when the see is vacant or impeded.

2. The administrator of the archiepiscopate when the see is vacant or impeded enjoys in regions where eparchies or exarchies are not established the rights, and is charged with, the duties of an administrator of a vacant eparchy.

3. In respect to the administrator of the archbishop's own eparchy the norms of c. 467 and c. 469 shall be observed.

CANON 338. No other right, except the prerogative of honor and the right of precedence, is due to bishops who have received the distinctive title of honorary archbishop or metropolitan.

CANON 339. # 1. An archbishop has precedence over other metropolitans, a metropolitan who is the head of a province has precedence over an honorary metropolitan or archbishop, who precedes bishops, save for the norm of c. 414.

A major archbishop precedes all metropolitans and minor archbishops, but, while according to the CIC all archbishops and metropolitans, resident or titular, are of equal rank, and precedence among them is established according to the rules of c. 106 CIC, in Oriental canon law resident metropolitans who are heads of an ecclesiastical province enjoy precedence over metropolitans who are not in charge of a province and over (minor) archbishops, whether resident or titular.

2. Among metropolitans who are not heads of a province and honorary archbishops he enjoys precedence who was first promoted to the metropolitan or archiepiscopal see; if they were promoted at the same time, who is senior by episcopal consecration; if they received episcopal consecration at the same time, who is senior by age.

CHAPTER EIGHT

SYNODS OF PATRIARCHATES, ARCHIEPISCOPATES, PROVINCES, OF SEVERAL RITES AND OF SEVERAL PROVINCES (cc. 340-351)

Convocation of Synods (c. 340; cf. cc. 281, 284, 1b CIC)
Membership:
   Members with Deliberative Vote (c. 341 # 1 = c. 282
    ## 1, 2 and cc. 285, 286 ## 1, 2 CIC)
   Members with Consultative Vote (c. 341 # 2 = c. 282
    # 3 and c. 286 § 3 CIC)
   Extraordinary Membership (c. 342; cf. 286)
   Excluded from Participation (c. 343 = new)
Time Limits (c. 344; cf. c. 283)
Absent Members and Proxies (c. 345 = c. 287 CIC)
Quorum c. 346)
Rules of Procedure (c. 347 = c. 288 CIC)
Prohibition of Leaving (c. 348 = c. 289 CIC)
Topics of Discussion (c. 349 = c. 290 CIC)
Confirmation of Apostolic See (c. 350 = c. 291 CIC)
Conferences of Bishops (c. 351 = c. 292 CIC)

Kinds of Synods

According to the tradition of the Church synods are gatherings of bishops, although they perhaps could be represented by simple priests, deacons or minor clerics. Therefore, a diocesan synod, composed of priests, with the bishop being the only legislator, is not called in Oriental law a synod, but a **conventus,** a convention, or — to take a term from English particular law — an eparchial **convocation.**

In **Cleri Sanctitati** the following assemblies of bishops are mentioned:

1. Ecumenical Synod (cc. 167-174).

2. Patriarchal (Archiepiscopal) Synods (cc. 340-351). According to their purpose, they can be a

(1) Legislative Synod, simply called **Patriarchal Synod.** It is the most important and largest gathering of the hierarchy. It is also called a **National Synod,** because the Rites in countries where Islam prevails were organized in the form of nations **(millet).**

If certain matters are to be brought before a patriarchal synod according to the demands of law, a gathering of all bishops can informally be transformed in a patriarchal synod (cf. c. 316).

(2) Synod for the election of the patriarch (c. 221 sq.)

(3) Synod for the election of bishops (c. 251 sq.)

(4) Permanent Synod, a body assisting the patriarch in the government of the patriarchate (cf. c. 288 sq.).

3. Synod of several ecclesiastical provinces (c. 340 # 4).

4. Synod of the hierarchy of several Rites (c. 340 # 3).

5. Metropolitan or Provincial Synod (c. 340 # 2).

Outside the sphere of synods is placed the Eparchial Convocation. (cc. 422-428).

CANON 340. # 1. Bishops and other Hierarchs subject to a patriarch or archbishop are called together to a patriarchal or archiepiscopal synod. Such a synod is convened and presided over by the patriarch or archbishop, and he also designates, with the advice of the permanent synod, the place of the meeting.

 # 2. Bishops and other Hierarchs of an ecclesiastical province who are outside the patriarchate and archiepiscopate are called together to a provincial synod. Such a synod is called by a metropolitan who is not subject to a patriarch or archbishop, and he, with the advice of all those who have the obligation to attend with a decisive vote, designates the place of the meeting within the territory of the province, and he also presides over it.

 # 3. Bishops and other Hierarchs of several Rites can convene in a synod after they obtained the permission of the Roman Pontiff, who designates the place where the synod shall meet, and appoints his legate who is to call together and preside over the synod.

 # 4. Bishops and other Hierarchs of several provinces, who are not subject to a patriarch or archbishop, can meet in a synod after the Roman Pontiff has designated his legate, who is to convene and preside at the synod.

5. In designating the place for the meetings of the synods mentioned in ## 1, 2, 4, unless there is a just reason, the patriarchal or metropolitan church shall have preference.

CANON 341. # 1. In each synod there must take part with decisive vote, besides the president, the resident bishops, who in their place can send their coadjutor or auxiliary, also the titular bishops, the apostolic administrators of eparchies, the exarchs, and the administrators of vacant sees.

According to the Code of the Latin Rite Church, titular bishops may take part in a plenary or in a provincial synod only if they received a special invitation (c. 282 # 2 and c. 286 # 2).

2. Other members of both clergy, if invited to the synod, possess only a consultative vote, unless the Apostolic See or the synodal fathers, by secret vote, have granted to the president of a monastical association or the president of a monastical confederation a decisive vote.

CANON 342. Besides those mentioned in c. 341 # 1 there must be called:

1. To a patriarchal synod, the president of an association of monastical confederations, the president of a monastical confederation, and the supreme superiors of clerical religious institutes;

2. To an archiepiscopal and provincial synod, all those mentioned in no. 1, the superiors of independent monasteries, without prejudice to particular law, and the other major superiors of clerical religious institutes who reside in the territory, and the eparchial consultors of every eparchy whose Hierarch must take part in the synod according to c. 341 # 1, who send to the synod two consultors, designated collegiately.

CANON 343. Those mentioned in c. 109 # 1 cannot participate in a synod.

CANON 344. The patriarchal, archiepiscopal and provincial synod is to be held as often as the patriarch or archbishop with the consent of the permanent synod, or the metropolitans with the consent of the bishops of the province, deems it necessary, and at least every twenty years.

CANON 345. # 1. If prevented from participation in the synod by a serious impediment:

1. all those who enjoy a decisive vote shall send a proxy and shall prove the existence of the impediment;

2. those mentioned in c. 342 must advise the synod of the impediment; and they can send to the synod a proxy in their place, with the exception of the delegates of the eparchial consultors.

2. If the proxy is one of the fathers who are entitled to a decisive vote, he does not enjoy a double vote; if he is not one of them, he has only a consultative vote.

CANON 346. For the validity of every synod, the absolute majority of the fathers who enjoy a decisive vote must take part.

162

CANON 347. # 1. In any synod, it is the president who determines the order to be followed in discussing the questions, with the consent of the fathers if it is the case of a provincial synod.

2. Each of the fathers can add to the proposed questions questions of his own after they have been approved by the president of the synod with the advice of the two bishops senior in rank.

2. Any synod may be opened, transferred, prolonged, or closed by the president after he has obtained, if he is not a legate of the Roman Pontiff, the consent of the fathers.

CANON 348. Once a synod has been opened, one who is obliged to take part is not permitted to leave, except for a serious reason, to be approved by the president of the synod, if he is the legate of the Roman Pontiff, or by the synod itself.

CANON 349. The fathers assembled in synod shall diligently study and decide what they deem, each for his own territory, suitable for the increase of faith, the improvement of morality, the correction of abuses, the reconciliation of controversies, the observation or introduction of the one and the same discipline.

CANON 350. # 1. The synod being terminated, the president shall submit all minutes and decrees to the Apostolic See, and they shall not be promulgated before they have been confirmed by the same; meantime all those who took part in the synod must observe secrecy on the decisions and matters discussed. The fathers of the synod, however, shall determine the manner of promulgation of the decrees as well as the time when the promulgated decrees shall take effect.

2. The decrees of the synod when promulgated oblige in the entire territory of each of the fathers, and the local Hierarchs cannot dispense from them except in individual cases and for a serious reason.

CANON 351. # 1. The metropolitan who is not subject to a patriarch or archbishop, and, in his absence, the bishop who is the senior in rank in the province, shall see that the local Hierarchs be called together whenever necessary at the seat of the metropolitan or of another bishop, in order to decide in mutual consultation what is to be undertaken in the eparchies to promote the welfare of religion, and they shall prepare the material to be acted upon by the future provincial synod.

2. It is expedient also that resident bishops, even if they have the honorary title of archbishop, who are not subject to a patriarch or metropolitan, exarchs who are in charge of a territory of their own, and apostolic exarchs, although they be of another Rite, take part together with the other Hierarchs of the same territory in the conferences mentioned in # 1.

3. The same Hierarchs shall determine in their meeting the place of the next conference.

CHAPTER NINE

APOSTOLIC ADMINISTRATORS
(cc. 352-361)

CANON 352. The government of a canonically established eparchy, whether the see be occupied or vacant, is sometimes committed by the Supreme Pontiff, for grave and special reasons, permanently or temporarily, to an apostolic administrator.

CANON 353. # 1. Any apostolic administrator, if he be appointed to an eparchy while the see is occupied, takes possession of his office by presenting his letters of appointment to the bishop, if the latter is sound of mind and residing in the eparchy, as well as to the college of eparchial consultors, according to c. 397 # 3.

2. If the see is vacant, or if the bishop is not of sound mind, or does not reside in the eparchy, the apostolic administrator takes possession of his office in the manner of a bishop according to c. 397 # 3, with the condition that he shows first the letters of appointment to the patriarch or archbishop, unless the Apostolic See itself has notified the patriarch or archbishop of his appointment.

CANON 354. The right, duties and privileges of an apostolic administrator are determined in his letters of appointment, or, unless expressly provided otherwise, in the norms of the canons that follow.

CANON 355. # 1. 1. The permanently appointed apostolic administration enjoys the same rights and privileges, and is bound by the same duties, as the resident bishop;

2. In respect to the appointment of a syncellus, the norms of cc. 432-437 shall be observed.

2. If he was appointed temporarily:

1. He has the same rights and duties as the administrator of a vacant see; but, even though the see is occupied, he can hold a visitation of the eparchy according to the norms of law; and he is not bound by the obligation of offering the Divine Liturgy for the faithful, which obligation is incumbent on the bishop.

2. In regard to honorary privileges, the norm of c. 387 obtains; but a bishop who was transferred to another see while retaining the

administration of the former see is entitled there also to all honorary privileges of resident bishops.

CANON 356. # 1. If the apostolic administrator was assigned to an eparchy while the see is occupied, the jurisdiction of the bishop and his syncellus becomes suspended.

2. Although the apostolic administrator is not subject to the authority of the bishop, he must not interfere in matters pertaining to the bishop himself, or institute proceedings or inquiries against the syncellus concerning acts of the former administration.

CANON 357. If the jurisdiction of the apostolic administrator is impeded, or if the administrator dies, the Apostolic See shall be notified at once; in the meantime, if the see is vacant or impeded in its function, the prescriptions of cc. 467 sqq. shall be in force; otherwise the bishops governs the eparchy, unless the Apostolic See provided differently.

CANON 358. # 1. The jurisdiction of the apostolic administrator does not cease with the death of the Roman Pontiff or the bishop.

2. It ceases, however, when the bishop of a vacant eparchy has taken possesion of his office according to the norm of c. 397 # 3.

CANON 359. If it happens that an apostolic administrator be given to the patriarchate or archiepiscopate itself during vacancy of the see, temporarily or permanently, for a very grave reason, or when the see was occupied, temporarily or permanently:

1. the administrator assigned to the patriarchate or archiepiscopate takes possession of his office by showing the letters of appointment to the patriarch or archbishop and to the permanent synod, unless the see was vacant, or the patriarch or archbishop is not sound of mind, or does not reside in the patriarchate or archiepiscopate, in which cases he presents the document to the permanent synod and the college of the consultors of the patriarch's or archbishop's own eparchy;

2. the notary of the permanent synod shall draw up a document attesting the taking of possession, which shall be preserved in the acts.

CANON 360. The apostolic administrator enjoys the same rights, but not the same privileges, and is bound by the same duties as the patriarch or archbishop, if he was permanently assigned to the patriarchate or archiepiscopate; otherwise the administrator given to a patriarchate enjoys the rights and is held by the obligations contained in cc. 309-312; that given to an archiepiscopate must observe the norms of c. 337.

CANON 361. What is decreed in cc. 356-358 in regard to the apostolic administrator of an eparchy shall apply to the apostolic administrator who governs a patriarchate or archiepiscopate.

CHAPTER TEN

EXARCHS

The term **Exarch** denotes a delegate. This was the official title given to the governor of a civil diocese of the late Roman empire, which again was divided into provinces. Parallel to the civil administrative division of the empire, the ecclesiastical organization was formed: the bishop was the ecclesiastical superior of a parish **(paroikia)**; the metropolitan headed the eparchy, while the chief bishop of a civil diocese took the title of exarch. Besides those sees which acquired later the patriarchal title, exarchical jurisdiction was enjoyed also by the metropolitans of Ephesus (Diocese of Asia), Neocesarea (Diocese of Pontus) and Heraclea (Diocese of Thrace). However, the bishop of the newly established imperial residence in Constantinople overshadowed them so completely, that these exarchs entirely vanished from the scene. The dignity of supra-metropolitan exarch is still known among the dissidents. The head of the Bulgarian Church took this title when his Church was formed in 1860 by a rebellious separation from the Patriarch of Constantinople; he now uses the title of patriarch. Dissident patriarchs sometimes appoint exarchs, who have subordinate bishops, for semi-independent groups of their jurisdiction, as the several exarch of the patriarchs of Constantinople, Antioch, Alexandria, and Moscow for the emigrants in various parts of the world.

The indefinite meaning of the term exarch (delegate) was the reason for calling by this title the representatives of patriarchs, archbishops, and even of bishops, and in some places it is a minor honorary title for diocesan priests conferred upon them by their bishop.

The visitors of monasteries with the title of exarch deserve special mention. While generally monasteries are under the jurisdiction of the bishop, who visits them in person or through a delegate, stauropegial or exempt monasteries are under the exclusive authority of the patriarch, who often, on account of distance or the number of monasteries, is prevented from performing the canonical visitation in person. Patriarchs established therefore a permanent office in charge of this duty, which was confided to an exarch, not rarely endowed with the episcopal dignity.

The Catholic Oriental canon law knows three kinds of exarchs:

(1) Exarchs with a territory of their own, who are equivalent to the abbots **nullius** of the Latin Rite.

(2) Apostolic Exarchs, who correspond to the apostolic vicars and prefects.

(3) Patriarchal and archiepiscopal exarchs, who govern a territory within the patriarchate or archiepiscopate where a diocese cannot yet be established for reasons which lead in the Latin Rite Church to the erection of apostolic vicariates and prefectures, and in the Oriental Church outside of patriarchates to the erection of apostolic exarchies.

Article One:

EXARCHS WHO ARE IN CHARGE OF A TERRITORY OF THEIR OWN OUTSIDE PATRIARCHATES (cc. 362-365)

Establishment of Exarchies (c. 362; cf. c. 319 CIC)
Appointment of Exarch (c. 363 = c. 320 CIC)
Rights and Duties of Exarch (c. 364)
Vacancy of Exarchies (c. 365)

The exarch with a territory of his own corresponds in all to the abbot **nullius.** The exarchy is an ecclesiastical circumscription established in a permanent manner. There is no equivalent in Oriental canon law to the **praelatura nullius,** which as a rule is not connected with a certain monastery. At the present time there is one such exarch with a territory of his own, the archimandrite or superior of the monastery of Grottaferrata near Rome (Italy), founded by St. Nilus in 1002. It was constituted an exarchy by Pius XI in 1937, and is limited to the premises of the monastery; it has one parish, to which, besides the religious community of the Italian Order of St. Basil the Great, belong only a few persons of the Byzantine Rite. Such an exarch governs his subjects in virtue of ordinary jurisdiction, but vicariously **(potestate vicaria),** i.e., on behalf of the Roman Pontiff.

Among dissidents there are extant today two instances where the superior of the monastery exercises jurisdiction over seculars as well. One is the superior of the Monastery of St. John the Theologian (Evangelist) on the Island of Patmos (Greece). The whole Island is under the jurisdiction of this stauropegial monastery, which again is dependent on the Patriarch of Constantinople.

A similar example is the St. Catherine's Monastery on Mount Sinai. Its superior was endowed with the episcopal dignity since the VII. century, and with the title of archbishop since the IX. century. In 1575 the archbishopric was recognized by the dissident patriarchs as an autocephalus Church, i.e., independent of any higher ecclesiastical authority, although the hegoumenus must receive episcopal consecration from the Patriarch of Jerusalem.

The jurisdiction of this archbishop-hegoumenus comprises St. Catherine's Monastery on Mount Sinai, a hospice in Cairo (Egypt), and a few Greek churches in India, founded by and under the care of his monks.

CANON 362. # 1. **Only the Apostolic See is entitled to erect or reestablish, change, or abolish an exarchy with a territory of its own.**

2. **The exarch who is a superior of an independent monastery and is in charge of a territory of his own, separated from every eparchy, with clergy and people, shall govern according to particular law, and where that is lacking, by the norms of the canons that follow.**

CANON 363. # 1. **The exarch who is superior of an independent monastery and in charge of a territory of his own is appointed by the Roman Pontiff, without prejudice to the right of election or presentation if it lawfully appertains to someone; in which case his confirmation and institution belong to the Roman Pontiff.**

2. To be qualified for this dignity, one must possess the same qualifications which the law demands for bishops.

3. For the validity of the election an absolute majority of the votes is required, not counting the invalid votes, save for particular law requiring a greater number of votes.

CANON 364. # 1. 1. The exarch who is superior of an independent monastery and in charge of his own territory shall not interfere with the administration of his exarchy before he himself has taken possession according to the norm of c. 397 # 3;

2. He must receive within three months from the day of receiving the apostolic letter of appointment the blessing or c h i r o t e s i a according to the norm of law, unless he was prevented by a serious impediment.

2. Such an exarch has the same ordinary authority and the same obligations with the same sanctions as a resident bishop in his own eparchy.

3. While he is in office, and within the boundaries of his territory, although he lacks episcopal dignity:

1. He can administer the sacrament of confirmation separately from baptism;

2. Without prejudice to the authority granted in common law to administer minor orders to his own subject religious, he can confer minor orders also on his own secular subjects, as well as on others who exhibit the dismissorial letters required by law, provided he received the blessing mentioned in # 1, n. 2; an ordination performed outside these limits is invalid;

3. He can impart blessings reserved to bishops, if there are such in his Rite, and grant indulgences of one hundred days;

4. He can perform those rites which require the use of the holy myron (chrism), unless in his own discipline this is forbidden to prelates who do not possess the episcopal dignity.

4. In respect to the appointment of a syncellus, the prescription of cc. 432-437 shall be observed.

CANON 365. # 1. When an exarchy ruled by a superior of an independent monastery becomes vacant the administration passes, until the new superior be appointed, to him who lawfully takes over in the meantime the government of the monastery.

2. If such an exarchy be impeded, the norm of c. 467 shall be observed.

Article Two

EXARCHS WHO ARE IN CHARGE OF A TERRITORY NOT OF THEIR OWN

I. APOSTOLIC EXARCHS (cc. 366-387)

Definition and Appointment (c. 366; cf. c. 293 CIC)
Limits of Rights (c. 367 = c. 294 CIC)

Power Over the Clergy:
    Exarch Grants Faculties to All the Clergy
        (c. 368 = c. 295 CIC)
    Supply of Clergy from the Patriarchate (c. 369 = new)
    Relationship of the Religious Clergy to the Exarch
        (cc. 370, 371 = cc. 296, 297 CIC)
    Controversies Among the Clergy (c. 372 = c. 298 CIC)
    Emergency Power of the Exarch (c. 373 = c. 307 CIC)
Law of Residence (c. 374 = c. 301 CIC)
Ad Limina Visit (c. 375 = c. 299 CIC)
Reports to the Holy See and the Patriarch
    (c. 376 = c. 300 CIC)
Exarchial Council (c. 377 = c. 302 CIC)
Annual Conference with the Clergy (c. 378 = c. 303 CIC)
Archives (c. 379 = c. 304 # 1 CIC)
Participation in Synods (c. 380 # 1; cf. c. 304 # 2 CIC)
Exarchial Convocation of the Clergy
    (c. 380 # 2; cf. c. 304 # 2 CIC)
Application of Mass for the Faithful (c. 381 = c. 306 CIC)
Duties Toward Faithful of a Different Rite (c. 382 = new)
Education of Native Clergy (c. 383 = c. 305 CIC)
Provisions for Case of Vacancy of Exarchy:
    Appointment of Pro-Exarch (c. 384 = c. 309 CIC)
    Power of the Administrator During Vacancy
    (c. 385 = c. 310 CIC)
    Termination of the Office of the Administrator
    (c. 386 = c. 311 CIC)
Honorary Privileges (c. 387 = c. 308 CIC)

Apostolic exarchies are in nearly all aspects equivalent to apostolic vicariates and prefectures. They are established outside the territory of patriarchates, in circumstances in which the erection of dioceses is not yet feasible.

Due to emigration, groups of Oriental Rite Catholics are now found in all continents, far from their native regions. If we inspect the various provisions which have been made for their pastoral care, we find the following situations:

1. If their number is sufficiently large, the Holy See might establish ecclesiastical provinces and dioceses for them, as it was done for the Ukrainians of the Byzantine Rite in Canada and the United States, or for the Byzantine Rite Catholics in Italy.

2. If this is not yet possible, they may be organized in apostolic exarchies, as, for instance, the Ukrainians in Germany, Australia, etc., with apostolic exarchs who are directly subject to the Holy See.

3. Sometimes all Oriental Rite Catholics in a country are subject to the chief bishop of the Latin Rite of that country in the capacity of apostolic exarch for them. He might then appoint vicars general for them, with episcopal dignity, as in Brazil for the Ukrainians, or a priest, as in England for the Ukrainian immigrants.

4. A similar arrangement places the Oriental Rite Catholics under the chief bishop of the country, granting him not vicarious jurisdiction as an apostolic exarch, but direct and immediate author-

ity, as the Archbishop of Vienna (Austria) enjoys in respect to the Byzantine Rite Catholics in that country.

5. If the Latin Rite is well organized in that region, while the Oriental Rite communities are few and scattered, making it impractical to organize them in an exarchy of their own Rite, they may be placed under the jurisdiction of the local Latin Rite ordinaries, as is the situation for most Orientals in the United States and Canada, with the exception of the Ukrainians and Ruthenians.

6. In the case where the respective Oriental Rite Catholics are the only Catholics in that region, or where they cannot be attached to the hierarchical organization of another Catholic Rite, while their number is still insignificant, they might receive as ecclesiastical superior a priest with the title of ordinary, as it was done with Armenian Catholics in Greece and Romania.

CANON 366. # 1. Apostolic exarchs govern on behalf of the Roman Pontiff a territory which is not subject to a patriarch or an archbishop, where because of the fewness of faithful or for some other grave reason eparchies are not established.

2. The appointment of the apostolic exarchs is reserved to the Apostolic See.

3. The apostolic exarch takes possession of the exarchy by presenting in person or by proxy the decree of appointment to him who rules the exarchy according to the norm of c. 384.

CANON 367. # 1. Apostolic exarchs enjoy the same rights and faculties in their territory as belong to resident bishops in their own eparchies, unless something is excepted by law or was reserved by the Apostolic See.

2. Even those apostolic exarchs who lack episcopal consecration, while they hold this office, and within the boundaries of their territory:

1. enjoy the rights and faculties mentioned in c. 364 # 3, nn. 1, 3. 4;

2. they can administer minor orders to their subjects as well as to others who present the dismissorial letters required by law, provided they have received the blessing, if they were obliged according to the norms of law or of liturgical regulations to do so, without prejudice to the norm of particular law that demands the blessing solely for lawfulness.

3. In regard to the appointment of a syncellus, the prescription of cc. 432-437 shall be observed.

The apostolic exarchs correspond in the Latin Rite canon law to the apostolic vicars and prefects. However, while the CIC has no provision for them concerning the appointment of vicar generals, although a letter of the Sacred Congregation for the Propagation of the Faith of December 8, 1919 (AAS 1920, 120) permits them to have vicar delegates, the present codification grants apostolic exarchs the right to have vicar generals in the same manner as bishops have them.

CANON 368. Priests and other clerics, even exempt religious, shall not dare to exercise the sacred ministry without authorization from the apostolic exarch.

CANON 369. # 1. The apostolic exarch can request the patriarch for qualified priests who are capable of undertaking the spiritual care of souls. The patriarch shall endeavor to satisfy the request of the exarch as far as possible.

2. Priests sent temporarily or permanently by the patriarch to the exarchy, after the approval of the Apostolic See has been obtained, shall be considered as assigned to the exarchy, and must be subject in everything to the authority of the apostolic exarch.

CANON 370. # 1. Religious, even if exempt, when assigned to the exarchy, are subject to the jurisdiction, visitation and correction of the apostolic exarch in all matters pertaining to the government of the exarchy, the care of souls, the administration of the sacraments, the management of schools, the offerings made for the benefit of the exarchy, the fulfillment of pious bequests made to the same exarchy.

2. Although the apostolic exarch is in no way, except in cases foreseen in law, to interfere in the religious discipline, which is dependent on the religious superior, if, however, a conflict should arise in respect to the matters mentioned in # 1 between an order of the exarch and an order of the superior, that of the former must prevail, without prejudice to the right of recourse to the Apostolic See, and save for special statutes and agreements approved by the Apostolic See.

CANON 371. In case of dearth of priests of the secular clergy, the apostolic exarch can, after having heard the advice of the superior, force religious priests, even if exempt, assigned to the exarchy, to take over the care of souls, without prejudice to special statutes and agreements approved by the Apostolic See.

CANON 372. If disagreements should perhaps develop in matters pertaining to the care of souls, either among individual clerics and religious, or between them and anyone else, or between various religious institutes, the apostolic exarchs shall endeavor as soon as possible to settle them, and if there is need, to decide them, without prejudice to the right of recourse to the Apostolic See.

CANON 373. # 1. Religious who are sent by their superiors, though they are assigned to the exarchy, can leave the exarchy after having lawfully obtained permission, and they can be dismissed from the exarchy for a grave reason by the apostolic exarch or supplanted by the proper superior, after mutual consultation between the apostolic exarch and the religious superior, if necessary, and with consideration of the good of the exarchy, the religious institute and of the religious.

2. 1. However, in case of public scandal and of very grave and imminent harm, they can, with the advice of their council, and, if it is the case of religious, notice having been given to the superior, remove the subject cleric or religious at once;

2. In respect to clerics sent by the patriarch, or in regard to religious sent by their superiors, to the exarchy and assigned to it, the same norm shall be observed, and the patriarch or religious superior, according to the case, shall be notified at once.

CANON 374. # 1. Apostolic exarchs shall reside in the exarchy, from which they are not permitted to be absent without grave and urgent reason, except for a brief time, without consulting the Apostolic See.

2. They must in person, or if they are lawfully prevented, through another, conduct a visitation of the region committed to their care, whenever this is necessary, and examine during the visitation everything which concerns the faith, the moral life, the administration of sacraments, the preaching of the word of God, the observation of holydays, the divine worship, the instruction of the youth, and the ecclesiastical discipline.

CANON 375. Apostolic exarchs are obliged to make a visit to the churches of Saints Peter and Paul in Rome as demanded in the same law obliging bishops according to c. 407. They can satisfy this obligation through a proxy, who possibly resides in Rome, if a grave reason prevents them from fulfilling the obligation in person.

CANON 376. # 1. Apostolic exarchs are obliged, according to the norm of c. 405, to submit to the Apostolic See a full and accurate report on their pastoral duties, and on everything which in any manner pertains to the situation of the exarchy, the clergy, the religious, the discipline of the faithful, the attendance at schools, and finally the welfare of the faithful committed to their care; which report must be signed by the apostolic exarch himself as well as by at least one of the councilors mentioned in c. 377.

2. Apostolic exarchs to whom the care of faithful of a different Rite was committed must in addition send a report on the personnel and religious situation of these faithful to the patriarchs and archbishops whose faithful was committed to their care.

CANON 377. Apostolic exarchs shall establish a council of older and wiser priests, their subjects, not less than three, for whose opinion they shall ask, at least by letter, in more serious and important matters.

CANON 378. When opportunity permits it, apostolic exarchs shall call together at least the more distinguished religious as well as secular priests of their own territory, at least once a year, in order to be able to decide with the help of the experience and counsel of each one what matters can be better regulated.

CANON 379. The laws which prescribe for bishops the establishment of archives bind in the same manner apostolic exarch, taking into consideration different circumstances of persons and places.

CANON 380. # 1. It is desired that apostolic exarchs take part in the synods convened by the patriarch or archbishop of the same Rite according to the norm of cc. 340 # 1, 344.

2. What is prescribed in cc. 422-428 in respect to the eparchial convocation, shall be applied, unless contrary to the nature of the matter, to the exarchial convocation, with the exception of the regulation demanding that the convocation be convened at least every ten years.

CANON 381. They must apply the divine liturgy for the people committed to their care at least ten times every year on the principal holydays.

172

CANON 382. Apostolic exarchs to whom the care of faithful of a different Rite is committed according to the norm of c. 22 ## 2-4 shall be vigilant that the various groups accurately observe their own liturgical and disciplinary regulations.

CANON 383. Apostolic exarchs shall consider their conscience most seriously burdened with the obligation of endeavoring with great zeal that from among their faithful or the inhabitants of their territory clerics be properly educated and admitted to the priesthood.

CANON 384. # 1. The apostolic exarch shall appoint, as soon as he arrives in his territory, a qualified secular or religious priest as pro-exarch.

2. The pro-exarch has no authority during the lifetime of the exarch except such as shall be granted to him by the exarch.

3. The pro-exarch must take over the direction of the exarchy until the Apostolic See decrees otherwise, and remain in this office:

1. at the cessation, for whatever reason, of the appointment of the exarch;

2. if there is no syncellus of the exarch or a priest designated by him according to the norm of c. 467 # 1;

3. if the exarch is prevented from the exercise of his authority according to the norm of the cited c. 467 # 2;

4. The pro-exarch who has taken over the direction of the exarchy shall at once appoint a qualified priest, who shall succeed in his office, as said in # 3.

5. If it should happen that no one was appointed according to ## 1, 4, the government passes by virtue of law in the meantime to the senior in the exarchy, i.e., who is residing in the territory and whose letters of appointment were presented there first; and among several of equal seniority, he who is older by priestly ordination.

CANON 385. # 1. He to whom the care of the exarchy passed according to the norm of c. 384 must as soon as possible notify the Apostolic See.

2. In the meantime he can make use of all faculties, ordinary according to c. 367, and delegated, to which the exarch was entitled, unless they were granted to the latter on account of personal qualities.

CANON 386. He who is temporarily in charge of the administration of the exarchy must continue in his office, with all faculties granted to him, although the predetermined time limit has passed, until a successor has taken over the administration of his office according to the norm of law.

CANON 387. # 1. Exarchs who have the episcopal dignity are entitled to the honorary privileges which the law grants to titular bishops; but if they lack the episcopal dignity, they have only, while holding office and in their own territory, the insignia and privileges of the prelatic title or the prelatic dignity which is the first after the bishop according to the rules of their own Rite.

2. The blessing which by particular law is prescribed in the granting of this dignity must be received within three months.

II. PATRIARCHAL AND ARCHIEPISCOPAL EXARCHS
(cc. 388-391)

Definition and Appointment (c. 388)
Taking Possession of Office (c. 389)
Report to the Patriarch or Archbishop (c. 390)
Extent of Rights and Duties (c. 391)

CANON 388. # 1. Patriarchal exarchs are appointed in patriarchates, archiepiscopal in archiepiscopates, for regions where eparchies are not established because of the small number of faithful or for some other serious reason. They rule the territory in the name of the patriarch or archbishop.

2. Patriarchal and archiepiscopal exarchs are appointed by the patriarch or archbishop with the advice of the permanent synod, and they cannot be removed from office without the consent of the permanent synod.

CANON 389. The patriarchal or archiepiscopal exarch takes possession of the administration of his territory by presenting in person or by proxy the letters of appointment from the patriarch or archbishop to him who rules the territory.

CANON 390. Patriarchal and archiepiscopal exarchs must submit every five years a full and accurate written report to the patriarch or archbishop on the religious and temporal state of the exarchy.

CANON 391. The norms enacted in respect to apostolic exarchs in cc. 367, 371, 372 (save for the right of recourse to the patriarch), 374 # 1 (save for the right of the patriarch or archbishop to grant to the exarch the required permission), 374 # 2, 377 — 379, 380 # 2, 381, 387, shall also be observed by the patriarchal and archiepiscopal exarchs.

PART TWO

THE EPISCOPAL AUTHORITY AND THOSE WHO TAKE PART IN ITS EXERCISE
(cc. 392-526)

CHAPTER ONE

BISHOPS

APPOINTMENT OF RESIDENT BISHOPS (cc. 392-397)

Definition — Power of Appointment (c. 392 = c. 329

1, 2 CIC)
Qualifications:
General Norm (c. 393 = c. 330 CIC)
Enumeration of Qualities (c. 394 = c. 331 CIC)
Canonical Provision (c. 395 = c. 332 CIC)

Episcopal Consecration (c. 396 § 1, 1 = c. 333 CIC;
§ 1, 2; § 2 = new)
Taking Possession of Eparchy (c. 397 = c. 334 CIC)

CANON 392. # 1. The bishops are the successors of the apostles, and are placed by divine law over the individual Churches, which they govern with ordinary power under the authority of the Roman Pontiff.

2. They are freely appointed by the Roman Pontiff, or if lawfully elected, confirmed by him.

CANON 393. Before one is elevated to the episcopate, proof must be furnished, according to the manner prescribed by the Apostolic See or by particular law approved by the Apostolic See, that he is qualified.

CANON 394. # 1. In order to be considered qualified, a candidate must be:

1. born of legitimate wedlock, excluding one who was legitimated, even by a subsequent marriage;

2. not bound by marriage bond;

3. at least thirty years of age;

4. at least five years in the priesthood;

5. of good moral character, piety, zeal for souls, prudence and other endowments which qualify for the government of the eparchy in question;

6. doctor or at least master in sacred theology or canon law, conferred by an institution of higher learning or university approved by the Apostolic See, or at least well versed in these sciences. If he should belong to a religious institute, he must have received from his major superiors either a similar title or at least a certificate attesting his learning.

2. One who is elected or designated by persons to whom the Apostolic See has granted or recognized the privilege to elect or designate must also possess the mentioned qualifications.

3. The Apostolic See alone judges definitely whether a candidate is qualified or not.

The requirement of legitimate birth was changed from "**natus ex legitimo matrimonio**" (c. 331 CIC) to "**legitimis natalibus praeditus**" because in c. 1015 CIC # 3 **legitimum matrimonium** was defined as "a valid marriage between n o n - b a p t i z e d persons," which definition, although supplied by the legislator himself, obviously could not be applied to a future bishop.

A bishop cannot be married according to the discipline of all Oriental Churches, but he could be a widower. However, his syncellus (vicar general) must be a celibate priest (cf. c. 433 # 1).

We find in the history of the Eastern Churches a vaccilating attitude in respect of candidates to the episcopacy, as regards their married status or their belonging to the secular or the regular clergy:

1. In apostolic times, and even later, celibate, widowed or married candidates were admitted, with the sole limitation that they

had not been married more than once, a demand imposed by St. Paul himself.

2. In the following era, secular celibate or widowed clerics and monks were appointed bishops, the latter gaining preponderance, since among the secular clergy there were few who possessed higher learning. Even a married candidate could become a bishop on condition that his wife separated from him and entered a monastery in an eparchy other than that of her husband.

3. When the various Oriental communities reunited themselves with the Holy See the law in force was that only religious could become bishops. Celibate secular priests were nearly non-existent. Widowed or celibate secular candidates had first to receive summarily the monastic habit and to make monastic profession. This state was reconfirmed even in the Catholic Provincial Synod of Zamoshch (1720) for the Ukrainian and Byelorussian Catholic Church of the Byzantine Rite. No protest was heard because of the lack of otherwise qualified secular clergy. However, when the number of properly qualified celibate and widowed candidates increased, the requirement of monastic profession was dispensed by the Holy See in each single case, and finally formally abolished by the Provincial Synod of Lwiw (1891).

The system of ordaining only monks to the episcopacy is still rigidly followed by all dissidents. The only candidate ever consecrated bishop in the Russian Church who had not taken religious profession was Marcel Popiel (1875), an apostate Catholic priest.

4. Among Catholics today celibate and widowed priests of the secular as well as of the religious clergy can become bishops. There have been a few appointments of widowers to the episcopacy as late as half a century ago, e.g., among the Ruthenians and Ukrainians, even with children sharing the living quarters of their father's bishop's palace.

CANON 395. # 1. Every candidate for the episcopate, even those elected or designated in virtue of a grant by the Roman Pontiff in concordats or otherwise, needs the canonical provision by which he becomes the bishop of the vacant eparchy, and which is granted solely by the Roman Pontiff, without prejudice to the prescription of c. 256, 2.

2. The candidate must take, before the canonical provision, besides the profession of faith, an oath of fidelity to the Apostolic See according to the formula approved by the Apostolic See, without prejudice to c. 260 # 1, 2, e.

CANON 396. # 1. 1. Unless prevented by legitimate impediment, the candidate promoted to the episcopate must within three months from the receipt of the apostolic document receive the episcopal consecration and within four months proceed to his eparchy.

2. Unless prevented by legitimate impediment, the candidate promoted to the episcopate in patriarchates must request episcopal consecration within two months from the election, and within four months proceed to his eparchy.

2. Having received episcopal consecration, the bishop:

1. Obtains episcopal jurisdiction and the right to receive the income from the m e n s a   e p i s c o p a l i s or episcopal estate;

176

2. Can grant indulgences of one hundred days in places of his jurisdiction.

According to traditional Eastern mentality it is the episcopal ordination what makes the priest a bishop, and not the granting of episcopal jurisdiction as such. Cleri Sanctitati has accepted this view in several instances, one of which is embodied in this canon: Episcopal jurisdiction can be exercised only after the priest has actually received episcopal consecration. However, he could take possession of the diocese before his consecration, because only in that case would the consecration itself confer upon him jurisdiction. If he has not entered into his office, he would obtain by consecration only radical jurisdiction of which he could make use only after having taken possession of the diocese.

3. If the promoted candidate already possesses episcopal consecration, the rights mentioned in # 2 are due to him from the moment of the canonical provision.

CANON 397. # 1. Resident bishops are ordinary and immediate pastors in the eparchies committed to them.

2. However, they shall not interfere, either in person or through others, with the government of the eparchy, under the pretext of any title whatsoever, before they have canonically taken possesion of the administration of the eparchy. However, if they were appointed administrators of the vacant eparchy, vicar judicials, or economes, before their designation to the episcopate, they can retain and exercise such offices also after their designation.

3. Resident bishops take canonical possession of the administration of the eparchy in the eparchy itself by presenting in person or by proxy the apostolic or patriarchal letters to the board of eparchial consultors, in the presence of the chancellor of the eparchy, who makes note of the fact in the official acts.

RIGHTS AND DUTIES OF RESIDENT BISHOPS (cc. 398-416)

Through a Representative (c. 408 = c. 342 CIC)
Visitation of the Eparchy:
 Time and Person (c. 409 # 1 = c. 343 # 1 CIC)
 Accompanying Aides (c. 409 # 2 = c. 343 # 2 CIC)
 Persons and Places Subject to Visitation
  (c. 410 = c. 344 CIC)
 Mode of Procedure (c. 411 = c. 345 CIC)
 Expenses of Visitation (c. 412 = c. 346 CIC)
Liturgical Commemoration of the Bishop (c. 413 = new)
Precedence of the Resident Bishop (c. 414 = c. 347 CIC)
Titular Bishops and Their Titular Eparchies
 (c. 415 = c. 348 CIC)
Honorary Privileges (c. 416 = c. 349 CIC)

CANON 398. The bishops themselves represent the legal personality of the eparchy and the m e n s a e p i s c o p a l i s or bishop's estate in all legal transactions which concern them according to the canonical norms.

CANON 399. # 1. They have the right and duty to govern the eparchy in spiritual as well as in temporal matters with legislative, judicial and executive power, to be exercised according to canonical norms.

2. Episcopal laws take effect immediately on being promulgation, unless provided otherwise in the law. The manner of promulgation is determined by the bishop himself.

CANON 400. # 1. They must endeavor with all their power that the purity of faith and morals be preserved in clergy and people, that the nourishment of Christian doctrine is offered to the faithful, especially to children and the unschooled, that the teaching in primary and secondary schools is given according to the principles of the Catholic religion.

2. Bishops shall urge the observation of the laws of the Church.

3. They shall watch lest abuses creep into ecclesiastical discipline, especially concerning the administration of sacraments and sacramentals, the worship of God and the saints, the preaching of the word of God, the sacred indulgences, the execution of pious bequests.

CANON 401. The bishops must see:
1. that in their own cathedral at least a part of the divine office is celebrated daily, where there is such a custom, according to the lawful usage of each Rite;
2. also that in every city, at least in one or other church. and at at least on Sundays and feastdays and on the chief holydays of saints according to the rules of their own calendar, and on their eves, the solemn divine office is celebrated, and that the pastor or rector and other ministers of the church assist at them in their official capacity. In regard to other priests and clerics of the city, the regulations of particular law shall be observed.

Concerning the public celebration of the divine office among Oriental Catholics cf. the commentary to c. 76.

CANON 402. # 1. The bishop can everywhere in his eparchy exercise the pontifical functions, even in exempt places, but not outside the eparchy without the express or at least the reasonably presumed consent of the local Hierarch, and if there is question of an exempt church, the consent of the superior.

2. The bishop can do the same in a stauropegial church with at least the presumed permission of the patriarch.

Postquam Apostolicis gave in c. 307 a definition what pontifical functions include (cf. commentary to c. 185 # 1, 15).

CANON 403. # 1. Although the bishops have a coadjutor, they are still obliged by law to reside in the eparchy.

2. Except for the occasion of the A d L i m i n a visit, or, according to the rule of particular law, of a visit to the patriarch, of synods in which they must participate, or because of the duties resulting from a state office lawfully attached to their Churches, they can be absent, in proportion to the occasion, not more than two, or at the utmost three months, either continuous or interrupted in a year, provided care is taken that no harm is caused by their absence to their eparchy. This time cannot be combined either with the time granted to them on the occasion of their promotion, or the A d L i m i n a visit, or the participation in a synod, or with the vacation time of the following year.

3. They shall not be away from the cathedral church from Christmas Eve till Epiphany, during Lent and on Easter and Pentecost, except for a grave and urgent reason.

Oriental Rite bishops are permitted, differently from those of the Latin Rite (c. 338 # 3 CIC), to be absent during the time preceding Christmas. Oriental Rites know a pre-Christmas penitential season, but the liturgical texts are not so developed toward the formation of an Advent as in the Latin Rite; Lent still retains its uniqueness in the annual liturgical cycle.

4. If they were unlawfully absent from the eparchy for more than six months:

1. the bishop subject to a patriarch shall be forced by the patriarch, even with suitable penalties if it is necessary, to resume residence; the bishop subject to an archbishop shall be denounced by the archbishop to the Apostolic See;

2. an archbishop shall be denounced to the Apostolic See by the highest-ranking metropolitan, or if there is none in the archiepiscopate, by the senior bishop of the province;

3. outside patriarchates and archiepiscopates the metropolitan shall be denounced to the Apostolic See by the highest-ranking bishop in residence; a bishop subject to a metropolitan, by the metropolitan; a bishop not subject to any metropolitan, or an apostolic exarch, by the metropolitan designated according to the norm of c. 323.

CANON 404. # 1. From the time of episcopal consecration, or, if the candidate promoted already possesses it, from the canonical provision, they must also apply the Divine Liturgy for the people committed to their care, on all Sundays and other holydays of obligation, save for particular law which prescribes that Divine Liturgy be applied at least fourteen times in a year, no attention being given to the smallness of the income or to some other excuse.

2. The bishop must apply the Divine Liturgy for the people on the above indicated days in person; if he is lawfully prevented from celebrating, he shall apply on the stated days through another; if he cannot arrange even that, he shall apply as soon as possible on another day either in person or through another.

3. Although the bishop governs two or more eparchies united a e q u e p r i n c i p a l i t e r, or, besides his own eparchy, administers one or more others, he satisfies the obligation by celebrating and applying one Divine Liturgy for all the people committed to his care.

4. The bishop who did not satisfy the obligation defined in the above paragraph shall apply as soon as possible as many liturgies as he has omitted.

CANON 405. # 1. All bishops, even those subject to patriarchs, must make every five years a report to the Supreme Pontiff on the state of the eparchies committed to their care, according to the form prescribed by the Apostolic See; special mention is to be made of catechetical instruction.

2. The bishops subject to a patriarch must also make such a report on the state of their eparchy every five years to their own patriarch.

3. The quinquennia are fixed and common to all, and are computed from January 1, 1954; in the first year of the quinquennium the report must be submitted by the bishops of Europe, in the second, by the bishops of Asia, in the third by the bishops of Africa, and in the fourth by the bishops of other regions.

4. If the year assigned for submitting the report should fall entirely or in part within the first two years of the governing of the eparchy, the bishop can for that term refrain from preparing and submitting a report.

CANON 406. Latin Rite bishops shall also inform the Sacred Congregation for the Oriental Church on the occasion of their quinquennial report of the situation and needs of groups of faithful of another Eastern Rite who reside in their territory and are deprived of a Hierarch of their Rite.

CANON 407. Every bishop must in the same year in which he submits his report come to Rome to venerate the graves of the Apostles Saints Peter and Paul, and must present themselves to the Roman Pontiff.

CANON 408. The bishop must satisfy the aforesaid obligation in person or through his coadjutor or auxiliary, if he has one, or, because of a just reason to be approved by the Apostolic See, through a qualified priest who resides in the eparchy of the same bishop.

CANON 409. # 1. In order to preserve sound and orthodox doctrine, to guard good morals, to correct the erring, to promote peace, innocence, piety and discipline among people and clergy, and to provide for other aspects of the welfare of religion, the bishops must make every year a visitation of the eparchy in its entirety or in part, in such a manner that they visit at least once in five years the entire eparchy either in person or, if they are lawfully prevented, through the syncellus or someone else.

2. The bishop may take two priests from his own clergy according to his personal choice as companions and aides on the visitation.

CANON 410. # 1. The persons, property and pious institutions, even though exempt, which exist within the limits of the eparchy, are subject to ordinary episcopal visitation, unless special exemption can be proved to have been granted by the Apostolic See or according to c. 263.

2. The visitation of exempt religious can be made only in the cases determined by law.

CANON 411. The visitator shall proceed in a paternal manner in matters that concern the scope and purpose of the visitation, without prejudice to the right to take recourse against his orders and decrees; in other matters the bishop, even during the visitation, must proceed according to the rules of law.

CANON 412. The bishops shall endeavor to perform the pastoral visitation with appropriate thoroughness but without undue delays. They shall beware of becoming a burden by causing superfluous expenses, nor shall they or anyone of their company demand or accept, for themselves or for anyone of their party, on account of the visitation, donations of any kind, every contrary custom being abolished. However, concerning the board and lodging to be provided for them and their company, or the transportation and traveling expenses, the local custom of the region shall be observed.

CANON 413. The bishop of the place must be commemorated in the Divine Liturgy and other divine services according to the rules of liturgical norms.

CANON 414. # 1. The bishop has precedence in his territory over all metropolitans and honorary archbishops and other bishops, but not over cardinals, papal legates, patriarchs, archbishops mentioned in c. 324, and his own metropolitan.

2. Outside of his territory, the rules given in c. 37 shall be observed, but in patriarchates, unless particular law decrees otherwise, precedence among bishops of the same grade is decided by the rank-order of the episcopal sees.

In certain Rites, as among the Melkites and Chaldeans, the rank of bishops was determined by the rank of the see usually established by the date of the erection of the see. Metropolitan sees, or sees of bishops who had this title although they were not heads of ecclesiastical provinces, preceeded, naturally, simple bishops. This criterion has now become a common law norm for bishops of a patriarchate; and can be superseded by particular law, which could establish another order of rank, for instance, that which prevails outside the patriarchate, and which is identical with that prescribed by the Latin Rite canon law (c. 347).

CANON 415. # 1. Titular bishops cannot exercise any authority in their eparchy, in whose administration they do not enter.

2. It is fitting that they sometimes apply the Divine Sacrifice for their eparchy out of charity but without any obligation.

CANON 416. Resident as well as titular bishops enjoy, from the receipt of episcopal consecration on, in addition to other privileges enumerated in corresponding sections, the privileges mentioned in c. 185 # 1, nn. 8-12; as well as in n. 2, in respect to censures reserved to the local Hierarch; n. 3, with at least the presumed consent of the local Hierarch; nn. 5, 6, always taking into consideration their own Rite.

CHAPTER TWO

BISHOPS COADJUTORS AND AUXILIARIES (cc. 417-421).

Definition of Office and Appointment (c. 417 = c. 350 CIC)
Limits of Rights and Duties (c. 418 = c. 351 CIC)
Taking Possession of Office (c. 419 = c. 352 CIC)
Duty of Residence (c. 420 = c. 354 CIC)
Expiration of Office (c. 421 = c. 355 CIC)

Resident bishops can receive assistant bishops from the Roman Pontiff or their patriarch. The Latin Rite knows three kinds: an auxiliary given as an aid to the person of the bishop, or one given to the diocese as such, and a coadjutor with the right of succession (c. 350 # 2, 3, CIC). The Oriental canon law has reduced them to two kinds: the coadjutor who is an assistant bishop appointed with the right of succession; the auxiliary who is one who does not have such a right. The auxiliary is in general given to the person of the bishop (c. 421 # 2).

CANON 417. # 1. It is in the competence of the Roman Pontiff to appoint a coadjutor or an auxiliary for a bishop, without prejudice to the prescription of cc. 248 # 1, 4; 327 # 1.

2. A coadjutor is assigned to a bishop with the right of succession; an auxiliary without the right of succession.

CANON 418. # 1. 1. The rights of a coadjutor are to be found in the letters of appointment by the Apostolic See, save for the norm of n. 2;

2. The rights of a coadjutor appointed according to the norm of c. 248 # 1, 4; c. 327 # 1, are determined by the patriarch or archbishop with the advice of the permanent synod.

2. Unless otherwise stated in these letters of appointment, the coadjutor given to a bishop who is totally incapacitated has all the rights and duties of a bishop; other coadjutors have only such as the bishop may have assigned to them.

3. Whatever the coadjutor can do and wishes to do the bishop should not habitually delegate to another.

4. The coadjutor who is not prevented by a just impediment must perform pontifical and other functions which the bishop himself would have to perform as often as it is requested by his bishop.

CANON 419. # 1. In order that the coadjutor and auxiliary may take canonical possession of their office it is necessary that they show the apostolic or patriarchal letters to the bishop.

2. The coadjutor must in addition show them to the board of eparchial consultors in the presence of the chancellor of the curia, who is to record this in the acts.

3. If the bishop's condition of health should progress to such a state that he is not capable of eliciting a human act, the prescription of # 1 is to be ignored, and only the prescription of # 2 shall be observed by the coadjutor and auxiliary.

CANON 420.. The coadjutor and the auxiliary are bound, like the bishop, by the obligation of residing in the eparchy, from which, outside the period of vacation according to the norm of c. 403 # 3, he is not allowed to be absent, except for a short time and with the permission of his bishop.

CANON 421. # 1. The coadjutor becomes immediately on the vacancy of the episcopal see the bishop of the eparchy for which he was appointed, provided he took lawful possession of his office according to c. 419.

2. The office of the auxiliary expires with that of the bishop, unless it is provided otherwise in the letters of appointment.

CHAPTER THREE

THE EPARCHIAL CONVOCATION (cc. 422-428).

Obligation and Time Limits (c. 422 = c. 356 CIC)
Convoking Prelate and Place of Convocation
   (c. 423 = c. 357 CIC)
Participants:
   Clergy to be Summoned (c. 424 = c. 358 CIC)
   Obligation of Participation (c. 425 = c. 359 CIC)
Preparation of the Convocation (c. 426 = c. 360 CIC)
Norms for Conducting the Convocation:
   Topics to be Discussed (c. 427 = c. 361 CIC)
   Confirmation of Resolutions (c. 428 = c. 362 CIC)

Diocesan synods are an institution of the Western Church. Since only bishops have legislative power, especially when assembled with other bishops, a gathering of diocesan clergy cannot be an ecclesiastical synod in the meaning of the Eastern tradition. This was the reason why the Oriental canon law calls this assembly a **conventus,** convention, translated by us as **convocation,** a term used in England for centuries to denote the assembly of the clergy of a diocese, as well as that of an ecclesiastical province.

The canons on the eparchial convocation follow in everything those of the C.I.C., with two additions: Bishops are urged to have an annual conference with their clergy (c. 424 § 4). This presupposes a number of priests, as in many dioceses of the Near East, smaller than found in many dioceses of America and Europe. The Byzantine

Rite Metropolitan of Philadelphia tries to satisfy this counsel by being present at the annual meeting held by the clergy of each proto-presbyterate (deanery).

Another regulation not found in the CIC is the possibility that the particular law of a Rite could entitle other functionaries within a diocese to participate in the eparchial convocation, who would then have a vote even if not invited by the bishop (c. 424 # 1, 8).

> CANON 422. # 1. In each eparchy an eparchial convocation shall be convened at least every ten years, in which only such questions shall be treated as refer to the particular needs and the advantage of the clergy and the people of the eparchy.
>
> # 2. If the bishop rules several eparchies which are united a e q u e   p r i n s i p o l i t e r, or if he has only one in title but another or others in perpetual administration, he satisfies this law by conven-ing only one convocation for all eparchies.
>
> # 3. The patriarch can, because of the particular situation of an eparchy, dispense bishops from the law of # 1, unless this is against a prescription of particular law.
>
> # 4. The custom is praiseworthy according to which the bishop calls together his clergy every year in order to consider with the aid of the experience and advice of each of them what should be done in the eparchy to promote the interest of religion.
>
> CANON 423. # 1. The eparchial convocation is convened and presided over by the bishop, not by the administrator of a vacant eparchy or the syncellus without a special mandate.
>
> # 2. It is to be held in the cathedral church, unless there is good reason to have it elsewhere.
>
> CANON 424. # 1. To the convocation are to be called and must take part, lay persons being excluded:
>
> 1. The syncellus;
>
> 2. The eparchial consultors;
>
> 3. The rector at least of the major seminary;
>
> 4. The protopresbyters;
>
> 5. The pastors of the city where the convocation is held;
>
> 6. One pastor at least from each protopresbyterate to be elected by all who have the active care of souls there, and who must have a   v i c a r i u s   s u b s t i t u t u s   for the time of their absence in ac-cordance with c. 506 # 4;
>
> 7. The superiors of independent monasteries and one of the superiors of each clerical religious institute, represented in the eparchy, to be designated by the major superior, unless he himself is residing in the eparchy and wishes to take part;
>
> 8. Other clerics designated by particular law.
>
> # 2. The bishop can, if he sees fit, call to the convocation also other, or all, pastors, religious superiors, even every secular priest of his eparchy, with the exception of those who are needed for the care of souls in the parishes. Those invited have the right to vote in all mat-ters just as the others, unless the bishop has expressly ordered other-wise in the invitation.

184

CANON 425. # 1. Those who are obliged to come to the convocation are not permitted to send, if they are prevented by a legitimate impediment, a proxy to take part in the convocation in their place, but shall notify the bishop of the impediment.

2. Those who are negligent can be compelled and punished by the bishop with just penalties, except exempt religious who are not pastors.

CANON 426. #1. The bishop may appoint, if he considers it advisable, at an opportune time before the convocation, one or several commissions composed of the clergy of the see city and the eparchy, which assemblage shall prepare the subjects for discussion at the convocation.

2. Before the sessions of the convocation open a schedule of the decrees to be enacted shall be given by the bishop to all who are invited and actually came.

CANON 427. All questions proposed shall be submitted in the preliminary sessions, under the presidency of the bishop in person or of his delegate, to the free discussion of the participants.

CANON 428. The only legislator in the eparchial convocation is the bishop, the others having only a consultative vote. He alone subscribes the laws passed in the convocation, which, if they are promulgated in the convocation, begin thereby their obligatory force, unless it is decreed otherwise.

CHAPTER FOUR

THE EPARCHIAL CURIA.

GENERAL PRINCIPLES (cc. 429-431).

Composition (c. 429 = c. 363 CIC)
Appointment (c. 430 = c. 364 CIC)
Secrecy (c. 431 = new)

The government of a diocese demanded always that the bishop be aided by certain officials, who constituted the diocesan, eparchial or episcopal curia. They were under the bishop's complete authority, not excluding the econome, although the bishop, according to the strict order of ecumenical councils, had to cede to him the actual handling of the temporal administration of property belonging to the diocese.

However, under the influence of Protestant ideas, which were directed against the monarchic status of the bishop, the Austrian and Russian governments introduced in the 18th century in the ecclesiastical administration of their respective countries a collegiate management of the affairs of the diocese. Each bishop had to have a consistory or board, composed of the members of his cathedral chapter, augmented by other consistorial councillors, some of whom were laymen. All business, including marriage dispensations, relaxation of fast, abstinence and dispensation from vows, etc., were

185

transacted **collegialiter** by majority vote, at weekly sessions of the consistory. The bishop could reject their resolutions, but he often was unable to enforce his own decisions.

A consistorial system of diocesan administration, guided by Catholic principles concerning the authority of the bishop, persisted till the end of World War II in the Ukrainian dioceses of Galicia, in the Byzantine Rite dioceses of Czechoslovakia, Hungary and Romania. Its existence is not reprobated by the new Oriental canon law, provided the authority and responsibility of the bishop is safeguarded. **Sollicitudinem Nostram** has in c. 41 # 2, the provision that eparchial judges shall be elected in an eparchial convocation, unless particular law stipulates that the office of judge be discharged by the members of the eparchial consistory.

CANON 429. # 1. The eparchial curia consists of those persons who assist the bishop, or whoever rules the eparchy in the place of the bishop, in the government of the whole eparchy.

2. To the curia belong therefore: the syncellus, the econome, the accountant, the vicar judicial, the chancellor, the promotor of justice, the defender of the bond, the eparchial judges and examiners, the pastor consultants, the auditors, the notaries, the bailiffs and constables.

3. These offices can be joined in the same person, if necessity or opportunity advises it, with other offices, not excluded those to which the care of souls is assigned, unless this is against their very nature or contrary to law.

CANON 430. # 1. The appointment of those who are to hold the aforesaid offices or positions shall be done in writing, according to the norm of c. 101.

2. Those appointed must:

1. take an oath before the bishop that they will faithfully attend to their office or appointment without respect of persons;

2. transact their respective duties under the authority of the bishop according to the rules of law;

3. keep the secret within the limits and according to the manner determined in law or by the bishop.

CANON 431. # 1. In addition to the offices mentioned in c. 429 # 2 the bishop can, even permanently, if the needs or the advantage of the eparchy demands it, also appoint other officials of the curia, in regard to whom the prescription of c. 430 # 2 shall be followed.

2. The bishop can demand secrecy from the officials, also from those appointed only for one matter, and even have them confirm it with an oath, if he sees fit.

Article One

THE SYNCELLUS AND THE ECONOME

THE SYNCELLUS (cc. 432-437)

Definition, Appointment, Plurality of Syncelli
(c. 432 = c. 366 ## 1, 2, 3 CIC)
Qualifications (c. 433 = c. 367## 1, 3 CIC; # 4 = new)

Power of Syncellus (c. 434 #1, 1; # 2 = c. 368 CIC;
1, 2 = new)
Duties (c. 435 ## 1, 2 = c. 369 CIC; # 3 = new)
Honorary Privileges (c. 436 = c. 370 CIC)
Expiration of Office (c. 437 # 1 = c. 371 CIC; # 2 = new)

CANON 432. # 1. Whenever the proper government of the eparchy demands it, a syncellus is to be appointed by the bishop, to help him in the entire territory with ordinary jurisdiction.

When monks were appointed bishops, and this became an exclusive rule quite soon in the whole East, they continued their monastic life by taking with them a companion, who stayed in the same living quarters, appropriately called a cell. This secretary and aide received the name of **synkellos**, i.e., one who lives in the same cell. It was natural that he as the confident of the bishop should occupy a very conspicuous position in the diocese, overshadowed only by that of the more important econome. However, when among Catholics, under the influence of the Latin Rite, the institution of the vicar general was introduced, the existing **alter ego** of the bishop, the syncellus, was vested with the new office, which gave him precedence over all other dignitaries.

Some groups among the dissidents have developed the office of a permanent delegate of the diocesan bishop, and they sometimes give him the title of syncellus, or protosyncellus, although in most dissident Churches these are honorary titles of lesser importance.

 # 2. The syncellus is freely appointed by the bishop, who can remove him at his will.

 # 3. One syncellus only shall be appointed, unless the size of the eparchy or another reasonable cause should require several. However, for an absent or impeded syncellus the bishop can appoint another, who will substitute for him.

 # 4. 1. If in a diocese of the Latin Rite there are communities of faithful of the Oriental Rite, a syncellus shall be appointed to take care of them. If possible, he should be of an Eastern Rite, otherwise, a Latin Rite priest may be appointed, who is qualified and well versed in Oriental matters.

2. This syncellus should show towards baptized non-Catholics of the Oriental Rite complete charity and prudent zeal.

The IV Lateran Council (1215), having in mind the ecclesiastical situation of Cyprus, demanded that the Latin Rite bishops should appoint a vicar or auxiliary bishop if the number of Oriental faithful of the diocese warranted it. The appointment of more than one vicar general in a Latin Rite diocese because of **"rituum diversitas"** was mentioned in c. 306 # 3 CIC.

Such a vicar general could be appointed for the care of all Oriental Rite Catholics, or of only one or several Rites. He should be preferably of the Oriental Rite, but we can envisage the case where a Latin Rite priest could be well suited, especially if he is to care for several Oriental Rites.

No such vicar general exists at this time in any Latin Rite diocese of the United States or Canada. The Archdiocese of Philadelphia had several decades ago a special vicar general for Oriental Rite Catholics. The reason for not making use of the appointment of such a vicar general is the small number of Oriental faithful under the jurisdiction of the individual Latin Rite ordinary. The Archdiocese of Boston, Mass., has the largest number of Oriental parishes under its jurisdiction, namely seven: Three Maronite, three Melkite, and one Armenian.

A vicar general for Orientals was appointed by the Archbishop of Vienna (Austria) to whom the Byzantine Rite Ukrainian-Romanian parish of St. Barbara was subjected by the Holy See. The territory of that parish extended over the entire Austrian Republic and eight dioceses. During World War II the number of faithful and clergy increased by immigration so greatly that its pastor was appointed vicar general for all Catholics of his Rite in Austria.

Another such appointment was made by the Archbishop of Paris. The vicar general was a Latin Rite priest who was soon elevated to the episcopacy and appointed auxiliary to the archbishop. An identical solution was adopted by the Holy See in 1959 for the Orientals in Argentina, now under the jurisdiction of the Archbishop of Buenos Aires.

When in 1952 the Holy See erected in Brazil an independent ordinariate for all Oriental Rite Catholics and appointed the Latin Rite Archbishop of Rio de Janeiro its titular, he in turn appointed for two of the several Oriental Rites distinct vicars general.

If the Latin Rite ordinary should not deem it necessary to appoint a vicar general for his Oriental Rite faithful, he may nevertheless wish to centralize their care and supervision, and may appoint instead a priest to whom he assigns certain defined tasks. Such a priest may be conveniently called a **delegate**. He may also be appointed from among the clergy of any Rite, for one, or all Oriental Rites represented in the diocese.

A delegate of this kind is mentioned in c. 87 # 3 of **Crebrae Allatae** as the rector of an Oriental Rite church or another priest in charge of faithful who do not have a pastor of their own Rite. Such a priest may be appointed especially to be in charge of all marriage cases of certain of the faithful, and receive a general delegation to assist at their marriages within the entire territory of the diocese.

CANON 433. # 1. The syncellus shall be a celibate priest of the secular clergy, not younger than thirty years, a doctor or master in theology or canon law, or at least truly versed in these disciplines, commendable for sound doctrine, probity of life, prudence and experience.

Cleri Sanctitati reflects faithfully the historical development of the institution of the Eastern Churches. Bishops could be assumed from among the monks, but also from the widowed secular clergy, and even married priests could aspire to become bishops if their wives entered a monastery while the husband took summarily monastic vows. Canon 69 demands that the candidate for the episcopal dignity simply be free of marriage bonds, i.e., either a celibate or widowed priest, or one whose previous marriage had

188

been dissolved according to the norms of Catholic marriage law. For the syncellus, who in former times was always taken by the bishop from among the monks, more is demanded, namely, that he be a celibate priest, one who has never been married, or perhaps at the most one whose marriage had been terminated before the reception of the subdiaconate.

A syncellus must be of the secular clergy. In an exarchy with a territory of its own (c. 364 # 4) he will be naturally a member of the monastery clergy. In other cases, a religious would need a dispensation to be appointable as syncellus. There are no dioceses in the Eastern Churches entrusted to a religious institute, and the corresponding provision of the CIC is not repeated here.

An oversight of the codificators of the CIC has been eliminated. In c. 331 # 1, 5, of the CIC, it was stipulated as a qualification for a future bishop that he should be a doctor or master in theology o r in canon law, while c. 367 # 1 demanded that his subordinate vicar general should preferably be a doctor or master in theology a n d in canon law. **Cleri Sanctitati** has now also for the syncellus the same requirement as for the bishop, and the "**and**" is changed to "**or**".

> # 2. **The office of syncellus shall not be given to blood relatives of the bishop to the third degree inclusive (Oriental computation), or, excepting the case of necessity, to a pastor and others having the care of souls.**

> # 3. **The bishop is not forbidden to take the syncellus from another eparchy.**

Canon 367 # 3 CIC has the rather odd provision that the bishop is not forbidden to appoint as vicar general a priest of his own diocese. Particular law, in force before the CIC, demanded in some regions, especially Italy with its numerous dwarf dioceses, that he be taken from another diocese. **Cleri Sanctitati** on the contrary permits explicitly in c. 433 # 3 that the syncellus be taken from another eparchy, also to offset contrary norms of particular law.

> **CANON 434. # 1. 1. Unless law provides otherwise, the syncellus has in the entire eparchy the same power of jurisdiction in spiritual and temporal matters as the bishop, with the exception of those matters which the bishop reserved for himself, or for which the law requires a special mandate of the bishop.**

> **2. The syncellus acts with ordinary power even in those matters that require a special mandate; and an act for which the law requires such a mandate is void if performed without it.**

A disputed canonical problem has found its solution in # 1, 2. It was not clear whether the vicar general who has, in accordance with c. 368 # 1 CIC, received a special mandate from his bishop, acts with ordinary or with delegated power. The answer has a bearing on the possibility of subdelegation. **Cleri Sanctitati** resolves the dispute by granting ordinary jurisdiction to the syncellus when he acts in virtue of a special mandate.

> # 2. **Unless law stipulates differently, the syncellus can execute apostolic and patriarchal rescripts which were addressed to the bishop**

or the preceding head of the eparchy, and in general he has also the habitual faculties granted to the local Hierarch.

CANON 435. # 1. The syncellus shall refer to the bishop the principal acts of the curia, inform him of what has been, or is to be, done, to safeguard discipline among the clergy and people.

2. He shall beware of making use of his powers against the intentions and the will of the bishop, without prejudice to # 3.

3. A favor asked of and refused by the syncellus, and then granted by the bishop without the fact of refusal being mentioned to the latter, is invalid; but a favor denied by the bishop cannot be granted by the syncellus even though the fact of refusal was mentioned, without the consent of the bishop.

CANON 436. # 1. The syncellus enjoys publicly and privately, even in the presence of the bishop, precedence over all clerics, whatever dignity or office they may hold, even though they appear as a college or in procession, unless such a cleric has episcopal rank and the syncellus has not.

2. If the syncellus is a bishop, he has all honorary privileges of titular bishops; otherwise he has, while in office, the privilege and insignia of the dignity which is first after that of a bishop.

Canon 370 # 1 CIC grants to the vicar general precedence over all clerics "of the diocese." Cleri Sanctitati has omitted the mentioning of the diocese, probably to include all possible clerics with a prelatic title, even those distinguished by the Roman Pontiff, or members of the retinue of a patriarch.

If the syncellus is a bishop, he enjoys precedence over other bishops, even of higher rank.

The syncellus who is a simple priest is entitled during his tenure of office to the honorary privileges and insignia of the highest dignity of simple priests known in that specific Rite or discipline or group.

Some examples: In the Armenian Rite he will be entitled to make use of the episcopal mitre and other pontifical appurtenances of the dignity of a **vartapet mitratus.** In the Syrian Rites he will be invested with the rank of a chorbishop. In the Byzantine Rite we have to apply the rules of each group separately. Those who belong to the Ruthenian discipline, including Ukrainians, Carpathoruthenians, Slovaks, Magyars, Croats, the syncellus will be entitled to the pontifical insignia as formerly used by the archimandrites of the Order of St. Basil the Great in imitation of Latin Rite abbots. Pius IX granted in 1875 to the two first dignitaries of the Byzantine Rite metropolitan chapter of Lwiw (Ukraina) the privileges of pontifical insignia "in the manner and form according to which the Basilian archimandrites used to wear." The same rule was adopted by the dignitaries of other Byzantine Rite chapters, and also by these priests who received either from the Holy See the honor of apostolic protonotaries or from the metropolitan that of **mitratus.** Syncelli of this discipline are therefore entitled to such insignia: Prelatic cassock, cincture and kolpak; purple mandyas with four **pomata,** decorated with four crosses instead of with the pictures of the four evangelists, but without the three **potamoi** or horizontal stripes; pectoral cross, ring, mitre, staff, hypogonation.

CANON 437. # 1. The jurisdiction of the syncellus expires by his resignation according to the norm of cc. 126-133, or by the revocation of the bishop made known to him, or by the vacancy of the eparchial see, save for the prescription of c. 469; it is suspended when the episcopal jurisdiction becomes suspended.

2. The jurisdiction of the syncellus of the patriarch's own eparchy does not expire with the death of the patriarch, but he is bound by law that during the vacancy of the see nothing new shall be undertaken.

According to the law of CIC the jurisdiction of the vicar general follows in all the vicissitudes of the jurisdiction of his bishop. If the bishop loses the jurisdiction by death, resignation, transfer, etc., his appointee ceases automatically to be vicar general. **Cleri Sanctitati** has the same rule for eparchies outside of patriarchates (c. 469). Within patriarchates it is the right of the patriarch, not of the diocesan consultors, to appoint the administrator of the diocese, and the syncellus consequently continues in his office until the arrival of the administrator. When the patriarchal see itself becomes vacant, the syncellus of the patriarch's own eparchy cannot expect the arrival of an administrator, but continues in his office till the enthronement of a new patriarch.

THE ECONOME

Accounting Office, Qualifications, Duties (c. 438).

CANON 438. # 1. For the administration of ecclesiastical property owned by the eparchy itself, an office is to be established in the curia, which shall consist of the econome in accordance with c. 429 # 2, an accountant, and other necessary officials.

The Latin Rite canon law knows an econome as a separate official in the diocesan administration only during the vacancy of the see, when the chapter of canons or the diocesan consultors must elect, besides a vicar capitular or spiritual administrator of the diocese, also an econome, although both offices can be united in the same person (cc. 432, 433 CIC). When the see is occupied, the titular is also the econome or administrator **ex officio** of the temporal property of the diocese.

In Oriental canon law a special, permanent office of diocesan econome existed from the very early days of the Church, dating back to the fourth century at least, i.e., to the time after the persecutions, when it became possible to own publicly real estate. A law of the Emperors Honorius and Arcadius, enacted in 398, mentions the office of the diocesan econome as if it were existing everywhere. The twenty-sixth canon of the Ecumenical Council of Chalcedon (451) demands strictly that each bishop must appoint an econome who is to have the actual management of the temporal goods belonging to the diocese, although under the authority of the bishop. Later councils established who of the higher hierarchs is to supply for the neglect of a bishop or metropolitan to appoint an econome in his diocese.

The office of an econome grew in importance when the Church property increased. He became soon the first dignitary in a diocese after the bishop. The econome was normally a deacon, following in that the apostolic tradition, and the reception of the presbyterate was regarded as rendering him disqualified for this office. There are known instances of forceful ordination of an econome to the priesthood in order to remove him from this influential position.

The development of the office of syncellus (vicar general) diminished the importance of the econome in the management of the diocese. In many Catholic Oriental groups Latin Rite principles were adopted, and the office of econome **sede plena** was eliminated. The renaissance of the diocesan econome in the new Oriental canon law codification is a return to an Eastern tradition and to the idea for which it stands, namely, that the bishop as head of the diocese should be relieved, in agreement with or against his personal inclinations, from the temporal management, always of mere incidental import, in order to be free to devote all his efforts to the pastoral aspects of his official duties.

 # 2. 1. The econome must possess the qualifications which are required of the patriarchal econome according to c. 299 # 2, n. 2.

2. The econome can have, if necessary, one or several associates or aides, even lay persons.

 # 3. It is the task of the econome under the authority of the bishop to administer the property of the eparchy, to supervise the administration of ecclesiastical property in the entire eparchy, to make provision for its preservation, protection and increase, to supply for the neglect of local administrators, and to administer in person whatever property lacks an administrator designated by law.

The existence of the office of an eparchial econome means that the bishop is not entitled to act as immediate administrator of the diocesan property. Although everything has to be managed according to the instructions of the bishop, who has the right and duty to control, inspect and supervise the temporal administration, it is the right and duty of the eparchial econome to be in direct charge of the administration.

 # 4. The econome must render an annual account of his administration to the bishop, and whenever else it is requested from him. The bishop, assisted by at least one consultor, shall examine the accounts submitted by the econome, check the cash on hand, conduct or have conducted appropriate inspections of the property, documents, securities, even unexpectedly.

Article Two

THE CHANCELLOR AND OTHER NOTARIES AND THE EPARCHIAL ARCHIVES

THE CHANCELLOR AND THE NOTARIES (cc. 439-441)

The Chancellor (c. 439 = c. 372 CIC)
The Notaries:
Definition, Duties, Qualifications, Appointment, Removal
(c. 440 = c. 373 CIC)
Limits of Authority (c. 441 = c. 374 CIC)

CANON 439. # 1. In every curia the bishop shall appoint a chancellor, who must be a priest, and whose office is principally to keep the acts of the curia in the archives, to arrange them in chronological order, and to make an index of the same.

2. If need be, a vice-chancellor or vice-archivist can be appointed to his assistance.

3. The chancellor is by his very office a notary.

CANON 440. # 1. The bishop can appoint, besides the chancellor, also other notaries, whose signature on documents shall give them public authenticity.

2. Such notaries can be appointed either for any acts or for judicial acts only, or for acts of a certain cause or affair.

3. If there is a dearth of clerics, notaries can be appointed from among laymen; however, the notary in criminal matters of clerics must be a priest.

4. The chancellor and the other notaries must be of irreprehensible reputation and above all suspicion.

5. The chancellor and the notaries can be removed and suspended by him who appointed them or by his successor or superior, but not by the administrator of a vacant eparchy, except with the consent of the eparchial consultors.

CANON 441. # 1. The office of notaries is:

1. to draw up the acts or instruments concerning decisions, requests, judicial citations and intimations, decrees, sentences, or other acts for which their help is required;

2. to consign faithfully to writing the proceedings, adding the place, the date, the month and the year, and their own signatures;

3. to transcribe the acts or instruments from the files on demand of those who lawfully request it, observing the pertinent regulations, and to declare their transcripts conformable with the originals.

2. The notary cannot draw up acts outside the territory of the bishop who appointed him, nor for affairs for which he was not lawfully appointed.

THE EPARCHIAL ARCHIVES

The Public Eparchial Archives:
Establishment and Structure (c. 442 = c. 375 CIC).
Catalogue, Preservation of Documents
(c. 443 = c. 376 CIC)

CANON 442. # 1. The bishop shall establish in a safe and suitable place the eparchial archives or records, in which the documents and writings that concern spiritual as well as temporal affairs of the eparchy are orderly and systematically preserved under lock and key.

2. An inventory or catalogue of the documents which are preserved in the archives shall be made with all care and consideration, containing a brief summary of each document.

CANON 443. # 1. Each year, within the first two months, the inventory or catalogue shall be brought up to date in respect to the documents which were written the last year or were otherwise neglected.

2. The bishops shall diligently inquire concerning documents withdrawn and kept elsewhere, and they shall make use of all necessary means to have these documents returned to the archives.

CANON 444. # 1. The archives must be kept locked, and no one is allowed to enter them without the permission of the bishop himself or of the syncellus together with that of the chancellor.

2. Only the chancellor shall have a key to it.

CANON 445. # 1. It is not allowed to remove documents from the archives without the bishop's or the syncellus' permission, and they shall be returned to their place as soon as possible, but always within three days. The bishop alone can prolong this time; however, such extension should not easily be granted.

2. Whoever takes any document out of the archives shall leave with the chancellor a receipt over his own signature.

CANON 446. # 1. The bishops shall in addition have other secret archives, or at least a chest or vault, well locked and closed, which cannot be moved from its place, and where secret documents shall be preserved with all caution. Each year, as soon as possible, the documents of criminal trials concerning immoral conduct shall be burned, if the guilty persons have passed this life, or if ten years have elapsed since their sentencing, in which latter case a brief summary of the case and the text of the final sentence shall be retained.

2. An inventory or catalogue of the secret archives or chest shall also be prepared according to c. 442 # 2.

3. These archives or chest should be so constructed that they can be opened only by the use of two distinct keys, one to be kept by the bishop or apostolic administrator, the other by the syncellus, or if there is no syncellus, by the chancellor of the curia.

 # 4. The bishop or apostolic administrator in person and alone, without any witness, can open and inspect the archives or secret chest when there is a need of it, and must lock them again with both keys.

CANON 447. As soon as the bishop has lawfully taken possession of the administration of the eparchy, he shall appoint a priest who in case of vacancy or impediment of the see shall take the key of the secret records or archives which was kept by the bishop.

CANON 448. **# 1.** Except if an apostolic administrator has been appointed for the eparchy:

1. in case the see is impeded in its jurisdiction as foreseen in c. 467 # 1, the priest mentioned in c. 447 shall deliver the key to the priest who was designated by the bishop to be in charge of the eparchy, but he retains the key if the syncellus is in charge;

2. in case the see is vacant or impeded as foreseen in c. 467 # 2, the priest mentioned in c. 447 shall deliver the key to whoever is in charge of the eparchy, immediately after his appointment. The syncellus or chancellor shall at the same time remit the other key kept by him to the first eparchial consultor.

 # 2. Prior to handing over the keys to those to whom they are to be delivered according to # 1, the syncellus or chancellor and the priest mentioned in c. 447 shall affix the curial seals to the archives or record chest.

CANON 449. **# 1.** The archives or record chest shall never be opened, nor shall the seals be removed, except in case of urgent necessity, and then by the administrator of the vacant eparchy himself in the presence of two eparchial consultors, who shall see that no document be removed from the archives. The administrator alone can inspect the documents preserved in the archives, in the presence of the same eparchial consultors, but never remove them. The archives shall be again resealed after the inspection.

 # 2. At the arrival of the new bishop, if the seals had been removed and the archives or record chest opened, the administrator of the vacant eparchy shall prove the existence of the urgent necessity which advised it.

CANON 450. **# 1.** The bishops shall see that inventories or catalogues of the archives of cathedral and parish churches, of confraternities, and of ecclesiastical institutions also, be set up in two copies, of which one is to be kept in the respective archives, the other in the eparchial archives.

 # 2. Original documents shall not be removed from the above mentioned archives, except according to c. 445.

CANON 451. **# 1.** Documents in archives of parishes and curias which are not of a secret character may be freely inspected, with the previous permission of the competent ecclesiastical authority, by those who prove their interest, and they can demand also that at their own expense authentic transcripts be made and delivered to them.

 # 2. The chancellors of curias, pastors, and other custodians of archives shall in exhibiting documents and in transcribing them and releasing such transcripts observe the regulations prescribed by the legitimate ecclesiastical authority, and shall consult the local Hierarch in doubtful cases.

Article Three

THE EPARCHIAL EXAMINERS AND THE PASTOR CONSULTANTS (cc. 452-457)

Appointment and Qualifications (c. 452 = c. 385 CIC)
Replacement (c. 453 = c. 386 CIC)
Expiration of Office (c. 454 = c. 387 CIC)
Removal (c. 455 = c. 388 CIC)
Duties (c. 456 = c. 389 CIC)
Compatibility of the Two Offices (c. 457 = c. 390 CIC)

CANON 452. # 1. 1. In every eparchy there shall be eparchial examiners and pastor consultants, who are all to be appointed in the eparchial convocation, the bishop proposing, the convocation approving them, without prejudice to particular law which orders that the duties of eparchial examiners and pastor consultants be performed by the members of the eparchial consistory;

2. Also a priest of another eparchy may be designated for the office of an eparchial examiner or a pastor consultant with the consent of his Hierarch.

2. As many shall be elected as the bishop judges necessary according to his opinion, but not less than four and not more than twelve.

CANON 453. # 1. For examiners and pastor consultants who have died or have gone out of office for another reason in the time between eparchial convocations the bishop may substitute others, with the advice of the eparchial consultors.

2. This rule shall be observed also in regard to examiners or pastor consultants whenever no eparchial convocation is held.

CANON 454. # 1. Examiners and pastor consultants, whether appointed in the eparchial convocation or outside of it, go out of office after ten years, or also sooner, if a new eparchial convocation is held. They can, however, finish an affair of their office which they had begun to handle, and they may be reappointed, provided the rules of law are observed.

2. Those who are appointed in place of examiners or pastor consultants who have gone out of office remain in office only as long as those would have remained in whose place they were chosen.

CANON 455. They can be removed by the bishop for a grave reason and with the advice of the eparchial consultors, except if the bishop judges this to be inopportune.

CANON 456. # 1. The eparchial examiners shall faithfully give their services, especially in the examinations for the appointment to parochial benefices as well as in trials prescribed by particular law, as the procedure for the removal or transfer of pastors and of clerics who do not fulfill the law of residence.

2. The bishop is free to make use of the eparchial examiners as well as of others in respect to the examinations of the candidates for ordination and of priests requesting to be approved for the hearing of confessions or for the preaching of sermons and in regard to the examinations mentioned in c. 66.

CANON 457. The same person can be both examiner and pastor consultant, but not in the same case.

CHAPTER FIVE

THE EPARCHIAL CONSULTORS

EPARCHIAL CONSULTORS (cc. 458-463)

Definition, Qualifications, Purpose (c. 458 # 1 = c. 458 CIC; c. 458 # 2 = cf. c. 427 CIC)
Relationship to the Appointing Hierarch (c. 459 = new)
Members ex officio and by Appointment (c. 460 = cf. c. 424 CIC)
Number (c. 461 = c. 425 CIC)
Duration of Appointment and Replacement (c. 462 = c. 426 CIC)
Removal (c. 463 = c. 428 CIC)

The institution of chapters of canons is a development of the Latin Rite, and was taken over only by the Oriental Catholics who lived intermingled with Latin Rite Catholics within the various parts of the former Austro-Hungarian Monarchy. In the meantime large parts of the Catholic Church, as in the United States, Canada, and in the mission countries had evolved a new system with diocesan consultors. The new Oriental canon law decided in favor of the latter, leaving the chapters of canons intact where they existed.

CANON 458. # 1. 1. In eparchies, even in those which are a part of a patriarchate, eparchial consultors shall be appointed by the bishop taking into consideration c. 460, who shall be priests recommended by piety, personality, learning and prudence, and who are to aid the bishop in the government of the eparchy by advice and assistance.

2. Religious can be appointed to the office of eparchial consultor with the consent of the patriarch, if necessity demands it.

Religious are here not per se excluded from the office of diocesan consultors, and should not be in circumstances where they constitute a considerable part of the pastoral clergy, as it happens in extraordinary circumstances. However, they need a dispensation from the patriarch for the appointment, who, outside the Eastern patriarchates, is the Roman Pontiff or the S. Congregation for the Oriental Church.

2. It is the right and duty of the college of eparchial consultors whenever this is not in the competence of the patriarch, also to take the bishop's place in the government of the eparchy according to c. 469 when the see is vacant or impeded.

Eparchial consultors have outside the patriarchate the same duties and rights as those of the Latin Rite. Within patriarchates they do not appoint the administrator of the vacant eparchy, which is a right of the patriarch (c. 469).

CANON 459. # 1. The bishop is obliged to request the consent or advice of the eparchial consultors according to the regulations of the canons.

2. The patriarch must in the government of his own eparchy seek the advice of the eparchial consultors whenever law decrees that a local Hierarch needs their advice or consent. The patriarch, however, shall highly value the unanimous opinion of the consultors, and shall not act against it without a prevailing reason according to his own judgment.

While the bishop cannot, under pain of nullity, act against the majority of his consultors whenever the law orders that he seek their consent, the patriarch is not bound to follow the decision of the consultors of his own eparchy even in such cases, although he is urged to do so.

CANON 460. The econome and first priest of the cathedral church are eparchial consultors ex officio; the other consultors are appointed by the bishop, without prejudice to c. 462.

The econome and the priest in charge of the cathedral clergy are ex officio members of the board of consultors. The syncellus is an alter ego of the bishop; as such he participates in the sessions and work of the consultors, but his vote does not count whenever a majority of the votes of the consultors is required. He is therefore not mentioned as an official member of the board of consultors.

The first priest of the cathedral could be its rector or pastor, or the first dignitary of the cathedral chapter, or a priest with some other title. A temporary administrator would not be in our opinion, a consultor. If for some reason, which must be beyond the limit of common law, a more or less permanent administrator of the cathedral church or parish should be appointed, he would qualify as first priest of the cathedral in the meaning of the canon.

CANON 461. # 1. The number of eparchial consultors shall be at least six; in eparchies with few priests, it is enough to have four; all of them must live in the eparchial city or in neighboring places.

2. Before they undertake this office, they must take an oath that they will faithfully attend to their office without respect of persons.

The econome and the first priest of the cathedral are included in the minimum number of consultors to be appointed. However, if the office of econome should be cumulated with that of head of the cathedral clergy, or either one with that of syncellus, the minimum number will have to be reached by appointing more consultors.

The distance of the domicile of the consultors from the bishop's residence is to be taken morally, and could mean hundreds of miles if this is offset by speedy means of communication and transportation, as it is the case in the United States and Canada.

CANON 462. # 1. The term of office of consultors is for ten years.

2. When the ten years have expired the bishop shall either appoint others in their place, or reappoint the same ones for another term of ten years, which rule shall be followed for subsequent decennia.

3. If any consultor goes out of office for whatever reason before the end of the decennium, the bishop shall appoint, with the advice of the other consultors, unless he deems it inopportune, another in his place, who shall remain in office until the end of the decennium.

4. If the decennium shall expire during the vacancy of the eparchial see, the consultors remain in office until the arrival of the new bishop, who is to attend to the matter according to the norms of this canon within the first six months after taking possession of the administration of the eparchy.

5. If during the vacancy any of the consultors dies or resigns, the administrator of the vacant eparchy shall appoint another with the consent of the other consultors, who, however, needs the confirmation of the new bishop to continue in the office after the vacancy has been terminated.

While consultors of Latin Rite dioceses are appointed for three years, Oriental Rite consultors must receive an appointment for ten years. This is a compromise between the short stay in office of the Latin Rite consultors and the lifelong tenure of the canons of the cathedral chapters.

It is the intention of the legislator that the consultors be appointed in a joint act of the bishop, and that the decennia thereby be established in a fixed and predetermined manner. Interim appointments are for shorter terms, i.e., till the expiration of the current decennium.

CANON 463. The bishop shall not remove consultors during their term except for a just cause and with the advice of the other consultors unless he deems it inopportune.

CATHEDRAL CHAPTERS OF CANONS

Purpose and Duties (c. 464 = cf. c. 427, c. 391 # 1 CIC)
Erection of Chapters and Appointment to Membership
(c. 465 # 1 = c. 392 CIC; # 2, 1 = cf. cc. 394 # 2;
396 # 1 CIC; # 2, 2 = c. 403 CIC; # 3 = cf. 410 CIC
Relationship to the Pastor of the Cathedral Church
(c. 466 = c. 415 CIC)

Chapters of canons were established in the Oriental Church only among those who in the former Austro-Hungarian Monarchy had adopted many features from the efficient administrative system of the Latin Rite, which was sanctioned by the civil government, and which had established a system of mutual support between Church and state. Before World War II ten Byzantine Rite dioceses had cathedral chapters: The three Ukrainian dioceses of Lwiw, Peremyshl, and Stanislawiw (Galicia), two in Czechoslovakia (Munkacevo-Uzhorod and Prejashev), one in Hungary (Hajdudorogh), and in Croatia (Krizhevtsi), four in Romania. Also the Armenian Rite Archdiocese of Lwiw (Ukraine) had a chapter. According to available information, only the cathedral chapter of Krizhevtsi (Croatia) is in existence at the present time.

For appointment as canon it was necessary that the priest were a celibate or at least a widower. There were also appointed honorary canons, who had no vote in the meetings of the chapter, but sometimes worked together with the other canons on equal terms in the eparchial consistories (cf. c. 429). There were also cases of married canons, appointed with a dispensation of the Holy See.

The S. Congregation for the Oriental Church erected in 1940 a chapter in the exarchical monastery (abbatia nullius) of Grottaferrata. This is an anomaly, since the entire clergy of the exarchy is composed of the members of the community, all of equal rights in their conventual chapter. The erection of the chapter qualified the monastery to receive the meager allowance which the Italian government allots to canons as a recompense for the confiscated church property.

CANON 464. # 1. The place of the college of eparchial consultors is taken in all aspects by the chapter of canons of the cathedral church, where one is established. Therefore, whatever the canons assign to the eparchial consultors in respect to the government of the eparchy, either during the occupancy of the see, or when the see is impeded or vacant, is to be understood as applicable also to the cathedral chapters.

2. It is in addition the task of the cathedral chapter to provide for more solemn divine services in the cathedral church.

CANON 465. # 1. The creation or erection, the re-establishment and the abolishment of chapters is reserved to the Apostolic See.

2. 1. The erection of dignities as well as the appointment to the first dignity is reserved to the Apostolic See;

2. However, it is the right of the bishop to appoint to each and every benefice and canonicate in the cathedral church with the advice of the chapter, every contrary custom being abolished and every contrary privilege being revoked, but without prejudice to a contrary stipulation of the foundation by-laws and to the norms of the law concerning benefices reserved to the Apostolic See.

3. Chapters, where they exist, shall be ruled by particular law.

CANON 466. # 1. If the cathedral is also a parish church, the juridical relationship between the chapter, if there is one, and the pastor, is regulated by the norms which follow, unless either an indult of the Apostolic See stipulates otherwise, or a special agreement was entered into at the time of the erection of the parish and lawfully sanctioned by the bishop.

2. It is the task of the pastor:

1. To apply the divine liturgy for the people and to preach at stated times and to instruct the faithful in Christian doctrine;

2. To be the custodian of the parish records, and to issue certificiates of entries therein contained;

3. To perform the parochial functions mentioned in c. 503. To officiate at the customary funerals, which are to be celebrated according to the regulations of law, belongs to the chapter only if it concerns the funeral of a dignity or a canon, even only honorary, or a beneficiary;

4. To perform other functions customary in parishes which are not strictly parochial, provided the choral office is not obstructed, and the chapter does not perform the same functions;

5. To collect alms in favor of parishioners, to accept, administer and disburse such alms, proferred directly or indirectly, according to the wishes of the donors.

3. It is the task of the chapter:

1. To be custodian of the Divine Eucharist; but the other key of the tabernacle or dove must be preserved by the pastor;

Here the ancient eucharistic dove is mentioned, which was suspended from a canopy or baldachin that covered the altar; it contained the Holy Eucharist for the sick. Such an eucharistic dove was recently installed in SS. Cyrillus and Methodius Seminary of the Byzantine Rite Apostolic Exarchy in Pittsburgh, Pa. (USA).

2. To see that the liturgical laws be observed in the functions performed in the church of the chapter;

3. To take care of the church and to administer its property together with the pious bequests.

4. The pastor shall not interfere with the functions and duties of the chapter, nor the chapter with those of the parish. However, in case of a conflict, the question shall be decided by the bishop, who shall especially see that the catechetical instruction and the explanation of the Gospel always be scheduled at an hour most convenient to the faithful.

5. Not only must not the chapters obstruct the pastor in the exercise of his pastoral duty, but they should in addition be aware that the canons are obliged out of charity, especially if there is a dearth of assistants, to lend him their aid according to the manner determined by the bishop.

CHAPTER SIX

THE GOVERNMENT OF AN IMPEDED OR VACANT SEE
(c. 467)

THE ADMINISTRATION OF A VACANT EPARCHY (c. 468-482)

Causes of Vacancy (c. 468 = c. 430 CIC)
Government before Appointment of an Administrator
(c. 469 = c. 431 CIC)
Appointment of Administrator (c. 470 = c. 432 CIC)

CANON 467. # 1. 1. When the government of the eparchy is obstructed because the bishop is in captivity, or banished, exiled, or otherwise inhabilitated, so that he cannot even by letter communicate with his subjects, the government of the eparchy chall rest with the bishop's syncellus, or with another qualified priest designated by the bishop, who acquires in virtue of law itself the authority, rights and duties of a syncellus, unless the Apostolic See has made other provisions.

2. The bishop may in such circumstances for grave reasons designate several priests who are to succeed each other in the office.

2. 1. If there are no such delegates, or if they are impeded in any of the ways described above, the college of eparchial consultors shall appoint an administrator according to c. 470 # 1, without prejudice to c. 249 # 1, 4;

2. This rule shall also be followed when the syncellus or the priest designated by the bishop was unable, for whatever reason, to assume the government of the eparchy;

3. The administrator mentioned in nn. 1, 2, has the authority of an administrator of a vacant eparchy.

3. He who has assumed the administration of the eparchy shall as soon as possible notify the Sacred Congregation for the Oriental Church and the patriarch or archbishop of the obstruction and of having taken over the government.

4. If the bishop should fall into excommunication, interdict or suspension:

1. in patriarchates, the patriarch himself shall meantime make the provision and notify the Apostolic See;

2. in archiepiscopates, the archbishop shall refer the matter to the Apostolic See; but if it concerns the archbishop himself, the highest-ranking metropolitan, or if there are no metropolitans in the archiepiscopate, the highest-ranking bishop shall do the same;

3. outside of archiepiscopates, the metropolitan, or if it con-

cerns him himself, the highest-ranking bishop of the province shall notify the Apostolic See;

4. if it is the case of a bishop who is not subject to any metropolitan, or of an exarch with an own territory, or of an apostolic exarch, the metropolitan designated according to c. 323 is obliged to bring the matter to the attention of the Apostolic See.

Although the possibility of a major archbishop having incurred excommunication, interdict or suspension is admitted, no provision is made for the case this should happen to a patriarch. This omission is an indication of the high esteem the legislator has for the dignity of patriarchs.

CANON 468. # 1. The episcopal see becomes vacant by the death of the bishop; by the express renunciation accepted by the Roman Pontiff, without prejudice to the norm of c. 248 # 1, 3, after the resigning bishop has been notified of the acceptance; by tacit renunciation according to the rules of c. 130; by transfer; and by removal made known to the bishop.

2. With the exception of appointments to benefices or ecclesiastical offices, all acts of the syncellus are valid until he has received definite notice of the bishop's death or of his tacit renunciation; also the acts of both of the bishop and his syncellus, until the authentic notification of the mentioned papal or patriarchal decisions has reached them, taking into consideration the norm of c. 469.

3. A bishop who is transferred to another eparchy must within four months from the receipt of the notice proceed to the eparchy and assume its administration according to the rules of cc. 396, 397. From the day he takes possession of the new eparchy his former eparchy becomes fully vacant, but in the meantime the bishop:

1. enjoys the jurisdiction of an administrator of the vacant eparchy and he is also bound by the same obligations; the authority of the syncellus ceasing entirely;

2. retains the honorary privileges of resident bishops;

3. retains the right to appropriate remuneration according to the rules of c. 479, n. 1.

CANON 469. In case of vacancy, whenever there is no apostolic administrator, or the Apostolic See has not provided otherwise, the government of the eparchy passes in patriarchates, without prejudice to particular law, to the patriarch, but the syncellus stays in office until the administrator approved by the patriarch according to c. 249 # 1, n. 4, has taken possession of his office; outside of patriarchates, it passes to the board of eparchial consultors.

Outside of patriarchates the eparchial consultors have the same duties and rights during the vacancy of the eparchial see as Latin Rite chapters of canons, or the diocesan consultors possess. In an apostolic exarchy the vacant exarchy is governed by the proexarch, and if none had been appointed by the exarch in neglect of c. 384 # 1, that active priest shall take over the administration who is the oldest by appointment to a pastoral office in the exarchy. Differently from the Law of the CIC (c. 371), where the jurisdiction of the vicar general ceases when he who appointed him departs from the diocese, that of the syncellus continues until the appointment of an administrator.

Within the patriarchate, it is the patriarch's right to appoint an administrator for the vacant eparchy. Until such an administrator has taken over, the syncellus appointed by the former bishop continues in his office. It is permitted that particular law provide otherwise even within patriarchates, either accepting the system whereby the eparchial consultors succeed in the administration, or some other mode of interim administration. The patriarch's own diocese will never be without an administrator, since the administrator of the patriarchate automatically also takes the place of the patriarch in the patriarchal diocese (c. 309).

CANON 470. # 1. The board of eparchial consultors must in case of the vacancy of the seee, within eight days from the receipt of the notice of the vacancy, elect an administrator, who is to replace them in the government of the eparchy.

2. If, within the prescribed time, they did not elect an administrator, for whatsoever cause, his designation becomes in patriarchates a right of the patriarch according to c. 249 # 1, n. 3; outside of patriarchates, of the metropolitan. However, if the metropolitan eparchy itself be vacant, or the metropolitan as well as the compro-vincial sees are vacant, it is the right of the archbishop, if the province is subject to him; otherwise of whoever among the actually residing bishops of the province is the senior in rank. However, if it is the case of the archbishop's own eparchy, the right of designation passes to the first metropolitan, or if there are no metropolitans in the archi-episcopate, to the first bishop of the province. The same rule shall be observed if the election of the administrator was invalid because of defect of form.

The patriarch is authorized to supply for the negligence of the eparchial consultors who did not elect an administrator in due time, or for an election which was valid. This provision applies only if particular law in that patriarchate grants such election to the diocesan consultors; otherwise c. 469 is to apply.

3. When an eparchy becomes vacant which is not subject to a patriarch, archbishop or metropolitan, and if the college of eparchial consultors has not elected an administrator within eight days, he shall be appointed by the metropolitan designated according to the rule of c. 323.

4. The eparchial consultors shall as soon as possible notify the Apostolic See of the death of the bishop, and he who was elected by them as administrator, of his election.

CANON 471. # 1. The board of eparchial consultors must elect the administrator of the vacant eparchy in a collegiate act according to the rules of cc. 102-124, without prejudice to specific norms contained in this chapter; and for validity a majority of votes is required, not counting any invalid votes.

2. The same person cannot be elected as administrator and hold the office of econome, any contrary custom being abolished.

The prohibition to elect more than one administrator (cf. c. 433 # 1 CIC) has not been repeated here, since the law is clear of itself; it speaks only in the singular when mentioning an administrator.

While c. 433 # 2 CIC permits joining the office of vicar capitular and econome in the same person, Oriental canon law expressly excludes it; i.e., the eparchial econome appointed by the former bishop continues in his office, but cannot be elected administrator. The separation of the government of the diocese into two departments, one spiritual or pastoral, incumbent upon the bishop or administrator, and the other temporal, with the actual management of which the econome is charged, remains in force even during the vacancy of the see.

CANON 472. # 1. A priest who is bound by marriage vows, as well as one who has not reached thirty years of age, or who was elected, nominated or presented to the same vacant see, is excluded from the office of administrator of a vacant eparchy under pain of nullity.

Only actually married priests are excluded from the office of administrator. Both celibate priests as well as widowers can be elected.

2. The administrator of a vacant eparchy shall in addition be a doctor or master in theology or canon law, or at least truly learned in these subjects, and shall be recommended by integrity of life, piety, and sound knowledge, joined with prudence.

3. If the conditions stipulated in # 1 have been ignored, the prescription of c. 470 # 2 shall be applied, and the acts of the one elected by the college of consultors are void by law itself.

CANON 473. # 1. During the vacancy of the see, without prejudice to norms of law in respect to certain forbidden transactions, the ordinary jurisdiction of the bishop in spiritual and temporal matters passes, prior to the designation of the administrator for the vacant eparchy, to the patriarch, save for particular law; outside the patriarchate, to the board of eparchial consultors; but once the administrator has been designated, the jurisdiction of the bishop passes to him.

2. Therefore, the board of eparchial consultors, and later the administrator of the vacant eparchy, may transact all the matters enumerated in c. 434 # 2.

This canon omitted an addition found in the corresponding c. 435 # 2, referring to the authority of the administrator, who is empowered either to exercise pontifical rites himself, if he is a bishop, or to permit other bishops to do so. The omission is justified, since the general assignment of all power of a bishop to the administrator contains also the above mentioned functions.

CANON 474. # 1. During the vacancy no innovations shall be made.

2. 1. The administrator and the eparchial consultors are forbidden to transact anything that could prejudice the rights either of the eparchy or the bishop.

205

2. The administrator and the eparchial consultors as well as other clerics or lay persons are forbidden to withdraw, destroy, hide or change any documents whatsoever of the episcopal curia.

CANON 475. Neither the patriarch nor the college of eparchial consultors can in the appointment of the administrator retain for themselves any part of the jurisdiction, nor can they put a time limit to the office, or attach other restrictions.

CANON 476. # 1. The administrator of a vacant eparchy designated by the patriarch obtains jurisdiction after he has made profession of faith before the patriarch, which he, however, is not to exercise before he has presented the document of appointment to the eparchial consultors; he shall see that this document be made known as soon as possible to the clergy of the entire eparchy.

2. The administrator of a vacant eparchy elected by the board of eparchial consultors obtains jurisdiction at once after he has made profession of faith, and he does not need confirmation from anyone.

CANON 477. The rules defined in c. 436 in respect to the syncellus are to be understood to apply also to the administrator.

CANON 478. The administrator is obliged to reside in the eparchy, and to apply the Divine Liturgy for the people according to the norm of cc. 403, 404.

CANON 479. Unless other legitimate provisions are made:

1. the administrator has a right to proper remuneration, determined in a synod of the patriarchate, archiepiscopate or province or, if particular law decrees it, by the patriarch with the consent of the permanent synod, or as it is established according to legitimate custom, which is to be taken from the income of the mensa episcopalis or the bishop's endowment or from other sources of income;

2. Other income accruing to the bishop during the time of vacancy of the episcopal see is to be reserved for the future bishop to be used for the needs of the eparchy, save for the norms of particular law which define the manner of expending such income.

CANON 480. # 1. The removal of an administrator of a vacant eparchy, who was elected by the eparchial consultors according to c. 469, is reserved to the Apostolic See. His renunciation, made in legal form according to c. 128, is to be presented to the same board, but for validity it does not need to be accepted by the board. However, the appointment of a new administrator after the former has resigned, died or was removed, belongs to the same eparchial consultors, and is to be performed according to the rules of c. 470.

2. The office of the administrator moreover expires when the new bishop takes possession of the eparchy according to the norms of c. 397 # 3.

CANON 481. # 1. 1. The econome shall discharge his duties under the authority of the administrator of the vacant eparchy;

2. To the econome himself passes the administration of the property which because of the vacancy of the see has been left without

an administrator, unless the patriarch or the board of eparchial consultors makes another provision.

2. 1. The removal of the econome during the vacancy of the see is reserved to the Apostolic See, without prejudice to what is said in n. 2;

2. In patriarchates, the removal mentioned in n. 1 is reserved to the patriarch;

3. His renunciation, made in legal form, is to be presented to the patriarch or the board of eparchial consultors. In order that the renunciation submitted to the patriarch become valid, it is necessary that it be accepted after he has heard the advice of the permanent synod.

3. When the econome loses the right to his office by whatever means, the election or appointment of a new one is a right of the patriarch with the consent of the bishops who have an office with residence in the curia, or of the board of eparchial consultors, by absolute majority.

4. Whatever rights were assigned to the patriarch in the preceding paragraphs are due to him insofar as he enjoys such rights in the appointment of the administrator of the vacant eparchy.

5. The econome must render an account of his administration to the new bishop, and after he has done this, his appointment expires except if he is confirmed in it by him.

CANON 482. # 1. The new bishop must demand from the eparchial consultors or the administrator, from the econome, and from other officials who during the vacancy of the see were appointed, a report of how they exercised their office, jurisdiction, administration, and the specific obligations of each of them, and must attend to those who in their office or administration have been deliquent, although they, having justified themselves, may have been in person or through others absolved and exonerated by the college of eparchial consultors.

2. The above mentioned persons shall also deliver to the new bishop all records pertaining to the eparchy, if there are such which came into their possession.

CHAPTER SEVEN

THE PROTOPRESBYTERS (cc. 483-488)

Definition (c. 483 = c. 445 CIC)
Appointment, Qualifications, Removal (c. 484 = 446 CIC)
Duties (c. 485 = c. 447 CIC)
Protopresbyterial Conferences (c. 486 = c. 448 CIC)
Report to the Bishop (c. 487 = c. 449 CIC)
Right of Precedence (c. 488 = c. 450 CIC)

Very early in the history of the Church the necessity developed of having an intermediary organ between the diocesan administration and the bishop on one side, and the pastoral clergy and pastors on the other. The solutions tried were many; what evolved in the Eastern Churches is the protopresbyter as head of the protopresbyterate.

Christianity was in the beginning a religion of the city and town, while the heathen held theirs in the village (pagus) for a long time, which earned them the name of pagans. For divine services and the administration of sacraments, Christians went to the nearby town or city, where their church was, and where perhaps several presbyters were residing, of whom the chief was the episcopus (superintendent, inspector). When later smaller congregations formed outside the city, priests were ordained for them, who, however, lacked the power of ordaining others. They were under the supervision of the urban bishop, who often exercised his authority through a chorbishop, a name derived from the Greek chora (country). The institution of such country bishops began in the 2nd century and lasted till the end of the 8th century. The synods of Ankara (314) and Antioch (341) endeavored to resolve the difficulties which developed between the country and the city bishops. The synods emphasized the dependence of the chorbishop from the city bishop; he was permitted to ordain deacons and priests only with the previous consent of his superior in the city. In later centuries the chorbishops lost the episcopal character. Wherever a consecrated bishop was needed, an eparchy was established, making the institution of chorbishops superfluous. The title continued, and is even today conferred on clerics in the Syrian Rites. The dignity is sometimes synonymous with that of the vicar general (Chaldeans) or that of the rural dean (Syrians); it is the highest honorary dignity for priests (Maronites). Besides being entitled to some of the pontifical insignia, they may administer certain sacramentals normally reserved to bishops, e.g., ordain lectors and cantors, consecrate churches.

Another way in which a bishop could supervise his parishes was to charge the chief priest of his cathedral church, the archpriest, with the supervision of the city clergy, while for the country parishes a circulating delegate, the periodeut (one who wanders about) was appointed. Because of the difficulties inherent in the coexistence of a chorbishop with the city bishop, synods demanded that the periodeut be substituted for the chorbishop. His faculties were considerably fewer, and he was more dependent on his superior. The periodeut remained as an institution among the Syrian Rites (Syrians, Maronites, Chaldeans).

The temporal administration of the property of the diocese was entrusted to the chief deacon of the diocese, the archdeacon. This position raised him to prominence, and he was often charged also with the supervision of the clergy, especially when he was an ordained priest, retaining — oddly enough — the title of archdeacon. The dignity is preserved among the Copts, Maronites and Chaldeans.

Among the Byzantine Rite Churches the duties of delegated supervision of the clergy were mostly entrusted to a parish priest with the title of protohiereus, protopresbyter, protopapas or protopopa, and even hegoumenos. However, this does not imply necessarily that the diocese was divided into districts. Catholic dioceses in the Near East were not divided into districts until the present time because of the small number of parishes and faithful. The Byzantine Rite diocese of Europe had adopted the Latin Rite system of deaneries and deans.

According to the new legislation, every diocese must be divided into protopresbyterates, headed by protopresbyters. Should this seem not feasible, the matter must be brought before the Holy See or the patriarch (c. 161 # 2). The rights and duties of the protopresbyters are identical with those enumerated in the respective canons of the C. I. C., concerning the **vicarii foranei**, although particular law can change them.

CANON 483. A protopresbyter is a priest who is put by the bishop in charge of the district defined in c. 161 # 1.

CANON 484. # 1. The bishop shall choose for the office of protopresbyter a priest whom he knows to be qualified, especially from among the rectors of parish churches.

2. The protopresbyter can be removed at the will of the bishop.

CANON 485. # 1. Besides the faculties which the patriarchal or provincial synod, or the bishop, either in an eparchial convocation or outside of a convocation, has granted to him, it is the right and duty of the protopresbyter to see especially:

1. whether the clergy of his district leads a life according to the rules of the canons, and satisfies diligently the demands of their duties, especially in respect to the law of residence, the preaching of the word of God, the catechetical instruction of children and adults, and the duty of assisting the sick;

2. whether the decrees which the bishop gave during the sacred visitation are carried out;

3. whether the rules concerning the matter of the Eucharistic Sacrifice are followed;

4. whether the decorum and neatness of the churches and sacred utensils, especially in the preservation of the Divine Eucharist and in the celebration of the Divine Liturgy is accurately preserved; whether the sacred functions are celebrated according to the liturgical regulations; whether ecclesiastical property is well administered, and the obligations attached to it, especially liturgies, faithfully carried out; whether parish records are properly kept and preserved.

2. In order to obtain knowledge of all these matters, the protopresbyter shall at times to be determined by the bishop visit the parishes of his district.

3. It is also the protopresbyter's duty to see to it, as soon as he hears of the serious illness of any pastor of his district, that he receives the necessary spiritual and temporal assistance, and, in case of death, not be deprived of a proper funeral. He has the duty to watch that during the illness and after the death the books, documents, sacred utensils, and other objects belonging to the parish church are not lost or removed.

CANON 486. # 1. The protopresbyter must on days determined by the bishop call together the priests of his district for the conferences of which c. 67 speaks, and preside at them. If such gatherings are held in various places of his district, he must see that they are properly conducted.

2. If he is not a pastor, he must reside in the territory of the protopresbyterate or in another place nearby according to the regulations to be made by the bishop.

CANON 487. At least once a year the protopresbyter must submit a report to the bishop on his protopresbyterate, disclosing not only the good that has been accomplished but also the evils that have crept in, scandals that have arisen, and what remedies have been employed to repair them, and what he has to suggest for drastically obliterating them.

CANON 488. # 1. The protopresbyter should have his own official seal.

2. He precedes all pastors and other priests of his district.

CHAPTER EIGHT

PASTORS

GENERAL PROVISIONS (cc. 489-495)

Definition and Classes of Pastors (c. 489 = c. 451 CIC)
Union of Parishes to Moral Persons (c. 490 = cf. c. 452 CIC)
Parishes Entrusted to Religious (c. 491 = new)
Relationship of Parish to Religious Community
    (c. 492 = new)
Qualities Requisite in a Pastor (c. 493 = c. 453 CIC)
Stability of Pastors:
    Principle of Stability (c. 494 # 1 = c. 545 # 1 CIC
    Degrees of Stability (c. 494 ## 2-5 = c. 454
    ## 2-5 CIC)
    Temporary Suspension of Irremovability (c. 495 = new)

The conditions peculiar to each country and Church were the reason why Catholic Orientals and their dissident counterparts evolved in various regions identical systems of pastoral organization, the chief of which were the following:

1. Dioceses divided into territorial units, presided by one pastor, possibily assisted by other priests and other clergy (deacons, cantors). Such an organization existed among the Oriental Rites in Europe: Ukrainians, Romanians, Russians, etc. It is identical with that existing in the Latin Rite according to the CIC, and that adopted by **Cleri Sanctitati.**

2. Several priests are attached to one church, each having as his parishioners certain families who selected them. For the pastoral care of the poor, the territory is divided into sections, according to the number of the parish priests, each of whom is to be considered to be a pastor, although one may be the rector of the church, possibly distinguished with some honorary dignity. Such a pastoral

organization is in existence in several countries of the Near East, e.g., Egypt, Lebanon, Syria, especially in city parishes.

3. Several priests may be connected with the same church. They take turns on alternate days or alternate weeks, during which time they are full pastors. One of them will be the rector of the church, although all enjoy the same parochial rights. This manner of care of souls is followed in Greece.

4. Several priests may be appointed to the clergy of a church. One of them is the rector of the church and the superior of the other clergy, insofar as he assigns them their share of the daily celebration of divine services, Divine liturgies on Sundays and holydays, etc. The territory of the parish is divided into districts of a few hundred houses or families, each assigned to one of the priests who is their exclusive pastor, the only one entitled to administer the sacraments of baptism, confirmation, extreme unction, and to assist at matrimony for his parishioners, as well as other functions, especially funerals and memorial services. Such a parochial organization is found in some dissident Churches in the Balkans.

Most Catholic Oriental Churches in the Near East had a parochial organization in which the faithful were assigned to pastors according to personal criteria, and one church had several priests. The reason for the evolvement of such a system is its suitability in conditions where the pastoral clergy is married, consequently lead a life apart from each other, and is chiefly subsistent on stole fees. To obviate misunderstandings, which in pecuniary matters arise so easily, and are unavoidable in the division of cumulative stole fees, the separation according to families or territorial districts was to be preferred to the system according to which there is only one paramount priest, the pastor, and subordinate priests, his assistants. However, **Cleri Sanctitati** adopted the parochial constitution of the Latin Rite Church because it has in so many countries proven to be the most advanced and suitable in the conditions of our times.

> **CANON 489. # 1. The pastor is a priest to whom a parish has been conferred i n t i t u l u m to attend to the care of souls under the authority of the bishop.**

The expression "local ordinary" was changed here to "bishop," since wherever there are parishes there is a bishop, and where there is no bishop, but another local Hierarch, namely an exarch, the pastoral units are quasi-parishes, and their rectors are quasi-pastors (c. 160 # 3).

> **# 2. Even when the parish is united with a religious house or with another legal person, a pastor must be appointed for the care of the souls.**

Since a moral person according to Oriental canon law cannot be **parochus habitualis,** the priest who exercises the pastoral duties of a parish which is united with a moral person is called a **parochus,** and not a **vicarius actualis** (cf. c. 471 # 1 CIC).

3. The following persons are considered equal to pastors, with all parochial rights and obligations, and come in law under the name of pastors:

1. Quasi- pastors who are in charge of the quasi-parishes mentioned in c. 160 # 3; and any other priests to whom the care of souls was committed in a certain territory after the manner of pastors.

Priests who are charged with the care of souls in a certain territory but lack the title and character of pastors are quasi-pastors, without consideration of the official title assigned to them. This includes certain temporary arrangements, found especially in Central Europe, which usually precede the erection of a parish, whereby the priest has such title as independent assistant, curate, rector, etc. If a certain territory has been exclusively assigned to such a priest, he will be a quasi-pastor. The question whether such priests enjoy, e.g., the authority to assist at marriages, has been thus resolved in the affirmative.

2. Parochial vicars, if they are endowed with full parochial power.

4. With regard to the major and minor military chaplains, the special regulations of the Apostolic See are to be observed, without prejudice to c. 260 # 4.

Until the present, no special jurisdiction for Oriental Catholics has been set up in any country for faithful in the service of the armed forces. There remains the question whether in countries with a multiple Catholic hierarchy in the same territory Catholics of the Oriental Rites come automatically under the jurisdiction of the military ordinariate, primarily established for Latin Rite Catholics, a situation found, e.g., in the United States and in Canada.

No problem can arise in regard to those Oriental Catholics, serving in the Armed Forces of the United States or Canada, who as civilians are subject to the jurisdiction of the local Latin Rite ordinaries, because they are certainly subject to the jurisdiction of the respective military ordinaries.

For Catholics who as civilians were under the jurisdiction of Ukrainian bishops or of the Apostolic Exarch of Pittsburgh the situation is the same. The military ordinaries have received jurisdiction over all Catholics in the respective armed forces, no distinction of Rite having been made by the Holy See, including also the subjects of the Byzantine Rite ordinaries in both countries.

From this consideration it follows that chaplains need no delegation or permission for marrying subjects of these ordinaries, and in virtue of general principles of interritual law, that they should commit the administration of the sacraments to Catholics of Eastern Rites to priests of the respective Rite, if such are available.

The dependants of the members or civil personnel employed by the armed forces are not excluded from the jurisdiction of military chaplains.

CANON 490. # 1. 1. Without an indult of the Apostolic See, a parish cannot be validly united in respect to spiritual and temporal aspects to a moral person, save for the prescription of c. 260 # 3;

2. By such a union the parish is actually united perpetually to the moral person, and if the latter is a religious one, the parish becomes a religious parish. However, it is excluded that the moral person itself be the pastor.

Oriental canon law does not admit the legal fiction of a moral person being a pastor, not even a so-called **parochus habitualis,** but demands that a priest with the title of pastor be appointed, who in virtue of ordinary jurisdiction and in his own name is in charge of the parish.

3. The property of the parish united to a moral person shall be in respect to administration kept distinct from the property of the moral person itself.

Another disputed question has been settled by the ruling that the property of the moral person with which a parish was united and that of the parish itself be kept apart. This establishes that the parish as such has a moral personality of its own, distinct from that of the **fabrica ecclesiae,** since the church building could easily be, and usually is, the property of the paramount moral person.

If the property of the monastery is exempt from the visitation of the local Hierarch, and subject exclusively to that of the religious superior, the bishop is still entitled to supervise the management of the parish real estate and monetary funds.

The bishop can prescribe, e.g., that a collection envelope system be introduced, and the proceeds thereof and their disbursement be submitted to his visitation. However, if the church is the property of the monastery, built or bought with the money of the religious community, whatever is collected for the building, renovation or decoration of the church, is outside the supervision of the bishop. The parish school, auditorium, social hall, etc., are presumed to be parish property. Whenever the bishop is entitled to levy assessments on parishes in general, he can do so also in regard to a parish united with a monastery, provided the levy can be derived from the income of the parish itself.

2. The union of a parish with a moral person in regard to a temporal property only is excluded.

CANON 491. # 1. The bishop can entrust a parish to a house of religious also for an undetermined time only.

2. The parish does not become a religious parish by such a trusteeship for an undetermined time, but remains a secular one, and for a reasonable cause, observing the stipulations contained in the agreement, the bishop can revoke the trusteeship, and the competent superior as well can give up the parish.

The union of a parish with a monastery is in recent times often replaced with a trusteeship arrangement, whereby the parish is entrusted to a house of a religious institute. The exact conditions under which the institute takes over the duties and rights, especially the relationship to the bishop, are stipulated in a bi-lateral contract.

CANON 492. The prescriptions of the canons on the parish which is united to a house of religious in spiritual and temporal matters are to be understood to apply also to a religious parish given in trusteeship, except if it is contrary to the nature of the matter or to the text or context of the law.

CANON 493. In order that a priest be appointed pastor, he must be of good moral character, possess learning, zeal for souls, prudence and other virtues and qualifications, which are required by common as well as by particular law for a laudable administration of the vacant parish.

CANON 494. # 1. Those who are put in charge of the administration of a parish as its proper pastors must enjoy stability in it, which, however, does not prevent that they all can be removed from it according to the rules of law.

2. However, not all pastors have the same stability in office; those of greater stability are called irremovable, those of lesser stability are usually called removable.

3. Irremovable pastors cannot be made removable without the consent of the Apostolic See, save for the prescription of c. 260 # 1, n. 2, f. Removable ones can be declared irremovable by the bishop with the advice of the eparchial consultors, but not by the administrator of the vacant see. New parishes which are erected are to be irremovable, unless the bishop prudently judges, with the advice of the consultors, that special circumstances affecting place or persons make it more advisable that they be removable.

4. Quasi-parishes are all removable.

5. Pastors belonging to religious communities are always, as far as the individual person is concerned, removable, and they can be removed at the will of the bishop, notifying the superior, as well as of the superior, notifying the bishop, both having equal rights, and the one does not need the consent of the other, nor has one to explain to the other, or to furnish proof, without prejudice to the right of recourse to the Apostolic See and to the prescription of c. 260 # 2.

The character of irremovability confers upon the pastor the right:

(1) to reject a transfer to another parish, provided his removal is not dictated by the good of the parish a quo, and he has not been found guilty of a delict for which the punishment is removal;

(2) to demand that in the case of removal against his will the special procedure contained in law for the removal of irremovable pastors be followed.

In every removal from any office or benefice, the superior has to attend chiefly to three points:

1. The existence of canonical reasons, which are either enumerated in law, or are accepted by legal custom.

2. Natural equity or justice must be observed. This is a demand of natural divine law. If the removal is a punishment, some suffering or pain will be inherent in the remedy adopted. However, the punishment must be commensurate with the delict, and must not affect others than the pastor. Therefore, there must be taken into consideration such circumstances as the age of the pastor, his state of health, his merits, how many years he had been in the respective

parish, etc. If he is married and has to care for a family, the repercussions which transfer will inflict on his family must also be reckoned with. This is a strict demand of canon law, beyond which there is in addition the broader law of charity.

3. A certain legal form, if a special procedure was set up by law.

In respect to the last point only, we can distinguish pastors as to their removability into several categories:

1. **Irremovable** pastors. The specific **procedure for the removal of irremovable pastors** of the Latin Rite is contained in cc. 2147-2156 CIC. No such procedure has been promulgated as yet by common law for the removal of Oriental Catholic irremovable pastors. However, since c. 134 # 2 demands that a cleric holding an irremovable office can be deprived of it by the Hierarch only according to legal procedure, the various Rites and their subdivisions have to follow in the meantime the procedure existing in their particular law, until the Holy See has promulgated the section of the Oriental Code, corresponding to cc. 2147-2156 CIC. If there is none, the Latin Rite CIC shall be followed in virtue of the legal analogy.

2. **Removable** pastors. The specific procedure for the removal of removable pastors of the Latin Rite is to be found in cc. 2157-2161 CIC. As to Oriental Catholic pastors, they can invoke such a procedure only if it exists in their own particular law (c. 134 # 3).

3. Secular pastors, where they exist, for whose removal no formal requirements of law are to be followed can be deprived of their parish without any specific solemnity.

4. A pastor who is a member of a religious institute can be removed by the local Hierarch without any specific procedure. A just and sufficient canonical cause must exist, although the removing Hierarch is obliged to reveal it only to the Holy See. The religious superior can remove his subordinate in addition also for other reasons, which are justified in view of the religious discipline.

However, it must be emphasized that these considerations concern only the formal procedure where prescribed. There is no instance of removal in which the superior (bishop) could dispense himself from taking into account the demands of natural equity. The same is to be said of the required canonical cause. The bishop may not be obliged to reveal it to the removed cleric, although this ought normally to be done, in order to avoid an unnecessary recourse to higher ecclesiastical authorities, but a sufficient cause must exist. The assigning of the legal character of major or minor irremovability to an office and office holder refers exclusively to a formal legal procedure where prescribed. Lack of a sufficient canonical cause would be arbitrariness, which is not admitted in canon law.

All Oriental Rite pastors in the patriarchates of the Near East were removable at the discretion of the bishop. Only the Ruthenian and the Romanian discipline of the Byzantine Rite in Central and Eastern Europe had adopted the respective Latin Rite legislation, and their pastors could be removed against their will only according to the strict procedures enacted for the removal of irremovable pastors. This procedure belongs to the particular law which has followed them in their migration to the American continent, and applies to the parishes of the Ukrainian dioceses of the United States and Canada.

The parishes of other Oriental Catholics in those two countries will have a somewhat different status. Latin Rite parishes are, in the dioceses of the United States, mostly removable benefices. The appointment and removal of Oriental Rite clergy other than those of the Ukrainian dioceses and the Pittsburgh Apostolic Exarchy are governed by special regulations of the Holy See, which will have to be applied to such parishes.

According to the new codification, the irremovable pastor is now also in the Oriental Rites the normal institution. How is this principle to be applied to the existing parishes? Removable parishes can be declared irremovable by the bishop with the advice of his consultors. Is it now necessary that the bishops issue such declarations for each existing parish? Not at all. The law itself declares parishes in general irremovable, provided they possess all the features stipulated in law as essential of an irremovable parish.

Therefore, irremovable parishes can exist only in eparchies, the parishes of apostolic and patriarchal exarchies are quasi-parishes. Among the existing parishes we will be able to distinguish three kinds:

1. Those which manifest unmistakenly all essential aspects of an irremovable pastoral benefice: Territory, faithful, church, pastor, and the necessary income for the upkeep of the parish plant, the support of the clergy, etc.

2. Those which unmistakenly lack one or the other essential characteristic of an irremovable parish, although there could be a well-founded hope that it will develop to one. Whenever a parish has not insured its perpetuity, or is not yet able to provide for all needs, it will be a quasi-parish, the pastor of which is removable.

3. Those where the factual state does not permit a clear decision. It will be the bishop's right to decide with the advice of his consultors to which category they belong.

Since the legal nature of irremovability has a practical application only in the case of the actual removal of the pastor against his will, the bishop is not obliged to make a decision concerning the parish and its pastor before the case presents itself. Most transfers or removals are either not against the will of the pastor, or dictated by reasons of ecclesiastical policy in which the pastor acquiesces, or the right to invoke the formal procedure has been voluntarily waived by the pastor for other reasons. There rarely will be instances in which the bishop will have to deal with this problem.

CANON 495. Local Hierarchs can confer a d n u t u m parishes or quasi-parishes which, according to the opinion of the patriarch with the consent of the permanent synod, have an insufficient endowment, but the Hierarchs shall take care that such parishes or quasi-parishes be provided as soon as possible with a sufficient endowment.

THE APPOINTMENT OF PASTORS (cc. 496-502)

Right of Appointment:
General Principles (c. 496 # 1 = c. 455 # 1 CIC)
During Vacancy of See (c. 496 # 2 = 455 # 2 CIC)
In a Parish United to a Moral Person
(c. 497 = c. 456 CIC)
In Respect to Quasi-Pastors (c. 498 = c. 457 CIC)
Time Limit for the Appointment (c. 499 = c. 458 CIC)
Manner of Appointment (c. 500 = c. 459 CIC)
Exclusion of Plurality of Parishes and Pastors
(c. 501 = c. 460 CIC)
Taking Possession of Office (c. 502 = c. 461 CIC)

CANON 496. # 1. The right to appoint and institute pastors belongs to the bishop, all contrary customs being abolished and any contrary privilege being revoked, with the exception of the privilege of presentation, if it belongs lawfully to somebody, and save for the norms of law in regard to benefices reserved to the Apostolic See.

2. When the eparchy is vacant or impeded in the meaning of c. 467, the administrator or he who governs the eparchy is entitled:
1. To appoint parochial vicars according to the rules of cc. 513-517;
2. To accept the presentation to a vacant parish, and to grant institution to the presented candidate;
3. To appoint to parishes of free appointment if the see has been vacant or impeded for at least one year.

CANON 497. For parishes united to a house of religious, the superior whose duty it is, according to the constitutions, presents a priest of his religious institute to the bishop, who shall give the investiture, observing the norm of c. 500 # 2.

CANON 498. Quasi-pastors of the secular clergy are appointed by the local Hierarch with the advice mentioned in c. 377, unless he judges it inopportune.

CANON 499. The bishop shall provide a vacant parish with a pastor according to the rule of c. 97, unless special local and personal circumstances, according to the prudent judgment of the bishop, advise delay in conferring of the pastorship i n t i t u l u m.

CANON 500. # 1. The bishop has a grave obligation in conscience to confer the vacant parish on the priest whom he judges best qualified for its management, without any favoritism.

2. In judging the candidates there must be considered not only learning but also all other qualities required for the proper administration of the vacant parish.

3. Wherefore the bishop shall:
1. not omit to examine documents which possibly are preserved in the archives of the chancery and regard the cleric who is to be appointed, and prudently gather information, even secret, if he should deem it advisable, even from places outside the eparchy;
2. be guided by the norm contained in c. 66 # 2;

3. subject the cleric to an examination as to his knowledge before himself and the eparchial examiners, from which he may dispense, with the advice of the same examiners, if it be the case of a priest well-known for his theological learning. The examination taken for the first parish suffices if the transfer is made on the proposal and advice of the bishop, but is to be repeated if the transfer occurs on request of the pastor, unless the bishop, with the advice of the synodal examiners, judges that his qualifications still perdure and that they suffice for the new parish. Neither the pastor who was removed from a parish and transferred to another parish, nor the pastor who is transferred ex officio to another parish, is to be subjected to an examination.

Oriental Rite parishes were conferred according to a general competitive examination only among the Ukrainians, Ruthenians and Romanians, in the dioceses of the former Austro-Hungarian Monarchy. At fixed terms priests who were otherwise qualified, because they had successfully undergone the junior clergy examinations and had the established minimum time of service in the clergy, could take the parochial competitive examination which entitled them to submit their request for appointment when the vacancy of a parish occurred.

The system of c. 500 # 3, 3, introduces the necessity of a parochial examination only

1. for the appointment to the priest's first parish, and this even if the appointment is made **ex officio,** without being requested by the candidate. The bishop can dispense the cleric therefrom on two conditions: (1) if he is eminent in his knowledge of theology and associate subjects needed in the pastoral care; (2) the bishop has heard the advice of the synodal examiners. The junior clergy examination cannot be substituted for the parochial examination (Code Commission on November 24, 1920; AAS 1920 574);

2. for successive appointments, if they are to take place on the request of the candidate. The bishop can dispense from this requirement if he judges, with the advice of the synodal examiners, that the knowledge of the candidate manifested in the first examination still persists.

4. In countries where the appointment to parishes is done by competitive examination, this form shall be retained, unless it be the case of the first appointment to a newly established parish.

CANON 501. # 1. A pastor shall have, according to what is said in c. 98, only one parish p r o t i t u l o, unless it be the case of two parishes united a e q u e p r i n c i p a l i t e r.

2. 1. In one and the same parish there must be but one pastor.
2. The local Hierarch shall see to it that customs contrary to n. 1, which are still observed, prudently be abolished.

We have said above (cf. commentary to c. 489) that among the Catholic Oriental Rites of the Near East the plurality of pastors, i.e., several in the same territory, is generally accepted as an institution dictated by practical considerations. Such situations existed before the Latin Rite code also in some dioceses of Italy and other countries, but were completely suppressed by c. 460 # 2. Cleri

Sanctitati takes into account the actual situation and possible difficulties in the application of the principle, and has therefore replaced in this canon the phrase "any contrary custom is rejected and any contrary privilege is revoked" with the admonition that the local Hierarch shall endeavor that contrary customs prudently be removed.

CANON 502. From the moment of the canonical appointment, the pastor assumes the care of the souls, which he is not permitted to exercise before he has, according to the rules of particular law, taken possession of the government of the parish. Before taking possession, or in the act of taking possession, he must make the profession of faith in accordance with the regulations of particular law.

Oriental law lacks in its genuine form the idea of benefice, and therefore also that of taking possession of the benefice or office in a bodily manner. The present canon has substituted for it canonical provision. It is left to particular law to establish rules according to which the pastor shall assume the administration of his office. However, for the validity of his acts only the fact of his having been appointed is significant, and jurisdictional acts performed before the assuming of the administration, as, e.g., assistance of marriage, will be valid, although unlawful.

In addition of making profession of faith, the pastor must also take the oath against modernism, as imposed by Pius X in **Sacrorum Antistitum** of September 1, 1910.

THE RIGHTS AND DUTIES OF PASTORS (cc. 503-512)

Functions Reserved to the Pastor (c. 503 = c. 462 CIC)
Remuneration of the Pastor (c. 504 = c. 463 CIC)
Persons Subject to the Pastor (c. 505 = c. 464 CIC)
Duty of Residence (c. 506 = c. 465 CIC)
Application of Mass for the Faithful (c. 507 = c. 466 CIC)
Celebration of Divine Services and Preaching
 (c. 508 = c. 467 CIC)
Pastoral Care of the Sick (c. 509 = c. 468 CIC)
Supervision of Religious and Moral Teaching
 (c. 510 = c. 469 CIC)
The Keeping of Parish Registers (c. 511 = c. 470 CIC)
The Pastor of the Cathedral Church
 (c. 512 = cf. c. 478 # 1 CIC)

CANON 503. The functions reserved to the pastor, unless common or particular law states otherwise, are the following:

1. To administer the sacrament of baptism with all the prescribed rites and ceremonies, and in conjunction with the baptism, the sacrament of confirmation;

Confirmation is administered in the Oriental Rites together with baptism by the baptizing priest. Two traditions developed during the first centuries of Christianity: one was the administration of confirmation by the chief presbyter, the bishop; and the other was the union of both sacraments in one rite, normally administered only to adult catechumens. Since both traditions could not be preserved at the same time, the West followed that one which reserved the administration of confirmation in normal cases to the bishop, while the East was intent on preserving the joint administration of the sacraments, and therefore had to empower the simple priest to confirm. Consequently, confirmation remained joined with baptism.

Under the influence of the Latin Rite some Oriental Catholic communities (Maronites, Malabarians, Ethiopians) took away the power of administering confirmation from simple priests, reserving it to the bishop or to such priests as had received a special authorization. It seems that this curtailment affected only the lawfulness and not the validity of confirmation by an unauthorized priest. The introductory words of the canon suggest the possibility that such a reservation could be continued.

The administration of confirmation separately from baptism is in several Rites reserved to the bishop, who usually authorizes the pastor for its administration.

2. Unless particular law decrees otherwise, to administer the sacrament of unction of the infirm to those who are in danger of death, and to carry the Divine Eucharist as viaticum to the sick. In case of necessity, or with the permission, at least reasonably presumed, of the pastor or the local Hierarch, every priest can administer these sacraments;

No general custom developed among Oriental Christians publicly to carry the Holy Eucharist to the sick, probably because, when the present form of the cult of the Blessed Sacrament evolved in the Latin Rite, the cradles of Oriental Christianity in the Near East had all come under the yoke of Islam, which excludes every non-Islamic public worship.

3. To announce the banns of sacred ordinations and of marriage, to assist at marriage and to impart the betrothal and the nuptial blessings;

Some Oriental Rites have preserved a special blessing of the betrothal. Human societies have nearly everywhere admitted a trial period before marriage. Since the state of matrimony was considered to be by its very nature perpetual, the trial period had to be in the form of a legal institution, including also the possibility of rescinding the conditional promise of marriage.

In order to give a religious character to the betrothal, Oriental Rites devised a special blessing. Religious fervor often endowed then the legal aspects of betrothal with certain juridical effects, in imitation of marriage, which also had a sacred character, which tended to render difficult or downright to prohibit the rescinding of the contract of betrothal. The result of this misguided zeal was the frustration of the primary purpose of betrothal as a period of trial. Nupturients, therefore, choose not to enter a formal religious betrothal, but formed an informal engagement, to preserve the right of a simple dissolution of the conditional promise of marriage.

Once the betrothal, blessed and entered before the Church, became adequated in essential legal consequences with matrimony, the rite of betrothal had to be performed before every marriage, and was therefore simply joined with the celebration of marriage (coronation) to one liturgical service.

Depending on how far the evolution progressed in each Rite, some Rites have retained a separate ritual of betrothal, while others, as the most numerous Oriental group, the Byzantine Rite, have joined it with the Rite of marriage as its first part.

In Rites which have a separate liturgical service of betrothal, the function is reserved to the pastor, as in all Rites the celebration of marriage itself.

4. To perform funeral services;

5. To bless homes on the days determined by the rules of liturgical books;

The blessing of homes is in Oriental Rites connected with the solemn blessing of water at the Epiphany. Beginning with that day, and continuing for as many days as is needed on account of the number of homes, or the distance at which the parishioners live, the pastor visits each house and sprinkles it with the "Jordan water" which was blessed publicly on Epiphany.

The Maronites, the only Oriental group which reestablished connections with the Catholic Church as a whole, leaving no dissident counterpart behind, were during the times of the Crusades under the powerful influence of the Latin Rite, from which they adopted, in addition to the Epiphany, also the Easter blessing of homes.

6. To bless the water according to the solemn rite of the feast of Epiphany, or on other days determined by law;

The solemn blessing of water on Epiphany is one of the most impressive public ceremonies of the Oriental Rites. It is, if possible, performed on the banks of a river, or at a fountain of a public square. In the residence cities of hierarchs patriarchs and bishops function at the blessing.

7. To conduct public processions outside the church, even from every church situated in the territory of the parish, although they are not filial churches and have their own rectors, without prejudice, however, to c. 522;

Mention of the baptismal font was omitted. Oriental Rites do not preserve the baptismal water but bless it for every baptism. Baptism is not performed in some special place or room, but in front of the altar, on a special table, the so-called **tetrapod** (Byzantine Rite). The imitation of the Latin Rite by some Oriental Catholics, who built separate baptistries, or at least preserved the baptismal water in some other place, was again reprobated, at least for the Ruthenian discipline (Ukrainians, Rusines, etc.) by the Holy See in 1952.

8. To give blessings outside the church with pomp and solemnity, to impart other blessings and to celebrate special prayers in accordance with lawful customs of the various Rites.

CANON 504. # 1. The pastor has the right to the revenue which legitimate custom or taxation, according to the regulations of common law, assign to him.

2. If he exacts more, he is held to restitution.

3. Although a parochial office may have been performed by another priest, the offering nevertheless accrues to the pastor, unless the contrary will of those making the offering is certain concerning the sum that exceeds the prescribed tax.

4. The pastor shall give his services gratuitously to those who are unable to pay for them.

CANON 505. # 1. The pastor is obliged in virtue of his office to exercise pastoral care over all parishioners who are not legitimately exempt.

2. The bishop can for a just and grave reason withdraw from the care of the pastor communities of religious and religious institutions which are situated in the territory of the parish and are not exempt by law.

CANON 506. # 1. The pastor is obliged to reside in the rectory near his church. However, the bishop can permit him for a just reason to live elsewhere, provided the house is not so far away from the parish church that the fulfillment of the duties of a pastor suffers thereby.

2. He is allowed to be absent for forty days in a year, either continuous or interrupted, unless a grave reason, in the judgment of the bishop himself, either requires a longer absence or permits only a shorter one.

The time allotted to Oriental Rite pastors for their annual vacation was reduced, in comparison with c. 465 # 1 CIC, from two months to forty days. This kind of absence does not include those needed for other unavoidable necessities, as, e.g., hospital treatment time for recuperating from an illness, etc.

3. The days spent by the pastor in the spiritual retreat once a year, according to the norm of c. 62 # 1, are not counted as part of the vacation spoken of in # 2.

4. Whether the vacation is taken in one stretch or several, whenever the pastor's absence lasts longer than one week, he must, in addition to a legitimate reason, have the written permission of the bishop and leave behind in his place a substitute vicar who is approved by the same bishop. If the pastor is a religious priest, he needs moreover the consent of the superior, and the substitute must be approved both by the bishop as well as by the superior.

5. If the pastor is forced because of an unexpected and grave cause to be absent for more than a week, he shall as soon as possible inform the bishop by letter, stating the reason for his absence, and indicating the substitute priest, being ready to follow his instructions.

6. Also, when the pastor's absence is to be shorter, he must provide for the needs of the faithful, especially when this is demanded on account of special circumstances.

CANON 507. # 1. The pastor and quasi-pastor are bound by the obligation to apply the Divine Liturgy for the people on all Sundays and other holydays of obligation, without prejudice to particular law which prescribes that the Divine Liturgy be applied ten times a year on the occasion of more important feasts.

2. The pastor who is perhaps in charge of several aeque principaliter united parishes, or who, besides his own parish, is administrator of another or of others, satisfies the obligation by celebrating and applying one Divine Liturgy for the entire people entrusted to his care.

3. The bishop can for a just reason permit that the pastor apply the Divine Liturgy for the people on another day than that prescribed by law.

4. The pastor shall celebrate the Divine Liturgy, when he is to apply it for the people, in the parish church, unless circumstances demand or advise that the Divine Liturgy be celebrated elsewhere.

5. The pastor who is lawfully absent can apply the Divine Liturgy for the people either in person in the place of his sojourn or through the priest who substitutes for him in his parish.

Christian antiquity and Oriental Rite traditions followed implicitly the doctrine that the **fructus ministerialis** of the Eucharistic sacrifice as offered by the priest, which **fructus** can be freely applied by the celebrant for whom he wishes, has indefinite value, which means that everyone for whom, and for as many as, the celebrant applied the sacrifice participated to the same full extent. This sentence was proposed also by some Catholic theologians, but rejected by the majority, which holds that the value is definite. It could, naturally, never justify the acceptance of several stipends for the application of one and the same Mass.

Oriental Rite tradition permitted the celebration of the divine liturgy only on Sundays and holydays, and on some other occasions, specified by law. Dissident Orientals still follow this practice. They accept one or several pecuniary offerings, obliging themselves to include the intentions of each donor in the sacrifice. This practice does not preclude, according to their conviction, that the Mass is also offered for the benefit of the parishioners.

When Oriental Catholics reunited themselves with the Holy See, they accepted the doctrine of Catholic theologians on the application of the **fructus ministerialis,** and followed the practice of the Latin Rite, of accepting only one stipend for each Mass, and of celebrating daily.

As a consequence, also, the Latin Rite legislation on the application of Mass for the faithful was imposed on bishops and pastors. Because of the exiguity of income, consisting only of Mass stipends and stole fees, the number of days of application among Oriental Catholics of the Near East was variously limited: Five times a year (Syrians), six times (Armenians, Melkites), twelve times (Maronites). A few followed the Latin Rite rule (Ukrainians, Ruthenians, Italo-Albanians): all Sundays and holydays of obligation.

The present canon has imposed two limits:

1. Where particular law does not object, the pastors are obliged to apply the Divine Liturgy on all Sundays and holydays of obligation. Which holydays are of obligation is established in their respective Rite, discipline or jurisdiction, by legal custom or by a decree of a synod. For the Ukrainans, e.g., from the former Galician Ecclesiastical Province, the Provincial Synod of Lwiw has

established which holydays are of obligation. Bishops and exarchs can order that a certain holyday be observed by their subjects as one of obligation only in individual cases, not perpetually or habitually.

A bishop can sometimes for an individual case, which does not automatically repeat itself, command his priests not only to celebrate on a certain day but also to apply the sacrifice for an intention of public nature. To order his priests to apply on certain days perpetually, or without a specific public intention, is beyond his powers.

2. Where the particular law does not determine any number, or less than ten applications a year, it is up to the hierarchs of that group: (1) either to establish the number, greater than ten, of annual applications, or (2) to raise the number to ten, and (3) to name the days of application.

CANON 508. # 1. The pastor must perform the sacred functions, administer the sacraments to the faithful, whenever they lawfully request it, preach to the people the word of God, know their flock, and prudently correct the erring, assist with paternal care the poor and the sick, and give his special care to the instruction of the children in the Catholic faith.

2. He shall celebrate in person or through his assistants on Sundays and holydays, besides the Divine Liturgy, at least a part of the office, according to the rules of his Rite and the instructions of the local Hierarch.

Concerning the celebration of parts of the divine office in Oriental Rite parochial churches cf. the commentary to c. 76.

3. The faithful should be admonished frequently to visit their parish churches, to assist there at the divine services, and to hear the word of God.

CANON 509. # 1. The pastor shall take special care, from the fulness of charity, of the sick in his parish, but especially when they are dying, assisting them frequently with the sacraments and commending their souls to God.

2. The pastor, and any other priest assisting the sick, has the faculty to impart the Apostolic blessing with a plenary indulgence at the moment of death, to be given according to the formula contained in approved liturgical books, and he shall not omit to give this blessing.

CANON 510. The pastor shall diligently see that nothing be taught contrary to the faith and morals in his parish, especially in public and private schools, and he shall advance and establish the works of faith, charity and piety.

CANO 511. # 1. The pastor shall keep parish records, i.e., registers of those who received baptism, who were annointed with the sacrament of chrism, of betrothals, of marriages, of those who died. He shall take care also to have the census books as accurate as possible, and he shall make the respective recordings in all these books, and shall keep them with great care according to the custom approved by the Church or the regulations of his own bishop.

2. In the baptismal register there should be noted, besides the administration of the sacrament of chrism, also the fact that the baptized person contracted marriage, unless it is the case of a so-called marriage of conscience, or that he has received the order of a subdeacon, or has made major profession, or has changed Rite, and these annotations shall always be included in baptismal certificates.

3. At the end of each year, the pastor shall send a transcript of the parish records to the episcopal chancery, with the exception of the census book.

4. A pastor to whom in accordance with c. 22 ## 2-5 the care of faithful of a different Rite was entrusted must avery year submit to their Hierarch a statistical report together with appropriate information concerning their condition.

5. He shall use a seal and shall have a depository for documents or archives, where the afore-mentioned books shall be kept together with the bishop's letters and other necessary or useful documents. All this shall be inspected by the bishop or his delegate on the occasion of a visitation or at another suitable time, and shall be conscientiously preserved by the pastor so as not to fall into the hands of unauthorized persons.

CANON 512. The pastor of the cathedral church has precedence over all pastors of the eparchy.

CHAPTER NINE

PAROCHIAL VICARS (cc. 513-518)

The Vicar Administrator:
   Appointment (c. 513 = c. 472 CIC)
   Rights and Duties (c. 514 = c. 473 CIC)
The Vicar Substitute .c. 515 = c. 474 CIC)
The Vicar Coadjutor (c. 516 = c. 475 CIC)
The Vicar Assistant (c. 517 = c. 476 CIC)
Removal of Parochial Vicars (c. 518 = c. 477 CIC)

CANON 513. During the vacancy of a parish:
1. The bishop shall as soon as possible appoint a suitable vicar administrator, with the consent of the superior if it is the question of a religious priest, who is to rule the parish during the vacancy, and to whom an appropriate share of the income shall be assigned for a suitable livelihood.

The vicarius oeconomus of the CIC is named in Cleri Sanctitati vicarius administrator, probably because the term econome denotes in other places the official in charge of the temporal management of church property alone, while the authority of the vicar administrator extends to spiritual as well as to temporal matters of administration.

2. Before the appointment of a vicar administrator the vicar assistant shall in the meantime assume the direction of the parish, unless some other provision was made; if there are several such vicars,

the first one, and if they are equal, the senior in this position. If there are no vicars, then the nearest pastor; finally, if it is a question of a parish united to a house of religious, the superior of the house to which the church is attached. The bishop shall in due time determine which parish is to be considered to be the nearest to each parish;

3. He wo takes charge of the parish according to the manner described in n. 2 must at once notify the bishop of the vacancy of the parish. .

CANON 514. # 1. The vicar administrator enjoys the same rights, and is bound to the same duties, as the pastor in all things that concern the care of souls. However, he is not permitted to do anything that might prejudice the rights of the pastor or of the parochial benefice.

2. The vicar administrator shall in the presence of the protopresbyter or another priest appointed by the bishop deliver to the new pastor or the succeeding administrator the key of the parochial archives and the inventory of the books and documents and other assets belonging to the parish, and shall give an account of the receipts and expenditures for the time of his administration.

CANON 515. The vicar substitute who was appointed according to the rules of c. 506 # # 4, 5, or in the case of a recourse permitted in law taken by the pastor who was removed from the parish, takes the place of the pastor in all matters concerning the care of souls, unless the bishop or the pastor has made some exception.

CANON 516. # 1. Unless it is decreed differently, or was appropriately provided in single cases:

1. if a secular pastor on account of old age, mental debility, ignorance, or other permanent reason, becomes unable to carry out his obligations, the bishop shall give him a vicar adjutor, who shall substitute for him, and there shall be assigned to the latter an appropriate share of the income;

2. however, if it is the case of a religious pastor, the rule of c. 494 # 5 shall be observed.

While c. 475 # 1 of CIC permitted that a vicar adjutor be given to a religious pastor, which in practice was not done, the Oriental codification orders his removal from the pastorate.

2. If the adjutor takes the place of the pastor in all matters, he has all the rights and duties of a pastor, with the exception of the application of the Divine Liturgy for the people, which remains an obligation of the pastor. If he replaces the pastor only partially, his rights and duties are to be defined in the letters of appointment.

3. If the pastor is sound of mind, the adjutor must give his assistance under his authority according to the appointment of his bishop.

4. If it is impossible to take care of the needs of souls by appointing a vicar adjutor, the pastor shall be removed in accordance to the prescriptions of law.

CANON 517. # 1. If the pastor cannot alone take adequate care of the parish, according to the judgment of the bishop, because of the great number of people or for other peasons, one or several vicars assistants shall be appointed, who shall receive a proper remuneration.

2. Vicars assistants can be appointed either for the whole parish or for a certain part of the parish.

3. Vicars assistants of the secular clergy are appointed by the bishop with the advice of the pastor, unless the bishop prudently decides otherwise.

Canon 476 # 3 CIC demands that the ordinary discuss with the pastor the appointment of a specific assistant. Because of the general dearth of priests, selection of an assistant by the pastor is usually impossible. A contrary custom is therefore everywhere in evolution, relieving the ordinary from seeking the previous advice of the pastor before the appointment of an assistant. **Cleri Sanctitati** has taken cognizance of this fact and has left it to the prudent discretion of the bishop whether or not he will approach the pastor before the appointment of an assistant.

4. Vicar assistants of the religious clergy are presented to the bishops, in whose discretion it is to approve them, by the superior who is so authorized by the constitutions, with the advice of the pastor, unless the superior prudently decides differently.

5. The vicar assistant is obliged to reside in the parish, in the manner prescribed by eparchial regulations or legitimate customs or by the bishop. Indeed, the bishop, according to the rule of c. 75, shall prudently see that he lives in the same rectory.

The bishop cannot force married clergy to live together in the same household, but has to procure for them separate living quarters, although they can be under the same roof. Celibate clerics cannot live, as a rule, in the household of married clergy or lay families, except with very close relatives.

6. His rights and duties are derived from eparchial regulations, from the letters of appointment issued by the bishop, and from the commission of the pastor himself. Unless otherwise expressly provided, he must in virtue of his office substitute for the pastor and assist him in the entire pastoral ministry, with the exception of the application of the Divine Liturgy for the people. However, he does not possess by virtue of his office the faculty of assisting at marriage.

7. He is subject to the pastor, who shall paternally instruct and direct him in the care of souls, supervise him, and report to the bishop at least once a year concerning him.

8. If it is impossible even by the appointment of vicars assistants properly to provide for the spiritual welfare of the people, the bishop shall divide the parish or shall apportion its territory.

CANON 518. # 1. If the parochial vicars mentioned in cc. 513-517 are religious, they can be removed according to the rules of c. 494 # 3; otherwise at the will of the bishop or the administrator of a vacant eparchy, but not of the syncellus unless he has a special mandate.

2. If there is anywhere a vicariate which is a benefice, the vicar assistant can be removed according to the norms of law not only for reasons required for the removal of pastors, but also for serious disobedience to the pastor in the due exercise of his duties.

CHAPTER TEN

RECTORS OF CHURCHES (cc. 519-526)

Definition (c. 519 = c. 479 CIC
Appointment (c. 520 = c. 480 CIC)
Rights:
    Negative Limits (c. 521 = c. 481 CIC)
    Positive Limits (c. 522 = c. 482 CIC)
Suppletory Duties in Parish Needs (c. 523 = c. 483 CIC)
Supervisory Rights in Church:
    Admission of Priests for Functions (c. 524 = c. 484 CIC)
    Celebration of Divine Services (c. 525 = c. 485 CIC)
Removal (c. 526 = c. 485 CIC)

CANON 519. # 1. The name of rectors of churches means here those priests to whom the care of a church was entrusted that is neither a parochial church, nor attached to a house of a religious community which celebrates therein the sacred functions.

2. In respect to the chaplains of religious women, of members of a lay congregation of men, of confraternities, or of other legitimate associations, the prescriptions of particular canons shall be observed.

CANON 520. # 1. Rectors of churches are freely appointed by the bishop, without prejudice to the right of presentation to which someone may be entitled; in which case the bishop is to approve the rector.

2. Even if the church belongs to an exempt religious institute, the rector nominated by the superior needs nevertheless the approval of the bishop, or of the patriarch if it is the case of a stauropegial church.

3. If the church is connected with a seminary or a college conducted by clerics, the superior of the seminary or the college is at the same time rector of the church, unless the bishop directs otherwise.

CANON 521. In the church committed to him the rector cannot perform parochial functions.

CANON 522. The rector of a church can celebrate divine services even solomnly, without prejudice to the legitimate terms of the foundation, and provided they do not infringe on the parochial ministry. In case of doubt as to whether such infringement exists, it is the bishop's duty to decide the matter and to prescribe appropriate instructions how it can be avoided.

CANON 523. If the church, in the bishop's judgment, is too far away from the parish church and the parishioners cannot without great hardship go to the parish church and assist there at divine services:

1. the bishop can command the rector, even by threatening grave penalties, to celebrate divine services at hours convenient for the people, to announce the holydays and fast days, and to give catechetical instruction and explanation of the Gospel;

2. the pastor may take the Divine Eucharist, which is perhaps kept there, from such a church for the communion of the sick.

CANON 524. Without at least the presumed permission of the rector or another legitimate superior, no one is permitted to celebrate in the church the Divine Liturgy, to administer the sacraments or to hold other sacred functions; but this permission must be given or denied in accordance with the norms of law.

CANON 525. # 1. The rector of the church must, under the supervision of the bishop and following legitimate statutes and acquired rights, see or invigilate that the divine services be celebrated in the church according to the order prescribed by the canons, the obligations faithfully be satisfied, the property properly administered, provisions be taken for the conservation and ornamentation of the sacred utensils and the sacred building, and that nothing be done which is repugnant to the holiness of the place and the reverence due to a house of God.

2. However, if it is the case of a church which belongs to a religious institute, it is the duty of the religious superior to take care of the administration of the property, the sacred utensils, and the conservation and ornamentation of the sacred building.

CANON 526. The rector of a church, although nominated by others, can be removed at the will of the bishop for any just reason. If the rector is a religious, the rule contained in c. 495 # 5 shall be observed.

THE MOTU PROPRIO

POSTQUAM APOSTOLICIS

THE LAW ON THE RELIGIOUS

The motuproprio **Postquam Apostolicis** is composed of three parts: The law on the religious (cc. 1 — 231), the law on the temporal property of the Church and its management (cc. 232 — 301), and the definitions of legal terms (cc. 302-325).

It was our purpose to collect in this book those canons which concern the law on persons as it is contained in the corresponding sections of the CIC, i.e., in the Second Book or cc. 87 — 725, and as it will appear later in the Code of Oriental Canon Law when it is published in its entirety. We have therefore omitted the canons on the temporal property of the Church, and have translated and commented only on those canons from the third part which concerned legal terms used in **Cleri Sanctitati** or in the law on the religious in **Postquam Apostolicis.**

THE DUALISTIC CHARACTER OF THE ORIENTAL LAW ON THE RELIGIOUS

As other institutions of the Church, so also religious life in community spread from the Christian East to the whole Church. But while in the Western Church it ramified in a gamut of various organizations, such as orders, congregations, societies without vows, dedicated to the most disparate tasks, in the Church in the East it never developed far from the beginnings of monachism in the Egyptian desert. Among Catholics, a number of religious institutes were established according to Latin Rite canon law principles, and others, originally Oriental religious, accepted norms taken from the same source. Only a few Catholic, but all dissident groups retained the characteristics of contemplative monks or nuns, and are governed by legal principles developed and defined during the first millenium.

The codification of the Oriental law on religious was urgently needed, not only because of the intention to produce a complete code of the entire Oriental canon law, but also to help the remnants of genuine Oriental tradition among the religious preserve, and sometimes recreate, their Oriental characteristics. Because of the uncertainty as to what constitutes essential Eastern tradition, and what was a dispensable borrowing from the Western Church, Oriental religious drifted farther and farther toward Latin Rite norms of religious life. The new codification in **Postquam Apostolicis** has permitted that Oriental religious life be organized both according to the Eastern as well as Western traditions. A clear line is drawn:

233

on one side is a complete preservation of the genuine ideals and norms of Oriental monachism, on the other side are the numerous religious institutes which could hardly be engaged in such variegated activities, indispensable to the Church in the circumstances of modern life, were it not for their institutional setup according to Western principles.

Although it is true that the Christian East has preserved the ancient structure of contemplative religious life, we must say that the same ideal is pursued in the Latin Rite Church by many monastical orders. However, essential organizational changes have been introduced, such as the establishing of classes among the members, of temporary or non-solemn profession, etc. Since it was the avowed purpose of the codification to preserve the genuine Oriental tradition in every branch of Church life, nay even to restore it where it had been subjected to the extraneous influence of the Western Church, **Postquam Apostolicis** had to make all such provisions which would permit the continued existence of the monastic state according to its ancient legal structure.

On the other hand, it could not be overlooked that the religious institutes of the Catholic Oriental Churches had undergone since their reunions with the Holy See of Rome a profound influence of the Latin Rite canon law. This should not be explained as a blind imitation, but is to be understood as an adoption and an adaptation of organizational features which had proven themselves as better suitable to tasks to which Oriental religious were called in novel situations. From monks leading a contemplative life in somewhat remote monasteries, living under the obedience of a superior elected for life, they were forced by circumstances to become missionaries and preachers, settled in a larger number of small residences in the midst of cities and towns. Such a way of life could not be conveniently reconciled with the **stabilitas loci,** with local superiors elected for life, or without introducing a legal distinction between monks capable of intellectual pursuits and those suitable only for manual work.

In consequence of such circumstances, most Oriental Catholic religious organized themselves into orders, with local superiors mostly appointed for a certain number of years, with a central novitiate and house of studies, with a superior general and with major superiors in charge of a number of monasteries, who received the corresponding title of provincials or protohegoumenoi, etc. That this transformation was justified and beneficial towards the goals of the religious state is demonstrated by the history, e.g., of the Ukrainian Order of St. Basil the Great, which after a temporary decline in the 19th century was reorganized, and before World War II was close to becoming an Oriental Rite religious institute represented in several branches of the Byzantine Rite, with a Ukrainian, Slovak, Hungarian, Yugoslav, Subcarpathian, American, Canadian, Brazilian province or vice-province.

Another group of Oriental religious institutes organized according to Latin Rite forms are various congregations of men and women established during the last centuries. They never experienced a structural transformation from the Oriental monastic tradition to that of the Latin Rite, but received from their very beginning the features of Latin Rite religious institutes.

The XIX century saw a number of Latin Rite orders and congregations form Oriental Rite branches of their institutes. The Redemptorists, the Jesuits, the Benedictines, the Franciscans (Observants and Conventuals), the Assumptionists, and others, have provinces or similar subdivisions of Oriental Rite. Although they endeavor to conform to the genuine Oriental traditions as closely as possible, they are governing their houses and membership according to the norms which they have in common with the Latin Rite members of their institutes.

There are Latin Rite orders and congregations which have started towards the establishment of Oriental Rite branches, either by accepting into their membership Oriental Rite candidates, who retain and practice their own Rite, or by permitting some members to transfer to an Oriental Rite, perpetually or temporarily.

The Church was thereby placed in a situation where it was found necessary on one hand to materialize the desire of favoring the continuation or revival of the ancient and genuine monastic traditions of the Eastern Churches, and on the other hand there was a need to provide legal norms for those institutes which had adopted the more modern structural features of Latin Rite institutes. The only solution was to introduce into the codification a dualistic character. For nearly every single institution special and separate norms for both kinds of religious institutes had to be defined. In order to hold the provisions apart and not to confuse them, it is therefore necessary to pay close attention to the definitions of legal terms in **Postquam Apostolicis,** since some fundamental ones have received a meaning quite different from that found in CIC, as, e.g., **monachus, monasterium, exemptio,** and several others.

The S. Congregation for the Oriental Church granted, after the promulgation of the motuproprio, to Oriental Rite religious institutes the opportunity once for all of chosing whether they would declare themselves for the category of monks, and then follow all pertinent legal norms, or would retain their present legal condition as orders or congregations. Most institutes found it not feasible to return to Oriental monastic forms because of the necessity of radical changes in their activities, which would have caused serious damage to numerous apostolic undertakings.

SOURCES OF ORIENTAL LAW ON THE RELIGIOUS

Owing to the dualistic character of the present codification of the law on the religious, the sources of the new legislation are twofold too. For the Oriental Rite religious institutes which are organized as orders, congregations or societies without public vows, the statutes and norms issued for them in the last centuries, which in their general structure as well as in many details conform to the norms of the CIC, provided a ready material for the codification. The collection and revision of the norms for the monks and nuns who follow Oriental traditions was more involved, since their present statutes had to be freed from influences alien to their genuine heritage. In addition, Oriental monks were never governed by rules that would contain all juridical and ascetical norms of their lives in such a thorough manner as we find in the Western Church in the Rule of St. Benedict and of the numerous other founders of religious institutes. The sources of their laws were widely scattered. De Meester (p. 3) enunmerates the following:

1. Norms and rules given by the fathers of monachism, foremost among them, as far as the Byzantine Rite is concerned, St. Pachomius, St. Basil the Great, and St. Theodore the Studite.

2. The canons of ecumenical and particular synods, of which the most important are that of Chalcedon (451) and Trullo (692).

3. Decrees of patriarchs and some other hierarchs.

4. Ordinances of the civil governments, in which they followed the example of Emperor Justinian (483-565), who legislated extensively on norms for the religious state.

5. Typica of individual monasteries, imposed either by the founders themselves, or by some reforming superior. Whoever established a monastery by endowing it was entitled to prescribe certain rules, not contrary to common law, which were to be followed by the monks forever. Such benefactors were lay persons as well as ecclesiastics, and sometimes they even entered their foundations as members.

An additional difficulty for the codification was presented by the dearth of canonical sources from some Oriental Rites, and the preponderance of material taken from the Byzantine Rite. However, this was not found to be a great disadvantage, since either many institutions were so ancient as to antedate the division of Churches, and were common to all Oriental Rites, or the other Oriental Rites had become permeated with the influence of the Byzantine Rite in quite remote times, with a consequent taking over of legal institutions from the Byzantine Church.

However, even within the Byzantine Rite we find that many traditions of monastic life were either best preserved or originally formulated on the Holy Mount Athos. It will be therefore necessary to say something of this remarkable relic of true Oriental monachism.

THE CONFEDERATION OF MONASTERIES OF THE HOLY MOUNT ATHOS

The Holy Mount Athos is the easternmost of the three promotories of the peninsula Chalcidice, which stretch like three fingers from the southern coast of Macedonia into the Aegean Sea, eastward of Saloniki in northern Greece. The Athos peninsula is some twenty miles long and three to six miles wide. It is extremely mountainous, culminating in the Mount Athos (6000 feet). Vegetation is mediterranean, with evergreen trees and bushes predominating, permitting however the cultivation of olive trees, and of small patches of vegetable gardens.

The Athos peninsula, or as it is officially called, the Holy Mountain Athos, is a separate political entity of Greece. It is truly a republic of monks. No woman is permitted to enter the Holy Mount Athos, and men can do so only with special permission of ecclesiastical and civil authorities.

This monastic republic was populated by several convents before the 9th century. The monks and their convents increased by time, until they had reached, before World War II, 6,400 inhabitants, of whom some 2,000 had come from the former Russian empire. The last forty years have seen a continuous decline of the number of monks, chiefly due to the restrictions placed by the chauvinism of Greece.

The Holy Mount Athos is now under the spiritual jurisdiction of the Patriarch of Constantinople, who does not enjoy that obedience which Catholics are wont to render their ecclesiastical superiors. The territory of the Holy Mountain is divided into 20 monastic territories, each owned by one of the ancient monasteries, of which today only three belong to monks other than Greeks: one to the Russians, another to the Serbs, and a third to the Bulgares. However, within the territory of each monastery there are other loosely dependent monasteries or convents, called **scetae,** and colonies of smaller groups of monks, two to six in one house, in addition to a number of hermits who live in caverns or cells precariously perched on the flanks of Mount Athos. These dependent convents are not rarely more numerous in monks than their suzerain monasteries.

Nine of the monasteries are today **idiorrhythmic,** i.e., the monks are permitted to possess property and have only the Church in common. The scetae are cenobitic as well as idiorrhythmic. In the cenobitic monasteries everything is common to all monks, who are ruled by a hegoumenus, while the idiorrhythmic convents elect a council of a few monks, the **epitropia,** for a limited time to govern the monastery.

The representatives of the 20 monasteries form the government of the Holy Mount Athos, with its seat in Karyes, the little capital of this tiny republic. The executive functions are delegated to a committee of four members, elected for one year, of whom one, the **protepistat,** is the head of the government.

The Holy Mount Athos enjoys full autonomy within the Kingdom of Greece, and has its own legislative, judiciary and coercive authority. No other Christians except those of the various dissident Orthodox Churches are permitted to settle on the Holy Mountain, but only Greeks actually receive such a permission.

The Holy Mountain is of interest to all Christians because it has quite faithfully preserved, although not free of symptoms of spiritual corruption, all the various stages of development of religious life, with anachorets who live in strict and austere solitude; hermits who live in small groups, often united by the loose bond of a common superior and church; strict cenobites who have not one aspect of their existence exempt from common life.

In addition, the Holy Mountain is a seemingly inexhaustible

treasure chest of medieval Christian art and of valuable manuscripts, which illuminate our understanding of the past.

Unfortunately, the Holy Mountain is not the spiritual force it once was. The cultural aspects are today negligible, since the great majority of the monks possess only the most rudimentary education, if they are not downright illiterates. The traditions of Oriental monachism are followed more as an external pattern than because of their spiritual value. Those who look for the standards according to which Western religious direct their lives and activities, will be disappointed, and there is no hope that the dissident Churches could on their own ever revive the pristine fervor of monachism on the Holy Mountain.

LEGAL CHARACTERISTICS OF ORIENTAL MONACHISM

1. There is no division of the religious into organizations, as orders, congregations, institutes without public vows, etc., but one only monastic state, to which belong all monks and nuns. To be a monk or nun has the same meaning as if a man belongs to the clergy, which knows different degrees but only one clerical state. The activity of all monks or nuns remained of a contemplative nature, although, as an exemption or a necessary adjunct to a complete monastery management, they had perhaps hospitals, guest houses or schools. Federations of monasteries were known also in the East, and one is still conspicuously in existence on the Holy Mount Athos, but the mutual bond among the member monasteries was rather loose, and they never selected one specific activity as a preferred task to be pursued by the entire organization, as did the various orders of the Latin Rite Church.

2. The organizational unit of the monastic state is the independent monastery **(monasterium sui iuris)**, the superior with the council composed of the monks or their elected representatives. Since the monastery is a self-contained unit, it has its own novitiate and house of studies.

The word monastery designated first the living quarters of a monk or a small group of monks, and only later it received the meaning of a convent or house separated from the habitation of other people, in order to permit a larger number of monks a common life in solitude. Eastern monasteries are usually very extensive buildings, with several large churches and numerous chapels, even if the number of members is not large. The reason for erecting more churches and chapels was not the need to accommodate the inhabitants, but to honor God under different titles or various saints.

The loose union of a number of separate cells, each populated by one to four or five monks, and under a common superior, was called a **laura**. In later times the term laura was applied to mother convents, which were renown either for being the founders of other monasteries, or for their large number of monks, or for their historic connection with the nation, etc. In the Ukrainian and Russian Church there were four such lauras: The Monastery of the Caves in Kiew, the mother convent of all other monasteries in Ukraina and

Russia, and the Assumption Laura of Pochayiw (Ukraine); St. Sergius's Laura close to Moscow and St. Alexander Newsky's Laura in the vicinity of Leningrad (Russia).

Sometimes a monastery might have colonies of small cells of monks organized in a **sceta**. The sceta has its own superior, a community church, and is subordinated to the mother monastery. Such scetas are numerous on the Holy Mountain Athos, because the number of monasteries in the strict sense is there fixed forever. A new foundation is by necessity therefore dependent on the monastery in the territory of which it is situated, and cannot receive the title of monastery even if it should surpass it by number of monks.

Metochion is a house pertaining to a monastery the purpose of which is to carry out a certain defined task. Since monasteries are always situated outside cities and towns, the management requires lodgings for the members who have to transact some business in the political or economical centers. The metochion has usually a small permanent community and a chapel or church. Some monasteries have sometimes possessions in distant countries which are taken care of by members living in a metochion close to the property.

3. Members of a monastery may be permitted to lead the life of anachorets or hermits, which frees them from some communal obligations, but does not withdraw them from the authority of the superior.

Ancient monasticism knew three kinds of monastic life:

(1) **Hermits, anachorets** or **hesychasts**, were living in perfect solitude. To these belonged also the so-called **stylites,** who had their abode on high exposed rocks or columns; the **recluses** who were sealed off from the world forever by a wall. No monk was permitted to start his monastic life as a hermit. He was obliged first to undergo a trial in a monastery of common life. After that he could be permitted to become a hermit for one year, to see whether he was qualified for this deprivation of companionship. If he had shown himself capable of anachoretic life, the superior of the monastery could grant then his final consent.

(2) **Lauriotes** were monks each of whom had a little hut or house as his own habitation, while all together were grouped into a so-called laura. They conducted their activities apart from each other, with the exception of the divine service and infrequent common meals. In the Latin Rite they are still represented by the Camaldoli Benedictines and the Carthusians. The name of laura was later reserved only for some distinguished monasteries of common life.

(3) **Cenobites** were those who in everything led a common life.

In the 14th century arose a new form of life among Eastern religious, the **idiorrhythmia,** which is still extant among some dissident Oriental groups, in spite of condemnation by synods, hierarchs and ecclesiastical writers. **De Meester** (p. 79) described the idorrhythmic manner of life as it is practiced on the Holy Mount Athos:

"The idiorrhythmic monastery is divided into 10, 12, 15 or 18 families of monks, according to the size of the premises. Each of these families is represented by a head with the title of **proistamenos** (director, superior), whose task it is to gather sons, i.e., monks, etc., either from among the yet unattached monks in the monastery, or from among the candidates, whom he can receive as novices. The number of the latter is usually small, and hardly exceeds six or seven. Each family stays in its own living quarters, and receives daily bread, wine and other necessities for life, which customarily are given by the monastery. Whatever else they need, the idorrhythmic monks procure themselves by the work of their hands or by paying for it with money. When they are approaching death, they call a companion, whom they call disciple, and leave to him in a last will the property they own within the monastery or outside the monastery, or they might donate it to the monastery. All **proistamenoi** are gathered once a year to elect from among themselves two or three, who are called **epitropi**, the duty of which is to manage the common property of the monastery and to preserve order. This **epitropia** takes the place of the hegoumenus of the monastery, who formerly ruled the monastery with the help of a few councillors. Idiorrhythmic monks are obliged to celebrate divine services in the common monastery church, and three times a year (on Christmas on Easter, and on the feast day of the patron of the monastery) they participate at a community meal, at which strict abstinence is observed. But in their private quarters the idorrhythmic monks eat meat, except on days designated by the Church, and do and say everything they like."

Some authors consider idorrhythmia a return to the second stage of monachism, when a number of small communities formed a loose union with a common church and a common superior, i.e., before the idea of the Egyptian-Syrian monastery monarch became established. However, all Church authorities, dissident as well as Catholic, regard idiorrhythmia a deterioration and mockery of true monachism, and endeavor to combat it, although often without success.

4. Monasteries may form higher organizations, federations, for the more efficient attainment of certain common goals, without losing thereby their individual independence. A still extant example of such a confederation of monasteries is the Community of the Holy Mount Athos, of which we have spoken above.

5. The superior of an independent monastery, being elected for life, receives a liturgical blessing, after which he is entitled to confer on his subjects the minor orders (cf. c. 174).

6. The monastic state is not a clerical nor a lay institute, but simply a monastic institute. Members possess in general equal rights, except that for certain offices, as, e.g., for that of the superior, the clerical state and the order of priesthood may be required.

Nor has there developed a distinction into clerical or choir and lay members among monks or nuns. The number of clerics, priests, called **hieromonks**, deacons, called **hierodeacons**, subdeacons and lectors in a given monastery was and is determined by liturgical needs of the community. While for priests some little higher education, gained perhaps through the reading of appropriate books, might be desired, other clerics need to possess only the qualities necessary for the proper fulfillment of the respective duties, primarily a good voice for singing or reading.

Because the number of monks who had received a higher education and who did not become bishops or superiors, but stayed as simple members of the community, was always very small, no classes of members developed on account of differences of personal culture.

The same is to be said of nuns. As mentioned in the first part of this book, the liturgical language is in the Oriental Rites either the actual vernacular, or at least an older form of the vernacular, as, e.g., ancient Greek, Old Slavonic, Syriac. Every member of the community, capable of reading, can fully participate in the recitation of the divine office. A distinction into choir and lay monks or nuns could thus not develop.

It might be very well that some members are more, or nearly exclusively engaged in liturgical activities or in manual work, but this happens rather on account of their individual capabilities, age, inclinations, etc., than because of distinction into classes. The poverty of the monasteries in the Near East forces all members, priests included, to give a considerable time to manual chores.

However, monasteries do not lack an order of ranks. Those who hold office have a higher position than their subjects. There are also the degrees of monastic profession: Simple candidate, novice or **archarios, rasophorus, microschemus, megoloschemus** (cf. c. 109). Another consideration which establishes rank is the time one has been in a certain degree of profession. Monks who have some special education will possess precedence over others on account of office, dignity or title they hold or were distinguished.

7. Postulancy or a definite period of trial preceding the novitiate is not known in the East (cf. c. 74).

8. Monks and nuns, as a general rule, do not make temporary profession, but after a novitiate of three years, they are admitted at once to perpetual vows (cf. c. 106).

9. Although every profession is perpetual and solemn, in the meaning of canon law, there are degrees of profession, the minor and the major habit or scheme, referring to degrees of ascetical obligations to which a monk or nun can oblige himself (cf. c. 109).

10. The chief duty of a monk or nun is to lead a contemplative life, with special emphasis on the solemn celebration of the divine office. The obligations of a true monk are:

(1) He must completely sever all bonds and connections he has with the world.

(2) He must lead a life of physical austerity, of which the perpetual abstinence from meat is one of the more conspicuous duties.

(3) He must participate in the celebration of the divine office, although the obligation as such is imposed in the first place upon the community as a whole. It is the duty of the superior to see to it that a sufficient number of religious are available for the divine

services, but also the individual monk is obliged to participate if so ordered by the superior.

(4) Manual and mental work, especially that which promotes his spiritual welfare.

(5) Stability in his vocation and in his monastery.

11. Because there are no classes among the members of a monastery, nor such organizations as orders, all monks wear the same habit, with the exception of differences following the degrees of profession (cf. c. 139).

12. Monasteries are as a rule subject to the local Hierarch, who is entitled to supervise the faithful observance of the monastic discipline (cf. c. 162).

13. Patriarchs enjoy the privilege of **stauropegia**, i.e., to exempt a monastery, under certain conditions, from the jurisdiction of the local Hierarch and subject it to their own immediate authority (cf. c. 164).

14. Since there is no division into orders or congregations or other institutes, the transfer from one monastery to another does not, in general, affect the legal status of the monk or nun. He always stays a member of the one monastic state. Repetition of novitiate or profession are not demanded by common law.

DEFINITIONS OF LEGAL TERMS

Definition of the Religious State (c. 1 = c. 487 CIC)
Dignity of Religious State (c. 2 = c. 487 CIC)
Definition and Kinds of Religious Institutes
(c. 312 = cf. c. 488 CIC)
Definition of Terms Applying to Monks
(c. 313 = cf. c. 488 CIC)
Definition of Terms Applying to Orders
(c. 314 = cf. c. 488 CIC)
Major and Minor Profession (c. 315 = new)
Definition of Rules and Constitutions (c. 316 = new)
Definition of Particular Law (c. 317 = new)
Division into Sexes (c. 318 = cf. c. 490 CIC)

CANON 1. The religious state is a stable manner of living in a society approved by the Church, and in which faithful undertake by public vows of obedience, chastity and poverty to observe, under a lawful superior, besides the common precepts, also the evangelical counsels, in accordance with the statutes.

Comparing this definition with that of c. 487 CIC, we find the following changes:

Since Oriental canon law permits that hermits, who are living apart from the community, belong to the religious state (c. 4), the expression "a stable manner of living **in community**" was replaced by **"in a society approved by the Church."** For the same reason it was added that the life of religious must be conducted **"under lawful superiors,"** and in "accordance with the statutes."

An improvement of minor importance is the addition of the qualifying adjective **"public"** to the vows.

CANON 2. The religious state shall be held in honor by all.

TERMINOLOGICAL DEFINITIONS

The motuproprio **Postquam Apostolicis,** probably following the example of the Justinian codification of the civil or Roman law (528-534) under the Emperor Justinian (483-565), which had a special section with definitions of legal terms, has as a third part definitions of terms used in the motuproprio, under the heading **De Verborum Significatione** (cc. 302-325). We are giving here those canons which contain definitions of terms of the law on the religious.

CANON 312. **# 1.** A religious institute is a moral person erected by the legitimate ecclesiastical authority, in which the members take public vows, perpetual or temporary, the latter however to be renewed after expiration, according to the particular statutes of the same moral person, thereby striving toward evangelical perfection.

Some stylistic improvements have been introduced in the definition of the religious institute. Instead of calling it (c. 488, 1 CIC) a **"society . . . approved** by legitimate ecclesiastical authority,"** it is defined as **"moral person . . . erected** by legitimate ecclesiastical authority." There are societies which have not the juridical nature of moral persons, and, at least today, tacit approval is not sufficient for the establishment of a religious institute, but a positive act of erection is required.

 # 2. A religious institute is:

1. Of e p a r c h i a l r i g h t if it is established by the Bishop and subject to him according to the rules of the canons;

This could be a monastery and a congregation of eparchial right, but not an order, which must be at least of patriarchal right.

2. Of p a t r i a r c h a l r i g h t, if the order or congregation was erected or approved by his decision, and is subject to him according to the rules of the canons;

An order is in Oriental law always exempt from the jurisdiction of the local Hierarch, but not necessarily also from the jurisdiction of the patriarch. Besides an order of patriarchal right, Oriental canon law knows also an order of papal right without papal exemption, in addition to an order endowed both with the quality of papal right and papal exemption.

A monastery of monks and nuns cannot be, strictly speaking of patriarchal right, although it can be under the immediate jurisdiction of the patriarch in virtue of the stauropegium (cf. c. 164).

3. Of p a p a l r i g h t, if either the approbation or at least a decree of praise was obtained from the Apostolic See in accordance with the norms established by the latter;

4. E x e m p t, if it is freed from the authority of the local Hierarch and subject to the patriarch or the Apostolic See alone.

3. 1. A d o m u s r e l i g i o s a is any house in general of a religious institute;

2. A d o m u s f o r m a t a is a house of religious in which live at least six members who have taken vows, of whom, if it is the case of a clerical order or congregation, at least four are in sacred orders;

Since monasteries are religious institutes which lack the juridical quality of being a clerical or lay institute, six members will suffice to make it a **domus formata** although they could be all lay.

4. A r e l i g i o u s is a person who has taken vows in a religious institute.

5. 1. Under the designation of m a j o r s u p e r i o r s are understood: The president of an association of monastic confederations, the president of a monastic confederation, the superior of an independent monastery, the highest superior of an order or congregation, the provincial superior, their substitutes and others who have power in the manner of provincial superiors;

The **monasterium sui iuris** was by us translated as **independent monastery**.

2. Under the designation of r e l i g i o u s s u p e r i o r does not come either the local Hierarch nor the patriarch, without prejudice to the canons which assign to the patriarch as well as the local Hierarch certain powers over the religious.

CANON 313. # 1. 1. A m o n a s t i c a l c o n f e d e r a t i o n is the union of several independent monasteries under the same president;

2. An a s s o c i a t i o n o f c o n f e d e r a t i o n s is the union of several confederations under the same president;

2. 1. M o n a s t e r y is a religious house of monks, and, provided nothing is decreed to the contrary, the house of an order of women;

In Latin Rite canon law **monasterium** is a house of certain orders, namely, of monks, canons regular, and of nuns (with solemn profession). In Oriental canon law it is a house of monks and nuns, and is not to be used for houses of orders. While, e.g., the Byzantine Order of St. Basil the Great of St. Josaphat can be considered a monastic order in a historical sense, juridically speaking it is an order, and its members are not monks in the meaning of **Postquam Apostolicis**.

As an exemption to this rule, the convent of women who are part of an order, i. e., not nuns in the meaning of Oriental canon law, is generally to be understood under the term of monastery.

2. A monastery is called:

(a) S t a u r o p e g i a l, if it is directly subject to the patriarch
,   in accordance with the canons;

(b) I n d e p e n d e n t, the superior of which has the rights and duties of a major superior according to the norms of the canons and the statutes. Other monasteries are d e p e n d e n t, of which some are a f f i l i a t e d and in preparation to the status of an independent monastery, others are s u b s i d i a r y.

244

 # 3. M o n k, or n u n, is a religious man or woman respectively who by profession becomes a member of a religious institute in which the religious life is led according to the traditions of the ancient East. Unless otherwise stated, as a n u n is also understood the religious woman who took profession in an order.

We have said under # 2, 1, that the term monk or nun has a different meaning than that found in the Latin Rite canon law.

 # 4. H e r m i t is a religious who according to the norms of the constitutions leads an eremitical life, without prejudice to his dependence from the superiors of his religious institute.

Although hermits will be chiefly found attached to a monastery, there is nothing to prevent their existence within an order or congregation, provided the rules and constitutions permit it.

CANON 314. # 1. A religious institute in which the members, although they are not monks, take vows which equal to the vows of monks is called an o r d e r.

According to the terms of **Postquam Apostolicis** Benedictine monks, for instance, of an Oriental Rite will not be monks in the meaning of Oriental law of religious.

The vows of monks are not called **solemn,** but they are said to make **major profession,** although from c. 115 it follows that they have the juridical effects of solemn vows of the CIC. It is not defined what vows are taken by monks, but they certainly include at least the three evangelical counsels.

 # 2. A r e l i g i o u s c o n g r e g a t i o n, or simply a c o n g r e g a t i o n, is a religious institute in which the members make only minor profession.

 # 3. An order or congregation is called c l e r i c a l if its members generally are to be raised to sacred orders, otherwise it is lay.

Only an order or congregation has the qualification of being either a clerical or a lay institute. The religious institute of Oriental monks and nuns, properly called a monastery, is a **religio monachalis,** which is neither clerical nor lay, although in general monks are treated in **Postquam Apostolicis** according to the norms enacted for clerical orders and congregations.

 # 4. The moral person which is a part of the order or congregation, consists of several houses, and is ruled directly by major superiors, is called a p r o v i n c e.

 # 5. S i s t e r s are religious women who take vows in a congregation.

CANON 315. M a j o r p r o f e s s i o n comprises both the monastical profession as well as the profession made in orders, which is equated to the monastical one. Every other profession is called m i n o r p r o f e s s i o n.

Major profession is equivalent, as far as juridical effects are concerned, to the solemn profession of CIC. Minor profession is every temporary profession, and the perpetual vows taken as simple profession either by all members of a congration, or by some members of an order.

CANON 316. Whenever it is the case of religious, as **s t a t u t e s** are understood the **t y p i c a** of monasteries as well as the **rules and constitutions of orders and congregations.**

The norms according to which a monastery and its members are regulating their life are called **typicum.** It consists of rules imposed upon the monastery by its founder, by the first superior, or some other authority, and contains usually disciplinary, liturgical and administrative regulations, which are to be followed by the monks or nuns. They are more or less equivalent to the constitutions of a particular monastery of monks of a Latin Rite order, which in general is governed by the **regula** of the order.

CANON 317. Under the designation of **p a r t i c u l a r l a w** come also the particular statutes or particular constitutions, lawfully approved, by which the moral person is governed, unless the contrary appears from the text and context of the law, or from the very nature of the matter.

CANON 318. The wording of a text in the masculine gender applies to both sexes, unless from the nature of the matter or the text and context of the law something else follows.

GENERAL PRINCIPLES (cc. 3-6)

Relationship of New Legislation to Rules and Constitutions of Religious Institutes (c. 3 = c. 489 CIC)
Norms for Hermits (c. 4 = new)
Norms for Religious Houses of an Institute of a Different Rite (c. 5 = new)
Rules of Precedence (c. 6 = c. 491 CIC)

CANON 3. All statutes of religious institutes retain their force in regard to those norms which are not contrary to regulations established by this law, while those which are contrary are repealed.

Statutes of institutions mentioned here include the rules and constitutions of orders and congregations, and the typica of monks (cf. c. 316).

Statutes must be changed to conform to the new codification only if they are contrary to norms of **Postquam Apostolicis.** If they are in conformity with them, or decide questions not treated in the new legislation, they are **secundum** and **praeter legem** and continue their legal force.

Canon 3 does not affect laws and customs enacted or approved for all Oriental religious, for those of a certain Rite, or for a certain institute, by the Apostolic See, synods or other legislators. However, they are taken care of by the closing words of **Postquam Apostolicis,** where Pius XII declares abrogated all contrary common or particular laws, customs and statutes.

While statutes of institutes contrary to the new legislation retain their legal force although they must be corrected, contrary common or particular laws simply lose their character of legislative acts, i.e., their very existence.

CANON 4. The canons concerning religious oblige also hermits, unless the contrary follows from the nature of the matter or from approved statutes of the respective religious institute.

Hermits can be religious if they are members of an institute. If they have no public vows, and are not living under superiors, they may lead a life of perfection, but they would not belong to the religious state according to the new law. In former times hermits could belong to the religious state even if they were not under the obedience of a superior and had not taken vows in an institute.

Although hermits are religious, all norms concerning religious cannot be applied to them on account of their peculiar way of life, as it is the case with obligations to be carried out in the community, e.g., the celebration of the divine office.

CANON 5. # 1. Houses of institutes of the Latin Rite which, with the approval of the Apostolic See, are attached to an Oriental Rite must observe the prescriptions established by this law, save for the prescriptions of statutes which refer to the internal government of the institute, and save for the privileges granted to the institute by the Apostolic See.

There are a number of Latin Rite religious institutes which have established houses of Oriental Rites, with members who either belong permanently or temporarily to that respective Rite. The house as such and the individual members are obliged to follow the laws of that Rite, with two exceptions:

1. The internal government continues to be conducted according to the norms of their rules and constitutions, although these might be contrary to Oriental law.

2. Privileges granted by the Apostolic See, as that of exemption from the jurisdiction of the local Hierarch or the patriarch, and enjoyed by the institute according to the norms of the Latin Rite canon law, continue in their force.

If the house is attached to an Oriental Rite, it is obliged to follow that Rite even if the majority of the members should perhaps at some time belong to some other Rite.

Prescriptions of the particular law of the institute, which establish obligations contrary to Oriental law, as, e.g., days of fast or abstinence, are to be disregarded, or commuted to corresponding Oriental Rite usages.

 # 2. An Oriental Rite institute which, with the consent of the Apostolic See, has houses and provinces of a different Oriental Rite, depends in respect to the government upon that ecclesiastical Oriental Rite hierarchy to which it was assigned by the Apostolic See.

Some Oriental institutes have spread out either to several Rites, or to several hierarchies of the same Rite, which are independent from each other. The originally Ukrainian Order of St. Basil the Great of St. Josaphat had before World War II organized, e.g., a Romanian province, which would have been attached to the Romanian hierarchy of the Byzantine Rite.

Paragraph 2 will find application chiefly in institutes which do not enjoy papal exemption, since institutes with such an exemption will not have often occasion to require the intervention of a local Hierarch.

This canon will be useful in the circumstances of the Near East, where in one territory several Oriental Rites and hierarchies are present, the faithful of all of them using the same vernacular and liturgical language. It has proven practical to have a house with members belonging to different Rites, who in their work are serving simultaneously the interests of all Catholic Orientals in a given place.

CANON 6. # 1. 1. Religious take precedence over the laity; monks over other religious; clerical institutes over lay; among clerical institutes, or among lay institutes, orders enjoy precedence over congregations.

2. Save for the rule of no. 1, institutes of papal right have precedence over institutes of patriarchal right; and these over institutes of eparchial right.

3. Among institutes of the same juridical condition precedence belongs to that which is in peaceful quasipossession of the precedency, and if this cannot be ascertained, that which was sooner established in the place where the question arose.

2. Secular clergy take precedence over the religious outside churches of the latter, and even in their churches if it is the case of a lay institute. The assembled eparchial consultors precede them everywhere.

3. Among individual clergy and religious the right of precedence in respect to each other is due to him who has authority over the other. If none of them has authority over the other: whoever holds a higher rank precedes him who is of lower rank. Among persons of the same rank but not of the same order: whoever holds a higher order precedes him who holds a lower one. If, finally, they are of the same rank and hold the same order, whoever was first promoted to that rank, and if they were promoted at the same time, whoever is senior in regard to ordination, unless the younger was ordained by the Roman Pontiff, and if they were ordained at the same time, whoever is older in age.

CHAPTER ONE

THE ESTABLISHMENT AND SUPPRESSION OF RELIGIOUS
INSTITUTES, PROVINCES AND HOUSES (cc. 7-22)

Definitions of the Term L o c a l H i e r a r c h
(c. 7 = cf. c. 492 # 1 CIC)
Monasteries:
Hierarchs Empowered to Establish (c. 8 = new)
Conditions of Permission to Establish a Monastery
(c. 9 = new)
Suppression (c. 10 = new)
Establishment of Confederations of Monasteries
c. 11 = new)

Suppression of Confederations (c. 12 = new)
Establishment of Congregations (c. 13 = cf. c. 492 CIC)
Suppression of Orders and Congregations
   (c. 14 = cf. c. 493 CIC)
Division into Provinces (c. 15 = cf. c. 494 CIC)
Establishment of Houses:
   Condition of Insured Support (c. 16 = c. 496 CIC)
   Houses of Eparchial Congregations
     (c. 17 = cf. c. 495 # 2 CIC)
Approbation of Constitutions (c. 18 ## 1, 2 = new;
   # 3 = c. 495 # 2 CIC)
Erection of Houses of Orders and Congregations
   (c. 19 = cf. c. 497 CIC)
Formalities in Suppressions (c. 21 = new)
Formalities in Permissions (c. 22 = new)

CANON 7. Neither the administrator of a vacant see, nor the syncellus, unless he received a special mandate, is to be understood in the canons of this chapter under the designation of l o c a l H i e r-a r c h.

CANON 8. # 1. The local Hierarch can establish independent monasteries, in which the members strive for evangelical perfection by observing the rules and the ancient traditions of Oriental monastic life, after he has asked the advice of the patriarch in patriarchates, and has consulted with the Apostolic See outside patriarchates.

2. The permission of the local Hierarch suffices for the establishment of a dependent monastery.

A local Hierarch cannot establish an order, as this term is understood in the meaning of Oriental canon law, but he can erect a monastery, which would be a religious institute, with members who take major or solemn profession, and as a rule (c. 162) are subject to the local Hierarch.

2. The establishment of any stauropegial monastery whatsoever is reserved to the patriarch after he obtained the consent of the permanent synod.
Concerning stauropegial monasteries cf. c. 164.

3. The approval of the Apostolic See is required for the establishment of any monastery endowed with papal exemption.

CANON 9. # 1. 1. The erection of a monastery or the permission to establish a new monastery implies, whether it is an independent monastery or a dependent one, the authorization to have a church or public oratory, and to exercise the sacred ministry, also to carry on works of piety proper to the rules of the statutes of the monastery, without violation of the conditions contained in the act of erection or permission itself, and with the strict obligation to obtain the consent of the local Hierarch before the church or public oratory is to be built in a certain and determined location.

2. Such erection or permission implies in the case of a subsidiary monastery the authority to have a semi-public oratory.

The three kinds of monasteries (independent, dependent, subsidiary) are defined above in c. 313 # 2, n. 2, b.

Strictly parochial functions (cf. c. 503 of **Cleri Sanctitati**) are as a rule excluded from monastery churches, except if the local Hierarch permitted some of them, or the monastery is in charge of the parish which has no church of its own (c. 155). The church of nuns cannot become a parish church (c. 156).

#2 1. The special permission of the local Hierarch is required for the building or opening of a school, hospice or a building of a similar nature separated from the monastery, even if this be endowed with papal exemption. In the case of a stauropegial monastery the permission of the patriarch is also required.

2. Such a permission of the local Hierarch carries with it the authority to have a semi-public oratory.

3. In order to convert to other uses a house already established, the same formalities as for the establishment of a house are required, except if it is the case of an alteration which, while being in conformity with the conditions of the foundation, affects only the internal government and religious discipline.

CANON 10. # 1. An independent or dependent monastery without papal exemption cannot be suppressed in patriarchates except by the patriarch, for grave reasons, with the consent of the permanent synod, and on request or after consultation with the local Hierarch if it is an eparchial monastery; and after consultation with the major superior of the monastery, and of the president of the confederation, if the monastery is confederated, without prejudice to the right of recourse with suspensive effect to the Apostolic See.

2. An independent or dependent monastery endowed with papal exemption, and, outside patriarchates, any independent or dependent monastery, even one of eparchial right, can be suppressed only by the Apostolic See.

3. A subsidiary monastery of whatever juridical condition can be suppressed by the superior of the independent monastery in accordance with the constitutions; if it is the case of a monastery enjoying papal exemption, after the approval of the Apostolic See has been obtained; if it is a stauropegial monastery, with the consent of the patriarch jointly with the permanent synod; in the case of another monastery, with the consent of the local Hierarch.

4. 1. Property of a suppressed independent monastery devolves upon the confederation, if it was confederated; otherwise to the eparchy, and, if it was a stauropegial one, to the patriarchate. To dispose of property of a suppressed monastery which was endowed with papal exemption is reserved to the Apostolic See, without prejudice to any possible wishes of founders.

2. Property of a suppressed dependent monastery devolves upon the independent monastery, without prejudice to the wishes of founders.

CANON 11. # 1. Several independent monasteries of men as well as of women, of the same juridical condition, and in the case of monasteries of eparchial right, if they belong to the same eparchy, may form a confederation with the permission of the lawful authority, to which it is also reserved to approve the constitutions of the confederation.

\# 2. This authority is vested in the local Hierarch if they are monasteries of eparchial right; in the patriarch if they are stauropegial; in the Apostolic See if they are of papal right.

CANON 12. \# 1. The aggregation of a non-confederate monastery to, or the withdrawal of a confederate one from, a confederation is reserved to the same authority mentioned in c. 11.

\# 2. A confederation can be suppressed only by the Apostolic See, or, if the confederation is of eparchial right, by the patriarch with the consent of the permanent synod, after having consulted the local Hierarch and the president of the confederation. The decision of the patriarch cannot be committed to execution before the approval of the Apostolic See.

\# 3. The disposal of the property belonging to the suppressed confederation itself is reserved to the Apostolic See, or, if the confederation was suppressed by the patriarch in accordance with \# 2, to the patriarch with the consent of the permanent synod, without prejudice to the wishes of the founders.

CANON 13. \# 1. 1. Local Hierarchs can erect congregations; they shall not, however, erect them without having consulted the Apostolic See.

2. Patriarchs can erect orders after having obtained the consent of the Apostolic See; congregations after consultation with the Apostolic See.

3. In the case of Third-Order members who live in community it is in addition necessary that they be affiliated by the superior general of the First order to his institute.

\# 2. A congregation of eparchial right, which in the course of time spread out into several eparchies, may become one of patriarchal right by a decree of the patriarch, after consultation with those who have an interest, and after having obtained the consent of the permanent synod.

\# 3. Neither the name nor the habit of an established order or of an established congregation may be assumed by those who do not lawfully belong to that institute or by a new institute.

CANON 14. \# 1. 1. An order, even one of patriarchal right, once lawfully established, even if it consists of one house only, can be suppressed only by the Apostolic See.

2. It is reserved to the Apostolic See itself to dispose of the property of the suppressed order, save for the wishes of the founders.

\# 2. A lawfully established congregation of patriarchal or eparchial right, even if it consists of one house only, can be suppressed only by the Apostolic See, or by the patriarch with the advice of those who have an interest in it, and with the consent of the permanent synod. The decree of the patriarch can be committed to execution only after the approval of the Apostolic See.

CANON 15. # 1. To divide an institute into provinces, to unite established provinces or to modify their boundaries, to establish new or to suppress established ones, pertains to the Apostolic See in the case of an institute of papal right, and in patriarchates to the patriarch in the case of an order of patriarchal right, or a congregation of patriarchal or eparchial right.

2. When a province becomes extinct, the right of disposing of its property, while safeguarding the laws of justice and the wishes of the founders, belongs, unless the constitutions decree otherwise, to the general chapter, or, in case of urgent necessity, to the superior general with the consent of his council.

CANON 16. No religious house shall be established unless it can be prudently presumed that it will be able to provide suitably for the habitation and maintenance of its members from its own income, or in some other manner.

CANON 17. # 1. A congregation of eparchial right cannot validly establish houses in another eparchy without the consent of the Hierarch of the place where the house is to be established, and, if it is the first house to be erected in another eparchy, without the consent of the Hierarch of the eparchy in which the superior general resides.

2. However, in patriarchates the Hierarch of the place where the house is to be established shall not grant his consent without the permission of the patriarch.

CANON 18. # 1. The patriarch approves the typicum of a stauropegial monastery and the constitutions of an order of patriarchal right after consultation with the permanent synod.

2. The patriarch approves the statutes of a congregation of patriarchal right after consultation with all local Hierarchs in whose eparchies there are houses.

#3. If a congregation of eparchial right spread to other eparchies, nothing can be validly changed in the constitutions without the consent of each single Hierarch in whose eparchies it has houses, with the exception of those matters which in accordance with c. 13 # 1, 1, 2, are subject to the Apostolic See.

CANON 19. # 1. 1. An order or congregation of papal or patriarchal right cannot establish houses without the permission of the Hierarch of the place where the house is to be established. If it is the case of the first house to be established in that place of an order or congregation or patriarchal right, the consent of the patriarch is required in addition.

2. An order or congregation endowed with papal exemption can establish houses only after the approval of the Apostolic See and the consent of the local Hierarch has been obtained.

2. The permission to establish a new house implies, for clerical institutes, the right to have a church or public oratory attached to the house and to exercise the sacred ministry in accordance with requirements of law, with the strict obligation to obtain the consent of the local Hierarch before the church or oratory is to be built in a certain

and determined location; for all institutes, to carry on the work of piety proper to the institute, without infraction of the conditions contained in the permission itself.

3. What provisions are prescribed in c. 9 # # 2, 3, in respect to monasteries shall be observed also in regard to orders and congregations.

CANON 20. # 1. The house of an order or congregation, whether a formal or an informal one, cannot be suppressed without Apostolic authority if it enjoyed papal exemption.

2. The house of an order or congregation, whether a formal or an informal one, of a papal institute without exemption, can be suppressed outside the patriarchate by the superior general with the consent of the local Hierarch.

3. The house of an order or congregation, whether a formal or an informal one, of a papal institute without exemption, as well as of one of patriarchal right, can be suppressed within the patriarchate by the superior general with the consent of the patriarch.

4. The house of a congregation of eparchial right, whether a formal or informal one, can be suppressed by authority of the local Hierarch alone, after having requested the opinion of the superior of the congregation, and save for the prescription of c. 14 # 2, if it is the case of the only house.

5. The decree of suppression of the house mentioned in # # 3, 4, can be committed to execution three months from the date of the decree, unless recourse was taken against.

CANON 21. The establishment, change or suppression of an institute or province or house, accomplished by a superior below the Apostolic See, must be done in writing. Copies of the decree shall be kept in the archives of the office of the superior who issued it, and in the archives of the moral person which was established or altered.

CANON 22. # 1. The approval, consent, permission, mentioned in the canons of this chapter are required for the validity of the act.

2. The consent and permission mentioned in the canons of this chapter shall be granted in writing.

CHAPTER TWO

THE GOVERNMENT OF THE RELIGIOUS

Article One:

SUPERIORS AND CHAPTERS (cc. 23-49)

Ecclesiastical Superiors:
The Roman Pontiff (c. 23 = c. 499 # 1 CIC)
The Local Hierarch and the Patriarch
    (c. 24 # 1 = c. 500 # 1 CIC; # 2 = new)
Subjection of Religious Women to Religious Men
    (c. 25 = c. 500 # 3 CIC)

CANON 23. All religious are subject to the Roman Pontiff as to their highest superior, to whom they are obliged to obey also in virtue of the vow of obedience.

No mention of the cardinal protector is made (cf. c. 499 # 2 CIC), probably because Oriental Rite religious can receive the same patronage from their respective patriarch.

CANON 24. # 1. Religious are subject also to the local Hierarch, excepting those who by statute or privileges are withdrawn from the authority of the local Hierarch and subject either to the patriarch or the Apostolic See alone, without prejudice to that authority which the law also assigns over them to the local Hierarch.

Pujol (p. 113) lists the following degrees of dependence of institutes from the local Hierarch:

"A) Exempt religious institutes of men (exempt monastery, order of men, clerical congregation) : They are as such subject either to the patriarch or the Holy See, and since their superiors, with the exception of a lay order, have also jurisdiction in both fora, their subjection to the local Hierarch is of minor degree, because they are in general not his subjects, and in addition only in the cases expressly mentioned in law.

B) Exempt lay order of men: Although the exemption is upheld, the dependence of such an institute from the local Hierarch is greater because the internal superiors lack jurisdiction.

C) Non-exempt institutes: In these institutes the principle of the general dependence on the local Hierarch holds true, and non-subjection is rather to be proved than to be assumed. However, among these institutes there are degrees of subjection, as it is stated by various canons and required by the juridical condition of each individual institute, and by the various participation of their superiors in the power of jurisdiction. Therefore

(a) independent monasteries of men, even those of eparchial right, as well as clerical congregations, both of papal as well as of patriarchal right, are subject to the local Hierarch, who is for them the immediate external superior, with the exception of those cases in which the jurisdiction shared by internal superiors is sufficient; and in regard to religious life, it is very much limited, as it appears, e.g., from cc. 167-168.

(b) Lay congregations of men, both of papal and of patriarchal right: Since they are not exempt, and their superiors lack the power of jurisdiction, their dependence upon the local Hierarch is greater, not only in their quality as faithful and clerics, but also as religious (c. 44, 2 ; c. 167 # 2).

D) Orders of women not subject to a superior of male religious, and the monasteries of nuns: They are subject to a larger extent to the local Hierarch, who is their immediate external ecclesiastical superior, upon whom they are totally dependent (according to the norm of law, c. 163, n. 1) as members of the faithful, and also in many aspects as religious. The same is true of a congregation of women of eparchial right.

Orders of women subject to a superior of male religious: They are in general exempt from the jurisdiction of the local Hierarch, in whose stead there is the religious superior, who can exercise jurisdiction in favor of the religious women if he has such. Therefore, they are subject to the local Hierarch only in cases expressly enumerated in law, and also as faithful their dependence will be regulated by the degree of jurisdiction possessed by the religious superior."

2. 1. Religious who do not enjoy papal exemption are subject in patriarchates also to the patriarch mediately in respect to those matters in which they are subject to a local Hierarch subject to the patriarch; immediately in other matters; save for cases in which they are subject solely to the Apostolic See in virtue of common law or privilege.

2. Religious enjoying papal exemption in patriarchates are subject immediately to the patriarch only in cases designated by law;

mediately, however, in those cases in which they are subject to the local Hierarch immediately.

CANON 25. No institute of men can have a congregation of women subject to it, or retain its care and direction as especially committed to it, without a special Apostolic indult.

CANON 26. # 1. Superiors and chapters have dominative power over their subjects in accordance with the rules of statutes and common law.

2. 1. The superiors and chapters have in an exempt monastery and in an exempt clerical institute ecclesiastical jurisdiction in the internal forum as well as in the external, in accordance with the regulations of statutes and common law.

2. The major superiors of non-exempt monks of whatever juridical condition and of non-exempt clerical congregations of papal or patriarchal right have ecclesiastical jurisdiction in both fora only in the cases expressly mentioned in law.

3. The major superiors of non-exempt monks of whatever juridical condition and of non-exempt clerical congregations of papal or patriarchal right can dispense in matters in which they are exempt from the local Hierarch, from general laws of the Church as well as from laws which were enacted by the Roman Pontiff specifically for a certain Rite or a particular territory or group of persons, within the limits of power of dispensation rightfully assigned by the same laws to Hierarchs below the Roman Pontiff.

Besides public dominative power certain religious superiors possess also jurisdiction:

1. The superior major and the synaxis (chapter) of an exempt monastery and of an exempt clerical institute (order or congregation). This includes institutes with papal as well as with patriarchal exemption.

2. The superiors major of non-exempt monks of whatever juridical condition (superior of an independent monastery of eparchial right, superior of a stauropegial monastery, president of a confederation of either type of monasteries), and the superiors major of clerical congregations of non-exempt papal or patriarchal right, also enjoy ecclesiastical jurisdiction in both fora, but only in the cases expressly enumerated in law.

In Latin Rite canon law such superiors wield only public dominative power, and ecclesiastical jurisdiction is reserved to the superiors of clerical religious institutes endowed with papal exemption.

CANON 27. All superiors are severely forbidden to interfere in matters pertaining to the competency of the Holy Office.

CANON 28. The president of a union of confederations. the president of a monastic confederation, and the superioress general of an order have not all the power and jurisdiction which common law assigns to major superiors, but their authority and jurisdiction is to be derived not only from the law, but also from the rules and statutes of each union of confederations or monastic confederation or order, save for the prescription of c. 207.

CANON 29. The superior general of an order or congregation obtains authority over all provinces, houses, members, to be exercised according to the statutes; other superiors enjoy it within the limits of their office.

CANON 30. Major superiors of monks and of an exempt clerical institute can appoint notaries, but only for the ecclesiastical affairs of their institute.

CANON 31. Without prejudice to the constitutions, which may demand a higher age or some more stringent requirements, the following are not qualified for the office of major superior:

1. those who are not of legitimate birth, without prejudice to particular law;

2. those who are not professed members of the same institute for at least ten years, counting from the first profession;

3. those who have not completed thirty-five years of age and are not ordained to the priesthood, if it is the case of monasteries of men;

4. those who have not completed forty years of age, if it is the case of a superioress of women;

5. those who have not completed forty years of age in orders and congregations if it is the case of the superior general of the institute; thirty years of age in the case of other major superiors.

Qualifications for other than major superiors are to be established by particular law. Oriental tradition does not require, among others, that the superior of a dependent monastery be a priest. He could be a deacon, or minor cleric, or a layman.

CANON 32. # 1. The superior of an independent monastery shall remain in office for life, unless the typicum states otherwise.

2. The major superiors in orders and congregations are temporary unless the constitutions decree otherwise.

3. 1. Minor local superiors shall not be appointed for more than six years, after the completion of which they can be reappointed to the same office if the constitutions permit it, but not for a third consecutive term in the same religious house.

The normal tenure of minor superiors has been increased from three years (c. 505 CIC) to six years.

2. The patriarch can in patriarchates dispense for a just cause from the prescription of no. 1 in institutes of whatever juridical condition on petition of the superior of the institute, after having asked the advice of the local Hierarch if the matter requires it.

CANON 33. The rule of c. 32 concerning minor local superiors applies also to superiors or rectors of schools, hospitals, and other pious houses when these superiors or rectors are at the same time religious superiors and have under their authority other religious in regard to religious discipline too.

CANON 34. # 1. Before proceeding in institutes of men to the election of major superiors, every single vocal has to promise under oath to give his vote to those whom he in God considers should be elected.

257

2. It is the right of the president of a monastic confederation of men to preside in person or by a delegate at the election of the superior of an independent monastery of the confederation.

3. 1. At the election of a superioress in a monastery of nuns, and at the election of a superioress general in orders of women, the local Hierarch or his delegate presides, with two priests as tellers, if the house of the nuns is not subject to a religious superior of men; otherwise this superior presides; but even in such a case the Hierarch must be informed in due time of the day and hour of the election, and he can assist at it in person or by another, together with the religious superior, and, if he is assisting, preside in person or through another.

2. In the case of a stauropegial monastery the authority and office of the local Hierarch belongs to the patriarch, to whose conscience it is entirely left to confirm or rescind the election.

3. The ordinary confessors should not be appointed tellers of votes of their nuns.

4. At the election of the superioress general of congregations of women the Hierarch of the place where the election is held presides in person or through a representatives, and, if it is a congregation of eparchial right, it is entirely left to his conscience to confirm or rescind the election.

CANON 35. # 1. In elections which take place in chapter common law is to be observed together with the statutes of the respective institute, provided the latter are not contrary to it.

2. All shall beware of seeking either directly or indirectly votes for themselves or for others.

3. Postulation can be admitted only in an extraordinary case, provided it is not forbidden by the constitutions.

CANON 36. The superiors shall reside each in his own house, and they are not to absent themselves from it except in accordance with the rules of the constitutions.

CANON 37. The superiors shall see that their subjects lead a life according to the statutes of their institute, and they shall aid them by example and encouragement in the accomplishing of the scope of the institute.

CANON 38. # 1. Every superior must promote among his subjects the knowledge and the execution of the decrees of the Apostolic See, of the patriarch, or of other legitimate authority.

2. The local superiors shall take care:

1. To have read publicly, at least once a year, on fixed days, the statutes, as well as the decrees ordered to be read publicly;

2. To have given at least twice a month, without prejudice to the prescription of c. 98 # 2, an instruction on Christian doctrine, adapted to the understanding of the hearers, to those monks who are not priests and are not in ecclesiastical studies, and to the domestics, and, in an order or congregation, to the lay members and domestics, and a pious exhortation to all the members of the house, especially in a lay order and congregation.

CANON 39. # 1. A report on the state of the institute shall be forwarded every five years or oftener if the constitutions prescribe it:

1. to the Apostolic See: by the president of a monastic confederation of papal right, by the superior of an independent monastery of papal right which does not belong to a confederation, and by the superior general of other institutes of papal right.

2. to the patriarch: those mentioned in n. 1, in accordance, however, with the formulary supplied by the Apostolic See, and by the superior of an order or congregation of patriarchal right.

2. The report shall consist in a document signed by the superior and his council and, in the case of an institute of women, also by the Hierarch of the place where the superioress general with her council resides.

CANON 40. The president of a stauropegial confederation and the superior of an independent stauropegial monastery shall follow the constitutions in the matter of the report.

CANON 41. # 1. The major superior designated to this office by the constitutions shall visit, either in person or by others, if they themselves are lawfully impeded, all the houses subject to their jurisdiction, at the times appointed by the constitutions.

2. The president of a monastical confederation shall visit, either in person or by another, if they are prevented by an impediment, each single monastery of the confederation, at the times appointed by the constitutions. The visitator for the monastery which is governed by the president himself must be designated by the statutes.

CANON 42. It is the right and duty of the patriarch to visit in person or through another stauropegial monasteries as often as he deems it advisable.

CANON 43. The bishop may visit exempt religious only in cases expressly specified in law.

CANON 44. # 1. The local Hierarch must visit every five years, either in person or by another:

1. each single monastery of nuns of whatever juridical condition not subject to a religious superior of men, with the exception of the stauropegial ones;

2. monasteries of men of eparchial right, and all houses of a congregation of the same juridical condition.

2. He must also visit every five years:

1. each single monastery of nuns of whatever juridical condition in respect to that which regards the law of enclosure;

2. each single monastery of men of papal right, and each single house of every clerical institute of papal or patriarchal right, in respect to that which pertains to the church, the sacristy, public oratory, the place for the administration of the sacrament of penance;

3. each single house of a lay congregation of papal and patriarchal right, not only in respect to matters mentioned in the foregoing number, but also in regard to others, pertaining to the internal discipline; however, within the terms of c. 167 # 2, n. 1.

3. The local Hierarch must visit all clerical as well as lay religious houses of papal or patriarchal right, exempt or not exempt, if the superior major to whom the right of visitation belongs has not visited them for five years, and having been admonished by the local Hierarch has neglected to visit them.

The local Hierarch receives in # 3 a mandate, i.e., not only the right but also the duty, to perform a suppletory visitation of all religious houses of any possible juridical condition, if their major superiors, although reminded by the Hierarch, have not made such a visitation during a period of five years. There is no such provision in CIC.

Pujol (p. 165) precludes such a visitation by the local Hierarch if the visitation by the major superior could not be carried out because of impossibility. Considering the general scope of all visitation, it seems to us that the legislator intended to include every reason, not only culpable negligence. Whatever the reason for the delay might be, a religious house not visited for five years is in dire need of being subjected to the searching eyes of an ecclesiastical superior. It seems therefore trivial to regard a visitation by the local Hierarch in such circumstances a "punishment of the negligence of the proper religious superior."

CANON 45. # 1. The visitator has the right and the obligation of interrogating the religious whom he deems it well to hear, and of informing himself on those matters that pertain to the visitation; all the religious, indeed, are under the obligation of replying according to the truth, and it is not lawful for superiors to divert them in any way from this obligation, or otherwise impede the scope of the visitation.

2. Recourse may be taken from the decrees of the visitator, but not with suspensive effect, except if he proceeded in judiciary form.

CANON 46. # 1. 1. It is the right and duty of the superior in every monastery and in every clerical institute to administer in person or by another the Eucharistic Viaticum and the sacrament of unction of the infirm to the sick professed, novices, and other persons who live day and night in the religious house for reason of employment, education, hospitality or impaired health.

2. The right and duty mentioned in no. 1 belongs to the superiors named in the same number in respect to sick religious and novices staying outside the house.

2. 1. In a house of nuns, the same right and duty is held by the ordinary confessor or his substitute.

2. If the confessor or his substitute is not of the Rite of the nun, and a priest of the same Rite can be summoned, he must be called, unless there be grave reason, in order to administer to the nun the Eucharistic Viaticum and the sacrament of unction of the infirm.

3. The right and duty mentioned in # 1 belongs in a lay congregation to the pastor of the place or to the chaplain who was appointed by the Hierarch in accordance with law for a just and grave reason to replace the pastor.

CANON 47. # 1. It is forbidden to confer on religious merely honorary titles of dignities or offices. If the constitutions permit it, the titles of higher offices which religious have discharged in their own institute are alone permitted, without prejudice to the prescription of # 2.

2. Religious who discharge offices outside their own houses can receive titles of dignities of their Rite only if the patriarch, having taken counsel from the superiors, gave his consent. After having given up the office, the title or the dignity also ceases, unless liturgical regulations provide otherwise.

CANON 48. # 1. The major superiors and the superior of any religious house, at least of a formal house, shall have their counsellors, whose consent or advice they must seek according to the terms of the statutes and the canons.

2. There shall be also econoemes for the administration of temporal goods: a general econome who administers the property of the entire institute; a provincial econome for the province; a local econome for each single house; all of whom shall discharge their duties under the authority of the superior.

3. The duties of the general and provincial econoemes cannot be discharged by the superior himself; the duties, however, of the local econome, although they should be separated from the office of the superior, may nevertheless be combined with it if necessity demands it.

4. The superior of an independent monastery shall not discharge the duties of the econome of his monastery.

5. If the constitutions are silent on the manner of appointing the econoemes, they shall be appointed by the major superior with the consent of his council.

CANON 49. # 1. 1. An institute of men enjoying papal exemption shall have a procurator general, who is appointed according to the statutes, to carry on the business of his institute with the Apostolic See.

2. The procurator shall not be removed from office before the time assigned in the statutes expires, without consulting the Apostolic See.

2. The prescription of # 1 shall be followed also by other institutes of papal right, to whom it was permitted by the Apostolic See to constitute a procurator general for transacting business with her.

Divergently from the provisions of the CIC, only institutes enjoying papal exemption are obliged to have a procurator general in Rome, while other institutes of papal right without such exemption may have one if this was permitted by the Holy See.

Oriental religious institutes might have, besides a procurator general representing them before the Roman Pontiff, also one representing them at the curia of the patriarch of their Rite.

Article Two

CONFESSORS AND CHAPLAINS

CONFESSORS (cc. 50-60)

CONFESSORS OF RELIGIOUS MEN

Confessors in Monasteries and Clerical Institutes
(c. 50 = c. 518 CIC)
Confession before an Extraneous Confessor
(c. 51 = c. 519 CIC)
Confessors in Lay Institutes (c. 60 = c. 528 CIC)

CANON 50. # 1. In every independent monastery of men as well as in filial formal or in subsidiary houses, and in every house of a clerical order or congregation, several lawfully approved confessors shall be appointed in proportion with the number of the members.

2. Religious superiors who possess jurisdiction for hearing confessions may hear the confessions of those subjects who freely and on their own accord request it, observing, however, what is to be observed according to law; moreover, they shall not do so habitually without a grave reason.

3. Superiors shall beware of inducing either in person or through another, by means of fear, importune persuasion, or in any other way, any subject to confess his sins to them.

CANON 51. Without prejudice to the statutes which prescribe or counsel that confession be made at stated times to designated confessors, if a religious, even exempt, for the peace of his conscience, makes confession to a priest approved by the local Hierarch, though not listed among those designated, the confession, every contrary privilege being revoked, is valid and licit.

No mention is here made of the reservation of sins or censures established by the superiors of institutes, and that a confessor who has received faculties from the local ordinary can grant absolution from said reservations (c. 519 CIC). According to Pujol (c. 180) this is an indication of the legislator's wish that such reservations should not be declared.

Canon 60, which concerns male lay religious, belongs in this place, but is found later.

CONFESSORS OF RELIGIOUS WOMEN (cc. 52-69)

Kinds of Confessors:
The Ordinary Confessor (c. 52 # 1 = c. 520 # 1 CIC)
The Special Ordinary Confessor
(c. 52 # 2 = c. 520 # 2 CIC)
The Extraordinary Confessor
(c. 53 # 1 = c. 521 # 1 CIC)
The Supplementary Extraordinary Confessor
(c. 53 ## 2, 3 = c. 521 ## 2, 3 CIC)

The ancient monasteries of nuns had as confessors aged priest monks, not infrequently hermits who lived close to the monastery. When monasteries of men and women were erected in the vicinity of each other for greater protection against marauders, the monks provided the confessors for the nuns. Confession was not made as often as in later times, and the services of a confessor were therefore less exacting.

It was also not infrequently demanded that a priest be employed as confessor of nuns who was an eunuch. Sometimes married priests were expressly excluded from hearing the confessions of nuns or the religious of both sexes, if they were not forbidden even to celebrate in churches of nuns.

CANON 52. # 1. Only one ordinary confessor shall be assigned to each community of religious women, who shall hear the sacramental confessions of the entire community, unless, because of their large number, or for another just reason, one or more additional confessors are needed.

2. If a religious woman, for the peace of her soul or for greater progress on the road to God, requests a special confessor or spiritual director, the Hierarch shall readily grant it, watchful, however, lest from this concession abuses arise; and if they do arise, he shall carefully and prudently eliminate them, safeguarding at the same time the liberty of conscience.

CANON 53. # 1. To every community of religious women there shall be given an extraordinary confessor who, four times at least in the year, shall go to the religious house, and to whom all the religious must present themselves, at least to receive his blessing.

2. The Hierarchs of the places where religious communities of women exist shall designate for each house several priests, to whom in particular cases, the religious may easily have recourse for the sacrament of penance.

3. When any religious woman asks for one of these confessors, no superioress, either personally or through others, either directly or indirectly, may inquire into the reason for the request, or show opposition to it by word or deed, or in any way manifest displeasure at it.

CANON 54. If, notwithstanding the prescription of cc. 52, 53, any religious, for the peace of her conscience, makes her confession before a confessor approved by the local Hierarch, this confession, whether made in a church or oratory, even a semipublic one, or in a place lawfully set aside for the confession of women or of religious, is valid and lawful, every contrary privilege being revoked; nor may the superioress forbid it, or make any inquiry into the matter, even indirectly; and the religious are under no obligation to inform the superioress of the matter. If the confession was made in a place not set aside for hearing the confessions, it is indeed valid, but the confessor acts unlawfully, except in the case some extraordinarily grave reasons should demand it.

Several clarifications, which had been made for the Latin Rite canon law by authentic interpretations of the Code Commission, were incorporated in this canon:

1. The word **"adeat"** was replaced with **"peragat,"** making it clear that the religious woman can both approach as well as have summoned to the religious house a confessor approved for women by the local Hierarch (cf. Code Commission, Dec. 28, 1927, AAS 1928, 61).

2. To the wording of c. 522 CIC, that this confession can be made **"in a church or oratory, even in a semi-public one,"** was added **"or in a place lawfully set aside for the confession of women or of religious"** (cf. Code Commission, Nov. 24, 1920, AAS 1920, 575).

3. It is said that the confession will be always valid irrespectively of the place, although it could be illicit. This is against the tenor of the explanation of the Code Commission of February 12, 1935 (AAS 1935, 92), which was interpreted as declaring invalid a confession heard against the norms of c. 522 CIC in regard to the place.

CANON 55. All religious women when seriously ill, even if not in danger of death, may, as often as they wish during their serious illness, invite any priest whatsoever approved to hear confessions, though not designated for religious women, and make their confessions to him, nor can the superioress either directly or indirectly prevent them from doing so.

CANON 56. # 1. The ordinary as well as the extraordinary confessor of religious women may be priests from among either the secular or, with the permission of their superiors, religious clergy, and who are known to be of blameless life and prudent. Moreover, they shall be at least forty years of age, except, in the judgment of the Hierarch, a just cause requires otherwise, and have no authority in the external forum over the religious in question.

2. An ordinary confessor cannot be appointed as an extraordinary one, except in the cases listed in c. 58, nor can he be re-designated as ordinary confessor in the same community, until after one year from leaving the office; but an extraordinary can be appointed immediately as ordinary confessor.

3. Both ordinary and extraordinary confessors of religious women shall not interfere in any manner either in the internal or the external government of the community.

CANON 57. # 1. Without prejudice to what is prescribed in # 2, the local Hierarch appoints priests both as ordinary and extraordinary confessors; if a monastery of nuns is subject to a religious superior, the latter is to present the confessors to the Hierarch, whose right it is to approve the confessors of these nuns, and to supply, if necessary, for the neglect of the superior.

2. The patriarch designates and approves priests as confessors in a stauropegial monastery, without prejudice to the right and duty of the local Hierarch to provide in individual cases, except if by particular law even this right and duty is reserved to the patriarch.

CANON 58. An ordinary confessor of religious women shall not discharge his office longer than three years; the Hierarch, however, can confirm him for a second, and even for a third, triennium, if because of the dearth of priests suitable for this office it is impossible to provide otherwise, or if the majority of the community, including those members who in other matters have no right to cast votes, agree in secret ballot on the re-confirmation of the same confessor; provision must be made in some other way for the dissenting members, if they so desire.

CANON 59. # 1. The local Hierarch can remove, without prejudice to what is prescribed in # 2, the ordinary as well as the extraordinary confessor of religious women, even if the house of religious women is subject to a religious superior and the confessor is a religious priest, and he is not obliged to reveal his reason for the removal to anyone except to the Apostolic See. should he be requested to do so. He must, however, inform the religious superior of the removal, if the house of religious women is subject to the religious superior.

2. 1. The local Hierarch or the religious superior shall not revoke or suspend the jurisdiction or permission for hearing confessions except for a grave reason;

2. Hierarchs are not permitted to deprive all confessors of a formal religious house at one and the same time of their jurisdiction without having consulted with the Apostolic See or the patriarch.

CANON 60. In a lay congregation of men the ordinary and extraordinary confessor shall also be appointed by the local Hierarch; and when a religious requests a special confessor, the superior shall grant it in no way inquiring into the reason or manifesting displeasure at it.

CHAPLAINS AND PREACHERS (cc. 61 = c. 529 CIC)

CANON 61. # 1. Without prejudice to # 2, it is the right of the local Hierarch to designate the priest for the performing of liturgical services and to approve the preacher in a monastery of women and in a lay order or congregation.

The corresponding c. 529 CIC grants to the male superior of nuns the right to designate, i.e., nominate or propose to the local Hierarch, the chaplain and preacher for the nuns. According to this Canon of **Postquam Apostolicis** this right does not belong to the male superior but exclusively to the local Hierarch.

2. It is for the patriarch to designate the priest for liturgical services and to approve the preacher in a stauropegial monastery of women, save for the right of the local Hierarch to grant the faculty of preaching in individual cases, unless by particular law this too is reserved to the patriarch.

265

DISCLOSURE OF CONSCIENCE (c. 62 = c. 530 CIC)

CANON 62. # 1. All religious superiors are strictly forbidden to induce their subjects in any way whatsoever to make a manifestation of conscience to them.

2. Subjects, however, are not forbidden to open their minds freely and spontaneously to their superiors; nay even more, it is desirable that they approach their superiors with filial confidence, and, if the latter are priests, expose to them their doubts and troubles of conscience also.

Article Three

TEMPORAL GOODS AND THEIR ADMINISTRATION (cc. 63-69)

Capacity of Ownership (c. 63 = c. 531 CIC)
Representatives of Moral Persons (c. 64 = c. 532 CIC)
Investment of Money (c. 65 = c. 533 CIC)
Norms of Alienation (c. 66 = c. 534 CIC)
Rendering of Accounts in Institutes of Women
(c. 67 = c. 535 CIC)
Responsibility for Debts (c. 68 = c. 536 CIC)
Giving of Gifts (c. 69 = c. 537 CIC)

CANON 63. # 1. A monastery, a monastic confederation, an association of confederations, an order and a congregation, a province or quasi-province, and the house of an order or congregation, are capable of acquiring and possessing temporal property of any kind, unless the capacity of acquisition be excluded or restricted by the statutes.

2. The limitations or extension of the capacity to acquire shall be expressly defined in the statutes.

CANON 64. # 1. The property which belongs to the moral persons listed in c. 63 # 1 is to be administered in conformity with the statutes.

2. Besides superiors, those officials also who are designated by the statutes can, within the limits of their office, validly incur expenses and perform the juridical acts of ordinary administration.

CANON 65. # 1. In respect to the investment of money, the statutes shall be observed; but the previous consent of the local Hierarch must be obtained for the validity of the act by:

1. the superioress of nuns and of a congregation of eparchial right for every investment of money; if the monastery of nuns is subject to a religious superior, his consent also is needed for the validity of the investment;

2. the superioress of religious in a congregation of papal or patriarchal right, if the money constitutes the dowry of the professed members, according to c. 81;

3. the superior or the superioress of every religious house, if the funds have been donated or bequeathed for the purpose of being applied to works of charity in the locality;

4. the superior of a house of a congregation of eparchial right and the superioress of a house of any institute whatsoever, if the funds have been donated or bequeathed for divine worship;

5. every religious, even exempt, if the money was given to the parish or mission, or to the religious for the benefit of the parish or mission;

A mission in the meaning of this canon is a part of the territory of an eparchy, with its faithful, which has not yet been established as a parish or quasi-parish. This is the conclusion drawn from the use of the term in several documents of the Holy See issued for the Oriental Rite Catholics in South and North America (cf. **Pujol,** p. 233).

2. The rights and duties of the local Hierarch as listed in # 1, 1, 2, belong exclusively to the patriarch, even if the monastery of nuns be subject to a religious superior.

3. The prescriptions of ## 1, 2 are to be observed also in every change affecting the investment.

CANON 66. # 1. For the alienation of precious objects or other property, or for the contracting of debts or obligations. the terms of canons 279, 280, 283, 288, 291, shall be observed, without prejudice to what is stated in the following ## 2-4.

2. The lawful superior whose consent is required by the terms of c. 279 # 1, 3, is:

1. the Apostolic See, if — outside the patriarchate — the objects are precious or the value of the property exceeds the sum of thirty thousand francs, or — in the patriarchate — the objects are precious or the value of the property exceeds the sum of sixty thousand francs;

2. the patriarch, if the objects are precious or the value of the property amounts to more than thirty thousand but less than sixty thousand francs;

3. the superior designated by the constitutions with the consent of his chapter or his council, manifested by secret vote in accordance with the terms of the constitutions, if the value of the objects or the property amounts from ten thousand to thirty thousand francs;

4. the superior designated by the constitutions, if the value of the objects or the property does not exceed ten thousand francs.

3. 1. In the case of nuns of whatever juridical condition, or of religious women of eparchial right, besides what is prescribed in # 2, the written consent of the local Hierarch is necessary for the validity of the act, and, if the nuns are subject to a religious superior, his written consent too is required, if the value of the property subject to alienation exceeds three thousand francs;

2. In stauropegial monasteries of women, the authority of the local Hierarch mentioned in 1 belongs to the patriarch.

4. The value referred to in # 2 is to be understood as that which has been established in the written appraisal of reputable experts.

5. In the petition for permission or consent to contract debts or obligations, the other debts or obligations with which the moral per-

son listed in c. 63 # 1 is — up to that day — burdened, must be expressed; otherwise the permission or consent obtained is invalid.

The above canon has been interpreted and slightly changed in the following decree of the S. Congregation for the Oriental Church (AAS 1952, 632-633) :

"Decree — Canons 66, 281, 283, 291 of the Motuproprio P o s t- q u a m A p o s t o l i c i s L i t t e r i s determine the sum above which Apostolic approval is required for the alienation of the precious valuables and other temporal property of the Church, as well as in contracting debts and obligations. However, since the aforementioned canons do not make any decision on the gold standard, this S. Congregation for the Oriental Church has deemed it fit to enact this Decree:

During the present circumstances Apostolic approval will be necessary in the alienation of precious valuables and other temporal property of the Church, as well as in contracting debts and obligations, if the price exceeds in patriarchates the sum of 30,000 gold francs; and outside patriarchates 15,000 gold francs.

Hierarchs subject to the jurisdiction of the patriarch, as well as other religious superiors in patriarchates, need permission of the patriarch, in accordance with the respective canons, if the price is between 15,000 and 30,000 gold francs . . .
May 10, 1952."

CANON 67. # 1. In every monastery of nuns, even if it enjoys papal exemption:

1. the superioress shall furnish an account of the financial administration once a year, or even oftener, if the constitutions so prescribe it, to the local Hierarch, as well as to the religious superior if the monastery is subject to the same. Nothing can be exacted for the auditing of the report;

2. if the Hierarch does not approve of the report of the administration, he can make use of the necessary remedies, even by removing, if the circumstances demand it, the econome and the other administrators; however, if the monastery is subject to a religious superior, the Hierarch shall admonish him to settle the matter; if the latter fails to do so, he himself may take care of the situation;

3. the right and duty mentioned in 1, 2, belong in the case of a stauropegial monastery to the patriarch.

2. In the other institutes of women, the account of the administration of the property which constitute the dowries shall be furnished to the local Hierarch on the occasion of the visitation, and even oftener if the Hierarch considers it necessary.

3. The local Hierarch has moreover the right of inquiring into:

1. the economic state of a religious house of eparchial right;

2. the administration of the property referred to in c. 65 # 1, 3, 4, 5.

CANON 68. # 1. When a moral person mentioned in c. 63 # 1 contracts debts and obligations, even with the permission of superiors, the same is responsible for them.

2. When a religious with major profession contracts debts and obligations with the permission of superiors, the moral person whose superior has given the permission bears the responsibility; when it is a religious with minor profession, he himself is responsible, unless he, with the permission of the superior, transacted business for the institute.

3. When a religious acted contrary to the prescription of # 2, he himself is responsible, not the moral person.

4. The permission referred to in ## 1-2 can be validly granted only by the superior whom the statutes of that institute designate, after the prescription of the same constitutions have been observed.

5. It shall be a fixed rule that suit can always be brought against him for whom the contract has been a source of profit.

6. Religious superiors must beware not to allow the contracting of debts unless it be certain that the interest on them can be met from current income, and that within a not too long time the principal can be paid off by installments in accordance with the stipulation.

CANON 69. Gifts from the property of the moral persons mentioned in c. 63 # 1 are not permitted, unless by way of almsgiving or for other just reasons. with the consent of the superior and in conformity with the constitutions.

CHAPTER THREE

THE RECEPTION OF MEMBERS

GENERAL NORMS (c. 70 = c. 538 CIC)

CANON 70. Every Catholic who is not debarred by any legitimate impediment, is inspired by a right intention, and is fit to bear the burdens of the religious life, may be admitted into religion.

Article One:

THE POSTULATE (c. 71-73)

Necessity and Duration (c. 71 = c. 539 CIC)
Place and Garb (c. 72 = c. 540 CIC)
Spiritual Retreats (c. 73 = c. 541 CIC)

CANON 71. # 1. In every order and congregation in which perpetual vows are taken, all the women, and, if it is the case of an order or congregation of men, the coadjutors, before being admitted to the novitiate, must make a postulancy of six entire months; in congregations with temporary vows the statutes can prescribe the postulancy, but not of longer duration than six months.

2. The major superior can prolong the time prescribed for the postulancy, but not beyond another term of six months.

CANON 72. # 1. The postulancy must be made either in the novitiate house or in some other house of the order or congregation where the discipline prescribed by the statutes is faithfully observed, under the special care of an experienced religious.

2. The postulate shall wear becoming dress, different from that of the novices.

3. In an order or congregation of women the postulants are bound by the law of enclosure which is prescribed in the order or congregation.

CANON 73. The postulants, before beginning their novitiate, must make a spiritual retreat of at least eight entire days; and, according to the discretion of the confessor, a general confession of their past life.

Article Two

THE NOVITIATE

REQUIREMENTS FOR ADMISSION TO THE NOVITIATE
(cc. 74-84)

Persons Excluded from Valid and Licit Admission
(c. 74 = c. 542 CIC)
The Admitting Superior (c. 75 = c. 543 CIC)
Documents Required of Aspirants:
Extent of Obligation and Kinds of Documents
(c. 76 = c. 544 CIC)
Norms for Granting Testimonials (c. 77 = c. 545 CIC)
Obligation of Secrecy (c. 78 = c. 546 CIC)
The Dowry of Religious Women:
Institutes Obliged to Require a Dowry (c. 79 = c. 547 CIC)
Forfeiture of Dowry by Death (c. 80 = c. 548 CIC)
Investment of Principal (c. 81 = c. 549 CIC)
Administration (c. 82 = 550 CIC)
Restitution to Members Leaving the Institute
(c. 83 = c. 551 CIC)
Canonical Examination of Women Aspirants
(c. 84 = c. 552 CIC)

CANON 74. #1. Without prejudice to the prescriptions of the statutes of each institute, the following cannot validly be admitted to the novitiate:

1. those who have defected from the faith and have joined a non-Catholic sect;

While c. 542, 1, spoke of those "qui sectae acatholicae adhaeserunt," the new codification made the meaning clearer by amplifying the text to "qui a fide defecerunt et sectae acatholicae adhaeserunt," thereby including only former Catholics who had fallen away from the Church, and excluding those who had been born outside the Church and had joined the Church as converts.

270

2. those who are threatened by punishment because of a grave crime committed by them, of which they have been accused or can be accused;

3. those who have not attained the age requisite for the novitiate;

4. those who enter the institute under the influence of violence, grave fear or fraud, or whom the superior receives under the same influence;

5. a spouse, while the marriage bond lasts;

6. those who are or who have been bound by the bonds of religious profession;

7. a bishop, whether resident or titular, even though only designated or elected;

8. clerics who by a disposition of the Apostolic See are bound by oath to dedicate their activity to the service of their eparchy or the missions, for the period during which their oath binds them.

2. Without prejudice to the prescriptions of the statutes of each institute, the following are unlawfully, though validly, admitted:

1. clerics ordained to the subdiaconate or to a major order, without the knowledge of the local Hierarch or against his objection that their withdrawal would cause grave loss to souls which cannot be prevented by other means;

2. those who are burdened with debts which they are unable to discharge;

3. those who are obliged to render accounts or are implicated in other secular business from which the institute may have reason to fear lawsuits and annoyances;

4. children whose parents, that is father or mother, grandfather or grandmother, are in grave need and who therefore must be supported by them; and parents whose help is necessary for the support and education of their children;

5. those destined for the priesthood in the institute but from which they are excluded by an irregularity or other canonical impediment;

6. Latins in Oriental institutes or even Orientals in Latin institutes — with the exception of those mentioned in c. 5 — or in Oriental institutes of a different Rite, without the written permission of the Sacred Congregation for the Oriental Church.

According to an authentic interpretation of the Code Commission of Nov. 10, 1925 (AAS 1925, 583) Oriental Rite faithful could be accepted into a Latin religious institute without permission of the S. Congregation for the Oriental Church if they intended to start a house or province of that Oriental Rite. **Postquam Apostolicis** has abrogated this decision, by confirming it only for those institutes which have already constituted such houses or provinces of an Oriental Rite (cf. **Pujol**, p. 273). This amounts practically to a prohibition to start with the establishment of houses or provinces of another Rite without the previous approval of the S. Congregation for the Oriental Church.

Candidates of an Oriental Rite can be received into the institute of another Oriental Rite only with a special permission of the same S. Congregation, since such a reception is tantamount to a transfer to another Rite, which is more objectionable among Oriental Rites, especially in the Near East, than it is between an Oriental and the Latin Rite.

We have to distinguish therefore the following cases:

1. a Latin Rite Catholic wishes to enter an Oriental Rite institute: permission of the Holy See required, except if the institute enjoys a special privilege to receive without any permission candidates of the Latin Rite, as the Order of St. Basil the Great of St. Josaphat.

2. a Latin Rite Catholic wishes to enter an established Oriental Rite house or province of a Latin Rite institute: no permission required.

3. an Oriental Rite Catholic wishes to enter a Latin Rite institute which has no house or province of his Rite: permission required.

4. an Oriental Rite Catholic wishes to enter a Latin Rite institute to become a member of a lawfully established house or province of his Oriental Rite: no permission required.

5. an Oriental Rite Catholic wishes to enter an institute of another Oriental Rite: permission required.

6. an Oriental Rite Catholic wishes to enter an Oriental Rite institute of another Rite, but which has a lawfully established house or province of his Rite (cf. c. 5 # 2): no permission required.

7. an Oriental Rite Catholic wishes to enter a Latin Rite institute which has a lawfully established house or province of an Oriental Rite different from that of the candidate, who intends to join this Oriental Rite: permission required.

CANON 75. The right of admitting to the novitiate and to the subsequent religious profession, whether temporary or perpetual, belongs to the major superior with the vote of the council or chapter, according to the statutes of each institute.

CANON 76. # 1. In every institute, all the aspirants, before being admitted, must present a certificate of having received the sacraments of baptism and chrism.

2. The male aspirants must in addition furnish testimonial letters from the Hierarch of the place of birth and of every other place in which, after completing their fourteenth year, they have lived for more than a year, morally continuous, any privilege or custom to the contrary being abolished.

3. When there is question of admitting aspirants who have been in a seminary, a college, or in a postulancy or novitiate of another institute, testimonial letters are also necessary, given, according to the circumstances, by the rector of the seminary or college, after consulting the local Hierarch, or by the major superior of the institute.

4. When there is the case of admitting a cleric, in addition to a certificate of ordination, the testimonial letters of the Hierarchs of the eparchies in which he has lived for more than one morally continuous year after ordination suffice, save for the prescription of # 3.

5. The testimonial letters of the major superior of his former institute suffice for a religious lawfully passing to another institute.

6. In addition to these testimonial letters required by law, the superiors who have the right of admitting the aspirants to the institute

may also demand others which seem to them necessary or opportune in this purpose.

7. Finally, women are not to be received until careful inquiry has been made regarding their character and conduct, save for the prescription of # 3.

CANON 77. # 1. Those who must give testimonial letters according to law may not consign them to the aspirants, but, closed and sealed, to the religious superiors, and this gratuitously within two months, to be counted from the date of request, and if the aspirants are persons who have been in a seminary, a college, or in a postulancy or novitiate of another institute, they must be signed under oath by the superior.

2. If for grave reasons they judge that they cannot furnish them, they must make known the reasons to the Apostolic See within the allotted time.

3. If they reply that the aspirant is not sufficiently known to them, the religious superior shall supplement the information by another careful inquiry and trustworthy report; but if they give no reply the superior who made the request shall inform the Apostolic See that he has received no response thereto.

4. In their testimonial letters, after having made diligent investigation, even by secret inquiries, they must furnish information, the accuracy of which they are under a grave obligation in conscience to ascertain, on the birth, the conduct, the character, the life, the reputation, the condition and the learning of the aspirant; whether he is suspect, or under any censure, irregularity or any other canonical impediment, whether his family has need of his help, and, finally, when there is a question of aspirants who have been in a seminary, a college, or in a postulancy or novitiate of another institute, the reasons for their dismissal or spontaneous withdrawal.

CANON 78. All those who have received such information are bound by a strict obligation to keep secret the information itself as well as the names of the persons that supplied it.

CANON 79. # 1. In monasteries of nuns aspirants must bring the dowry prescribed by the constitutions or determined by lawful custom.

2. This dowry must be handed over before the taking of the habit, or at least surrender shall be guaranteed in a form valid according to civil law.

3. In religious congregations the statutes are to be observed in respect to the question of the dowry.

4. The prescribed dowry cannot be remitted entirely or partially without the consent of the local Hierarch if it is the case of an institute of eparchial right; otherwise only with the consent of the Apostolic See or, in patriarchates, of the patriarch in respect to an institute which is not of papal right.

CANON 80. The dowry is by law irrevocably acquired by the institute on the death of the religious, even though she had taken only temporary vows.

CANON 81. After the first profession of the religious, the superioress, after she has obtained — for the validity of the act — the consent of her council, of the local Hierarch and of the religious superior, if the house is dependent on a such one, must place the dowry in a safe, lawful and productive investment, without prejudice to what is prescribed in c. 65 # 2; it is under no circumstances allowed to make use of it in whatsoever manner, not even for the building of a house or for paying debts.

CANON 82. # 1. The dowry shall be administered by the monastery or house in which the superioress general or the provincial superioress habitually reside.

2. The local Hierarchs are diligently to supervise the conservation of the dowries of religious women; they must demand an account of them, especially on the occasion of the canonical visitation.

CANON 83. # 1. If, for whatever cause, a religious woman of whatsoever profession leaves the institute, her dowry must be restored in its entirety, but without the interest already accrued therefrom.

2. 1. If the professed religious woman lawfully passes to another institute, the interest on the dowry belongs, during her novitiate, to that institute, in accordance with c. 104 # 1; but after the new profession has been made, the dowry itself devolves upon it.

2. If a religious woman passes from a dependent monastery to an independent monastery, or vice versa, or if she passes from a house of an order or congregation to another house of the same order or congregation, the dowry is due to that independent monastery or house from the day of transfer.

3. If the dowry has been spent against the prescription of c. 81, the obligations mentioned in ## 1, 2, remain notwithstanding.

CANON 84. # 1. The local Hierarch must be informed by the superioress of religious women, even though exempt, at least two months in advance, of the approaching admission to the novitiate as well as to the first and to the perpetual profession.

2. 1. The local Hierarch or, if he is absent or prevented, a priest designated by him, shall search diligently and gratutiously the mind of the aspirant, at least thirty days before admission to the novitiate or the profession, without however entering the enclosure, as to whether she is forced or deceived, whether she understands what she is about to do; and only then can an aspirant be admitted to the novitiate or a novice to the profession after it has been ascertained that she is doing so from a pious and free state of mind.

2. The same right and duty belongs in a stauropegial monastery to the patriarch, without prejudice to particular law which assigns the same to the local Hierarch.

TRAINING OF NOVICES (cc. 85-105)

THE NOVITIATE:

Mode of Beginning the Novitiate (c. 85 = c. 553 CIC)

The Novitiate in Monasteries (c. 86 = new)
The Novitiate in Orders and Congregations
(c. 87 = cf. c. 554 CIC)

274

Conditions for a Valid Novitiate (c. 88 = c. 555 CIC)
Duration (c. 89 = c. 556 CIC)
The Use of the Religious Garb (c. 90 = c. 557 CIC)
Novitiate for Different Classes of Members
(c. 91 = c. 558 CIC)

CANON 85. The novitiate begins with the reception of the habit, or in any other manner prescribed by the constitutions.

CANON 86. # 1. Each independent monastery is entitled to have its own novitiate.

2. Aspirants may make the novitiate for a just reason by order of the superiors in another independent monastery of the same confederation.

3. If a confederated monastery is judged by the chapter of the confederation to be unable to satisfy the canonical prescriptions in respect to the education of novices, the chapter can direct that monastery to send the aspirants to another monastery of the same confederation.

4. 1. Confederated monasteries may agree to have one common novitiate.

2. If several confederated monasteries are judged by the chapter of the confederation not to be able to have each its own novitiate, it can impose on them one common novitiate.

5. If a non-confederated independent monastery cannot fulfill the prescriptions relative to the education of novices, the superior is bound by a grave obligation to send the aspirants to another monastery where these prescriptions are conscientiously observed.

CANON 87. # 1. 1. In orders and in congregations the novitiate house shall be erected in accordance with the statutes.

2. For its valid erection the permission of the Apostolic See is required if the house belongs to an order or congregation which enjoys papal exemption, or to a congregation of papal right, or, in patriarchates, the permission of the patriarch is needed if it belongs to an order subject to the patriarch or to a congregation of patriarchal right, or of the local Hierarch if it belongs to a congregation of eparchial right.

The novitiate of a monastery does not need for its erection a special permission from any hierarch, since each independent monastery is authorized by law (c. 86 # 1) to have its own novitiate.

A dependent monastery that is in preparation to become independent can establish a novitiate only with the approval of that hierarch to whom it is subject.

3. If an institute is divided into provinces, more than one novitiate house cannot validly be erected in the same province, except for grave reason and with the permission obtained in accordance with 2.

2. The superiors shall permit in the novitiate house and in a house of study only religious who are exemplary in their zeal for regular observance.

CANON 88. # 1. In addition to the conditions enumerated in c. 74 # 1, in order that the novitiate be valid, it must be made:

1. after at least the fifteenth year of age has been completed.
2. for an entire and uninterrupted period of three years, if it is the case of monks. However, the superior of an independent monastery can dispense, with the consent of his council or chapter in accordance with the statutes, for a sufficient and justified reason, from the third year of the novitiate, without prejudice, however, to the prescription of c. 107;

The duration of the novitiate was fixed as early as in the 6th century as a period of three years, although for candidates of mature age, who had as seculars led an exemplary life, the novitiate could be shortened to six months. This norm is still followed by Oriental dissidents of the Byzantine Rite. Students of schools of theology or widowed secular priests, especially if they are to be promoted to the episcopacy, are permitted to receive the little habit, i.e., to make monastic profession, at once, after a very short novitiate, possibly of one day only.

3. for an entire and uninterrupted year, if it is the case of an order or congregation;
4. in the monastery or house of the novitiate.

2. If in an order or congregation the statutes prescribe a longer time for the novitiate, this is not required for the validity of the profession, except the constitutions expressly declare otherwise.

CANON 89. # 1. The novitiate is interrupted and must be recommenced and completed: if the novice, having been dismissed by the superior, leaves the house, or, without the permission of the latter, leaves the house with the intention of not returning, or, even with the permission of the superior, and from whatever motive, during the first year of novitiate, has remained for more than thirty days, whether continuously or not, outside the house, although with the intention of returning.

2. If the novice during the first year of the novitiate, with the permission of the superiors or constrained by force, has passed more than fifteen days but not more than thirty days, even interruptedly, outside the precincts of the house under the obedience of the superior, it is necessary and sufficient for the validity of the novitiate that he supplement the number of days so passed outside; if for a period not exceeding fifteen days, the supplementing for this period can be prescribed by the superiors, but is not necessary for the validity.

3. Superiors shall not grant permission to remain outside the precincts of the novitiate except for a just and grave reason.

4. If the novice is transferred by the superiors to another monastery of the same confederation in accordance with c. 86 ## 2-4, or in another novitiate house of the same institute, the novitiate is not interrupted, save for the prescription of # 1.

The corresponding paragraph of c. 556 CIC does not contain the reference to the first paragraph, and a novice, therefore, who for the transfer from one to another novitiate took more than one month was not, strictly speaking, obliged to repeat the novitiate or supplement the time lost.

CANON 90. The habit prescribed for novices by the statutes shall be worn throughout the whole period of the novitiate, unless special local circumstances demand otherwise.

Eastern monachism does not know the postulate as a specific period which preceeds the novitiate. According to St. Theodore the Studite a candidate should be kept for two or three weeks in the guest house, in order that he may get to know the monastery and the monastery know him. He was then at once accepted into the monastery as a novice, without any specific ceremony. This corresponds to the tradition preserved in some Latin Rite monastic orders, as the Carthusians. Other orders also, as, e.g., the Benedictines, have the real clothing with the monastic habit at the time of profession.

Sometimes the novice (archarios, dokimos) is permitted to wear certain parts of the monastic garb, perhaps the tunic, cincture, headdress, and the rason. From the last garment novices were called rasophori, which led to confusing them with the first degree of monastic profession, the rasophorate (cf. c. 109). It will be up to the constitutions to decree whether novices shall wear lay garb, or shall change to a somewhat more sober form, or shall receive certain parts of the general monastic garments.

CANON 91. In orders and congregations where there are two classes of members the particular law shall be observed in the matter of the passing of a novice from one class to the other.

The present canon speaks only of the transfer of novices from one class to another. The transfer of professed members from the class of clerics or choir members to that of lay brothers or sisters, and viceversa, is to be regulated by particular law.

While c. 558 CIC simply declares that the novitiate has to be repeated if a member of an order or congregation transfers from one class to the other, Oriental canon law lets particular law enact suitable norms for such cases.

Monks do not know a division in classes, and there is only one novitiate for all candidates, whether they are clerics, or laymen, who either are to be promoted at some later time to orders, or are to stay forever simple monks.

THE MASTER OF NOVICES:

Number and Qualifications (c. 92 = c. 559 CIC)
Appointment (c. 93 = c. 560 CIC)
Relationship to other Superiors (c. 94 = c. 561 CIC)
Duties Toward the Novices (c. 95 = c. 562 CIC)
Report to Superiors (c. 96 = c. 563 CIC)

Novices in Eastern monasteries were not under the direction of one master of novices, but they were individually assigned to certain older monks, who were known for their exemplary life and knowledge, who acted as their teachers in the spiritual life, less by oral instruction than by their daily example.

CANON 92. # 1. The formation of the novices must be entrusted to a master, who shall be at least thirty-five years of age, professed for at least ten years from the date of his first profession, be distinguished for prudence, charity, piety and regular observance, and, if it is the case of a monastery of men or a clerical institute, he must possess the order of priesthood.

2. If it is deemed expedient, on account of the number of novices or for any other just cause, an associate shall be assigned to the master of novices, immediately subject to him in all matters pertaining to the direction of the novitiate, who shall be at least thirty years of age, professed five years from the first profession, and have the other necessary and suitable qualities.

3. Both must be free from all other occupations which could hinder them in the care and direction of the novices.

CANON 93. The master of novices and his associate shall be appointed in accordance with the terms of the statutes and, if these prescribe a fixed term for the duration of their office, they shall be removed only in accordance with the statutes for a just and grave reason. However, if the fixed term has expired, they may be reappointed.

CANON 94. # 1. The master alone has the right and duty of providing for the formation of the novices, and he alone is charged with the direction of the novitiate, so that no one, under whatever pretext, may interfere in these matters, except the superiors to whom this is permitted by the statutes and the visitors. However, as to the general discipline of the house, the master, in the same way as the novices, is subject to the superior.

2. The novice is subject to the authority of the master and of the superiors of the institute, and he must obey them.

CANON 95. The master of novices is bound by a grave obligation to employ all diligence in assiduously forming his novices in the discipline of religious life, conformably to the statutes and to the terms of c. 98.

CANON 96. During the term of the novitiate, the master shall present, comformably to the statutes, to the chapter or the major superior a report concerning the conduct of each of the novices.

ACTIVITY OF NOVICES:

Segregation of Novices (c. 97 = c. 564 CIC)
Required Training (c. 98 = c. 565 CIC)
Second Year of Novitiate (c. 99 = new)
Confessors of the Novices (c. 100 = c. 566 CIC)

CANON 97. The novitiate shall be, as far as possible, separated from that part of the house which is inhabited by the professed members, so that, without a special reason and the permission of the superior or master, the novices may have no communication with the professed members, nor the latter with the novices.

The # 2 of c. 564 CIC, which orders for the novices separate living quarters according to classes (clerics — lay brothers; choir nuns — lay nuns), was not taken over into **Postquam Apostolicis.**

CANON 98. # 1. The term of the novitiate under the direction of the master must have for its object the forming of the mind of the novice by the study of the statutes, by pious meditations and assiduous prayer, by instruction in matters which pertain to the vows and the virtues, by suitable exercises in rooting-out vices, in regulating the movements of the soul, in acquiring virtues.

2. The lay novices are in addition to be carefully instructed in Christian doctrine, and to this end a special conference should be given them at least once a week.

3. During the year of novitiate the novices shall not be employed in preaching, or hearing confessions, or in the external charges of the institute, or even in the study of literature, the sciences or arts; the lay members may perform within the religious house itself all their duties, not, however, in a supervisory capacity, in so far they do not prevent them from taking part in the exercises of the novitiate prescribed for them, without prejudice to c. 90.

CANON 99. # 1. The novices of monasteries are permitted, after the first year of novitiate has expired, and unless the statutes provide otherwise, to carry on studies in their monastery, or — if it is the case of confederated monasteries in accordance with c. 123, ## 2, 3 — in the monastery where the house of studies is located, without prejudice to the prescription that they must two months before the profession return to their monastery, and, having put aside their studies, prepare themselves for the taking of the profession.

2. The prescription of # 1 shall be observed in those orders and congregations whose statutes establish a term of novitiate longer than a year. The novices may carry on their studies also in another novitiate house of the same institute.

CANON 100. # 1. In the novitiates of women the prescriptions of cc. 52-59 are to be observed in respect to the priest-confessor.

2. In institutes of men, without prejudice to what is prescribed in c. 51:

1. There shall be, according to the number of novices, one or more ordinary confessors, safeguarding the prescription of # 3.

2. In a monastery or in a clerical order or congregation the ordinary confessors shall live in the novitiate house itself; in lay congregations they shall at least frequently come to the novitiate house to hear the confessions of the novices;

3. Besides the ordinary confessors other confessors shall be designated to whom in particular cases the novices may freely have recourse; nor may the master manifest any displeasure at this;

4. At least four times a year the novices are to be given an extraordinary confessor to whom all are to present themselves at least to receive his blessing.

3. The master of novices and his associate shall not hear the confession of their subjects with whom they live in the same house, except in particular cases, if the novices request it for a grave reason of their own accord.

RIGHTS OF NOVICES:

Privileges of Novices (c. 101 = c. 567 CIC)
Dispositions Concerning Property of Novices:
During the Novitiate (c. 102 = cf. c. 568 CIC)
At the Termination of the Novitiate (c. 103 = c. 569 CIC)
In Relationship to the Institute (c. 104 = c. 570 CIC)
Freedom of Leaving the Institute (c. 105 = c. 571 CIC)

CANON 101. # 1. The novices enjoy all the privileges and spiritual favors granted to the institute; and if they should be overtaken by death, they have a right to the same suffrages as are prescribed for the professed members.

2. During the novitiate they may not go through the sacred rite by which one is received into the clergy, nor be promoted to orders.

CANON 102. A novice cannot licitly or validly renounce in any way whatever his benefices or his property, or burden them with obligations.

CANON 103. # 1. Before the novice makes the minor profession in whatever institute, he must cede, for the whole period during which he will be bound by this profession, the administration of his property to whomsoever he prefers, and dispose freely of its use and usefruct, except the constitutions determine otherwise.

2. If this cession and disposition was omitted because of lack of property and something came subsequently into his possession, or if after making the provision other property was acquired under whatever title, it should be made now or repeated in accordance with # 1, although he may have already made the profession.

3. The novice shall before the profession freely dispose by a last will of all the property he presently posseses or may subsequently acquire.

CANON 104. # 1. Unless the statutes or a formal agreement require the payment of a certain sum for food and clothing during the postulancy or novitiate, nothing can be exacted to defray the expenses of the postulancy or novitiate.

2. What a postulant or novice has brought with him and has not been consumed by use shall be returned to him if he leaves the institute without making profession.

CANON 105. # 1. The novice can freely leave the institute, or he may for any just cause be dismissed by the superiors or the chapter, in accordance with the statutes, and the superior or chapter are not bound by any obligation to make known to the dismissed the reason for the dismissal.

2. The novitiate completed, the novice shall be admitted to profession if he is judged suitable, otherwise he shall be dismissed; but if there remains a doubt whether he is suitable, the time of his probation can be prolonged in orders and congregations by the major superiors, but not for more than six months.

No prorogation of the time of novitiate can be accorded in a monastery. If a novice after three years of novitiate still has not proved his worthiness to become a professed member of the monastery, there is no sense in expecting that it could happen in the next six months. He is to be dismissed at once, or admitted to profession, except if he has not yet completed his twenty-first year of age (cf. c. 108).

 # 3. The novice shall make a spiritual retreat of at least eight entire days before pronouncing his vows.

Article Three

RELIGIOUS PROFESSION (cc. 106-122)

Conditions for Validity of Profession (c. 106 = cf. c. 572 CIC)
Age Required:
    General Norm (c. 107 = c. 573 CIC)
    In Monasteries (c. 108 = new)
Degrees of Monastical Profession (c. 109 = new)

Monastic profession was in the East compared to baptism, and following this analogy, the superior receiving it was compared with the baptizing priest, the master from among the monks, who had guided the novice and now presented him for profession, had the role of the godfather. Further analogies with baptism were the change of the name, the vesting with the monastic habit, the inauguration of a new life.

Profession can be major or minor, the latter again either a temporary or a perpetual one (cf. c. 315, inserted after cc. 1, 2). Major profession is equivalent in its juridical effects to the solemn profession of CIC, while minor profession is the same as simple profession.

Eastern monks make major profession, to be pronounced after the novitiate. The only minor profession among Eastern monks and nuns is that mentioned in c. 108.

CANON 106. # 1. For the validity of any religious profession whatsoever it is required:

1. That he who is to make it be of legal age according to c. 107; that he made a valid novitiate, according to c. 88; that he be admitted to profession by the legitimate superior in accordance with the statutes.

2. That the profession be expressed in formal terms, that it be free from violence or grave fear or fraud; that it be received by the legitimate superior according to the statutes, either in person or through another.

Profession of the monastic vows was not always in the Christian East an act expressed by some formula. Sometimes signs were considered a satisfactory expression of the intention, as, e.g., free participation in the liturgical act, listening to the contents of the liturgical prayers, tonsure, reception of the habit, etc. Today a clear expression of the will to accept the obligations of the vows is prescribed for all Oriental religious.

However, even the express profession is not necessarily an explicit enumeration of all obligations, i.e., of each vow. Not all Oriental formularies contain a taxative listing of the obligations.

281

It is not required that the profession be expressed in one concise declaration; it suffices that the candidate answers affirmatively to the various questions put to him by the superior during the liturgical services.

2. For the validity of the perpetual profession in orders and congregations, it is in addition required that it be preceded by a temporary simple profession according to the prescription of c. 110.

3. 1. A novice who is in danger of death can be admitted to profession by the major superior, or, if time does not permit recourse to him, by the local superior.

2. Such a professed member enjoys the same indulgences, privileges and spiritual favors gained by the professed members; if he, however, regains his health, the profession lapses in its force.

CANON 107. Whoever makes a religious profession must have completed for the temporary profession his sixteenth year of age; for the perpetual profession his twenty-first year.

CANON 108. Whoever in monasteries, after having completed the triennium of novitiate, is admitted to religious profession, but has not yet reached the age required by law for the major profession, must make without any delay temporary profession in the same monastery, which will be valid till he has reached the legal age, except if the interval between the end of the novitiate and the prescribed age is shorter than six months; in this case the superior of an independent monastery can decide that the temporary profession be omitted.

CANON 109. In respect to the different degrees of the monastic profession, the constitutions shall be observed, safeguarding the canonical force of the monastic profession in the different degrees.

A peculiarity of Eastern monachism are the degrees in the monastic profession. All degrees induce the same legal effects, and make the monk or nun juridically incapable of acts contrary to the vows or, in other words, all degrees of the profession have the effects of solemn profession of the Latin Rite canon law. What distinguishes one degree from the other are ascetical obligations, and as a consequence, also some limitations as to appointment to certain offices.

It cannot be ascertained when the originally single profession was divided into degrees. The 8th century knew the distinction, and St. Theodore the Studite († 825) fought valiantly against it, however, without success. It is now accepted everywhere, and **Postquam Apostolicis** permits its existence.

According to liturgical formularies and the witness of ancient authors, there are three degrees:

1. **Rasophorate,** so-called because these monks wore **(phorein)** the **rason,** a black coat with wide sleeves, donned over the cassock **(sub-rason).** The liturgical formulary has no explicit profession, and is therefore not clear what obligations are induced by these vows. It was therefore always debated whether the rasophor is a true, professed monk or only a novice, or perhaps a monk who observes the vows, has a moral obligation to persevere in the mon-

astery, but may leave the monastery without legal consequences. The rasophorate can be regarded as a juridical institution which has not gone through its complete evolution. What kind of obligation is effected by the reception of the rasophorate, if it exists in a Catholic religious institute, will depend on the stipulations of the constitutions.

Among dissident Orientals rasophors are usually not promoted to orders, although sometimes widowed priests, who took monastic tonsure as rasophores, have been ordained bishops in the Russian Church.

2. The **Little Habit** (**mikron scheema**) is so called from the vestments the monk receives in the liturgical ceremony. He again is tonsured, even if he has received previously the rasophorate, and his answers to the questions of the superior contain the usual monastic vows. Besides the garments specific of the rasophors, the **rason** and the **camelaucum,** a high hat of cylindrical form, the mikroscheemus receives the **mandyas,** a wide black cloak, the **supercamelaucum,** a veil which covers the camelaucum and falls down over the shoulders, and a small wooden cross to be worn under the vestments. Such a monk was forbidden ever to eat meat, and was obliged to all monastic duties, but he was qualified for the office of superior, and could become a bishop.

It is not necessary to go through the ceremony of the rasophorate if a person wishes at once to become a full monk.

3. The **Grand** or **Angelic Habit** (**mega scheema**) gives the monk or nun a new garment, the **paramandyas.** It has the form of a Latin Rite scapular, reaching in front and back down to below the knees. The paramandyas, also called **analabion** or **paraman,** is adorned with many crosses, therefore also called **polystaurion** (many crosses), with the inscription "Holy, Holy, Holy," and with other symbols. The megaloscheemus exchanges the camelaucum and supracamelaucum with a cowl or hood (**koukoulion**). Such monks are obliged to devote more time to prayers and meditation. They are usually not admitted to this profession, except at an age of at least fifty years, and after a number of years (in Russia thirty) as monks of the little habit. Because of their ascetical duties they cannot be superiors or become bishops. A bishop who would take the grand habit would thereby resign his dignity, since they are considered incompatible with each other. The grand habit is often taken by monks on the death bed.

When Oriental Rite monks became organized according to the manner of Latin Rite orders, as, e.g., the Ukrainian Basilian Fathers, they declared the temporary profession in the order as little habit, and the perpetual and solemn profession as grand or angelic habit. This adaptation does not, of course, correspond with the use of the same terms in Oriental canon law.

TEMPORARY VOWS:

General Norms (c. 110 = c. 574 CIC)
Effect of Expiration of Temporary Vows (c. 111 = c. 575 CIC)
Rite of Profession (c. 112 = c. 576 CIC)
Anticipation of Profession (c. 113 = c. 577 CIC)
Rights and Duties (c. 114 = c. 578 CIC)

CANON 110. # 1. In orders and congregations in which perpetual vows are taken the novice must, after he has completed the novitiate, and has been admitted to profession, without any delay make in the novitiate house itself a profession to endure for a triennium, before taking perpetual vows, save for the provision of c. 184, or for a longer period, if the age required for perpetual profession will be attained at a latter date, unless the statutes require annual professions.

2. The legitimate superior can prolong this period for a just reason, the religious meanwhile renewing the temporary profession, provided the interval from the end of the novitiate till the making of the perpetual profession does not exceed in any event six years.

CANON 111. # 1. In any institute whatsoever with perpetual vows, when the period of temporary profession has expired, the religious, according to the terms of c. 187, must return to secular life if he does not make the perpetual profession; but even during the period of temporary profession he can, if he be not judged worthy to pronounce perpetual vows, be dismissed by the legitimate superior conformably to c. 199.

2. The vote of the council or chapter is a deliberative one, both for the first profession as well as for the subsequent perpetual profession.

While c. 575 # 2 CIC decrees that the vote of the chapter or council is a decisive one at the admission to the first profession, and at the admission to perpetual profession it has only consultative force, **Postquam Apostolicis** narrows the authority of the superior, and declares in both circumstances the vote of the synaxis as decisive, forcing the superior to follow the majority.

CANON 112. # 1. In making religious profession the prescriptions of the statutes and of the liturgical books are to be observed.

2. The temporary profession shall in monasteries be made privately, namely, without a gathering of the faithful.

Temporary profession in a monastery is prescribed only for candidates who have terminated their three years of novitiate, but have not yet completed their twenty-first year of age, or will not complete it for a period of more than six months. It is not in harmony with the Eastern tradition. In order not to diminish the singularity of the monastic or major profession, this temporary profession is to be performed in a private manner.

3. The document of the profession, signed by the professed member himself and at least by him before whom the profession was made, shall be preserved in the archives of the institute; and in addition, if it is the case of a major profession, the superior accepting it

must notify the pastor where the baptism of the professed religious should have been recorded according to the prescriptions of the canons.

CANON 113. # 1. In orders and congregations no interval shall be interposed before the renovation of the vows if the time for which the vows had been taken has expired.

2. The superiors can permit for a just reason a brief anticipation of the renewal of the temporary vows, but only so that the anticipation does not exceed one month.

CANON 114. In an institute of perpetual vows, those who are bound by temporary profession:
1. enjoy the same indulgences, privileges, and spiritual favors as the members professed of perpetual vows, and if they be overtaken by death, they have the right to the same suffrages;
2. they are held by the same obligation as the perpetually professed to observe the constitutions;
3. they lack both active and passive voice, except the statutes expressly declare otherwise.

JURIDICAL EFFECTS OF PROFESSION

General Norm (c. 115 = c. 579 CIC)
Property Rights After Minor Profession
  (c. 116 = cf. c. 580 CIC)
Abdication Before Major Profession (c. 117 = c. 581 CIC)
Property Accruing After Major Profession
  (c. 118 = c. 582 CIC)
Acts Forbidden Those in Minor Profession
  (c. 119 = c. 583 CIC)
Loss of Benefices and Offices (c. 120 = c. 584 CIC)
Loss of Original Eparchy (c. 121 = c. 585 CIC)
Invalid Profession (c. 122 = c. 586 CIC)

CANON 115. Minor profession, whether temporary or perpetual, renders acts contrary to the vows illicit, but not invalid, unless it be otherwise expressly provided for; while the major profession renders them also invalid if they can be nullified.

CANON 116. # 1. The minor profession, whether made temporarily or perpetually, does not deprive the religious either of the ownership of his property nor of the capacity to acquire other property, except if the statutes declare otherwise.

2. But whatever the religious acquires by his own industry or in respect of his institute, he acquires for the institute; and it shall be presumed that the religious acquires it in respect to the institute, except the contrary was lawfully proven.

The text of c. 580 CIC was expanded by the insertion of the legal presumption that whatever a religious acquires he acquires for his institute, except if the contrary is lawfully proved.

3. Regarding the cession or disposition treated in c. 103 ## 1, 2 the professed religious can modify it, not however on his own

authority, except if the statutes permit so, but with the consent of the superior general, or of the superior of the independent monastery, or, if it is the case of religious women in monasteries or in orders bound by minor profession, with the consent of the local Hierarch, and, if the institute of women is subject to a regular superior, of this superior also, provided the modification is not to be made in favor of the institute, at least for a notable part of the property; in the case of withdrawal from the institute, this cession and disposition ceases to have effect.

CANON 117. # 1. 1. A candidate for major profession must within sixty days preceding the profession, save for special indults granted by the Apostolic See, renounce in favor of whomsover he wishes all the property he actually possesses, on condition that his profession subsequently takes place.

2. A renunciation which is made before this time is null and void by law.

2. Immediately after the profession has been made all necessary measures shall be taken to make the renunciation effective in civil law.

CANON 118. All property which comes in any way to the religious after major profession, save for special indults of the Apostolic See, accrues to the monastery or order, province, quasi-province, house, according to the statutes.

Canon 582, no. 2, CIC was not reproduced in this canon, since there are no religious institutes in the Oriental Church incapable of acquiring property, as we find them in the Latin Rite Church in the various branches of the Franciscans.

CANON 119. Those who are bound by minor profession are not allowed:

1. To renounce gratutiously the dominion over their property by a voluntary deed of conveyance;

2. To change the last will made according to the terms of c. 103 # 3, without the permission of the superior general, or, if the case be urgent and time does not admit of recourse to him, without the permission of the major superior, or, if not even he can be reached, of the local superior.

While c. 583, 2, CIC permits the change of a last will only with the consent of the Holy See, Postquam Apostolicis requires solely that of the superior general.

CANON 120. With the making of the religious profession all offices whatsoever of the professed religious become vacant by this very act, without any special declaration; his parish benefice becomes vacant after one year; the other after three years.

This canon has added to the text known from c. 584 CIC the clause that, besides benefices, also offices held by the religious became vacant only at the moment of his profession.

CANON 121. After a religious has made his perpetual profession, either a solemn or simple, and in an institute without perpetual vows, after six years from the first profession have elapsed, he loses by law itself his own eparchy to which he belonged as a secular.

Differently from c. 585 CIC provision was here made for members of institutes in which no perpetual vows are taken; they lose their original eparchy after six years of temporary profession.

CANON 122. # 1. The religious profession which is null because of an external impediment is not rendered valid by subsequent acts, but needs to be validated by the Apostolic See, or, the nullity having been discovered and the impediment removed, a new profession must be lawfully made.

2. If it be null on account of a purely internal defect of consent, it becomes valid when this is given, provided that the consent on the part of the institute has not been revoked.

3. If there are serious arguments against the validity of the religious profession, and the religious refuses as a means of precaution either to renew the profession or to apply for its convalidation, the matter shall be referred to the Apostolic See.

CHAPTER FOUR

THE SYSTEM OF STUDIES AND MATTERS PERTAINING TO THE RECEPTION OF ORDINATION IN MONASTERIES AND IN OTHER CLERICAL RELIGIOUS INSTITUTES

STUDIES FOR MEMBERS OF THE CLERICAL STATE
(cc. 123-130)

Home of Studies of Monks (c. 123 = new)
House of Studies of Clerical Institutes
   (c. 124 = c. 587 # 1 CIC)
Discipline in Houses of Studies (c. 125 = c. 587 # 2 CIC)
Provisions in Case of Lack of a House of Studies
   (c. 126 = c. 587 ## 2, 3 CIC)
Spiritual Director of Students (c. 127 = c. 588 CIC)
Course of Studies (c. 128 = c. 589 CIC)
Junior Clergy Examinations (c. 129 = c. 590 CIC)
Monthly Conferences (c. 130 = c. 591 CIC)

Extensive norms for regulating the studies of Oriental Rite clergy in the Near East were issued by the S. Congregation for the Oriental Church in the decree of Jan. 27, 1940 (AAS 1940, 152-157) "De recta cleri orientalis institutione in territoriis patriarchalibus," which orders the preparation of the secular as well as the regular clergy.

CANON 123. # 1. Each individual independent monastery may have its own house of studies.

2. Several monasteries of the same confederation may agree to have a common house of studies.

3. If a monastery of a confederation is judged by the chapter of the confederation not to be able to have its own house of studies properly established, the same chapter can order that the religious for their studies be sent to another monastery of the confederation where a course of studies is properly established.

CANON 124. Every clerical institute shall have its house of studies established by the general chapter or by the superiors in accordance with the terms of the statutes.

CANON 125. In the house of studies monastic and religious disipline is to be perfectly observed, as similarly prescribed in c. 87 # 2.

The threat that "students cannot be promoted to orders" (c. 587 # 2 CIC) if perfect religious discipline is not observed in the house of studies, is not repeated here. The warning is too indefinite and vague as to when the discipline ceases to be perfect and which superior is to apply the sanction, so that it would remain without effect.

CANON 126. # 1. If a monastery or a confederation, a clerical institute or province, is unable to have a house of studies properly established, or in the case there is one but access to it, in the judgment of the superiors, is difficult, the religious shall be sent for their studies either to another house of studies, properly conducted, of another monastery or province or institute, or to the courses of the episcopal seminary, or to a public Catholic university.

2. Religious who are sent for their studies far from their own house are not allowed to live in private homes, but must necessarily go to a house of their own institute, or, if this is not possible, to a religious institution of men, or to a seminary or a pious house which is under the direction of a priest, and is approved by ecclesiastical authority.

CANON 127. # 1. The religious are to be entrusted for the entire curriculum of studies to the special care of a spiritual director or prefect, who shall lead their minds towards the religious life by suitable admonitions, instructions and exhortations.

2. The spiritual prefect or director must possess those qualities which are required for the master of novices according to the terms of c. 92 # 1.

3. The superiors shall seduously watch that what is prescribed in c. 137 for all religious be observed most perfectly in the house of studies.

CANON 128. # 1. After the religious have received proper instruction in preparatory disciplines, they shall apply themselves to the study of philosophy for at least two years and of sacred theology for at least four years, in accordance with # 2, in the manner prescribed by the Apostolic See.

2. 1. The professors shall in their teaching of theological disciplines have as a guide the doctrine of the holy fathers and teachers of the Church.

2. The same professors shall in explaining the teaching of philosophy and theology and in the education of their pupils in these dis-

ciplines follow and conscientiously apply the manner, doctrine and principles which were taught and professed by the Angelic Doctor St. Thomas as follower of St. John Damascene.

In order to emphasize the respect the Western Church feels toward the theological traditions of the Christian East, c. 589 # 2 CIC has been amplified by mentioning, as sources and guides in theological studies, the fathers and great teachers of the Church, and specifically St. John Damascene, who in some aspects was a precursor of St. Thomas Aquinas.

3. During the studies occupations which are in any manner an obstacle to the teachers in carrying out their duties, or to the students either in the attendance of classes or in their studies, shall not be assigned to the teachers and students; but the superior of an independent or dependent monastery, the superior general, and in particular cases, other superiors too, may, according to their prudent judgment, dispense them from one or the other common duty, even from the celebration of the divine office, especially during the night hours, as often as this is considered necessary for the success of their studies.

CANON 129. Religious priests, with the exception only of those who are dispensed by the major superiors for a grave reason, or who teach either theology or canon law or scholastic philosophy. after having finished the curriculum of studies, shall, each year, for five years at least, undergo an examination before learned and worthy fathers in the various disciplines of the sacred sciences to be assigned in advance.

Deacons and minor clergy, especially if permanently promoted to these orders, are exempt from the junior clergy examinations, since they are usually without any systematic theological studies.

CANON 130. In every formal house at least, as a minimum once a month, there shall be held a meeting or conference on moral and liturgical problems, to which may be added a lecture concerning a dogmatical question or kindred subjects; and all professed clerics who are engaged in the study of sacred theology or have completed such a course, and are living in the house, must attend, unless the constitutions provide otherwise.

RECEPTION OF HOLY ORDERS (cc. 131-134)

Dismissorial Letters (c. 131 = cf. c. 964 CIC)
The Competent Bishop (c. 132 = c. 965 CIC)
Inavailability of the Local Bishop (c. 133 = c. 966 CIC)
Prohibition of Fraudulent Avoidance of the Local Bishop
(c. 134 = c. 967 CIC)

CANON 131. Major superiors. in accordance with the statutes, can grant to their subjects dismissorial letters for minor orders after they have made their first profession; for major orders, in institutes with perpetual vows after they have made the perpetual profession, in institutes without perpetual vows after the completion of six years from the first profession.

289

CANON 132.# 1. The bishop to whom the religious superior must address the dismissorial letters is the bishop of the eparchy in which the religious house is located, to the family of which the candidate for orders belongs.

2. The superior of a stauropegial monastery must address the dismissorial letters to the bishop designated by the patriarch.

CANON 133. # 1. The religious superior may direct the dismissorial letters to another bishop only in the case that the eparchial bishop has given his permission, or that he is of another Rite, or is absent, or, finally, the eparchy is vacant and he who is governing it does not possess the episcopal consecration.

2. It is necessary that this be ascertained to the satisfaction of the ordaining bishop by an authentic document of the episcopal curia.

CANON 134. Religious superiors shall beware of deceiving the eparchial bishop by sending their subjects candidates for orders to another religious house, or purposely of postponing the issuance of dismissorial letters to the time they know the bishop will be absent.

CHAPTER FIVE

OBLIGATIONS AND PRIVILEGES OF RELIGIOUS

Article One:

OBLIGATIONS OF RELIGIOUS

Obligations Common With the Clergy (c. 135 = c. 592 CIC)
Striving After Perfection (c. 136 = c. 593 CIC)
Common Life (c. 137 = c. 594 CIC)
Practice of Piety (c. 138 = c. 595 CIC)
Prescribed Attire (c. 139 = c. 596 CIC)

CANON 135. All religious are bound by the obligations to which clerics are obliged by common law, except it appears otherwise from the nature of the matter or from the text and context of the law.

CANON 136. Each and every religious, the superiors as well as subjects, is obliged not only to observe faithfully and integrally the vows which he has pronounced, but also to order his life according to the rules and constitutions of his own institute, and thus tend to the perfection of his state.

CANON 137. # 1. In every institute all shall carefully observe the common life, even in matters of food, clothing and furniture.

2. Whatever is acquired by the religious, including the superiors, according to the terms of c. 116 # 2 and c. 118, must be added to the property of the corporate entity listed in c. 63 # 1; and all the money and all securities shall be deposited in the common safe, every contrary custom being abolished.

3. The furnishings of religious shall correspond with the poverty of which they made profession.

CANON 138. # 1. Superiors shall take care that all religious:

1. make every year for several days a spiritual retreat in accordance with the constitutions;

2. who are not lawfully prevented, assist daily at the Divine Liturgy according to the prescription of the Rite, make a meditation on divine matters, and faithfully perform other exercises of piety prescribed by the rules and constitutions;

3. approach the sacrament of penance at least once a week.

2. The frequent, even daily, reception of the Divine Eucharist shall be possible to all religious properly disposed; and the superiors shall promote this practice among their subjects.

3. If, however, a religious has since his last sacramental confession given grave scandal to the community, or committed a serious, external fault, the superior can forbid him to receive Holy Communion until he shall have again approached the sacrament of penance.

4. If in any institute the statutes or customs assign or prescribe certain days for the reception of Communion, such regulations have merely the force of counsel.

CANON 139. All religious shall wear the habit of their institute both inside and outside the house, except if in the judgment of the major superior, or in case of urgency even of the local superior, a grave cause excuses.

The habit of monks and nuns who live according to the ancient Eastern heritage is determined by the liturgical and historical traditions of the Rite.

Religious whose constitutions prescribe a specific habit must wear that habit.

Religious who have no habit prescribed in their constitutions wear the garb of the secular clergy of that Rite, if they have orders, while lay members follow the custom of their institute.

ENCLOSURE (cc. 140-153)

General Rules (c. 140 = c. 597 CIC)
Monasteries of Men (c. 141 = c. 598 CIC)
Institutions Conducted by Religious (c. 142 = c. 599 CIC)
Monasteries of Women (c. 143 = cf. c. 600 CIC)
Admission of Extern Women (c. 144 = new)
Exit of Nuns (c. 145 = cf. c. 601 CIC)
Seclusion from Sight and View (c. 146 = c. 602 CIC)
Supervision of the Enclosure of Women (c. 147 = c. 603 CIC)
Enclosure of Houses of Orders (c. 148 = new)
Effect of Non-Observation of Strict Enclosures (c. 149 = new)
General Norm of Lesser Enclosure (c. 150 = c. 604 CIC)
Supervision of Visiting (c. 151 — c. 605 CIC)
Prevention of Abuses (c. 152 = c. 606 CIC)
Exit of Religious Women (c. 153 = c. 607 CIC)

Although they were not systemized, nor uniformly applied, the Christian East had very explicit norms concerning the enclosure of monasteries.

The enclosure affected, even in convents of men, the whole building, garden, and even the churches or chapels, which prompted some monasteries to build a church outside the enclosure (**exoekklesion**) for the needs of visitors and pilgrims of the other sex. The enclosure extended not infrequently to the cemetery of the monastery.

The law of enclosure excluded persons of the other sex, but did not go so far as to forbid the visiting of persons of the same sex. We find often the prohibition of keeping eunuchs or beardless boys in a monastery of men because they made the monks reminiscent of women. A monk was permitted to leave a monastery on his own decision if the superior became a heretic, if women were admitted habitually to the monastery, or if boys who were not aspirants to the religious state were educated there.

Some peculiar norms of enclosure were, e.g., the prohibition to have animals of the opposite sex in the precincts of the convent, not excluding fowl; married women to enter the church of a monastery of men; to employ in the monastery handymen who were married; married men to stay overnight; celibate monk priests to bless a marriage; married priests to perform any function in a church of nuns; women over sixty years of age to be permitted to stay in a convent in order to nurse the sick or infirm monks.

The new codification did take cognizance of the changes introduced in the meantime by the Holy See concerning the enclosure of Latin Rite nuns, especially the Constitution of Pius XII **Sponsa Christi** of November 21, 1950 (AAS 1951, 5-24), and the pertinent instruction of the S. Congregation for the Religious (AAS 1951, 37-44). The most significant change was the creation of two classes of papal enclosure for Latin Rite nuns: the major or stricter, and the minor or relaxed enclosure.

The S. Congregation for the Oriental Church, taking into consideration the difficulties of our times for monasteries of nuns with strict enclosure, who are prevented from activities which could insure their economic support, and also the desire of others to engage in some form of extern apostolate, published June 2, 1953, later augmented by a letter of the same S. Congregation of January 18, 1956, (reprinted in **Pujol**, p. 543-548) the "**Instruction pour les moniales qui dèsirent se consacrer aux oeuvres d'apostolat externe**". The significant concession was the permission for the nuns to have free access from their strict enclosure to the school or boarding house of students adjoining to their convent.

> CANON 140. # 1. In monasteries either of men or of women which have been canonically erected, although they are not formal, the enclosure shall be observed.
>
> # 2. The house inhabited by the religious community is subject to the law of enclosure, together with garden and orchards, admittance to which is reserved to the religious, excluding not only the church with the adjoining sacristy, but also the house for guests and the parlor, which last should as far as possible be situated near the entrance of the house.

3. 1. The parts of the house subject to the law of enclosure shall be clearly indicated as such.

2. It is up to the major superior with the consent of his council, or the patriarch if it is the case of a stauropegial monastery of nuns, or the local Hierarch if the monastery is subject to him — to determine the exact limits of the enclosure or to change them for lawful reasons.

CANON 141. # 1. All women of whatsoever age, class or condition, except the wives of those who actually are the ruling heads of the state together with their retinue, shall not be admitted into the enclosure of monasteries of men.

2. The major superiors can dispense from this law for a grave reason, after taking the prescribed precautions, and on the condition that these women from the entrance on be accompanied by at least two virtuous monks.

A very practical norm has been added here to the text we know from c. 598 CIC, whereby the superior can permit women to enter the enclosure of men, as, e.g., the relatives of a sick monk.

CANON 142. # 1. When the monastery of men or women has annexed to it a house for boarding pupils, or for other works proper to the institute, a separate part at least of the house should be reserved for the habitation of the monks, subject to the law of enclosure.

2. Persons of the other sex shall not be admitted except for a just reason, and with the permission of the superior, even to places outside the enclosure reserved for extern or intern pupils or for works proper to the institute.

CANON 143. # 1. Into the enclosure of monasteries of women no person of the other sex of whatsoever age, class or condition may be admitted, except the following persons:

While Latin Rite canon law excludes most severely from the enclosure of nuns men and women alike, the enclosure of Oriental nuns prohibits only men.

1. the patriarch with his retinue, if the monastery belongs to his Rite, wherever it be situated; the archbishop, but only if the monastery is in his archiepiscopate, not however, if it is outside of it;

The patriarch can enter a monastery of nuns of his Rite also outside the patriarchate, i.e., when it is not subject to his jurisdiction.

2. the local Hierarch or the regular superior, when visiting the monastery, or other visitors delegated by them, solely for the purpose of the inspection, and with the precaution that they be accompanied by at least one cleric or male religious of mature age; save for the right of the local Hierarch to enter in person the enclosure, taking the same precautions, also on an occasion other than the visitation, when the necessities of his pastoral duty require so;

The local Hierarch and the male superior of nuns cannot enter the enclosure with an entourage, as the patriarch is permitted to do, but must be accompanied by at least one cleric or male religious,

293

and they can visit the enclosure only of monasteries which are under their jurisdiction.

In addition, the local Hierarch, but not the male superior of nuns, can in person enter the enclosure for other reasons, pertaining to the proper fulfillment of his pastoral duty, as, e.g., to see a sick nun, to inspect the enclosure, etc.

> 3. the confessor or whoever is substituting for him, with the necessary precautions, for administering the sacraments of the sick, or to assist the dying;
>
> 4. who actually are heads of states and their consorts and retinue; also cardinals of the Holy Roman Church;
>
> 5. physicians, surgeons and others whose work is necessary, if the superioress permits them to enter, due precautions having been taken, and at least the habitual approval of the local Hierarch has been obtained; but if urgent necessity does not allow time to seek this approval, the permission may rightfully be presumed.
>
> # 2. The local Hierarch can dispense in monasteries of whatever juridical condition from the law of enclosure treated in # 1 for a grave reason, observing the precautions established by the constitutions; the same can be done in patriarchates by the patriarch.

A useful addition to the text of c. 600 CIC is this paragraph, which gives local Hierarchs outside of patriarchates the power of dispensation, while within patriarchates this can be done also by the patriarch.

> CANON 144. Although the law of enclosure as contained in c. 143 does not extend to women, the superioress shall nevertheless beware of admitting without grave reason women to sojourn in the monastery even for a brief period of time.

Since c. 143 forbids only men from entering the enclosure of nuns, this canon cautions against the admittance of women, who can be permitted only for a brief visit.

> CANON 145. Religious women in monasteries are not permitted, after they made their profession, even minor profession, to leave the monastery under whatever pretext, even for a short time, without a grave reason and the approval of the local Hierarch, which may be rightfully presumed if necessity does not allow time to seek this approval.

Here again is a relaxation from the strictness of Latin Rite canon law. While c. 601 CIC reserves to the Holy See the granting of an indult to a cloistered nun to leave the monastery, this canon empowers the local Hierarch to such a permission, which in case of danger in delay can be lawfully presumed.

> CANON 146. The part of the monastery of nuns which is subject to the law of enclosure shall be protected in such a way as to prevent, as far as possible, anyone from having a view of the inside, or someone from the inside seeing persons outside.

> CANON 147. # 1. The enclosure of nuns of whatever juridical condition, even if their institute be subject to a regular superior, is

under the supervision of the local Hierarch, who can correct and coerce, even with penalties and censures, the delinquents, not excepting exempt religious men; after having informed the patriarch, if these religious men belong to a stauropegial monastery.

2. The custody of the enclosure of nuns is confided also to the regular superior, who can likewise inflict punishment on the nuns or his other subjects, if in this matter they should have been delinquent.

CANON 148. The regulations of cc. 140-147 on the enclosure in monasteries either of monks or of nuns shall be observed also in the matter of enclosure in the houses of orders of men as well as of women.

The foregoing canons concerned only monks and nuns in the meaning of Eastern tradition. This canon extends them to all orders, i.e., institutes with solemn profession. It should be pointed out that, although such orders are governed by principles borrowed from the Latin Rite canon law, the enclosure of Oriental nuns-members of an order is less strict than that of Latin Rite nuns of the same juridical condition, because of the divergent norms of c. 143.

CANON 149. Whenever the rules of cc. 143-145 cannot be permanently observed in a monastery or order of women, major profession cannot be made.

Which hierarch is entitled to make the decision that a monastery of nuns or a house of nuns-members of an order, is incapable of observing the enclosure, which in consequence forbids the members to make major profession, is not said here. **Pujol** (p. 405) considers it a **causa maior** and as such reserved to the Apostolic See. Matters of this kind were certainly heretofore transacted by the S. Congregation for the Oriental Church. However, it seems to us that the patriarch would not be excluded from making such a decision in orders of nuns under his jurisdiction.

CANON 150. # 1. Also in the houses of congregations, though they are only of eparchial right, the law of enclosure shall be observed, so that no one of the other sex may be admitted there, excepting those mentioned in c. 143, and others whom the superiors decide, for a just and reasonable motive, to admit.

2. The prescription of c. 142 shall apply also to houses of congregations.

3. For grave reasons and in particular cases the local Hierarch can, except in the case of an exempt clerical congregation, safeguard the enclosure by censures; he shall, however, always be vigilant in seeing that it is duly observed and in correcting any abuses that may arise in this respect.

CANON 151. All those who have the custody of the enclosure shall carefully guard that the discipline be not relaxed from intercourse with outsiders and the religious spirit weakened by useless conversation.

CANON 152. # 1. Religious superiors shall take care that the prescription of their constitutions be accurately observed regarding the going out of their subjects from the cloister, or the visits made to or paid by outsiders.

2. Except in cases of major importance, and save for the prescription of cc. 171-173, and what is provided otherwise in approved statutes concerning the exercise of the holy ministry under the direction of the superiors, the superiors cannot permit their subjects to stay outside the house of their own institute, except for a just and grave cause and for as brief a period as possible according to the statutes; but for an absence of more than six months, unless for motives of study, the permission of the patriarch is required, or, outside the patriarchate, of the president of the monastic confederation, or of the superior general of the institute.

This canon again shows an accommodation to factual exigencies, by granting to the patriarch and certain major superiors the faculty, in c. 606 CIC reserved to the Apostolic See, to permit subjects an absence from the religious house of more than six months.

CANON 153. The superioresses and the local Hierarch shall watch that no religious woman go out alone except in case of necessity.

RELATIONSHIP TO THE EPARCHY AND ITS CLERGY

General Norm (c. 154 ## 1, 2 = c. 608 CIC;
    # 3 = c. 1334 CIC)
Parishes in Care of Religious (c. 155 = cf. c. 609
    and c. 415 # 2 CIC)
Prohibition of Erecting Parishes in Churches of Religious
    Women (c. 156 = cf. c. 609 # 2)

CANON 154.# 1. The superiors shall take care that their religious subjects, designated by them, shall willingly lend their aid, without prejudice to the monastic observance and the religious discipline, when their ministry is required by the local Hierarch or pastors for providing for the needs or the advantage of the people, within as well as outside their own churches or public oratories.

2. Likewise, the local Hierarch and pastors shall willingly make use of the help of the religious, especially of those who are staying in the eparchy, in the sacred ministry and above all in the preaching of the word of God and in the administration of the sacrament of penance.

3. When in the judgment of the local Hierarch the help of religious is needed for the catechetical instruction of the people, religious superiors, even exempt, must, if requested by the Hierarch, give such instruction to the people, especially in their own churches, without detriment, however, to the monastic observance and the religious discipline.

CANON 155. # 1. If the church where a religious community resides is at the same time a parish church, unless it is provided otherwise by the indult of the Apostolic See or in the individual agreement entered into at the erection of the parish and lawfully approved by the bishop:

1. the pastor is:

(a) to apply the Divine Liturgy for the people and, at due time, to preach and teach Christian doctrine to the faithful;

(b) to have custody of the parish registers and to issue documents therefrom;

(3) to perform the parochial functions;

What the parochial functions are is stated in c. 503 of **Cleri Sanctitati.**

(d) to perform other functions which, although they are not strictly parochial, are customarily performed by pastors, provide they do not interfere with the celebration of the divine office, and the religious community does not perform the same functions;

(e) to collect alms for the aid of parishioners, to receive and administer them when they are directly or indirectly offered, and to distribute them according to the instruction of the benefactors;

2. the religious community is

(a) to preserve the Divine Eucharist, but a second key of the tabernacle or the dove must be left in the church;

(b) to watch over the pastor that the liturgical regulations be observed in the functions celebrated in the church;

(c) to take care of the church and to administer its property together with the pious bequests.

2. The superiors shall see to it that the celebration of the divine offices in their own churches be not a hindrance to the catechetical instruction or the explanation of the Gospel given in the parochial church; it pertains to the local Hierarch to judge whether or not this hindrance exists.

CANON 156. In no church of any religious women can a parish be established.

> Recitation of the Divine Office (c. 157 = cf. c. 610 CIC)
> Correspondence of Religious (c. 158 — c. 611 CIC)
> Public Prayers Prescribed by the Local Hierarch
> (c. 159 = cf. c. 612 and c. 1345 CIC)

CANON 157. # 1. In each monastery of men as well as of women in which there are as many monks (nuns) as required for the celebration of the divine office according to the proper Rite, actually not impeded, the divine office must be celebrated daily, in accordance with the statutes or lawful custom.

2. The prescription of # 1 shall be observed in orders and congregations of men as well as of women, with the exception of those which, in accordance with the statutes, have no obligation of celebrating the divine office.

3. In institutes mentioned in ## 1, 2, professed members who were absent from the celebration of the divine office are not obliged to recite the canonical office privately, unless and as far as their own statutes or lawful custom provide so.

4. The Divine Liturgy must be celebrated daily in the house of religious men unless liturgical laws provide otherwise, and also in the houses of religious women, if it is possible.

Concerning the divine office and its celebrations in the Christian East cf. the commentary to c. 76 of **Cleri Sanctitati.**

As to the obligation of religious in respect to the recitation of the divine office the following principles apply:

1. The obligation burdens the community and not the individual members. It is the duty of the superior of every monastery of men or women to satisfy the obligation with as many members as are needed.

2. The minimum number of members needed for the recitation of the divine office is to be determined by particular law.

3. There is no obligation deriving from common law of private recitation of parts of the divine office, whether the monk or nun has culpably — and therefore sinfully — or inculpably been absent from the public recitation.

CANON 158. All religious, whether men or women, can freely send letters, exempt from all control, to the Holy See and its legate in the country, to the patriarch, the archbishop, to their own major superiors, to the superior of their house when absent, to the local Hierarch in matters in respect to which they are subject to him, and, in the case of religious women subject to the jurisdiction of religious men, also to major superiors of the latter; and from all these persons the religious, men or women, can also receive letters which nobody is permitted to open.

CANON 159. # 1. If the local Hierarch prescribes for a public reason certain prayers or liturgical solemnities, all religious, even exempt, must obey, without prejudice to constitutions and privileges of each institute.

2. It is desirable that at Divine Liturgies, which are celebrated on holydays of obligation, in all churches or public oratories of religious, when members of the faithful are present, a short explanation of the Holy Gospel or of some article of Christian doctrine be given; if the local Hierarch prescribes it and gives suitable instructions, also the exempt religious are bound by his law, even in their own churches.

Article Two

PRIVILEGES OF RELIGIOUS (cc. 160-174)

General Norms:

Original Source and Communication (c. 160 = c. 613 CIC)
Relationship to Clerical Privileges (c. 161 = c. 614 CIC)

CANON 160. # 1. Each institute enjoys those privileges only which either in virtue of a general law are due to all institutes, or have been directly granted to it by the Apostolic See, every communication of privileges henceforth being excluded, safeguarding, however, the privileges acquired and peacefully possessed by institutes before the promulgation of this common law for the religious.

2. The privileges which monks enjoy belong also to the nuns

who are governed by the same constitutions, insofar they are capable of enjoying them; likewise, the privileges of orders of men are extended to the religious women of the same order.

CANON 161. Religious, even those who are not clerics, and novices enjoy the privileges of clerics defined by common law.

JURISDICTIONAL RELATIONSHIP TO VARIOUS HIERARCHS (cc. 162-170)

Exemption of Monks from the Local Hierarch an Exception
(c. 162 = new)
Exemption of Orders from the Local Hierarch the Rule
(c. 163 = cf. c. 615 CIC)
Stauropegial Monasteries (c. 164 = new)
Exempt Religious Outside Their Houses (c. 165 = c. 616 CIC)
Suppletory Supervision of the Local Hierarch
(c. 166 = c. 617 CIC)
Non-Exempt Religious Institutes (c. 167 = cf. c. 618 CIC)
Religious Institutes of Patriarchal Right (c. 168 = new)
Coercive Power of the Local Hierarch (c. 169 # c. 619 CIC)
Dispensative Power of the Local Hierarch
(c. 170 = c. 620 CIC)

Exemption denotes that a religious institute is not subject to the local Hierarch except in the instances expressly mentioned in law. In the Latin Rite canon law only one kind of exemption is known, namely, papal exemption, while Oriental canon law has two kinds, papal and patriarchal.

Either type of exemption can be obtained only in virtue of common law or an indult of the Holy See. Patriarchs can grant only one species of exemption, the stauropegia (cf. c. 164).

Oriental monastic law followed the maxim that the religious and their houses are subject to the local Hierarch. Since this is clearly not always to the advantage of the Church and her aims that surpass the boundaries of dioceses, the institution of stauropegia developed, especially when monasteries grew in the number of members and importance for a whole region, and their activities began to reach beyond the boundaries of the eparchy. This is the reason Oriental religious law was not forced to evolve the principle of the Latin Rite canon law, whereby orders as a rule are exempt from the local Hierarch (c. 615 CIC).

However, those Oriental religious institutes which were organized as orders in the meaning of the Latin Rite accepted thereby also the principle of exemption from the local Hierarch, but with the difference that such orders, even though they are of papal right, may be subject to the patriarch or to the Roman Pontiff. Nuns of orders who are subject to the superior of religious men are not exempt from the jurisdiction of the local Hierarch (c. 163).

Stauropegium is a liturgical rite belonging to the blessing of the ground or corner stone, or the consecration of a church. The officiating bishop or priest sets up or lowers into the ground (**peg-**

nytai) a cross **(stauron)** in that place where later the altar will be erected. If the bishop could not perform himself the ceremony, he might send the cross, which was considered as a symbol of the subjection of the church to his jurisdiction.

When the patriarch himself sent the cross at the erection of a monastery church, the monastery became dependent on the patriarch, and exempt from the jurisdiction of the bishop. Patriarchs were later wont to send their cross also to monasteries which were in existence for a considerable time; the cross was then affixed in the sanctuary as a sign of the exemption.

It cannot be established when the patriarchal stauropegium was begun, but the Byzantine canonist **Balsamon** regarded it in the 12th century as a very old privilege, and we can assume that it goes back to the 7th or 8th century.

Stauropegium is known to Catholics as well as to dissidents. Catholic patriarchs can establish a stauropegium only at the founding of a new monastery, and cannot grant the privilege to an existing one. However, if the monastery changes from the juridical condition of a dependent to an independent monastery, this could be done, because such change is tantamount to a new establishment in the legal sphere.

In stauropegial monasteries only the patriarch's name is commemorated in divine services; only he is entitled to perform a visitation of the monastery in person or through another cleric, usually called an exarch; the patriarch supervises the administration of the property. He exercises the judicial and coercive power in the monastery; confirms the election of the superior and gives him in person or through another the appropriate liturgical blessing **(chirotesia)**; is entitled to a contribution as sign of subjection **(kanonikon).** He designates the bishop for all ordinations to the diaconate and presbyterate.

The superior, usually invested with the dignity of archimandrite, or with that of a hegoumenissa in the case of a stauropegial monastery of women, and the monks and nuns are considered as belonging to the clergy and religious of the patriarch's own eparchy.

Stauropegium is not identical with the juridical condition of an institute of patriarchal right. The former is a nearly total exemption from the intervention of the local Hierarch and subjection to the patriarch. It takes a position intermediate between an institute of patriarchal right, and an exarchical monastery **(abbey nullius).** Stauropegium differs from an exarchical monastery in that the former has as bishop the patriarch, while the latter has in its superior a quasi-bishop.

Stauropegium of a religious house can be granted only to a certain monastery, but not to the house of an order or congregation. According to the new legislation, to grant it the patriarch needs the consent of the permanent synod.

The stauropegial exemption is also territorial, and extends to everything within the precincts of the convent, including churches, garden, etc., and excluding outlying buildings, fields, etc.

As far as persons are concerned, monks and novices enjoy full exemption from the local Hierarch within and outside the monastery. Other persons, such as chaplains, confessors, teachers, servants, provided they are residing in the monastery, are only exempt in matters pertaining to their relationship with the monastery.

DIVISION OF ORIENTAL RITE RELIGIOUS INSTITUTES ACCORDING TO THEIR JURISDICTIONAL RELATIONSHIP TO VARIOUS HIERARCHS.

Because of the existence of an intermediary hierarchical authority between the bishop and the Roman Pontiff, namely, the patriarch, there are more classes of relationships of religious institutes to the different degrees of hierarchy. Not all are actually in existence at this time, but theoretically the following are possible:

I. M o n a s t e r i e s, in which the ancient rules and traditions of Eastern monachism are observed, could have the following juridical conditions:

1. A single monastery or confederation of monasteries of papal right, endowed with papal exemption.

2. A single monastery or confederation of monasteries of papal right, but without enjoying papal exemption.

3. Stauropegial monasteries or monasteries of patriarchal right.

4. Monastery of eparchial right.

II. O r d e r s, in which major or solemn profession is made, but the constitution of which is that found in Latin Rite orders:

1. Order of papal right, endowed with papal exemption.

2. Order of papal right, without papal exemption.

3. Order of patriarchal right.

III. C o n g r e g a t i o n s, in which the members take minor or simple profession:

1. Congregation of papal right, endowed with papal exemption.

2. Congregation of papal right, without papal exemption.

3. Congregation of patriarchal right.

4. Congregation of eparchial right.

CANON 162. Monasteries and clerical congregations do not enjoy the privilege of exemption from the jurisdiction of the local Hierarch unless it has been specifically granted to them.

CANON 163. # 1. In orders, the religious and novices, either of men or of women, with their houses and churches, but not those nuns who are not subject to the regular superior of the order, are exempt from the jurisdiction of the local Hierarch, excepting the cases provided for by law; in patriarchates these religious are immediately subject to the patriarch, unless it is the case of an order which enjoys papal exemption.

2. A confederation or monastery which obtained from the Apostolic See the privilege of exemption is equal in everything to an exempt order according to the terms of # 1.

CANON 164. # 1. Stauropegial monasteries are exempt in accordance with the canons from the jurisdiction of the local Hierarch, and are subject to the immediate and exclusive jurisdiction of the patriarch.

2. 1. The patriarch can grant at the time of its foundation, for a grave reason and with the consent of the permanent synod, the stauropegial privilege to a certain monastery, but not to a house of an order or congregation;

2. Unless it is determined otherwise in the decree of the patriarch, this privilege affects only the monastery, the persons belonging to it, and other members of the household who day and night stay in the house, without prejudice to the prescription of 3;

3. Any persons not belonging to the stauropegial monastery are exempt from the jurisdiction of the local Hierarch for the time they are attached to it, and subject to the patriarch alone in all those matters which pertain to their employment or office or are related to the discipline of the monastery.

CANON 165. # 1. Exempt religious do not enjoy the privilege of exemption or stauropegium when unlawfully staying outside their convent, even under the pretext of going to superiors.

2. If they have committed a delict outside their convent and were not punished by the superior although he was notified by the local Hierarch, they can be punished by the latter, even if they left the house lawfully and have already returned to the convent.

3. If the religious mentioned in ## 1, 2, belong to a stauropegial monastery or to an order subject to the patriarch, the local Hierarch shall notify the patriarch at once.

CANON 166. # 1. When in houses of exempt religious or in their churches abuses have crept in, and the superior, although admonished by the Hierarch, neglected to correct them, the same local Hierarch is obliged to bring the matter at once to the attention of the Apostolic See, or, in patriarchates, to the patriarch, if the monastery is stauropegial, or the house or the church belongs to an order subject to the patriarch.

2. An exempt non-formal house remains under the special vigilance of the local Hierarch, who may take provisional measures in case of abuses which have crept in and are a source of scandal to the faithful.

CANON 167. # 1. In institutes of papal right which do not enjoy papal exemption, neither the patriarch nor the local Hierarch can make any change in the statutes or inquire into the temporal administration, save for the prescription of cc. 65-67.

2. They are not permitted to interfere in the internal government and discipline in these institutes, except in the cases expressed by law; nevertheless:

1. in a monastery of women or in an order and in a lay congregation, the local Hierarch can and must inquire whether discipline is

302

maintained conformably to the statutes; whether sound doctrine and good morals have suffered in any way; whether the enclosure has been violated; whether the sacraments are received regularly and frequently, and if superiors, having been warned of the existence of grave abuses, have failed duly to remedy them, he himself shall provide; if, however, something of greater importance which will not suffer delay should occur, the Hierarch shall decide immediately; but he must report his decision to the Apostolic See;

2. If in monasteries of men of papal right and in a clerical congregation of papal right abuses have crept in and the superior, although admonished by the local Hierarch, has neglected to correct them, the same Hierarch can provisionally do so, if they have been a source of scandal to the faithful. If it is the case of a formal house, he shall report the matter to the Apostolic See.

CANON 168. The local Hierarch possesses in orders and in congregations of patriarchal right the same rights and is bound by the same duties to which he is entitled or bound, in accordance with the terms of c. 167, in respect to an order or congregation of papal right which does not enjoy papal exemption.

CANON 169. In all matters in which religious are subject to the local Hierarch, he can coerce them even with penalties.

CANON 170. When an indult was lawfully granted by the local Hierarch, the obligation of common law ceases also for all religious living in the eparchy, without prejudice to the vows and particular statutes of their own institute.

Pujol (p. 440) expresses the opinion that the indults granted by the local Hierarch cannot be enjoyed by a religious who stays within the territory of that local Hierarch, but who resides in a place which belongs to the exclusive jurisdiction of another Rite. Examples of such places can be found in a territory with multiple jurisdiction, as, e.g., in the Near East, the United States of America, Canada, etc.

However, a distinction is necessary here. Whenever the validity of an act is involved, the favor cannot be made use of in a place of exclusive jurisdiction of another Rite; in other instances there can be no objection. Otherwise absurd consequences would follow. There is no reason why an Ukrainian Byzantine Rite religious, who stays in a Latin Rite house of his institute in the United States, could not utilize, e.g., a dispensation from the law of abstinence granted by the local Ukrainian bishop.

THE PRIVILEGE OF BEGGING (cc. 171-173)

Various Hierarchs Entitled to Grant This Privilege
(c. 171 = cf. cc. 621, 622 CIC)
Qualities of Religious Assigned to Begging
(c. 172 = c. 623 CIC)
Norms for Begging Issued by the Holy See
(c. 173 = c. 624 CIC)

CANON 171. # 1. The habitual collection of alms is forbidden:

The laws which regulate begging apply only to the indiscriminate visiting of homes for the purpose of asking for contributions. It is not begging in the meaning of the law, if certain persons known for their generosity are visited, nor if unknown persons are approached for alms by letter.

    1. To the religious of papal right, without a special permission of the Apostolic See, save for 2.

    2. To members of a stauropegial monastery, and of an institute of papal right which does not enjoy papal exemption, or one of patriarchal right, without the written permission of the patriarch;

    3. To members of an institute of eparchial right, without a written permission of the Hierarch of the place where the house is situated.

    4. If the alms are to be collected outside Oriental regions in accordance with c. 240 # 3, without a permission of the Sacred Congregation for the Oriental Church.

The permission for habitual, continued, begging is to be granted only exceptionally, and only by the highest extern superior of the particular religious institute (c. 171 # 1, 1-3). For begging outside Oriental regions permission of the Holy See is required in every case (c. 171 # 1, 4). Oriental regions are countries where the Oriental Rite is established since ancient times, although no ecclesiastical hierarchy may be in existence today (c. 303 # 1, 2).

    # 2. The members of institutes mentioned in # 1 need in addition the written permission of the Hierarach of the place where they wish to collect alms, except it has been provided otherwise in the granting of the permission by the Apostolic See, or, in respect to the members mentioned in # 1, 2, by the patriarch, save for the prescription of # 5.

    # 3. The members of an institute of whatever juridical condition must obtain only the written permission of the Hierarch of the place where they wish to collect alms, if they intend to collect alms for a transitory need.

Religious institutes and their houses do not need the permission of their own local Hierarch when they intend to beg for a transient purpose in another diocese, but they must obtain the consent of the bishop (c. 171 # 3) of the place in which they wish to beg.

    # 4. Patriarchs and local Hierarchs shall not grant permission for collecting alms, as mentioned in ## 1-3, unless they are convinced of the true need of the house or the pious work, which cannot be provided for by other means; if the need can be satisfied by collecting alms within the place or eparchy where the religious are living, he shall not grant a more ample permission.

While c. 621, 2, CIC urges local ordinaries not to deny their permission for begging whenever the circumstances warrant it, c. 171 # 4 takes a more negative attitude, and reminds the ordinaries not to grant their consent except if necessity compels.

304

 # 5. **For the collecting of alms in an eparchy of the Latin Rite the permission of the Hierarch of this eparchy is required.**

For begging in a diocese of the Latin Rite, whether within the patriarchate or outside, the permission of its ordinary is required, in addition to whatever authorization is prescribed by the foregoing paragraphs.

In territories with a multiple hierarchy the permission of one's own local Hierarch is sufficient if only his subjects are visited. When indiscriminate begging among all Catholics is planned, the permission of the own as well as of all those Hierarchs is to be obtained, whose faithful are likely to be approached in a significant number.

CANON 172. **Superiors are forbidden to entrust the collection of alms to others than professed members of mature age and character, especially in the case of women, but never to those who are still in studies.**

CANON 173. **In whatever concerns the method to be followed in seeking alms and the discipline to be observed by those who seek them, the religious of both sexes must conform to the instructions given by the Holy See on this subject.**

CHIROTSIA OF SUPERIORS (c. 174 = cf. c. 625 CIC)

CANON 174. **# 1.** **Superiors of monks, whose Rite or typicum prescribe that they receive a benediction, must receive within three months after their election the benediction in accordance with particular law from the patriarch or bishop of the eparchy where the monastery is situated, or also from another minister, if the liturgical prescription provide so.**

A special blessing, which is called a **chirotesia** (imposition of hand), the same term which applies to minor orders, in distinction from the ordination to major orders, which is called **cheirotonia** (stretching out of hand), of the new-appointed superior became a standard procedure when the evolution of Eastern monachism had progressed to the stage in which such superiors had become entitled to ordain subdeacons and lectors, and to perform other liturgical functions. While before that time often simple monks, deacons, or minor clerics, were elected superiors, now priests became considered the best, or even the only, qualified candidates. The new codification rules that candidates for the office of superiors of monasteries, independent as well as dependent ones, must be priests (c. 31, 3).

Which superiors of religious are obliged to receive a special benediction is to be decided by particular law. Generally speaking, superiors of independent monasteries of men and the superioress of full monasteries of women receive such a blessing. In the religious institutes organized according to the manner of orders, usually only the superior general is entitled to the benediction, since other superiors are not independent **(sui iuris)** and are generally appointed only for a certain time.

The title given to the superiors who receive the liturgical blessing is most commonly that of archimandrite (arch-shepherd). The dignity is not lost when he ceases to hold the office. The liturgical insignia, which are more fully described above in the commentary to c. 41 of **Cleri Sanctitati,** are the following:

1. **Archimandrites of the Byzantine Rite in the Near East:** Pectoral cross; supracamelaucum, with the right to wear it also in the sanctuary during the celebration of the Divine Liturgy and other divine services; the epigonation; commemoration of his name in his churches by all celebrants in all divine services.

2. **Archimandrites in the Ukrainian, Russian, Ruthenian, a.o. Churches:** The same liturgical privileges as enumerated under 1; and in addition: Purple mandyas with pomata, but without potamoi; mitre; crozier; ring; sometimes also enkolpion or panagia, especially in a stauropegial monastery or in an exarchical monastery (abbey **nullius**); rarely also **dikirium** and **trikirium,** candle-sticks with two or three candles for imparting the blessing during Mass.

The Ukrainian and Russian Churches know also the **hegoumenus** as a superior entitled to a liturgical blessing. He has as the sign of his rank the insignia granted to archimandrites in the Near East, in addition to a crozier.

The superioress of a monastery, who is entitled to receive the blessing, has as signs of her dignity: Pectoral cross and crozier. Here title is always **hegoumenissa.**

Some Churches, especially among the dissidents, know also the title of titular hegoumenus and titular archimandrite, who are not superiors at all, sometimes not even monks but secular clerics, who receive the same blessing and are entitled to the same insignia.

The titles of the superiors of the Ukrainian Basilian Fathers, **protoarchimandrite** for the superior general, **protohegoumenus** for the provincial superior, and **hegoumenus** for the superior of a convent, are mere titles, and are surrendered with the loss of the office.

> # 2. **The superior of an independent monastery may confer minor orders provided the candidate is his subject in virtue of at least minor profession, and he himself is a priest, and has lawfully received the benediction, if he was obliged to receive it according to # 1. An ordination conferred by him which transgresses these limits is invalid, except if the ordaining superior possesses the episcopal consecration.**

The superior of an independent monastery is entitled to confer the minor orders on his subjects, under the same conditions which are prescribed in c. 625 CIC for Latin Rite abbots.

The number of minor orders is not the same in all Rites. The Armenians, for instance, have now the minor orders of the Latin Rite, while the majority of the Eastern Churches know only the double order of lector-cantor, and the subdiaconate. Cf. also c. 45 of **Cleri Sanctitati.**

OBLIGATIONS AND PRIVILEGES OF RELIGIOUS PROMOTED TO ECCLESIASTICAL DIGNITIES OR ASSIGNED TO ADMINISTER PARISHES (cc. 175-181)

Permission for Accepting Dignities (c. 175 = cf. c. 626 CIC)
Religious Promoted to the Hierarchy:
   Relationship to Institute (c. 176 = c. 627 CIC)
   Property Rights (c. 177 = c. 628 CIC)
   Return to Institute After Resignation (c. 178 = c.629 CIC)
Religious in Charge of Parishes:
   Relationship to the Institute (c. 179 = c. 630 CIC)
   Relationship to the Local Hierarch (c. 180 = c. 631 CIC)
Norms for Religious Employed Outside Their Houses
   (c. 181 = new)

CANON 175.   # 1.   A religious cannot be promoted to dignities, offices and benefices which are incompatible with the religious state, without permission granted by legitimate authority.

While dissidents freely confer honorary titles, dignities and insignia upon their monk-priests, which can be explained by the norm that bishops must necessarily belong to the religious state, Catholics have always considered honorary distinctions of whatever kind as alien to the religious spirit of abnegation (c. 47).

This canon speaks of offices to which a dignity or a benefice is joined, and which are incompatible with the obligations of the religious state. The incompatability will differ for the members of different religious institutes. The office of eparchial judge may be compatible for a member of an active order, but incompatible for a member of a contemplative monastery with strict rules of enclosure.

Generally speaking, offices are considered incompatible which are reserved to secular clerics, as eparchial econome, chancellor, advocate; etc. Others, as eparchial censor, examiner of clergy, judge of the eparchial tribunal, are as a rule not excluded from being given to religious.

The authority entitled to grant permission for a religious to accept the appointment to an extern ecclesiastical employment will be, for generally incompatible offices, the highest extern superior of the institute (Roman Pontiff, patriarch, or local Hierarch), with the exception of the appointment as syncellus (c. 433 of **Cleri Sanctitati**), where the patriarch is competent within the patriarchate, and the Roman Pontiff in other places.

2.   A religious elected by a college cannot accept the election without the permission of the superior.

3.   In patriarchates, however, a religious can be promoted to offices and benefices which are conferred by the synod, if elected by the synod. In such a case he does not need the permission mentioned in # 2 in order to give his consent to the election of his person.

The religious needs no one's permission for offices conferred by the patriarchal synod. The reason is that such an electoral college considers all possible consequences for the religious institute as well as for the whole particular Church or Rite, arising from the appointment.

Canon 626 # 3 CIC mentioned the need of a dispensation to be obtained from the Holy See whenever a religious, who has taken the special vow of not accepting dignities, is to be promoted to one. The omission designates the wish of the legislator that the matter be decided according to particular law. Such a vow is made by the members of the Ukrainian Order of St. Basil the Great.

CANON 176. # 1. A religious promoted to the dignity of cardinal, patriarch, or bishop, resident or titular, remains a religious, but without active and passive voice, sharing in the privileges of his institute, and bound to the vows as well as the other obligations of his profession, with the exclusion of those which he himself prudently judges incompatible with his dignity, without prejudice to c. 177.

2. He is withdrawn from the authority of his superiors and remains by reason of his vow of obedience subject to the Roman Pontiff alone.

The wording of c. 627 # 1 CIC did not decide whether a religious who was appointed cardinal or bishop continues to enjoy an active and passive vote in his institute. However, since c. 629 # 2 CIC mentioned that such religious, when they have retired from their office, and reside in a house of their institute, are deprived of any vote, it was legitimately inferred that active dignitaries are even more so. The present # 1 of c. 176 states this expressly.

CANON 177. A religious promoted to the dignity of cardinal, patriarch, bishop or another one outside of his own institute:

1. If he lost by profession the capacity of acquiring the ownership of property, he has the use, the usefruct and the administration of property which falls to him; but the ownership is acquired by the patriarch, the resident bishop, the exarch, for the patriarchate, the eparchy, the exarchy; others for the monastery or order, in accordance with c. 118, save for the privilege of the cardinals of the Holy Roman Church.

2. If he did not lose by profession the ownership of property, he regains the use, usefruct and the administration; what comes to him later he acquires it with full ownership.

3. In both possibilities, if property came to him in his official capacity, he must use it in accordance with the intention of the donors.

CANON 178. # 1. If he renounces the dignity of cardinal, patriarch, bishop, or after he has discharged the office or duty outside his institute entrusted to him by the Apostolic See, the religious must return to his institute.

2. The religious who has renounced the dignity of cardinal, patriarch or bishop may choose as his residence any house of his institute, but he lacks active and passive voice.

3. The institute is bound by the obligation to supply the religious mentioned in # 1 with all necessities for a mode of life corresponding with his dignity.

CANON 179. # 1. The religious who is in charge of a parish remains bound to observe the vows and statutes insofar as the observance is compatible with the obligations of his office.

2. Therefore, in matters which pertain to the monastic observance and religious discipline, the afore-mentioned religious is subject to his superior, whose duty it is, and not that of the local Hierarch, to inquire into his behavior, and, if need be, to correct him.

3. Property which comes to him in behalf of the parish whose charge he has he acquires for the parish; other property he acquires in the same way as other religious.

4. Notwithstanding the vow of poverty, he is permitted to accept or collect alms by any means to the advantage of the parish or Catholic schools or pious institutions attached to the parish or for the profit of parishioners or parochial purposes, and to administer such accepted and collected alms, and to use them according to the intention of the donors, and his prudent and free choice, without prejudice to the right of vigilance of his superior. However, to accept, safeguard, collect or administer alms for the building, preserving, repairing, adornment, of the parish church, or for the exercise of divine worship in it, belongs to the superiors if the church belongs to the religious community, that is, if the community claims the church as its property, or the right of perpetual use at least for an unlimited period; otherwise the norm of c. 264 shall be observed.

CANON 180. # 1. The afore-mentioned religious pastor, although he may carry out his duties in the house or place where the major superiors of the institute have their ordinary seat, is directly and in all subject to the jurisdiction, visitation and correction of the local Hierarch, not otherwise than secular pastors, with the sole exception of the monastic observance and the religious discipline.

2. When the local Hierarch discovers him to be deficient in his official duties, he can order suitable remedies and inflict deserved punishments. This power of the Hierarch does not exclude the same power of the superior, but it is to be exercised jointly in such a way that in case the superior has perhaps rendered a decision different from that of the Hierarch, the decision of the Hierarch is to prevail.

CANON 181. # 1. Duties to be discharged outside the house of his institute, even if consisting in the care of souls, can be entrusted to religious only for a limited time.

2. 1. The same religious must go at the time assigned by the general chapter to the house designated by the superior, where monastic observance and religious discipline is known to flourish, and there remain for a period of at least three months.

2. Religious who are in charge of a parish distant from a house of their institute shall have a fellow member of the same institute living with them, except in case of necessity.

CHAPTER SIX

TRANSFER TO ANOTHER INSTITUTE (cc. 182-186)

Hierarchs Granting Permission (c. 182 = c. 632 CIC)
Novitiate in the New Institute (c. 183 = c. 633 CIC)
Effects of Transfer between Institutes (c. 184 = c. 634 CIC)
Effects of Transfer between Monasteries (c. 185 = c. 635 CIC)
Extinction of Major Profession (c. 186 = c. 636 CIC)

CANON 182. # 1. No religious can, without permission from the Apostolic See, validly pass to another institute, except in the case of a transfer from one independent monastery to another of the same confederation, in which case the authorization of the president suffices, without prejudice to ## 2, 3.

Postquam Apostolicis has simplified the procedure for religious who wish to leave their monastery or institute and enter another. The permission of the Holy See is required only outside the patriarchate, and, in respect to monks, only if they wish to transfer to a monastery of another confederation, or to an order or congregation. In other instances the permission can be granted by the patriarch, and in some cases even by the local Hierarch.

2. In patriarchates, religious can pass from an independent monastery to another independent monastery, from an order or congregation to another order or another congregation with the consent of the superiors of both monasteries, or the superior general of both institutes, and with the permission of the patriarch.

3. A religious can pass from a monastery or congregation of eparchial right to a monastery or another congregation of eparchial right with the permission of the local Hierarch of the monastery from which he passes and of the local Hierarch of the monastery or house to which he is to pass, after they have requested the opinion of the superior of the institute from which he passes and the consent of the superior of the monastery or house to which he is to pass.

CANON 183. # 1. 1. He who passes to another institute must make a novitiate, save for what is prescribed in # 2. During the novitiate the vows remain intact, while the rights and particular obligations which he had in the institute he left are suspended, and he is bound to obey the superiors of his new institute and the master of novices even by virtue of the vow of obedience;

2. If he does not make profession in the new institute, he must return to his former institute, except if in the interval the terms of his vows expired.

2. 1. He who passes to another independent monastery of the same confederation does not make either the novitiate or a new profession.

2. He who passes from an independent monastery to another independent monastery which does not belong to any, or to another confederation, shall observe in respect to the obligation of making a novitiate or profession the requirements of the typicum of the monastery to which he passes. In case the typicum has no provision, he does not

make either a novitiate or profession. The superior, however, can request him to pass in the monastery a probational period of time, not longer than six months, which time the mentioned superior may prolong, but not for more than another six months, if after completion there remains a doubt whether he should be admitted. After completion of the probational period, the religious who was to pass must either return to his former monastery, or he shall be accepted, with the deliberative vote of the council or chapter, permanently into the new monastery.

We have stated above that Eastern monachism knows only one monastic state, with no distinction into separate religious institutes. Consequently, no new novitiate or profession is prescribed by common law for a transfer between monasteries. If two monasteries are involved which do not belong to the same confederation, a new novitiate and profession will be necessary only in case this is expressly stipulated by particular law.

CANON 184. The religious who is bound by any perpetual profession whatsoever shall, if he passes to another institute of perpetual vows, after the novitiate omit the temporary profession spoken of in c. 110, and either be admitted to perpetual profession, or return to his former institute; the superior, however, has the right to prolong the period of probation, but not beyond one year after the completion of the novitiate.

CANON 185. Those who pass to another independent monastery of the same confederation, from the day of transfer, but if to another institute, from the day of their new profession or from the day of admission treated in c. 183 # 2, 2:

1. Lose the rights and are released from the obligations toward the former monastery or institute, and assume the rights and duties of the other institute;

2. The monastery or institute which such a religious left keeps the property that he may have acquired in the capacity of religious; as to the dowry and its interest and other personal property, if the religious had such, the prescription of c. 83 # 2 is to be observed.

CANON 186. The solemnity of the major profession in respect to a religious who lawfully made, in accordance with the above mentioned canons, minor profession in a religious congregation, is by that fact extinguished, except the apostolic indult expressly provide otherwise.

CHAPTER SEVEN

VOLUNTARY LEAVING OF THE RELIGIOUS INSTITUTE
(cc. 187-196)

Leaving After Expiration of Vows (c. 187 = c. 637 CIC)
Exclaustration:
    Hierarchs Granting Indult (c. 188 = cf. c. 638 CIC)
    Effect of Indult (c. 189 = cf. c. 649 CIC)

Secularization:

Hierarchs Granting Indult (c. 190 = cf. c. 639 CIC)
Effect of Indult (c. 191 = c. 640 CIC)
Secularization of Religious Clerics
  (c. 192 = cf. c. 641 CIC)
Incapacity for Certain Ecclesiastical Employments
  (c. 193 = c. 642 CIC)
Financial Severance Assistance (c. 194 = c. 643 CIC)
Unlawful Leaving of the Institute:
Apostasy and Flight from the Institute
  (c. 195 = c. 649 CIC)
Obligation of Return (c. 196 = c. 645 CIC)

CANON 187. He who made a profession of temporary vows may, when the term of the vows has expired, freely leave the institute; likewise, the institute, for just and reasonable motives, can exclude him from renewing the temporary vows or from making perpetual profession, not however because of ill health, except it be clearly proved that the religious, before profession, had fraudently hidden or dissimulated the illness.

CANON 188. # 1. 1. The indult of exclaustration may be granted by the Apostolic See;

2. The same indult may be granted in patriarchates to religious who belong to an institute which does not enjoy papal exemption by the patriarch, save for the prescription of # 2.

2. In an institute of eparchial right the indult of exclaustration may be granted also by the Hierarch of the place where the house is situated, of which the religious is a member.

While c. 638 CIC reserves the granting of the indult of exclaustration in all institutes of papal right to the Holy See, Oriental canon law narrows the reservation to institutes of papal right who are endowed with papal exemption. Outside of Oriental patriarchates, the competent patriarch is the Roman Pontiff as Patriarch of the Occident.

CANON 189. He who obtained the indult of exclaustration according to c. 188, remains bound by the vows and other obligations of his profession which are compatible with his condition; he must, however, put off the external form of the habit of the institute; while the indult is in force he lacks active and passive voice, but he enjoys the merely spiritual privileges of his institute, and he is subject to the Hierarch of the region where he resides, who takes the place of the superiors of his own institute, also by virtue of his vows of obedience.

CANON 190. # 1. The indult of secularization may be granted by the Apostolic See, save for # 2.

2. The same indult may grant, provided it is the case of religious bound by minor profession:

1. The patriarch, in patriarchates, to religious of every juridical condition, without prejudice to 2;

2. The Hierarch of the place where the house is situated whose member the religious is, if the religious pertains to an institute of eparchial right.

CANON 191. # 1. One who, having obtained the indult of secularization, leaves the institute:

1. becomes separated from his institute, must put off the external form of its habit, and returns to the secular state;

2. remains free of his vows, without prejudice to the obligations connected with the subdiaconate or a major order, if he had been promoted to such order; he is not bound by the statutes of the institute.

2. If he should in virtue of an indult be re-admitted to the institute, he has to repeat the novitiate and profession, and receives his place among the professed members from the date of the new profession.

CANON 192. # 1. A religious who had been promoted to an order below the subdiaconate and had belonged to the institute as a cleric, on leaving the institute leaves the clerical state in virtue of law, except if he be admitted by a Hierarch willing to accept him into the clergy of his eparchy.

2. If a religious who had been promoted to the subdiaconate or a major order has not lost his proper eparchy, he, not having renewed his vows, or having obtained the indult of secularization, must return to his proper eparchy and be received back by his proper Hierarch; if he lost it, he cannot exercise the subdiaconate or major orders outside the institute as long as he did not find a local Hierarch willing to accept him or the Apostolic See did not provide otherwise.

3. The Hierarch may accept the religious either permanently or for a period of three years to subject him to probation; in the first possibility, the religious becomes at once enrolled into the eparchy; in the other possibility, the Hierarch can prolong the period of probation. If after three years of probation had been completed he does not expressly prolong the period, the religious is considered dismissed. He cannot prolong it for a third triennium. After this too has been completed, the religious, unless he has been dismissed sooner, becomes by this very fact incardinated in the eparchy.

Canon 641 # 2 CIC has a somewhat different provision for the religious priest who is accepted by a bishop on probation. If after three years the candidate is not accepted for permanent, the probationary period is considered prolonged. If he was not dismissed before the end of the second triennium, he is automatically incardinated.

Postquam Apostolicis declares the candidate dismissed automatically after the first triennium if the bishop either does not incardinate him or prolong expressly the probationary period for another triennium.

CANON 193. # 1. A professed member who returns to the world, though he is permitted, within the terms of c. 192 ## 2, 3, to exercise the subdiaconate or major orders, is excluded:

1. from any benefice in cathedral churches;

2. from any appointment as teacher or to any other office in major or minor seminaries or colleges in which clerics are educated,

as well as in the universities and other educational institutions which enjoy the apostolic privilege of conferring academic degrees;

3. from any office or employment in a patriarchal or episcopal curia, and in religious houses, whether of men or women, even though the institute is of eparchial right;

4. from receiving an honorary title.

2. The prescription of # 1 applies also to those who have taken temporary vows, or an oath of perseverance, or certain special promises according to their constitutions, and have been dispensed from them, if they were bound by them for six full years.

3. The patriarch may dispense from the prescription of # 1, 2, 3, for a grave reason and having obtained the consent of the permanent synod, professed members of institutes of any juridical condition whatsoever who returned to the world.

To the legal inabilities which affect a religious dispensed from the vows was added the prohibition to be the recipient of a honorary prelatic title (c. 642 # 1 CIC).

Because of the dearth of clergy in patriarchates, especially of those with some specialized knowledge, patriarchs can dispense from the prohibitions contained in c. 193 ## 1, 2, and 3; outside patriarchates this can be done by the Holy See.

CANON 194. # 1. Those who leave their institute, whether on the expiration of the term of temporary vows, or by virtue of an indult of secularization, or who have been dismissed, cannot seek compensation for any services rendered by them to the institute.

2. If the religious woman was received without dowry and is unable to provide for herself out from her own resources, the institute has the obligation from charity to furnish her with the means of returning home in a secure and becoming manner, and to take provisions, in the observance of natural equity, that she may be able to have a respectable livelihood for some time, to be determined by mutual consent, or, in case of disagreement, by the local Hierarch.

CANON 195. # 1. An apostate from religion is one who, having made profession of perpetual vows, unlawfully leaves the religious house with the intention of not returning, or who, with the intention of withdrawing himself from religious obedience, though he has lawfully left the house, does not return.

2. The malicious intention, referred to in # 1, is legally presumed when the religious within a month has neither returned nor manifested to his superior his intention of returning.

3. A fugitive is one who, without the permission of his superiors, deserts the religious house but with the intention of returning to the institute.

CANON 196. # 1. Neither the apostate nor the fugitive is freed from the obligation of his constitutions and vows, and they must without delay return to their institute.

2. The superiors must seek them with solicitude and receive them if they return animated by a sincere repentance; the return of an

apostate or fugitive religious woman bound by major religious profession shall prudently be sought after by the local Hierarch and, if she belongs to a religious house subject to a regular superior, also by this superior.

CHAPTER EIGHT

DISMISSAL OF RELIGIOUS

Automatic Dismissal (c. 197 = c. 646 CIC)
Dismissal in Urgent Cases (c. 198 = cf. cc. 653, 668)

CANON 197. # 1. The following religious are i p s o f a c t o regarded as lawfully dismissed:

1. Who have publicly professed apostasy, heresy, schism;

2. Who have run away with a person of the other sex, even though they did not go to the same place;

3. Who attempt or contract marriage, even the so-called civil marriage.

2. In these cases it suffices that the major superior with his council, according to the prescriptions of the statutes, make a declaration of fact; but the superior shall take care to preserve in the archives of the house the collected evidence of the fact.

CANON 198. # 1. 1. In the case of a grave external scandal or of very grave danger threatening the community, the religious can be returned to the world by the major superior with the consent of his council, or, if there is a danger from delay and time does not permit to approach the major superior, even by the local superior with the consent of his council; the religious shall immediately put off the habit;

2. The return to the world, treated in 1, produces the effects assigned by c. 200 to the dismissal; recourse may be taken against it with suspensive effect according to c. 199 # 3, 4.

2. 1. If it is the case of a religion with perpetual vows in a non-exempt clerical congregation or in a lay, or of a religious woman with perpetual vows in a monastery or in an order, and the discharge is decreed by a local superior in accordance with # 1, 1, the latter needs in addition the consent of the local Hierarch.

2. When a religious has been returned to the world, the major superior or the local Hierarch, if he intervened in accordance with 1, shall submit the matter without delay to the judgment of the Apostolic See.

3. If it is the case of a religious of perpetual vows in a monastery of men of whatever juridical condition, or in an order, or in an exempt clerical congregation, the return of the religious to the world having been accomplished, the judicial procedure shall be instituted at once, if it has not been already instituted, in accordance with cc. 206-219.

Article One

DISMISSAL OF RELIGIOUS WHO TOOK TEMPORARY VOWS IN ANY RELIGIOUS INSTITUTE (cc. 199-201)

Dismissing Authority and Reasons of Dismissal
(c. 199 = cf. c. 647 CIC)
Effects of Dismissal (c. 200 = c. 648 CIC)
Dismissal of Religious With Indefinite Vows (c. 201 = new)

CANON 199. # 1. A religious man who is bound by profession limited as to time may be dismissed:

1. In an independent monastery, by the superior of the monastery with the consent of his council, manifested by secret ballot;

2. In an order or in a congregation of papal or patriarchal right, by the superior general with the consent of his council, manifested by secret ballot;

3. but in a congregation of eparchial right, by the Hierarch of the place where the religious house is located, who, however, shall not make use of his right without knowledge or against the will of the superiors if they are justly opposed.

2. A religious woman bound by temporary profession can be dismissed:

1. In a monastery or an order of papal right or in an order of patriarchal right, by the local Hierarch, or, if the monastery is subject to a regular superior, by the same superior, after, in either possibility, the superioress of the monastery with her council has faithfully recorded in writing the reasons;

2. In a stauropegial monastery, by the patriarch, after the superioress of the monastery with her council has faithfully recorded in writing the reasons;

3. In a congregation of papal or patriarchal right, by the superioress general with the consent of her council, manifested in secret voting;

4. In a monastery or a congregation of eparchial right, by the Hierarch of the place where the house is located to which the religious belongs, who, however, shall not make use of his right without the knowledge of the superiors or against them if they are justly opposed.

3. All those mentioned in ## 1, 2, can dismiss a religious, under a grave obligation in conscience, only on the following conditions:

1. The motives for dismissal must be grave, whether they exist on the part of the institute or on the part of the religious;

2. The absence of the religious spirit which is a cause of scandal to others is a sufficient motive for dismissal when a repeated admonition, together with a salutary penance, has produced no effect. Ill health is not a sufficient motive for dismissal, unless it is proved with certainty that it had been fraudulently hidden or dissimulated before profession;

3. Although these motives must be really known to the superior who effects the dismissal, it is not necessary, however, that they be

proved by a judicial procedure. But they must always be manifested to the religious, and full liberty to reply given to him; and his replies must be faithfully submitted to the superior effecting the dismissal;

4. The religious has the right to take recourse to the Apostolic See with suspensive effect, within ten days, or, in the case of an institute which is not of papal right, to the patriarch, except the case when he himself issued the decree;

5. If it is the case of women, the prescription of c. 194 # 2 must be observed.

CANON 200. The religious dismissed in accordance with c. 199 is ipso facto freed from all religious vows, but not from the obligations connected with the subdiaconate or a major order, and without prejudice to cc. 192 # 2, 193; a cleric below the subdiaconate is ipso facto reduced to the lay state.

CANON 201. The rules of cc. 199, 200, shall be observed in the dismissal of religious who took vows in a congregation with the following or a similar stipulation "as long as I shall live in the congregation," in such a way that a member who either spontaneously withdrew or was dismissed by the superiors shall be ipso facto freed from the vows.

Article Two

DISMISSAL OF RELIGIOUS WHO TOOK PERPETUAL VOWS IN A NON-EXEMPT CLERICAL OF LAY CONGREGATION OR IN A MONASTERY OR ORDER OF WOMEN (cc. 202-205)

Dismissal of Religious Men:
Required Reasons (c. 202 = c. 649 CIC)
Procedure (c. 203 = c. 650 CIC)
Dismissal of Religious Women:
Required Reasons (c. 204 = c. 651 CIC)
Confirmation by Hierarch (c. 205 = c. 652 CIC)

CANON 202. In a non-exempt clerical, or in a lay congregation of men, the dismissal of a member who has taken perpetual vows must necessarily be preceded by three offenses with a double admonition and failure to amend, according to the terms of cc. 208-214.

CANON 203. # 1. When the facts mentioned in c. 202 are ascertained, the superior general of the institute with the consent of his council, to be given in secret ballot, shall decide whether the case is one for dismissal.

2. If the majority of the votes are in favor of dismissal:

1. In a congregation of eparchial right, the entire question shall be forwarded to the Hierarch of the place where the religious house of the professed member is located, who is to issue, according to his prudent judgment, a decision within the limits of c. 199 # 1, 3.

2. In a congregation of papal or patriarchal right, the superior general himself of the institute issues the decree of dismissal; but in order that it have effect, it needs to receive confirmation from the Apostolic See, or, if it is the case of an institute which is not of papal right, of the patriarch, unless he himself has issued the decree.

3. The religious is entitled freely to expose his reasons; and his replies shall be faithfully recorded in the acts.

CANON 204. # 1. 1. To dismiss religious professed of perpetual vows grave external causes are required together with defect of repentance had from previous experiment, so that hope of emendation is lacking in the judgment of the superioress of the monastery or the superioress general of the congregation, with the consent of her council, manifested by secret ballot;

2. In confederated monasteries or in an order which has a superioress general the constitutions shall be observed, besides the prescription of no. 1, concerning the intervention of the president of the confederation or the superioress general.

2. The prescription of c. 203 # 3 shall be observed in the dismissal also of religious women.

CANON 205. # 1. 1. If a religious woman belongs to a monastery or a congregation of eparchial right, the Hierarch of the place where the religious house is located shall examine the motives for dismissal and issue the decree of dismissal;

2. When the monastery is subject to a regular superior, he is called to issue the decree of dismissal, which needs to be confirmed by the local Hierarch.

2. If there is a question of nuns of papal right, the entire matter shall be submitted by the local Hierarch to the Apostolic See together with all acts and documents; if the religious woman belongs to a congregation of papal right, this shall be done by the superioress general.

3. Likewise, the superioress of the monastery or the regular superior, if the monastery is subject to him, shall submit the entire matter with all acts and documents to the patriarch; this shall be done also by the superioress general of an order according to c. 204 # 1, 2, if the religious woman belongs to a stauropegial monastery or an order subject to the patriarch; and the superioress general of a congregation, if the religious belongs to a congregation of patriarchal right.

4. In the case the local Hierarch is obliged to forward the acts of dismissal to the Apostolic See according to # 2, or to the patriarch according to # 3, he shall add to the acts and documents his own opinion; such an opinion is to be added also by the regular superior if the monastery is subject to him.

Article Three

THE JUDICIAL PROCEDURE IN THE DISMISSAL OF RELIGIOUS MEN WHO TOOK PERPETUAL VOWS IN A MONASTERY OF WHATEVER JURIDICAL CONDITION OR IN AN EXEMPT CLERICAL ORDER OR CONGREGATION

CANON 206. A professed member of perpetual vows in a monastery or order of men and in an exempt clerical congregation may be dismissed only after judicial proceedings have been instituted, but without prejudice to canons 197, 198, every contrary privilege being revoked, and contrary customs being suppressed.

CANON 207. # 1. For the issuance of a sentence of dismissal the president of the monastic confederation, the superior of a non-confederated independent monastery, the superior of an independent stauropegial monastery is competent, unless, in the last case, the patriarch, having been notified by the superior concerning the matter, has himself taken over the case; also the superior general of an order or congregation; each with his council composed of at least four religious; and if this number be lacking, the president shall designate, with the consent of the other members, the needed number of religious, who will constitute with him a collegiate tribunal.

2. The president shall with the consent of the other members appoint a professed member of the same institute as prosecutor.

CANON 208. The procedure may not be begun before the following requirements preceded:
1. grave crimes against either common law or against the special law of the religious;
2. admonitions;
3. incorrigibility.

CANON 209. The offenses must be three of the same kind, or if they are different, such that taken together they manifest a perverse will resolved on evil, or continued and persisting if it is only one, which, because of repeated admonitions, becomes equal to a threefold one.

CANON 210. # 1. In order that a warning be given it is necessary that either the violation is notorious or established by extrajudicial confession of the culprit or by other sufficient proofs furnished by previous investigation.

2. In conducting the investigation the legal prescriptions concerning the investigation in criminal judicial trial shall be observed, unless it is against the nature of the case.

CANON 211. The warning must be made by the immediate major superior in person or through another at his order; but the superior shall not issue the order before the fact was established according to c. 210 # 1; the mandate issued for the first warning is valid also for the second.

CANON 212. Two warnings must be given, separately for each of the first two violations; in continuous or persisting violations an uninterrupted period of at least three days must have elapsed between the first and second warning.

CANON 213. # 1. The superior will add to these warnings suitable counsel and admonitions, prescribing additional penances and penal remedies, which are considered capable of procuring the amendment of the culprit and the reparation of the scandal.

2. The superior must in addition remove the culprit from the occasion of relapse, if necessary even by transferring him to another house where vigilance is easier and the opportunity of committing the violation is more remote.

3. Each warning shall be accompanied by the formal threat of dismissal.

CANON 214. The religious is considered not to have amended if he after the second warning committed a new violation, or, if in the case of permanent or continuous violation, if he persisted in it; after the last warning at least six days must elapse before further steps be taken.

CANON 215. The immediate major superior, after the warnings and admonitions have been abandoned as useless, shall collect all acts and documents and forward them to the president of the confederation or to the superior general. The latter then shall deliver them to the prosecutor, who shall examine them and submit his conclusions. In the case of a non-confederated independent monastery the superior himself shall the collected acts and documents deliver to the prosecutor for the above mentioned purpose.

CANON 216. # 1. If the prosecutor, who may also conduct further investigation if he judges it opportune, institutes an accusation, the proceedings shall be begun with observation of the canons concerning the judicial trial.

2. The proceedings are to establish that the violations had

been committed. that a double warning had preceded and that emendation was lacking.

CANON 217. After the tribunal has pondered the allegations of the prosecutor as well as of the culprit, and if they judge the suppositions mentioned in c. 216 # 2 to be sufficiently proved, the sentence of dismissal shall be pronounced.

CANON 218. # 1. The sentence rendered by a tribunal of an institute of papal right cannot be committed to execution before it has been confirmed by the Apostolic See.

2. If the religious belongs to a stauropegial monastery or one of eparchial right or to an order dependent on the patriarch, the sentence cannot be committed to execution before it has been confirmed by the patriarch.

3. The president of the tribunal shall see that the sentence as well as the acts of the trial be forwarded to the Apostolic See or the patriarch respectively.

CANON 219. In distant regions the superiors mentioned in c. 207 # 1 may commit the authority of dismissal, with the consent of their council, to reliable and prudent religious who must be at least three, without prejudice to the prescription of cc. 215-218.

Article Four

CONDITION OF RELIGIOUS WITH PERPETUAL VOWS WHO WERE DISMISSED (cc. 2201223)

Legal Effects of Dismissal (c. 220 = c. 669 CIC)
Penalties for Clerics:
    Clerics Dismissed for Major Delicts (c. 221 = c. 670 CIC)
    Clerics Dismissed for Minor Delicts (c. 222 = c. 671 CIC)
Obligation and Right of Return to the Institute
    (c. 223 = c. 672 CIC)

CANON 220. # 1. The professed religious who has taken perpetual vows and who has been dismissed from the institute remains bound by his religious vows, unless the constitutions or apostolic indults determine otherwise.

2. A cleric below a subdeacon is by the fact of dismissal reduced to the lay state.

CANON 221. A cleric who is a subdeacon or in major orders, and who has committed the violation mentioned in c. 197, or has been dismissed because of a violation which by common law is punished with infamy of law or with minor or simple deposition or with major deposition or degradation, is forever forbidden to wear the clerical garb.

Differently from the provision of this canon, which has as an automatic sequel of minor deposition also the prohibition of wearing the clerical garb, c. 2304 CIC deprives of the ecclesiastical garb the culprit punished with minor deposition by a special act of the Hierarch only if he gives no sign of repentance.

CANON 222. If the cleric who is a subdeacon or who is in major orders has been dismissed because of the lesser violations mentioned in c. 221:

1. He remains i p s o f a c t o suspended until he obtains absolution from the Apostolic See, or the patriarch, in case the sentence or decree of dismissal has not been submitted to the Apostolic See for confirmation;

2. The Apostolic See may, should it be judged expedient, order the dismissed to stay in a specified eparchy and to wear the garb of the secular clergy, informing the local Hierarch of the reason for which he has been dismissed;

3. If the dismised should not obey the order mentioned in 2, the institute will not be bound by any obligation towards him, and the dismissed is deprived by the fact itself of the right to wear the ecclesiastical garb;

4. The Hierarch of the eparchy where he is assigned to stay shall send the religious to a house of penance, or he shall commit him to the care and vigilance of a pious and prudent priest; and if the religious does not obey, the prescription of 3 shall be observed;

5. The institute shall provide the dismissed, through the mediation of the Hierarch of the place of his stay, with the necessities of life, by giving him out of charity a subsidy for support, except if he is capable of providing for himself from other resources;

6. If the dismissed does not lead a life fitting a man in ecclesiastical service, he shall be deprived after the lapse of a year, or even sooner if the Hierarch decides so, of the charitable subsidy, and shall be ejected from the house of penance, and the right of wearing the ecclesiastical garb shall be taken away from him by the Hierarch himself, who shall take care that a corresponding report be sent to the Apostolic See, or, in the case treated in 1, to the patriarch, as well as to the institute;

7. But if the dismissed has shown during the foregoing time such laudable behavior that he may be deservingly considered reformed, the Hierarch shall recommend his petition to the Apostolic See, or, in the case mentioned in 1, to the patriarch, for the absolution from the censure of suspension, and, having obtained it, shall permit him to celebrate, with suitable precautions and limitations, the Divine Liturgy in his eparchy, and also in his prudent judgment permit him other parts of the sacred ministry, to provide for his honorable support; in which case the institute may stop the charitable subsidy. If it is the case of a deacon or subdeacon, the matter shall be submitted to the Apostolic See.

CANON 223. # 1. Except in case of dismissal mentioned in c. 197, the dismissed religious who has not obtained the dispensation from the vows is not free from the obligation of returning to the convent; and if he gave proofs of reformation during a period of three years, the institute must receive him back; should this be opposed by reasons existing either on the part of the institute or on the part of the religious, the matter shall be submitted to the decision of the Apostolic See.

2. When the vows taken in the institute have expired, the dismissed shall remain under the jurisdiction and special vigilance of the local Hierarch, if he has found one willing to accept him, without prejudice to the prescription of c. 193; otherwise, the matter shall be referred to the Apostolic See.

CHAPTER NINE

SOCIETIES OF MEN OR WOMEN LIVING IN COMMON ACCORDING TO THE MANNER OF RELIGIOUS BUT WITHOUT PUBLIC VOWS

Definition and Kinds of Societies (c. 224 = c. 673 CIC)
Establishment and Suppression (c. 225 = c. 674 CIC)
Government (c. 226 = c. 675 CIC)
Holding and Administration of Property (c. 227 = c. 676 CIC)
Reception, Education and Ordination of Members
  (c. 228 ## 1, 2 = c. 677 CIC; # 3 = new)
Obligations of Members (c. 229 = c. 678 CIC)
Privileges of Members (c. 230 = c. 679 CIC)
Separation of Members from the Society (c. 231 = c. 680 CIC)

CANON 224. # 1. A society of men or of women in which the members, under the rule of superiors, in accordance with approved constitutions, imitate the mode of life of religious, although they are not bound by the three customary public vows, is neither a religious institute in the strict sense, nor do its members come under the name of religious properly so called.

2. Such a society may be clerical or lay, of papal, patriarchal or eparchial right, according to cc. 312 # 2, 314 # 3.

CANON 225. In respect to the erection and suppression of a society and its provinces or houses, the same prescriptions obtain which are established for religious congregations.

CANON 226. The mode of government is to be defined in the constitutions of each society. In all, however, the norms of cc. 23-62 on congregations shall be applied, unless this be against the nature of the matter.

CANON 227. # 1. The society, its provinces and houses are capable of acquiring and possessing temporal property.

2. The administration of the property shall be governed by the norms of cc. 64-90.

3. Whatever the members acquire in respect of the society is acquired by the society; other property is retained, acquired and administered by the members in conformity with the constitutions.

CANON 228. # 1. In regard to the admission of candidates, the constitutions shall be followed, save for the norm of c. 74.

2. In respect to matters pertaining to studies, the members are under the same laws as secular clerics, save for special provisions made by the Apostolic See.

3. In the matter of the ordination of members, the major superiors can grant, according to the statutes, to their subjects dismissorial letters for minor orders after their first acceptance; for major orders after their final acceptance, if the society has such; if it does not have such, then after six years have elapsed since the first acceptance.

The corresponding c. 678 CIC did not make any specific provision for such societies. In order to obviate the many difficulties which were experienced by such organizations, the S. Congregations for the Propagation of the Faith and of Religious adopted in 1947 a plan according to which indults are granted to superiors major so requesting in virtue of which they can grant dismissorial letters for ordination to their subjects. Oriental canon law has incorporated this provision as a part of its common law.

CANON 229. # 1. In addition to the obligations to which they are subject according to the constitutions as members, the members of the society are bound by the common obligations of clerics, unless the nature of the matter or the text or context of the law decrees otherwise, and they must also observe the prescriptions of cc. 138-148, 150-159, which respect congregations, unless the constitutions should order differently.

2. The enclosure shall be observed according to the terms of the constitutions and under the vigilance of the local Hierarch.

CANON 230. The members of the same, even if lay, enjoy the clerical privileges as defined in common law and others which were directly granted to the society, but not, without a special indult, the privileges of the religious.

CANON 231. In addition to the constitutions of each society, the norms of cc. 182-185, 196, shall be observed, unless the nature of the matter demands otherwise, in respect to transfer to another society or a religious institute, or to the departure of members of a society even of papal right; the prescriptions of cc. 197-223, in regard to their dismissal.

THE MOTU PROPRIO

CLERI SANCTITATI

ON

THE LAITY

TITLE FIVE

THE LAITY

(cc. 527-558)

THE LAITY IN GENERAL

Relationship to Clergy (c. 527 = c. 682 CIC)
Participation of Laity in the Work of the Clergy
(c. 528 = new)
Wearing of Clerical Garb by Lay Persons
(c. 529 = c. 683 CIC)

CANON 527. The laity have the right to receive from the clergy the spiritual benefits and especially the necessary means of salvation, according to the rules of ecclesiastical discipline.

CANON 528. # 1. Local Hierarchs shall see, by issuing appropriate instructions, observing the norms enacted in this matter by the Apostolic See, that the laity under the leadership of qualified priests render to the clergy, as far as it is in their power, assistance in the defense of the Christian laws, and that they confirm their words with the example of their life, in order that the whole way of life of the people be modeled according to these laws.

2. The laity, especially those who are eminent on account of learning, shall not omit to illuminate with the light of Christian doctrine and brotherly love, by employing appropriate reasoning, the more important problems pertaining to the province of social questions.

Since the promulgation of the CIC in 1917, the idea of organized Catholic Action has been advanced by the Roman Pontiffs, notably Pius XI, which demanded recognition in written law. **Cleri Sanctitati** has taken legislative cognizance, and the present canon defines the role of lay people in the apostolate of the Church.

CANON 529. Laymen are not allowed to wear the ecclesiastical garb, unless it is the case of students of seminaries and other candidates to orders, or of laymen legitimately appointed to the service of the church while they take part in some ecclesiastical ministry, either within the church building or outside.

ASSOCIATIONS OF THE FAITHFUL IN GENERAL (cc. 530-547)

CANON 530.   The faithful deserve praise who join associations erected, approved or at least recommended by the Church. They shall beware of associations that are secret, condemned, seditious, suspected, or those which strive to withdraw from the legitimate supervision of the Church.

CANON 531.   Associations distinct from religious institutes or from societies of men or women living without public vows according to the manner of the religious can be established by the Church either for promoting a more perfect Christian life, or for the practice of works of piety or charity, or, finally, for the advancement of the public worship.

CANON 532.   # 1.   In order that an association be recognized as canonical it is necessary that it is erected or at least approved by legitimate ecclesiastical authority.

2.   Although some associations of the faithful are neither erected nor approved by the Church, they nevertheless are under the supervision of the local Hierarch, who must see to it that no abuses creep in, and if they crept in, he must correct and amend them.

CANON 533.   # 1.   To erect or approve associations is the right of the Roman Pontiff, the patriarch or the local Hierarch, with the exception of those whose erection is by law, in virtue of an apostolic privilege, reserved to others.

2.   Though it can be proved that a privilege was granted, it is nevertheless necessary for the validity of the erection or approval, unless it is stipulated otherwise in the privilege, that the patriarch or local Hierarch give his written consent. The consent of the patriarch

or local Hierarch given for the erection of a religious house is valid also for the erection, in the semi-public oratory of the house or in the church attached to it, of an association belonging to this religious institute, which however is not organized in the form of an organized body.

3. A syncellus without a special mandate and an administrator of a vacant eparchy cannot erect an association or grant approval or consent for its erection.

4. The letters of erection or approval granted by those who erect the association in virtue of an apostolic privilege shall be granted gratis, with the exception only of a tax for the necessary expenditures.

CANON 534. The associations of faithful acquire legal personality in the Church by special grant of the legitimate ecclesiastical superior, given by a formal decree.

Those associations which have not received such a decree from the ecclesiastical superior may still possess the juridical quality of moral persons in virtue of natural law (cf. P. Rayanna, S.J., Moral or Juridical Person, in **The Jurist**, XVIII, 1958, p. 465).

CANON 535. # 1. An association shall not assume a name or title which savors of levity or unseemly novelty, or gives expression to a form of devotion not legitimately approved.

2. The local Hierarchs shall watch lest, in connection with the title and name of associations, somethings less appropriate to the Rites and traditions of the Oriental Church be introduced.

CANON 536. #1. Every association shall possess statutes, examined, approved or confirmed by the Apostolic See, the patriarch or the local Hierarch.

2. Statutes which were confirmed or approved only by the local Hierarch remain subject to the authority of the Hierarch, who can change them.

CANON 537. The banner and the insignia of the association need to receive special approval of the legitimate authority according to the rules of c. 536.

CANON 538. # 1. All associations, even those erected by the Apostolic See or the patriarch, are subject, except if this is opposed to a special privilege granted or recognized by the Apostolic See, to the jurisdiction and supervision of the local Hierarch, who has the right and duty to supervise them according to the norms of the canons.

2. In respect, however, to associations which were erected in virtue of an Apostolic privilege by exempt religious in their churches, the local Hierarch of the same Rite can direct and inspect them in matters which concern the Rite, but not in matters which refer to the internal government or spiritual direction.

CANON 539. # 1. An association legitimately erected can, unless the contrary has been expressly ordered, possess and administer temporal property under the authority of the local Hierarch, to whom it must render an account of the administration at least once a year, according to the rules of law, and not to the pastor, although it is established in his territory, except if the Hierarch himself has ordered differently.

2. The association can, according to the prescriptions of the statutes, receive offerings, and spend the receipts for the pious purposes of the association, always according to the intentions of the donor.

3. No association is permitted to collect alms, except if it is either permitted by the statutes, or necessity demands it, or the permission of the local Hierarch is granted, and the form prescribed by him is observed.

4. For collecting alms outside the eparchy in which the association is established, the permission of each Hierarch, given in writing is required.

5. The association must render account of the faithful use of the offerings and alms to the local Hierarch.

CANON 540. In order to participate in the rights, privileges, indulgences, and other similar favors of the association, it is required that a person be validly received into the association according to the association's own statutes, and that he remain enrolled at that time.

CANON 541. # 1. Into associations of the faithful:
1. there cannot be validly received non-Catholics and members of condemned societies or those who are known to be under ecclesiastical censure;
2. there cannot be licitly received public sinners.

2. The same person can be enrolled in several associations.

3. Absent persons cannot be enrolled in associations which are established in the form of an organized body, and those present cannot be enrolled except with their knowledge and consent.

4. Religious may enroll in pious associations, with the exception of those whose laws, in the opinion of the superior, are incompatible with the observance of the constitutions of the religious institute.

CANON 542. # 1. The reception shall take place in accordance with the norms of law and the statutes of the individual association.

2. In order that the reception be ascertainable, it must be duly recorded in the membership roll of the association. This recording is necessary for validity if the association is erected as a legal person or is established in the form of an organized body.

CANON 543. On the occasion of the reception into the association no payment shall be demanded, either directly or indirectly, except what is established by the legitimately approved statutes, or expressly permitted by the patriarch, in respect to an association of patriarchal right, or by the local Hierarch, in favor of the association, in view of special circumstances.

CANON 544. # 1. No lawfully enrolled member shall be dismissed from the association except for a just reason in accordance with the rules of the statutes.

2. Those who fall into a cause mentioned in c. 541 # 1 shall after previous admonition be deprived of membership in the manner prescribed by the statutes of the association, and without prejudice to the right to take recourse to the Hierarch.

3. Although no express mention is made in the statutes, the patriarch or local Hierarch in respect to all associations, and the religious superior in regard to associations established by the religious in virtue of an apostolic indult, can dismiss members.

CANON 545. # 1. Lawfully established associations have the right, in accordance with the rules of their statutes and the canons, to hold meetings, to enact specific regulations that concern the association itself, to elect economes of their property, officials and assistants, without prejudice to the norm of c. 558.

2. In regard to the convening of meetings and elections, the rules of cc. 103-124 and of the statutes, insofar they are not contrary to common law, shall be observed.

CANON 546. # 1. 1. The appointment of the spiritual director and of the chaplain is a right of the local Hierarch in respect to associations which were established or approved by him, the patriarch or the Apostolic See, and in associations established by religious in virtue of an apostolic indult outside their own churches.

2. In associations, however, established by religious in their own churches, the appointment in question belongs to the religious superior, but if a spiritual director and a chaplain of the secular clery are to be appointed, the superior must prior to the appointment obtain the consent of their Hierarch;

3. In a case where nearly all members belong to a Rite different from that of the religious, the spiritual director and the chaplain will be of the Rite of the members, and the pious practices of the association shall be conducted in the parish church or in another church of the Rite of the members, unless it is arranged differently with the consent of the local Hierarch of the members.

2. The spiritual director and the chaplain can while holding this office bless the habit and the insignia of the association, and invest new members with them.

3. The spiritual director and the chaplain can be removed for a just reason by those who have appointed them, their successors or superiors.

4. The same priest can be both spiritual director and chaplain.

CANON 547. # 1. 1. For serious reasons and without prejudice to the right of recourse to the Apostolic See, the local Hierarch can suppress not only an association established by him or his predecessors, but also an association established in virtue of an apostolic indult by religious with the consent of the local Hierarch, save for the prescription of c. 260 # 2;

2. The recourse taken against the decree of the local Hierarch by which he abolishes an association established by religious in accordance with the rule of 1, suspends the execution of the decree.

2. An association established by the Apostolic See can be abolished only by it; those established by the patriarch also by the patriarch.

CHAPTER TWO

ASSOCIATIONS OF THE FAITHFUL IN PARTICULARS
(cc. 548-558)

CANON 548. There are four different kinds of associations in the Church: Aggregations to a monastery, third orders secular, confraternities, and pious unions.

CANON 549. # 1. The order of precedence among the pious lay associations is, without prejudice to the rule of c. 37, 5, 6, the following:

1. Aggregations to monasteries;
2. Third orders;
3. Confraternities;
4. Pious unions.

2. The confraternity of the Divine Eucharist enjoys precedence over all other confraternities in a procession in which the Divine Eucharist is carried.

3. However, all these have the right of precedence only when they take part in a body, under their own cross or banner, and vested with the habit or insignia of the association.

CANON 550. # 1. Aggregations to monasteries are associations of the faithful who strive in the world after Christian perfection, under the direction of the superior of monks, in accordance with legitimately approved rules.

2. The rules mentioned in # 1 must be approved by the local Hierarch if the monastery is of eparchial right, or of papal right but not exempt; by the patriarch if it is a stauropegial monastery; by the Apostolic See if it is endowed with papal exemption.

CANON 551. # 1. 1. Secular tertiaries are persons who in the world strive after Christian perfection, under the direction of an order and in harmony with its spirit, in accordance with the rules approved for them by the Apostolic See;

2. The approval of the rules mentioned in 1 is a right of the patriarch if the order is subject to him.

2. If the third order secular is divided into several associations of whom all are legitimately established, each of them is called an association of tertiaries.

CANON 552. # 1. Without prejudice to the privilege granted to some orders, no religious institute can erect or affiliate a new third order.

2. Religious superiors can enroll, it is true, in their third order individual persons, but they cannot, even with an apostolic indult, validly establish an association of tertiaries without the consent of the local Hierarch, in accordance with the rule of c. 533 # 2.

3. Nor can they grant without special permission of the same local Hierarch to sodalities established by them the use of a special garb to be worn in public religious functions.

CANON 553. # 1. Associations of the faithful set up in the form of an organized body, which were established, besides for the purpose of practicing some work of piety or charity, for the promotion of public worship, are called confraternities.

2. Associations of the faithful whose aim is only the practice of some work of piety or charity are called pious unions, and those which are set up in the form of an organized body are called sodalities.

CANON 554. Confraternities can be established only by a formal decree of erection. For pious unions the approval of the legitimate ecclesiastical authority suffices, to the extent that, when they have received it, although they are not legal persons, they become capable of obtaining spiritual favors, especially indulgences.

CANON 555. Local Hierarchs shall see to it that in every parish is established the confraternity for the promotion of the Eucharistic devotion and the sodality for the spreading of the knowledge of Christian doctrine, although they are empowered to establish, on account of the exceptional circumstances, in place of the confraternity, a pious union or sodality for the promotion of the Eucharistic devotion.

CANON 556. # 1. Confraternities or pious unions shall be established only in a church, or public or at least semi-public oratory.

2. The local Hierarch can permit in the churches or oratories of religious women the erection only of an association of women, or of a pious union which is engaged only in the recitation of prayers and enjoys merely communication of spiritual favors.

CANON 557. Confraternities shall not abandon or change their habit or insignia without the permission of the local Hierarch, save for the right of the patriarch in respect to confraternities of patriarchal right.

CANON 558. # 1. 1. The local Hierarch has the right to preside in person or through a delegate at the meetings of confraternities, even if they are held in churches and oratories of the religious, but without the right of voting, to confirm the election of worthy and qualified officials and assistants, to reject or remove unworthy or incapable ones, to correct and approve or confirm the statutes and other regulations, unless they were approved or confirmed by the Apostolic See.

2. If the confraternity is of patriarchal right, the local Hierarch is not empowered to correct, approve or confirm statutes or other regulations which were approved or confirmed by the patriarch.

2. The confraternity shall in due time inform the local Hierarch or his delegate if they plan to hold an extraordinary meeting, otherwise the Hierarch is entitled to disband the meeting or to annul its decisions in their entirety.

INDEX

The numbers refer to pages of the book.

patriarchates 127; confirmation in patriarchates 128; titular, appointment in patriarchates 129; supervision by patriarch 139; consecration by metropolitan 153; appointment by Pope 175; qualifications 175; canonical provision 176; taking possession of office 177; rights and duties 178; pontifical celebrations 179; residence duty 179; report 180; quinquennial report 180; liturgical commemoration in eparchy 181; titular bishops 181; visitation of eparchy 181; auxiliary 182; coadjutors and auxiliaries 182; ordaining religious 289.

BOND furnished by clerics 73.

BRAZIL, Ukrainians 6.

BUDKA, BISHOP NICETAS 17.

BULGARIANS, Byzantine Rite Catholics 7; celibacy 68.

BYZANTINE RITE, definition 13; subgroups 13; initiation into clergy 61; celibacy 68.

BYZANTINE-SLAVONIC 16.

CANADA, Ukrainians 6, 12, 17; celibacy of clergy 69.

CANONS AND CHAPTERS 57, 59, 197, 199.

CANTORATE 61.

CAMELAUCIUM 144, 283.

CAMERA APOSTOLICA 109.

CARDINAL of Oriental Rite 97, 98.

CATHOLICUS 159.

CASES, THEOLOGICAL, solution 66.

CELIBACY in general 67; among Orientals 68; Armenians 68; Byzantine Rite 68; of syncellus 188.

CENOBITES 239.

CURATE, cf. **VICAR ASSISTANT.**

CURIA, EPARCHIAL 185.

CURIA, PATRIARCHAL, definition, composition 145; upkeep 150.

CURIA, ROMAN, composition, competence, norms for transaction of business 102.

CHALDEANS 7, 12, 68, 132, 159.

CHANCELLOR, EPARCHIAL 193.

CHANCELLOR, PATRIARCHAL 149.

CHANCERY, APOSTOLIC 109.

CHAPLAINS, MILITARY 212.

CHAPLAINS of religious 265.

CHAPTER OF CANONS 57, 59, 197, 199.

CHASTITY and clergy 70.

CHIROTESIA 143, 300, 305.

CHIROTONIA 143, 305.

CHORBISHOP 208.

CHRISM, consecration privilege of patriarch 140.

CICOGNANI, CARDINAL AMLETO GIOVANNI, 3.

CLASSES, among religious 242.

CLERGY, Oriental Rite — subjection to Latin Rite ordinary 25; authority of accepting into 55; rite of acceptance into 5, 61; minor clerics, permanent 56; patriarchal 62; exclusive rights 62; privileges 63; financial aid to retired 63; obligations 64; junior clergy examinations 66; married candidates 67; celibacy of minor clergy 70; keeping of women 70; beard 72; dress 72; occupations alien 73; unbecoming occupations 73; bond furnished by clerics 73; negative obligations 73; unbecoming spectacles 73; clericus vagus or acephalus 75; return to lay state 91; readmission 91.

CLERICAL RELIGIOUS INSTITUTE, definition 245.

"CLERI SANCTITATI" 4.

CLOISTURE, cf. **ENCLOSURE.**

COADJUTOR of bishop 182.

CODIFICATION of Oriental canon law, history 3.

COLLEGE, rector of church 228.

COLLEGIATE PERSONS, rules of actions 51.

COLOR of clerical dress 58.

COMMEMORATION, LITURGICAL, of bishop 181; of metropolitan 153; of patriarch 138; of Pope 95.

COMMISSION, PATRIARCHAL LITURGICAL, 149.

COMMON LIFE of clergy 70.

COMPUTATION of degrees of relationships 49.

CONFEDERATIONS OF MONASTERIES, association of, 244; monastical 244; 251, 256.

CONFERENCES, PROTOPRESBYTEREAL, 66.

CONFERENCES, EPISCOPAL, in patriarchate 127.

CONFESSORS, appointed by patriarch 136; privilege of patriarch 140; in stauropegial monastery 265; of religious men 262; of religious women 262.

CONFIRMATION, parochial function 220.

CONFRATERNITIES 332.

CONGREGATIONS, SACRED: general norms 103; Holy Office 103; Consistorial Congregation 103; Oriental Congregation 104; territorial jurisdiction of Oriental Congregation 105; of Sacraments 105; for the Religious 106; for the Propagation of the Faith 106; of Ceremonies 107; of Sacred Rites 107; for Seminaries and Universities 108; for Extraordinary Ecclesiastical Affairs 108.

CONGREGATION, RELIGIOUS, definition 245; erection 251; of women and institute of men 256.

CONSANGUINITY 49.

CONSCIENCE, DISCLOSURE, 266.

CONSENT to actions of superiors 53.

CONSISTORY, EPARCHIAL, 185.

CONSULTANTS, PATRIARCHAL, 150.

CONSULTORS, EPARCHIAL, qualifications 197; number, 198; term of office, removal 199; religious appointed 197; ex officio members 198; during vacancy 203.

CONSTITUTIONS OF RELIGIOUS, definition 246.

CONVERSION and Rite 27; informal conversion 28.

CONVOCATION, EPARCHIAL, 183.

CONVOCATION, EXARCHIAL, 172.

COPTS, 5, 68.

CORRESPONDENCE by religious 298.

COUNCIL, PATRIARCHAL, 148.

COUSSA, MONS. ACACIUS, 3.

"CREBRAE ALLATAE" 3.

CROATS, 14, 68.

CROSS, PECTORAL, 58.

CROZIER, cf. STAFF, PASTORAL.

DAMAGE, compensation for, 53.

DATARY, APOSTOLIC 109.

DEACON, permanent, 60, 65.

DEAN, cf. PROTOPRESBYTER.

DEANERY, cf. PROTOPRESBYTERATE.

DEBTS, contracted by religious, 269.

DECREES OF APOSTOLIC SEE, to be read in religious houses 258.

DEGREES of religious profession 282.

DELEGATES, APOSTOLIC, 110.

DELEGATION of jurisdiction 89.

DEPRIVATION of office 86.

DIGNITIES and offices for religious, incompatibility 307.

DIOCESAN, cf. EPARCHIAL.

DISCIPLINE, subdivision of Rite, 8.

DISCLOSURE OF CONSCIENCE 266.

DIGENEIA 50.

DISMISSAL of clerics, 61; of religious 315.

DISMISSORIAL LETTERS for the ordination of religious 289.

DISPENSATION, power of patriarch, 135.

DOMICILE 44.

DOMINATIVE POWER, cf. PUBLIC ECCLESIASTICAL AUTHORITY.

DOVE, EUCHARISTIC, 201.

DOWRY of religious women, 266, 273; restitution 314.

DRESS, CLERICAL, obligation of wearing 72; color 58.

ECONOME, EPARCHIAL, 191; ex officio eparchial consultor 198; distinct from administrator 205; during vacancy 206.

ECONOME, PATRIARCHAL, 149.

ECONOMES, in religious institute, 261.

ECUMENICAL SYNOD 95.

ELECTION, norms 79; convocation 80; plurality of votes 80; tellers 81; compromise 81; acceptance 82; renunciation 82; confirmation 82.

ENCLOSURE of religious 291; monasteries of men, of women; institutions, admission of externs, 292; supervision 294; houses of orders and congregations 295; exit 296.

ENCOLPION 142.

EPANOKAMELAUKION, cf. SUPRACAMELAUCIUM.

EPARCHY, dismissal of clerics by administrator 61; definition 93; establishment in patriarchates 127; supervision of vacant eparchies by patriarch 127; patriarchal 139; visitation by bishop 181; archives 192; administration of vacant or impeded eparchy 201; administrator 205; religious and eparchy 296.

EPIPHANY, water blessing, 221.

ERROR 53.

ETHIOPIANS 5, 68.

EUCHARIST, DIVINE, dove 201; viaticum 220.

EXAMINATION, competitive for parishes 218; junior clergy 289.

EXAMINERS, EPARCHIAL, 196.

EXARCHY, definition 93.

KANONIKON 300.
KOLPAK 58.
KOUKOULION 283.

LADYKA, ARCHBISHOP BASIL VLADIMIR, 17.
LAITY, relationship to clergy; assistance to clergy; wearing of clerical dress, 327.
LANGUAGE, LITURGICAL, and Rite 9; and parishes 94; and divine office 241.
LAURA and LAURIOTES, 238, 239.
LAW, PARTICULAR, of religious, definition, 246.
LEAVING, voluntary, of religious institute, 311.
LECTORATE 61.
LEGATES, in general 110; and patriarchs, 111.
LEVYTSKY, CARDINAL MICHAEL, 98.
LIFE, COMMON, of parish clergy, 227.
LWIW, Ukrainian Metropolitan 6, 57; synod of 1891, 71; Armenian archbishop 8.

MAGYARS of the Byzantine Rite 7, 14, 68.
MAJORITY (Age) 44.
MAJOR ARCHBISHOPS, cf. ARCHBISHOP, MAJOR.
MALABARIANS 8, 11, 68, 131, 154.
MALANKARIANS 6, 61, 132, 155.
MANDYAS 142, 283.
MAPHRIAN 159.
MARONITES 6, 12, 61, 68.
MARRIAGE ASSISTANCE, parochial function, 220.
MATRIMONY, LAW OF, cf. CREBRAE ALLATAE.
MULTIPLE HIERARCHY 46.
MULTI-RITUALISM 24.
MYRON, HOLY, cf. CHRISM, HOLY.
MEGALOSCHEMUS 241.
MELKITES 6, 12, 13, 68, 116.
MENSA EPISCOPALIS 178.
METROPOLITAN, in patriarchate 125; appointment 127; ordination and enthronement 129; definition 152; liturgical commemoration 153; consecration of bishops 153; jurisdiction 153; authority over eparchies 153; pallium 154; independent, outside patriarchates 154; suppletory 155; titular 160.

METROPOLITAN SYNOD, cf. SYNOD, PROVINCIAL.
METOCHION 239.
MILITARY CHAPLAINS in patriarchates 131; in general 212.
MILITARY SERVICE and clergy 74.
MINOR CLERICS, permanent 56; celibacy 70; and subdeacons ordained by religious superior 306.
MICROSCHEMUS 241, 283.
MINOR SCHEME 144.
MITRE 57.
MONACHISM, ORIENTAL, legal characteristics 238.
MONASTERIUM SUI IURIS, cf. MONASTERY, INDEPENDENT.
MONASTERY, exarchical 167; Grottaferrata 200; definition and kinds 244; erection 249; suppression 250; confederation of 251; jurisdiction of president of confederation 256; stauropegial, confessors 265.
MONASTIC STATE, unity, no division into institutes 238.
MONEY, investment by religious 266.
MONK, definition 245.
MORAL PERSONS 51.

NOTARIES, patriarchal 140; eparchial 193.
NATIONAL PARISH 93.
NATIONAL SYNOD, cf, SYNOD, PATRIARCHAL.
NOVITIATE, admission, qualifications 270; mode of beginning 275; in monasteries 275; in other institutes 275; duration 276; habit to be worn 277; classes of members 277; master 277; segregation 278; training, studies, confessors 279; privileges of novices, property rights, leaving 280.
NUN, definition 245.
NUNCIOS 110.

OBEDIENCE of clergy 66.
OFFICE, DIVINE, obligation of private recital 70; public recital 72; in secular churches 178; celebrated by pastors 224; kind of obligation in monasteries 241; recitation by religious 297.
OFFICE, ECCLESIASTICAL, definition 76, kinds of appointments 76; non-vacant 77; qualifications of candidate 77; time limit 78; incompatible 78; modes of vacancy 78; modes of loss 84; renunciation 84;

vacancy 85; tacit renunciatioon 85; removal 86; irremovable offices 86; transfer to another office 86; deprivation 86.

OFFICE, HOLY, 103.

OFFICES OF THE ROMAN CURIA 109.

OMOPHORION 121, 123.

ORDER, religious institute, definition 245; erection 251.

ORDERS, HOLY, diriment impediment 67; ordination of married candidates 67; power of confering 91; reception by religious 289.

ORDERS, THIRD, 332.

ORDINARY, cf. HIERARCH.

ORDINARY, LATIN RITE, Oriental Rite subjection 25; limits of jurisdiction over Orientals 48; and Orientals 48; subjection to Latin Rite hierarchy of Orientals 47.

ORIGIN 44.

ORTYNSKY, BISHOP SOTER STEPHEN, 15.

PALLIUM 121.

PANAGIA 58, 142.

PARAMAN 283.

PARAMANDYAS 283.

PARISH, in general 93; national parish 93; personal parish 94; Oriental, territorial, 94; liturgical language 94; kinds among Orientals 210; union to moral persons 212; entrusted to religious 213, 296.

PAROCHIAL VICARS, cf. VICARS.

PASTOR, Latin Rite pastors and suppletory jurisdiction over Orientals 45; in general 210; removability 214; appointment 217; rights and duties 219; vacations 222; missa pro populo 223; parochial functions: baptism 219; betrothal 220, marriage assistance 220; confirmation 220; celebration of divine office 224; religious pastor and community 297; religious pastor 309.

PASTORS CONSULTANTS 196.

PATRONAGE, RIGHT OF, 76.

PATRIARCH, precedence in regard to Papal Legates 111; history of title 112; Catholic patriarchal titles 113; non-Catholic patriarchal titles 114; canonical definition 114; jurisdiction 115; personal titles 115; precedence among patriarchs 116; apocrisiary 117; election 117; qualifications of candidate 120; acceptance and confirmation 120; electors 118; rights and obligations 123; limits of jurisdiction 124; gen-

eral delegation 125; legislative power 125, 126; dispensative power 126; teaching authority 126; encyclical letters 126; appointment of local hierarchs 127; supervision of vacant eparchies; visitation of patriarchate 127; ordination of metropolitans 129; relationship to faithful outside the patriarchate 131; power over holydays 135; power over fast and abstinence 135; power of sanation 136; appointment of preachers and confessors 136; financial support 136; liturgical commemoration 138; duties 138; supervision of bishops 139; patriarchal eparchy 139; privileges 140; title "Apostolic" 141; title "Pope" 141; title "Beatitude" 142; precedence over other bishops 142; appointment of exarchs 174.

PATRIARCHATE, administrator and dismissal of clerics 61; erection 93; ecclesiastical provinces 125; territorial division 127; metropolitans 127; eparchies 127; exarchies 127; visitation by patriarch 127; episcopal conferences 127; supervision of hierarchy 130; administrator 150; synod 161; military chaplains 131.

PENITENTIARY, SACRED, 108.

PERIODEUT 208.

PERSONAL STATUTES, cf. STATUTES, PERSONAL.

PERSON, COLLEGIATE, rules of actions 51.

PERSONS, MORAL, definition 51, classification, establishment 51; duration of existence 51; extinction 52.

PHILADELPHIA, Byzantine Rite metropolitan 15, 17.

PIOUS UNIONS 332.

PITTSBURGH, Byzantine Rite Apostolic Exarchy 18.

POLYSTAURION 283.

PONTIFICAL FUNCTIONS, definition 100; by bishops 179.

PONTIFICAL INSIGNIA 57.

POPE, definition of authority 94; liturgical commemoration 95, 158.

POSTQUAM APOSTOLICIS 4, 233.

POSTULATE of religious 269.

POSTULATION in election 83.

POWER, cf. JURISDICTION.

PREACHERS for religious 265.

PRECEDENCE, rules 53; among archbishops and metropolitans 160; rank of see 181; among religious 248; among lay associations 332.

PRELATE, definition 68.

PRELATIC TITLES, Oriental 56, religious 56; and Latin Rite clergy 60; conferred by patriarch 56; cf. Mitre, Staff, Hypogonation, Cross, Color.

PRESBYTER, definition, 65.

PRIVILEGES, of clerics, of religious: original source, communication, 298; and clerical privileges 299.

PROCEDURAL LAW, cf. SOLLICITUDINEM NOSTRAM.

PROCURATOR GENERAL of religious 261.

PRO-EXARCH 173.

PROFESSION, RELIGIOUS, major and minor 245; requirements for validity 81; in monasteries 282; degrees 282; temporary 284; juridical effects, property rights 285; renunciation of property 286; abandonment of offices 286; loss of eparchy 287; invalid profession 287.

PROPERTY, temporal of religious 266; alienation by religious 267.

PROTOARCHIMANDRITE 59.

PROTOHEGOUMENUS 59.

PROTOPRESBYTERATE, conferences of clergy 66; division of eparchy 94; protopresbyters 209.

PROTOSYNCELLUS 59.

PROTOTHRONOS 150.

PROVINCE, ECCLESIASTICAL 152.

PROVINCE, RELIGIOUS, definition 245.

PUBLIC DOMINATIVE POWER, 76, 91, 256.

QUASI-PARISH 93.

QUINQUENNIAL REPORT of bishops 180.

RASON 58, 283.

RASOPHORATE 241, 282.

RECOURSE against decrees 89.

RECTORS OF CHURCHES 228.

REGION, ORIENTAL, definition 47.

RELIGIOUS, prelatic title 56; eparchial consultors 197; law of: dualistic character 233; sources 235; Oriental monachism 238; relationship to former law 246; definition of religious 244; religio monachalis 245; papal exemption and local Hierarch 255; papal exemption and patriarch 255; reservations 262; financial administration 268; debts 269; holy orders 289; obligations 290; habit 291; and eparchy 296;

divine office 297; privileges 298; exemption 299, 302; begging 303; promoted by patriarchal synod 308; incompatible offices and dignities 307; pastors 309; transfer to another institute 310; dismissal 315.

RESIDENCE, law for clergy 74; outside of eparchy 74; outside of Oriental regions 74; outside of religious houses 74.

RETREATS 64.

RITE, definition of Postquam Apostolicis 9; liturgical 8; subdivision 10; number 10; acquisition 26; by adults 27; by children 28; baptism 30; change of Rite (cf. TRANSFER); Oriental, preservation 23; prevalent 25.

ROMANIANS 12, 13, 68, 154.

ROTA, SACRED ROMAN, 108.

RUSSIANS 7, 12.

RUTHENIANS, definition 16; in U.S.A. 12, 14; celibacy 68.

SACERDOS, definition, 65.

SANATION, power of sanation of patriarch, 136.

SECRETARIATE OF STATE 109.

SECULARIZATION of religious 312.

SEMBRATOWYCH, CARDINAL SYLVESTER, 98.

SEMINARY, rector of church, 228.

SIGNATURA APOSTOLICA 108.

SISTERS, RELIGIOUS, definition 245.

SLOVAKS of the Byzantine Rite 14.

SOCIETIES WITHOUT PUBLIC VOWS 323.

"SOLLICITUDINEM NOSTRAM" 4.

STAFF, PASTORAL, 57, 141.

STATES, RELIGIOUS, definition, 242.

STATUTES, PERSONAL, 136, 137.

STATUTES OF RELIGIOUS, definition, 246.

STAUROPEGIUM, patriarchal privilege 133; local Hierarch and stauropegium 134; confessors 265; origin 299; stauropegial monastery 302.

STUDIES OF RELIGIOUS, house of studies 287; spiritual director 288; schedule and duration 288; freedom from occupations 289; junior clergy examinations 289.

SUBJECTION to another Rite 41.

SUBDIACONATE 55, 58, 61, 306.

SUNDAY MASS, in which Rite, 24.

SUPERIORS, ECCLESIASTICAL, seeking consent or advice 53.

SUPERIORS, RELIGIOUS, definition 244; Roman Pontiff, local Hierarch 254; superiors general of orders and congregations 257; major superior, qualifications 257; tenure 257; election of, 258; supervision of subjects 258; report to Apostolic See and patriarch 259; liturgical insignia 306.

SUPRACAMELAUCIUM 142, 144, 158, 283.

SURETY furnished by clerics 73.

SYNCELLUS, origin 59; dismissal of clerics 61; Oriental Rite syncellus of LATIN RITE bishops 187; definition, appointment, number, 187; qualifications 188; authority 189; honorary privileges 190; expiration of appointment 191; celibacy of syncellus 188; during vacancy of see 203.

SYNODS, species 161; ecumenical 95; patriarchal 124, 161; archiepiscopal 161; metropolitan or of ecclesiastical province 161; diocesan synod, cf. Eparchial Convocation; synod of election of patriarch 118; permanent synod 158, 145.

SYRIANS 5, 61, 68, 132, 159.

TAPPOUNI, CARDINAL IGNATIUS GABRIEL, 98.

TERRITORY OF ORIENTAL RITE 20, 47.

TERRITORIAL DIVISIONS 93.

TETRAPOD 221.

THEOLOGICAL CASES 66.

THIRD ORDERS 332.

TITLES, PRELATIC, Oriental 56; for religious 56; and Latin Rite clergy 60; conferred by patriarch 56; for religious 261, 307.

TONSURE 55, 61.

TRANSFER OF RITE, prohibition of proselytism 31; permission 33; reasons 36; children, wife, 37; Oriental dissidents, Protestants, 38; infidels 39; legal effects 40; recording 41; between Rites 33; between subgroups 33; illegal transfer 35.

TRAVEL of clergy, limitations, 74.

TRIBUNALS OF ROMAN CURIA, 108.

TRIBUNAL, PATRIARCHAL, 148.

TRIGENEIA 50.

TURKEY, Byzantine Rite Catholics, 7.

TYPICUM 236, 246, 252.

UNCTION OF INFIRMS, administered to religious, 260.

UNIONS, PIOUS, 332.

UNITED STATES OF AMERICA, Byzantine Rite eparchies 6; celibacy 69.

UNITY AMONG RITES 23.

UKRAINIANS, dioceses 6; subgroup of Byzantine Rite 14; in U.S.A. outside their parishes 46; celibacy 68; divine office, private recitation 71; metropolitans 154; in various countries: Argentina 7, Australia 6, Austria 7, Brazil 6, Canada 6, 12, 17, 19, France 7, Great Britain 7, Germany 6, Philadelphia, Pa., 15, 17.

VACANCY of patriarchate 150.

VACATION TIME for pastors 222.

VIATICUM 220, 260.

VICAR ADJUTOR 226.

VICAR ADMINISTRATOR 225.

VICAR ASSISTANT 226.

VICAR FORAINE, cf. PROTOPRESBYTERATE.

VICAR GENERAL, cf. SYNCELLUS.

VICAR, PATRIARCHAL, 133.

VICAR SUBSTITUTE 226.

VOTING on request of superior 53.

VOTE, requirements for validity, 80.

VOWS, OF RELIGIOUS, cf. PROFESSION, RELIGIOUS.